BACKSTAGE

BACKSTAGE

THE STORY BEHIND INDIA'S HIGH GROWTH YEARS

MONTEK SINGH AHLUWALIA

RUPA

Published by
Rupa Publications India Pvt. Ltd 2020
7/16, Ansari Road, Daryaganj
New Delhi 110002

Sales Centres:
Allahabad Bengaluru Chennai
Hyderabad Jaipur Kathmandu
Kolkata Mumbai

ISBN: 978-93-5333-821-3

First impression 2020

10 9 8 7 6 5 4 3 2 1

Printed at Parksons Graphics Pvt. Ltd., Mumbai

*This book is dedicated to Isher,
my life partner and companion
over the past fifty years,
without whose encouragement and
intellectual support
this book would never have been written.
And to our five grandchildren —
Veer, Angad, Arjun, Meher and Mahira.
Theirs is the generation that has the
greatest stake in the India story
continuing to move forward.*

CONTENTS

PROLOGUE

This book is not a memoir. I was turned off the idea of writing a memoir after I heard someone refer to them as 'selfies in book form'. I present this book to the reader as a travelogue of India's journey of economic reforms, in which I had the privilege of being an insider for 30 long years. My own story is interwoven with the narrative, but the personal experiences are not the principal focus; they are offered to the reader as an additional insight into what influenced my decisions and, quite possibly, my biases, as I saw India's growth and development story unfold.

In a country with a history of over 3,000 years, there is always a danger of overestimating the importance of individual events. Nevertheless, I believe the acceleration of economic growth that occurred in India between the early 1990s and the late 2000s was of crucial importance. India's GDP grew at over 7 per cent per annum in real terms from 1993-94 to 2011-12 and poverty declined from 37 per cent in 2004-05 to 22 per cent in 2011-12. Only a handful of developing countries have achieved rapid growth of this order over a prolonged period and none of them were large democracies. In this sense, India's accomplishment during this period is unique in the economic history of developing countries.

Part I of this book is largely personal. It is about my years growing up in Secunderabad and Delhi in the 1950s and early '60s, my time at Oxford in the mid-60s, and the eleven years I spent at the World Bank in Washington DC as a young development economist. It is during this period that I met my wife Isher when she was a summer intern at the International Monetary Fund (IMF) in 1970, studying the impact of the 1966 devaluation of the rupee on the Indian economy. This is the period when I took the two most important decisions in my life: to marry Isher in 1971 and, a few years later, to return home and take up a position as economic advisor in the Ministry of Finance.

By the time I returned to India in 1979, I had acquired extensive experience looking at economies all over the world, the development strategies employed by these countries and how those strategies interacted with political constraints. I looked forward to the opportunity to deploy that experience in shaping India's economic policy.

Part II of this book is about the decade or so leading up to the economic reforms that were launched in 1991. At the start of this period, India was widely seen—by those outside the country—as a laggard in growth, locked into an outdated economic strategy that would not deliver rapid growth. Indian planning had all the right objectives. It recognized the need for rapid growth to raise income levels because mere redistribution of income would not suffice to lift Indians out of poverty. There was some success initially— in raising the rate of investment, creating an industrial base and improving agricultural productivity; but the model had run out of steam. Crucially, productivity in Indian industry had stagnated.

From the late 1960s through the '70s, the growth performance of the Indian economy deteriorated while other countries in Southeast Asia fared much better. And yet, surprisingly, there were no voices in India advocating or demanding change—not civil servants, not academics, not the press, and not even Indian industry. They all saw that economic performance was not satisfactory but they did not view this as a consequence of the strategy deployed. They knew the public sector was performing very poorly and soaking up a lot of resources instead of generating surpluses for investment, but they saw the solution as pushing the government to somehow make the public sector more efficient. They could see that export performance was consistently falling short of targets, but they did not see the link between poor export performance and the import substitution strategy. That strategy raised the domestic cost structure and created an environment in which businesses would lobby for more protection from import competition rather than strive to lower costs to build export competitiveness.

I was convinced that if we liberalized the economy and gave greater freedom to the private sector, while opening up the economy to import competition, our economic performance would improve. Over the 1980s, some incremental steps were taken to ease controls in some individual areas. In 1990, I got the opportunity to prepare a paper that presented an integrated strategy for reform of fiscal policy, industrial policy, trade policy and exchange rate policy. This paper came to be known as the 'M Document'. It excited a great deal of controversy but I was delighted when much of what it proposed was implemented in the reforms that were started in 1991 under the leadership of Manmohan Singh.

Part III of this book is about the reforms that began in 1991 and continued thereafter. They were remarkable because they dismantled an extremely restrictive policy of controls on industry, foreign trade, foreign investment, the exchange rate and the financial sector. I was commerce secretary and finance secretary in those years and was directly involved in planning and executing those reforms.

The scale of reforms unleashed in 1991 would never have been possible without a cast of characters at both the political and bureaucratic level, all of whom were convinced about the need for change. Among the politicians, the most notable were Prime Minister (PM) P.V. Narasimha Rao, Finance Minister Manmohan Singh and Commerce Minister P. Chidambaram. The United Front government continued the reforms, helped by the continuity provided by Chidambaram under PMs H.D. Deve Gowda and Inder Kumar Gujral. The National Democratic Alliance (NDA) government under PM Atal Bihari Vajpayee, with the support of Yashwant Sinha, Jaswant Singh and Arun Shourie, stuck to the same course. At the bureaucratic level, there were a number of trained economists and highly competent IAS officers who held key positions at different times; A.N. Verma, C. Rangarajan, Bimal Jalan, Nitin Desai, Vijay Kelkar, N.K. Singh, Shankar Acharya, S.S. Tarapore, Y.V. Reddy, D.R. Mehta, S. Ganeshan, Rakesh Mohan, N. Vittal, Jayanta Roy and Gajendra Haldea come readily to mind.

They were a well-knit team that knew and respected each other. Domain experts like Raja Chelliah were roped in to provide a medium-term agenda for tax reforms and M. Narasimham to plan reforms of the financial sector.

While all these people made several important contributions to the reform effort in the 1990s, none of it would have happened without the clear and decisive leadership of Manmohan Singh. The success of the reform efforts in the initial years and the atmosphere of frank discussion and mutual respect across political parties helped to create a broader political consensus. This enabled successive governments to continue with these reforms. I remained finance secretary under the United Front government and, initially, under the NDA government until I was shifted out to be a member of the Planning Commission in 1998.

Part III of the book ends with a three-year interlude when I was on leave from the government to take up an appointment as director of the Independent Evaluation Office (IEO) of the IMF. That interlude came at a time when our children had grown up and were away at university. In many ways, Isher and I returned as empty-nesters to Washington DC where we had started our life as a young couple 22 years earlier. My job at the IEO was very challenging and exciting professionally, but Washington DC felt very different from the Washington of our youth in the late 1960s and '70s. Our memories were of anti-Vietnam war protests, impeachment proceedings, and the progressive anti-establishment songs of Joan Baez, Tom Lehrer and others. All this had changed in the post 9/11 atmosphere of the 2000s and the ascendancy of the neoconservatives.

Politics aside, Isher felt far too rooted in India to spend any extended period abroad. The surprise election result of 2004 in India, the appointment of Dr Manmohan Singh as PM and his offer to me to return to the government gave us an opportunity that I was quick to take up.

Part IV of the book is about the United Progressive Alliance (UPA) years, which were very much a second innings for me. As a civil servant, I would have retired in 2003 at the age of 60. Instead, I ended up serving for a full 10 years as deputy chairman of the Planning Commission in both the UPA 1 and UPA 2 governments.

My role at the Planning Commission was very different from my earlier assignments. I was given cabinet rank and made a special invitee to all cabinet meetings, giving me a seat at the table when important economic issues were discussed. I was also a part of many Groups of Ministers (GoMs) constituted to take important economic decisions. The Planning Commission enabled me to interact with different ministries as well as all state governments. The PM also nominated me as his sherpa for G20 meetings, which allowed me to interact with officials in other countries at the sherpa level. These interactions proved very valuable in the years after the global financial crisis in getting a sense of how other countries were dealing with the crisis.

The UPA years were, in many ways, a tale of two governments. UPA 1 and the initial period of the UPA 2 were a remarkable success. The first seven years recorded a growth rate of 8.5 percent. Indicators such as export growth, private investment and reduction in poverty also showed excellent performance. There were many reasons for this. The cumulative effect of the first-generation reforms, started in 1991 and continued and sustained by different governments for over a decade, played a role. The global environment was also very favourable. Above all, the UPA took a number of policy initiatives including a successful attempt at reducing the fiscal deficit, a special focus on agriculture, new initiatives in public-private partnerships (PPPs), a general impetus to infrastructure development, and continued opening up to foreign direct investment (FDI) in a range of sectors. The government also dealt effectively and decisively with the immediate aftermath of the global financial crisis, injecting a fiscal stimulus.

This positive economic picture turned at the mid-point of UPA 2. GDP growth started decelerating and inflation rose on the back of high global oil and commodity prices. However, many of the problems related to the downturn were domestic and I reflect on these at length in the book. Regulatory clearances were slow in coming, thus holding up private investment. Corruption scandals dominated the press and the investment climate was soured by both court interventions in public interest litigations (PILs) and retroactive amendments of tax laws by the government.

I must admit the last few years were disheartening for me as a policymaker. However, an important success at the time was the management of the taper tantrum in 2013. In the end, the declining trend in growth was reversed in 2013 as the economy began to pick up but the public mood against UPA 2 remained adverse and the government was voted out in 2014.

The economic reforms introduced in 1991 have fundamentally transformed the economy, society and politics of India. This book tells the story of how that change came about, and how policies that were once reviled came to be accepted. While the pace of change was slow, the direction was unmistakeable. The approach to change was a combination of gradualism and what I have called 'reform by stealth'. Personally, I always thought we should have moved much faster but I recognized that given the constraints of Indian politics, the best we could do was to create a pragmatic consensus on small steps forward, and then wait for windows of opportunity to push big changes through. Over the decades, these small changes and occasional big pushes resulted in a transformation of the economy. In 2010, India moved out of the group of low-income countries as classified by the World Bank and into the group of middle-income countries, albeit at the bottom end.

The past two years have seen an evaporation of optimism as the economy has slowed down very considerably. In the epilogue of this book, I look at the challenges ahead and steps we can take to get back onto a high-growth path. The road to high growth has never been free of potholes and there is no doubt that we face some major challenges in the years ahead. However, I believe we can draw strength from the fact that we have encountered—and overcome—similar if not greater challenges before. There is no reason why we cannot do so again.

Part One

1

MY FORMATIVE YEARS

I was born in Rawalpindi, now in Pakistan, four years too early to qualify as one of Salman Rushdie's 'Midnight's Children' but close enough to have gone through similar aspirations for Independent India.

My father Jagmohan Singh graduated from Khalsa College, Amritsar, and joined the Department of Defence Accounts as a clerk. He was a reclusive person with a strong moral conscience and an abiding sense of duty. He put whatever little savings he had in a bank account, strictly avoiding investments in stocks, which he viewed as a form of speculation.

My first years of childhood were spent in Saharanpur and Ambala, both towns with a military establishment, which naturally included an accounts department. In September 1948, the Indian Army moved into Hyderabad to deal with growing violence by the Razakar movement against the Hindu population. There was very little resistance and soon thereafter, the Nizam of Hyderabad acceded to India, retaining a titular position as Rajapramukh (head of the state). With the Indian Army ensconced in Hyderabad, the accountants could hardly be far behind and that is how, in 1950, my father moved with the Defence Accounts office from Ambala to Secunderabad, the twin city of Hyderabad.

I spent much of my childhood in Havelock Lines next to Karkhana village in Secunderabad. The village was home to both Hindus and Muslims with a Kali temple in one half of the village and a mosque in the other. I started my schooling in Secunderabad at St. Anne's Convent, an admirable all-girls school that admitted boys only until they reached the dangerous age of eight! I then moved to St. Patrick's English High School, a brother institution for boys run by the Jesuits. The 'mission schools' had a reputation for providing good education at low cost to children from low to upper middle classes.

My father largely left the supervision of my education to my mother Pushp and she shouldered the burden cheerfully. My mother was one of the first generation of women in northern India who studied beyond high school, graduating from DAV College, Lahore, in 1940. She had entertained hopes of becoming a 'lady doctor' but as her family could not afford a medical education, she 'settled down' to the pleasures and challenges of married life and parenting. She was also vivacious, loved mixing with people, and was confident she could break class barriers given half a chance. She devoted a great deal of her considerable energies to bringing up her children. As her first child, I received a disproportionate share of her affection and more than a little pressure to do well. I later realized some of her effort to push me was a sublimation of her own unfulfilled ambitions.

I discovered in an entirely unexpected way how my father also cared deeply for my education when I had to miss school for a week because my mother had taken me out of town for a family wedding. As I had recently got 'double promotion', taking me to a class above the one I would normally have entered, he worried the prolonged absence may make it difficult for me to keep pace. He took special permission from the principal to sit in my class for math and science so he could help me catch up when I return. It was an important signal—early in life—that studies had to be taken seriously.

My father was extremely well regarded by his superiors and as his retirement approached, they told him they were willing to recommend him for promotion into the Indian Defence Accounts Service (IDAS), which was a matter of professional dignity and some pride. This would enable him to retire as an IDAS officer but it would mean moving to head a small unit in a small town. They also gave him the option of a transfer to Delhi to spend the remaining years before retirement in his present grade. My father chose to forego promotion and opted for Delhi as it would mean a better education for us. It is only much later that I realized the significance of his sacrifice.

A CAPITAL MOVE

Our move to the capital in 1957 was exciting. I was 14 and enjoyed the sights: Red Fort, Old Fort, Qutub Minar, Parliament House, Rashtrapati Bhavan, and many more. The roads were much less crowded and it was possible to explore a good bit of South Delhi on a bicycle from our rented two-room flat in Lajpat Nagar III. Humayun's Tomb, Safdarjung's Tomb and Lodhi Gardens were only a good cycle ride away.

The change that affected me most directly was my new school. Delhi Public School (DPS) at Mathura Road was established shortly after Independence and was still operating out of tents, though a building was coming up. The principal, Dr K.C. Khanna, was a distinguished educationist with a towering presence. He had an infectious smile, but one that left no doubt that he would tolerate no nonsense. Fortunately, he readily agreed to admit my sister Anjali and me to the school. My younger brother Sanjeev joined a few years later.

I liked my new teachers. There were two in particular who inspired me to read and develop an appreciation for literature. Mrs Menon, a cherubic and affectionate motherly figure, encouraged me by lending novels from her own small collection, a book at a time, to be returned after a few days. She had the whole set of Alexandre Dumas novels that I devoured. And Mrs Snehlata Sanyal pushed me towards greater intellectual effort by making me aware of A.C. Bradley. His *Shakespearean Tragedies* was too esoteric a book to be stocked in the library; she lent me her copy so I could appreciate literary criticism.

Thanks to the quality of teaching and the inspiration provided by my favourite teachers, I did well in the Senior Cambridge

Examination, topping the DPS class with a distinction in six subjects. My class teacher at St. Patrick's had told me he was sorry to see me leave because he thought I could get distinction in at least two subjects! The fact that I did much better vindicated my father's decision to forego promotion and move to Delhi.

Just about when I finished school, my mother landed the job of secretary to the director of the India International Centre (IIC), a newly founded, non-government society that had become a favourite haunt for the intellectually oriented and top bureaucratic elite of the capital. For my mother, it was an ideal opportunity — she knew my father was due to retire in two years and a regular salary would supplement his pension and assure us of comfort, if not luxury, as we completed our education. It was also an ideal workplace for her because her social skills could be put to good use.

The limited access I had to the IIC provided me a peek into the life of the Delhi elite. IIC was not very far from our home in Lajpat Nagar. But if the geographical distance was small, the cultural distance was huge.

I had to wait a year before I could join Delhi University because I was two months short of the minimum age. I used the time to delve into some books on economics that I borrowed from the British Council Library on Rafi Marg. This gave me a feel for the subject and helped convince me to opt for the BA Honours course in economics in Delhi University. I also enrolled for French lessons at Alliance Française. As the time to apply to colleges approached, I took the examination for the All India Merit Scholarship.

I was delighted when I was awarded one of the residential scholarships of ₹100 per month, as I scored among the top five in the competitive examination. It assured me admission into St. Stephen's College in residence — not a small privilege as residential places were normally reserved for those outside Delhi.

KOOLER DAYS AT ST. STEPHEN'S

In those days, St. Stephen's was a men-only college and the natural choice for children of the Delhi elite. The privileged progeny behaved as if they owned the college, often parading a family tradition of older relatives who had gone there. But it was also a place where middle-class children who had done well in school could hope to get in. Once in, there was no sense of class discrimination. Being part of the student community was all that mattered. The self-image of St. Stephen's was not of an institution that would produce students who would go on to have a distinguished academic career. Instead, it took pride in providing an education that would help students do well in civil services examinations. The civil service in those days was the prime career choice for middle and even upper middle-class youth who did not have family businesses to slip into.

Coming from a middle-class family I knew I had to get a good job, and this meant much of my time was taken up studying to get a good degree. But there was much more of college life open to me because I was in residence. Debating was my favourite extracurricular activity and I was good at it. Most debates were organized by individual colleges and some by university departments. Some debates organized by the older colleges, like the Mukarji Memorial Debate at St. Stephen's, were especially prestigious and attracted large audiences. In my student career in Delhi, I won almost all the prestigious debates, some more than once.

Although I enjoyed debating, the subjects were rather staid and unexciting: for example, 'Progress depends on unreasonable men' or 'Agriculture must be the centrepiece of a successful development strategy'. They were not controversial subjects on which people might be expected to have strong preconceived views. This was in sharp contrast with the practice at the Oxford Union, which in 1938 famously debated the proposition, 'This House will not fight for King and Country'. That pacifist proposition was carried, and severely criticized by the political establishment at the time as undermining national unity in Britain. However, it established the principle that students should be given freedom to explore sensitive subjects.

The real problem with debating in Delhi was that it did not really hone the art of persuading people to change their minds, or even rethink their positions. It certainly taught us the art of public speaking. Later in life, when faced with the challenge of having to persuade senior people in government to change their way of thinking on economic policies, I realized the art of persuasion is very different from the art of debating, and much more challenging.

Whatever its limitations, debating in Delhi University enabled me to make many friends among prominent debaters of the time, some of whom became colleagues and friends in later life. N.K. Singh, Mani Shankar Aiyar, Aftab Seth, Prabhat Patnaik, Jayant Das, Deb Mukherjee and Ram Chopra are some names that come to mind.

St. Stephen's College took pride in keeping itself out of the politics of the Delhi University Student's Union. In retrospect, I feel that the notion behind this was that the technocratic elite could make its contribution to nation-building in an apolitical manner, leaving the dirty business of politics to politicians. This makes little sense in a democratic society. Even the elite group of students in St. Stephen's was not entirely immune to the call from politics. In the 1970s, a few students left the college to join the extreme-Left Naxalite movement in the backward district of Naxalbari in West Bengal. That particular protest got nowhere and those who joined the movement may have come to regret their decision later, but it indicated a desire to be part of active politics.

My other extracurricular activity was student journalism. There were two student journals: *The Stephanian*, the official bi-annual college journal, and the much more gossipy *Kooler Talk*[1].

---

[1]The magazine took its name from a large water cooler located next to the college administrative offices, which was a natural watering hole for students to gather and exchange small talk.

I ended up editing both in different years. *The Stephanian* was a ponderous and somewhat pretentious publication, full of articles on heavy issues such as world peace and Indian culture, and travel or mountaineering experiences, leavened at times by poetry of dubious quality. It was read mainly by the contributors and perhaps their closest friends.

Kooler Talk was started by Sarwar Lateef, who went on to have a distinguished career in journalism, which he abandoned during the Emergency to join the World Bank in Washington DC. The other founding editors were Peter Philip from the Kerala-based family owning the Malayalam Manorama group of publications and Roshan Seth, who went on to achieve acclaim in films and television. *Kooler Talk* had a snappy style and carried short pieces on current student life and events, with irreverent comments on prominent students. We were careful to steer clear of criticizing the college authorities but disparaging remarks about the food were tolerated. Interestingly, the students covered didn't mind being mentioned in print, even when good-natured fun was poked at them. It was an early revelation that those who enjoy public prominence value being in the news, even if the stories about them are not adulatory.

No account of St. Stephen's in the 1960s can be complete without a reference to Balbir Singh, a young Sikh lecturer in the Economics Department. Balbir had spent a year at Cambridge and viewed his job as providing an intellectually stimulating environment, leaving it to the students to pick up the essential information they needed for their exams from textbooks! He was single and had a two-room 'resident tutor' suite in Rudra North, one of the student hostels. He was fond of Indian classical music and would invite a few of us to have tea in his rooms and listen to music while savouring Marmite on toast. Those who didn't like Marmite were told it was the food of the intellectuals. Most of us were bullied into acquiring the taste in order to belong!

The biggest difference in St. Stephen's of those days was that most students, even from wealthy families, had much smaller spending allowances. Students generally travelled by bus and only a few had scooters. Sarwar Lateef, whose parents lived in Hyderabad, told me that on one occasion, when some friends of his parents drove him back to college—after he had gone to meet them by bus—he insisted on being dropped off half a mile from the gate because it 'wasn't done' to be seen coming to college in a private car. Today, the college parking lot is full of student-driven cars! Though the number of poorer students has increased because of affirmative action, the rich are much less discreet.

The basic economics syllabus at St. Stephen's was a mixture of microeconomics and macroeconomics, history of economic thought, economic history of the major economies and Indian economic issues. Looking back, I am struck by how little we were exposed to what I realized later were the controversial issues in India's economic policy. In the early 1960s there was still a broad consensus on economic policy, with an acceptance of the Nehruvian vision that the Government had to play a very active role in promoting development, with a correspondingly large role for the public sector. This view was not popular in the United States (US) but similar to the views of the Left of the spectrum in the United Kingdom (UK), where the same Fabian Socialist ideas that inspired the Indian National Congress held sway in the Labour Party. Much the same was true in most European countries. However, there were dissenting views in India on government policies that we learnt about only through our extracurricular activities.

C. Rajagopalachari, the first Indian Governor General and a stalwart freedom fighter, had important differences with Nehru on the direction of economic policy, which led him to resign from the Congress in 1959. He joined Minoo Masani and N.G. Ranga to establish the Swatantra Party as a Right-wing alternative to the Congress. Many who use the phrase 'Licence Permit Raj' today do not know that it was coined by 'Rajaji' and not some latter-day, market-oriented critic of economic controls! Rajaji had remarked in the late 1950s that we had not struggled to get rid of the British Raj only to have it replaced by the Licence Permit Raj.

We had a system of regularly inviting speakers to the college common room for lectures on different topics; this helped sensitize us to alternate views. Minoo Masani was once invited to talk at this forum. He spoke about his early days with Nehru and Gandhi but later lit into Nehru and the socialist path he was following. He argued vehemently against cooperative farming, which Nehru was strongly supporting at that time. When the students, who were generally pro-Nehru, attacked Masani on this, he offered to come back for a full-scale debate on the subject. He was duly invited back for a second round. Arun Shourie, then very much a Nehruvian socialist like everyone else, took him on. Masani valiantly defended his position and gave Arun and others as good as he got.

On the academic side, B.R. Shenoy was a vocal critic of the Government's policy. His minute of dissent to the report of the Panel of Economists on the Second Plan questioned both the reliance upon deficit financing as a method of funding public investment, and the resort to controls and licences that interfered with market forces. These arguments were to surface strongly in the public debate in the 1990s but we left St. Stephen's with no idea they had been hotly debated because planning was all the rage.

At the end of my three years, I applied for admission to the MA programme in economics at the Delhi School of Economics, where luminaries such as Amartya Sen, Jagdish Bhagwati and Sukhamoy Chakravarty were teaching. I also decided to apply for a Rhodes Scholarship to Oxford University. I never thought I had much of a chance because Rhodes scholars were traditionally expected to have strong credentials in sports. Fortunately, by the time I applied, the Rhodes Trust Selection Committee had decided that insisting on excellence in sports as a precondition could imply a considerable weakening in academic standards and that candidates could be 'well rounded' through other extracurricular activities as well. I found myself on the shortlist of candidates; the interviews went on for several hours and we hung around for the committee to complete its deliberations. Sometime around 5 p.m., the secretary of the committee, Ranjit Bhatia, a lecturer in mathematics at St. Stephen's, came out to announce the results. I was delighted to hear I was one of the two candidates selected, the other being Karna Dev Bardhan, a doctor from Christian Medical College, Vellore.

I was excited that I would be at a great university. I came to appreciate even more the significance of my father's decision—I would never have got the Rhodes Scholarship if my father had taken up the offer of promotion and moved us all to a small town. I promptly telephoned my mother at her office at IIC; she was overjoyed. My father had retired and we did not have a telephone at home. In those days, telephones were a luxury, with long waiting lines to get one. I took the bus to go home and give him the good news. He did not give me a typical Punjabi hug but just shook my hand solemnly and said, 'Congratulations'. He was not a very demonstrative person but I could detect an ever-so-slight smile behind the twitch of his white beard. Parental pride can be hard to suppress.

On 27 May 1964, a few months before my departure for Oxford, Jawaharlal Nehru, the then PM, passed away. He had towered over the nation's political life for decades, first as Mahatma Gandhi's most trusted colleague and designated successor in the Freedom Movement and then as India's first PM who symbolized everything the nation stood for and aspired to achieve. I was sufficiently moved to go to Teen Murti House on that hot day in May to join the crowd waiting for his cortege to move out and head to the site of the cremation. The crowds were massive but, as it happened, the young police officer at the gates of Teen Murti was an alumnus of St. Stephen's who had joined the Indian Police Service only a year earlier! He recognized me and helped me get a good vantage point from where I could bid a final adieu.

OXFORD

I was keen to study economics at Oxford but unlike Cambridge, which offered a Tripos in economics, then regarded as the gold standard of economics degrees, Oxford did not have a degree in economics alone. Instead, it offered the Philosophy, Politics and Economics (PPE) degree, a unique cocktail introduced in 1920 and called 'Modern Greats', to distinguish it from the traditional 'Greats', which covered Greek and Roman (Latin) literature and history. Greats had been the traditional route to joining the civil service in Britain but opinion had come around that however uplifting the knowledge of Greek and Roman philosophy and history might be for the soul, it was of limited relevance for a career in the civil service. PPE was the obvious choice.

Magdalen College at Oxford fully lived up to my expectations. I was given surprisingly spacious rooms in cloisters, the oldest part of the college, adjoining the chapel and the tower. My years at Oxford gave me the opportunity to experience traditional ways of making merry such as balls, punting on the Cherwell, spending time with friends in pubs, and playing croquet on the college lawns. I made lots of good friends, with many of whom I have remained in regular touch. Among these are Richard Danzig, a Rhodes scholar from the US who later became secretary of the Navy in the Clinton administration, and Michael Spence, another Rhodes scholar and good friend who was awarded the Nobel Prize in economics in 2001. In later years, I served with Mike on the Growth Commission set up by the World Bank. Among the Indian students who became very good friends were Sudhir Anand, a mathematician-turned-economist who joined the World Bank but returned to teach at St. Catherine's College at Oxford; Shankar Acharya, who overlapped with me in the World Bank and later in the Ministry of Finance; and Kumar Advani from Bombay. Others whose friendship I have valued include Michael Jay, whom I tutored at Oxford and who went on to become the permanent undersecretary in the Foreign Office in the UK, and Torquil Dick Erikson, a scholar of modern languages who now lives in Rome.

I also got to meet Aung San Suu Kyi, who later gained global recognition for fighting a prolonged battle against the military regime in Myanmar—although her reputation was to suffer later because of Myanmar's handling of the Rohingya situation. Years later in 2013, I called on her in Nay Pyi Taw on an official visit to Myanmar. I recall asking our ambassador whether I should address her as 'Your Excellency' or simply 'Madam'. A few minutes later, 'Sue', as she was known in Oxford, breezily entered the room and threw all formalities to the wind, saying, 'Montek, how nice to see you. You haven't changed at all!' Then, turning to my wife Isher, who had accompanied me, she said, 'I always knew Montek would make an excellent choice of life partner.' Our ambassador was a little taken aback at this camaraderie, and I am sure it gave him an exaggerated respect for the value of Oxford networking!

DEBATING AT THE OXFORD UNION

Having debated a lot in Delhi University, I wanted to continue at Oxford and joined the Oxford Union Society in my very first week. The Union, founded in 1825 and still flourishing, describes itself (with some justification) as the most famous debating society in the world. But it is also a club. Debates were held only once a week in term time but the Union offered much more. It had spacious buildings at Frewin Court in the centre of town, providing members a range of facilities through the term, with a slightly reduced range during the holidays for those who remained in Oxford, like many of us foreign students. It had an excellent formal dining room and bar open through the week and an elegantly furnished Gladstone Room, where we could have a very British tea with scones while reading newspapers or books. The room was lined with bound volumes of the *Illustrated London News* going back to the early 19th century as well as *Punch*. There was a billiards room for those inclined to that particular diversion. It also had its own library stocked with non-academic books and some very attractive frescoes by William Morris (then desperately in need of restoration, which has since been done).

I stood for election to the position of president of the Oxford Union in the Michaelmas term of 1966 — the same term I took the PPE final exam. I was elected to serve as president for the term that began just after the summer holidays. The other candidate, Simon Head, was supported by the more conservative segments of the membership whereas I had the support of the Left and the liberals, which won me the election. Simon went on to become a well-known journalist, author and academic. There had been Indian presidents of the Oxford Union before me — Raghavan Iyer in 1954 and Girish Karnad in 1963 (both incidentally from Magdalen) — but it was a rare enough event to attract some attention in the press in India and a brief mention in some of the London papers.

The debates in the Oxford Union imitated those in the House of Commons and the debating hall was designed accordingly. The seats in the front half were arranged along its length so members sat facing each other, those for the motion on the right-hand side of the president and those opposing on the left. The back half of the hall had seats along the width, rather like the cross benches in the House of Lords. There was a gallery along the top of the hall to accommodate an overflow.

I was pitted on several occasions against Larry Pressler, a Rhodes scholar who later became the Republican senator for South Dakota, and I got to know him well. Larry had sponsored the Pressler Amendment, which banned US aid to Pakistan unless the president certified each year that Pakistan did not possess a nuclear weapon and that the proposed assistance would significantly reduce the risk of Pakistan possessing such a weapon.

CONGRATULATORY FIRST

I was determined to do well academically as well as savour Oxford's extracurricular life to the full. It is to the credit of the education we had received in India that I was able to take the academic challenges in my stride even though the system of teaching was very different. There were no compulsory lectures. Sir John Hicks and Sir Roy Harrod were the most famous economists lecturing in Oxford at the time. They were not good lecturers but we dutifully attended so we could say we had done so. Historian Hugh Trevor Roper and political philosopher Isaiah Berlin were other famous scholars whose lectures I attended just for the experience.

Despite the distractions—notably time spent at the Oxford Union—I did well academically and got a first-class degree in PPE. A day later, I received a letter from Sir Roy Harrod, chairman of the Board of Examiners, conveying I had done exceptionally well, even among those who got a First, and that the Board of Examiners had asked him to convey their congratulations to me. This made it a Congratulatory First, which was much prized academically. In earlier times, all candidates were called for an interview but those being awarded congratulatory firsts experienced a special ritual. No questions were asked and the examiners simply stood up and doffed their academic caps as a form of congratulations! I thought it a charming ritual and regretted that it had been replaced by a letter.

After completing my PPE, I was convinced I wanted to get deeper into economics. The two-year BPhil seemed to be ideal; it was later renamed the MPhil to avoid any misperception that the 'B' connoted an undergraduate degree. In the course of my first year, I was offered a job in the private sector in London by Maurice Zinkin, formerly of the Indian Civil Service, who had worked for several years in the Government of India, leaving shortly after Independence to join Unilever. I had never met Maurice but his son John Zinkin was a student at Magdalen and I was his tutor for a term.

I received an invitation to meet Maurice Zinkin for dinner in a fancy London restaurant. Towards the end of the sumptuous meal, he asked whether I would be interested in joining Unilever in London. After spending some time working in London, they would then place me in India on terms that would be very attractive. I was naturally very pleased at being offered such an opportunity, that too without even applying. But the idea of working in the private sector had never appealed to me. My wife Isher thinks my father, who was an uncompromising government servant, had subconsciously influenced me, as well as my brother and sister, as we all ended up in government! She may well be right. In any case, I thanked Zinkin profusely and declined on the grounds that I wanted to work on issues of development policy, either returning to India to join the civil services or taking a detour into an assignment that would prepare me for that.

At the end of my first year of the BPhil, the World Bank sent a recruiting team to Oxford to attract suitable students to apply for its Young Professionals Programme, the avenue through which it planned to recruit younger staff, fresh from universities. I had not thought of working at the World Bank but I realized it would give me first-hand experience of development problems in a range of developing countries. I could then hope to return to India not just in a generalist Indian Administrative Service (IAS) cadre but in one of the few specialist positions for economists that existed in a few ministries. I met the Bank's recruiting team in Oxford and was invited to a job interview in Paris. Shortly thereafter, I was offered a position in the programme and readily accepted.

I left Oxford in July 1968 to return to India for a brief holiday before joining the World Bank in September. I had made many friends during my four years and enjoyed many typical Oxford distractions. I had also honed my analytical skills as an economist and read widely about development economics. There was much I did not know, though, and the full extent of my ignorance only seeped into my consciousness in the years ahead. But at that time, I felt ready to take on the World Bank with confidence.

2

DEVELOPMENT IN PRACTICE

I arrived in Washington DC towards the end of September 1968 to start my assignment as a Young Professional (YP) at the World Bank. It was my first job and I was greatly looking forward to getting practical exposure on how different countries addressed their development challenges. It was also my first exposure to the US. I was pleasantly surprised at how easy it was to find accommodation for renting. I quickly decided on a functionally adequate one-bedroom apartment, a comfortable 15-minute walk from the Bank. I had yet to learn to drive a car!

I was particularly interested to see how countries navigated the complex maze of designing policies in politically constrained situations. We had all learnt as students how a particular policy that made sense in a 'first-best' situation, where all other policies were properly deployed, may not work in a second-best situation where other policies were suboptimal. As developing countries suffered from innumerable constraints, their policymaking had to be of the second-best variety and I was particularly keen to observe how this worked in practice.

LEARNING THE ROPES

YPs had to go through an 18-month period of probation during which we were rotated through three different departments.

The 18 months went very fast. My first assignment in the Projects Department was in Peru to assess whether a specific irrigation project was proceeding on schedule. I thought the skills needed for the assignment were not related to economics but management or engineering. To my lasting regret, I passed up the chance to visit Machu Picchu. The round-trip airfare was about $150 and as I had just transited from a severely budget-constrained student life, I failed to realize it was a steal.

My second assignment was an economic appraisal mission of a new project in Ethiopia where coffee was grown by farmers with small landholdings. The visit to Ethiopia—my first to an African country—was fascinating but the experience also convinced me that project appraisal was not my cup of tea.

I then moved to the Economics Department from where I went on a mission to Jakarta in Indonesia to assess the progress made in setting up an effective external debt reporting system. I reviewed Indonesia's effort to set up a data monitoring system. It was more a job for an accountant than an economist, though it gave me a sense of the extent to which critical economic analysis and assessment depend on having proper data systems in place.

My last probationary stint was with the Middle East Department and involved participating in country missions to North Yemen and Egypt. There were no official GDP statistics but the national accounts expert on our team managed to produce an estimate by piecing together two bits of information. A UN report included a reference to a UN official saying the population of North Yemen was 'most probably around x million'. Another UN official had speculated that North Yemen 'seemed to be a country of per capita GDP of about $y'. The product of x and y was used by our expert as the best available estimate of GDP for North Yemen!

I was finally assigned to the Fiscal Division in the Economics Department. This gave me the opportunity for research on fiscal issues and to participate in country missions as a fiscal economist.

I found Yugoslavia particularly interesting because of its similarities with India. A common slogan in Yugoslavia in those days was 'Seven frontiers, six republics, five nationalities, four languages, three religions, two alphabets but one nation'. In the more impolite version, one nation was substituted by 'one leader'. I was saddened when Yugoslavia broke up into six different countries in the late 1990s, that too with a highly fratricidal civil war and reports of ethnic cleansing.

Turkey and Malaysia were two developing countries with a much higher level of per capita income than India. Both were significantly more open economies with much lower levels of trade protection and a policy of welcoming FDI. Both had governments that were proactive but encouraged private sector activity much more than we did. Both countries also had a much better economic performance than India in the 1970s, which gave me food for thought.

A PARTNERSHIP FOR LIFE

There were many reasons why I stayed longer in Washington DC than the three years or so I had originally intended. The most important was Isher, whom I first met in 1970. She arrived in Washington DC from the Massachusetts Institute of Technology (MIT) for a summer assignment with the IMF. She was pursuing her PhD in economics and had just completed her coursework. Her classmate Brendan Horton, an English student who knew me from Oxford, telephoned me to say there was a 'really nice Indian girl' spending the summer at the Fund (as it was popularly known), and that I should get in touch with her. I promptly followed up. I took her out a few times and was soon convinced that in Isher I had found my life partner. Brendan clearly turned out to be an expert matchmaker.

I remember our first meeting when I had asked Isher to lunch at the executive dining room of the World Bank, hoping to impress her with my access to this important perk. We discussed her summer project at the Asian Department of the IMF, which involved studying the effect of India's devaluation of 1966 on the economy. While I was impressed by her intellectual commitment to the subject, I was focusing less on economics and more on her charm and personality. In her simple salwar kameez, she looked every bit a demure young Indian woman but she had surprisingly strong feminist convictions and, at the end of the lunch, complained when she discovered that only I could sign for the two of us. I assured her she could invite me out to even the score, thereby hoping to create one more opportunity to get to know her better.

Like me, Isher was from a middle-class Indian family but there was a lot of difference in our upbringing. She came from a conservative Sikh family and received a strong foundation in religion. She studied in an all-girls Marwari school in Calcutta where the medium of instruction was Hindi; English was taught only as a second language. She had rebelled against the social conservatism of her family and insisted on studying at the famous co-educational Presidency College in Calcutta, and then the Delhi School of Economics, from whence to MIT—all the way on scholarship. I would not have realized it from our first meeting but she told me later that it took her a few years after she went to university to be comfortable speaking English.

Isher was supposed to return to MIT after the summer but luckily for me she was offered a regular job as an economist at the Fund that she decided to take up, persuading MIT to let her defer work on her PhD thesis. We had a whirlwind courtship, going to plays and movies and for long drives and picnics in the many scenic spots the Washington area had to offer. I had bought a car a year earlier: a scarlet red Karmann Ghia, which was actually a Volkswagen Beetle dressed up in a low-slung sportscar body designed by Ghia of Italy and manufactured by the Karmann Wagen Werks in Austria. We both enjoyed driving in my red 'faux' sports car through the roads crisscrossing the Blue Ridge Mountains of Virginia.

As we got to know each other better, Isher confessed that she was originally deeply suspicious of Indians from Westernized English-speaking backgrounds who had attended elite colleges like St. Stephen's. She felt they tended to cloak academic mediocrity with social snobbery towards students from schools where the medium of instruction was not English. I was lucky these prejudices had moderated by the time we met; otherwise my St. Stephen's background, topped by Oxford, might have proved to be a devastating 'no-no'! She later told me what saved the day for me was the fact that I wasn't just academically bright—an essential requirement in her mind—but fun loving with a great sense of humour. Today, she complains that decades of being a senior official in the Government of India have practically effaced this trait.

We were married in October 1971 in a civil ceremony by a district judge in Washington DC. We started our married life drawing international salaries and living in a very congenial, if somewhat cocooned environment of highly educated professionals from different countries. Coming as we both did from families of modest means, we enjoyed the opportunity to indulge in a bit of consumerism. We soon moved from my modest bachelor apartment to a somewhat larger and much better located apartment in elegant Georgetown. It overlooked Montrose Park where we would spend hours on weekends enjoying a pizza lunch and reading *The New York Times*, *The Washington Post* and other newspapers—they were a bulky lot with many more pages with advertisements and comics than our Indian newspapers. While reading newspapers in print is now becoming passé everywhere, to me the idea of lounging lazily in a park and reading the news on a smartphone seems singularly unrelaxing.

Georgetown was a pleasant neighbourhood with many choices for impromptu dining. We were especially fond of a French bistro on M Street that served excellent onion soup and green salad with a great dressing. We were sufficiently fond of the soup for me to learn the recipe. Even today, in the Delhi winters I am called upon by the family, including our grandchildren, to whip up my French soupe à l'oignon gratinée!

My work at the World Bank gave me the opportunity to travel to many developing countries and engage in policy discussions with the governments. Isher worked as an economist in the Western Hemisphere Department of the IMF on the US economy and a number of small countries in the Caribbean. Her work on the US involved little travel, mostly walking across to the US Treasury only two blocks away. However, her responsibilities in the Caribbean involved visits to some of the most exotic holiday spots: Barbados, Trinidad and Tobago and Guyana.

The IMF and the World Bank have very generous provisions for home leave every two years; we would visit India every year, taking advantage of the home leave from each organization. One of our favourite stopovers during these visits was Paris, where we routinely spent a day by the side of the Seine, looking for old India maps from the bouquinistes who lined the river. In those days you could pick up really good old maps for less than $10. We would bring them to India, get them framed and take them back to DC. To this day, these maps adorn the walls of our dining room, keeping the memories alive.

After four years of this blissful reverie, Isher decided it was time to get back to her studies. She took study leave from the Fund and got a one-year research fellowship at the Brookings Institution in Washington DC to work on her PhD thesis, which she completed in 1976.

POVERTY REDUCTION, THE PRIORITY

In 1973, former US defense secretary Robert S. McNamara, then president of the World Bank, decided to position the Bank as an institution devoted to promoting development strategies that would help the poor, especially small farmers. He persuaded Hollis B. Chenery, a well-known development economist, to leave his professorship at Harvard and join the Bank as chief economist and vice president for development policy. Hollis initiated work on poverty and inequality and a new Income Distribution Division was created in the economics complex.

I was appointed the first chief of this division at the age of 28. The job was originally offered to Arun Shourie but he was keen to go back to India where he was to distinguish himself as editor of *Indian Express* and launch the paper on the path of investigative journalism. When the Bank tried to persuade him about the importance of measuring the extent of poverty, Arun told them he didn't find it very challenging: 'What is there to say other than that the poor are very poor and there are very many of them?'

McNamara had picked on poverty reduction as the dominant mission of the World Bank primarily to persuade the liberal end of the political spectrum in developing countries to continue supporting the Bank. Many people also believed he was motivated by the desire to assuage the guilt he may have felt about his role in the Vietnam War. Whatever the motivation, Hollis Chenery refocused World Bank research on how development strategies should be refashioned to help the poor. We kicked off our work by organizing an international brainstorming conference on poverty and income distribution.

The conference was held at the beautiful Villa Serbelloni in Bellagio overlooking Lake Como in northern Italy. The luxurious setting was somewhat incongruous with the idea of discussing poverty; but perhaps because of it we were able to bring together a galaxy of renowned international experts who had worked on these issues. Following the conference, a group of us under Hollis Chenery produced a book, *Redistribution with Growth*[2], which for many years became a semi-official policy document of the World Bank.

Ten years earlier, the Planning Commission of India had prepared a paper titled 'Perspectives on Development: Planning for a Minimum Level of Living', at the direction of PM Jawaharlal Nehru. It outlined a 15-year strategy from 1960–61 to 1975–76, which would bring the living standard of every Indian up to a minimum level. The paper suggested the need for a combination of high growth (7 per cent per annum) and some redistribution targeted at the bottom 20 per cent of the population who could not benefit sufficiently from growth. The scale of taxation needed

---

[2]Chenery H.B., et al., 1975, *Redistribution with Growth*, The World Bank.

to finance this redistribution could be accommodated without disrupting the incentive to invest.

Redistribution with Growth outlined the broad framework of policies to achieve a more equally distributed growth. It recommended a combination of efficiency-oriented policies and other policies that would lead to faster growth and more employment generation. Faster agricultural growth, in particular, was most likely to benefit the poor and this called for larger investment, greater efficiency in resource use and better technology induction in agriculture. In his introduction to the book, Chenery acknowledged the intellectual debt to the Indian Planning Commission for having produced the first quantitative planning exercise in a developing country explicitly aimed at raising the population above a minimum level of living.

Ironically, even as the Planning Commission paper was being acknowledged internationally, its core message regarding the centrality of growth in any process for eliminating poverty was being diluted at home. Economic growth in India in the 1970s dropped to very low levels. Policymakers keen to reduce poverty should have focused on why growth was stuck at such a low level. Instead, they reacted by emphasizing the need for stronger redistribution through a direct attack on poverty.

Much of the pessimism about reducing poverty in India at that time was triggered by a paper by Pranab Bardhan showing that rural poverty had worsened considerably between 1960 and 1968. However, 1968 was a drought year when agricultural incomes would have been abnormally low and rural poverty abnormally high. I looked at poverty estimates for a number of years between 1956 and 1968 for which survey data was available; using this information, I tested the hypothesis that the per capita agricultural GDP is inversely correlated with the percentage of the rural population in poverty. Having found evidence in support of this hypothesis, I argued that the way to reduce rural poverty over time was to accelerate the growth of per capita agricultural GDP.

I was invited to make a presentation of my findings at the Planning Commission in 1976. I was flattered to find that the deputy chairman of the commission, D.T. Lakdawala, decided to chair the seminar himself, and my results were well received. It was my first involvement in an official event in India and my first exposure to the Planning Commission. Little did I realize that I would end up as deputy chairman three decades later!

INDIA AS VIEWED BY THE WORLD BANK

India was the Bank's largest borrower and the Bank had been reviewing the country's policies for many years. The Bank had consistently supported India with long-term soft loans through the International Development Association (IDA), which was set up to provide aid to low-income countries with interest rates close to zero and a repayment period of 40 years, compared to normal World Bank loans that carried a market interest rate and repayment period of 15 years.

By the mid-1960s, international opinion became highly critical of India's economic policies, which were seen as limiting the effectiveness of foreign aid. In 1964, the World Bank sent a large economic mission to India under the leadership of Bernard R. Bell, a well-known agricultural economist from the US, to make an assessment of India's foreign aid requirements and the corrective policies needed to justify additional aid.

The 14-volume report of the Bell Mission provided an updated version of all the policy inadequacies noted in earlier Bank reports. It became the basis for negotiations in which donors were to offer a substantial increase in foreign aid over a five-year period, linked to policy changes. These changes included liberalization of various controls and a devaluation of the rupee. The package had been negotiated during the prime ministership of Lal Bahadur Shastri but it was finally accepted by Indira Gandhi when she became PM in 1966 after Shastri's sudden demise.

The devaluation of the rupee by 36 per cent in June 1966 triggered a vigorous debate in India. Jagdish Bhagwati, then a professor at the Delhi School of Economics, argued in favour of devaluation and liberalization, while K.N. Raj, another highly respected Indian economist, took the opposite view. As it happened, the foreign aid that was meant to be part of the package — about $900 million per year for five years — never came. US President Lyndon B. Johnson, possibly irritated at India's continued opposition to the Vietnam War, went back on the agreement. Other aid donors also refused to deliver. In the absence of expected funding, some steps to liberalize imports that had already been taken were reversed. Most importantly, Mrs Gandhi lost faith in the reliability of Western promises. In the years to come, many in the Indian political establishment would remind her of this perfidy.[3]

By the time I arrived at the World Bank in 1968, all this was in the past and it was accepted that the policy changes the Bank was hoping for at the time of the Bell Mission would not materialize. The World Bank settled down to do what it could within the policy framework adopted by the Government of India. A significant positive development in the late 1960s and early 1970s was the Green Revolution, which enabled India to become self-sufficient in foodgrains. This was recognized globally as a major achievement, disproving the forecasts of the Club of Rome[4] that India would not be able to feed herself and was too large to be fed by the rest of the world.

The political credit for the success of the Green Revolution must go in large measure to Mrs Gandhi, who took bold decisions in the late 1960s to make it happen. Agriculture Minister C. Subramaniam vigorously argued for import of large quantities

---

[3]In *The Price of Aid: The Economic Cold War in India* (Harvard University Press, 2018), David C. Engerman provides a fascinating blow-by-blow account of how aid diplomacy in those days played out.

[4]Founded in early 1968 by a group of European businesspeople and scientists, this nonprofit NGO serves as an international think tank on global issues.

of high-yielding varieties of Mexican wheat seed from International Maize and Wheat Improvement Center, a research institute (part of CGIAR) in Mexico, to allow Indian agricultural scientists to develop hybrid seeds suitable for Indian conditions. He was ably supported by B. Sivaraman, agriculture secretary, and M.S. Swaminathan, director-general, Indian Council of Agricultural Research. They were opposed by the Planning Commission on the grounds that the ongoing Intensive Agricultural Development Programme, which relied on domestic seeds but with improvements in cultivation practices, was good enough. The Ministry of Finance opposed it on the grounds that the import of seeds would take up scarce foreign exchange. The Left opposed the idea because the Mexican wheat was actually developed by American agronomist Norman Borlaug working under a grant from the Rockefeller Foundation, and it was perceived as adoption of US technology. To her credit, Mrs Gandhi decided to overrule the opposition from these formidable quarters and allow the import as she was determined to avoid any vulnerability with respect to India's food security.

While the country's success in achieving food self-sufficiency was applauded, its failure to reconfigure policy for the industrial sector remained a point of criticism. This was widely used to explain India's poor growth compared to other countries. The original East Asian 'Gang of Four' (Korea, Taiwan, Hong Kong and Singapore) experienced rapid growth in the 1960s, at about 9 per cent per annum. By the 1970s, the Southeast Asian countries were also taking off. Growth in Malaysia, Indonesia and Thailand accelerated from an average rate of 5.9 per cent in the 1960s to an average of 7.6 per cent in the 1970s, but India's growth decelerated from 4.2 per cent in the 1960s to 2.9 per cent in the 1970s. With the population growing at over 2 per cent, this meant per capita GDP was growing at less than 1 per cent per year in the 1970s.

Had we asked why growth had slowed down in India when other countries were able to do well, the search for an answer would almost certainly have highlighted the shortcomings in our policies that could have been corrected. In 1975, in an article titled

'Economists: Diminished Role' for *Seminar*, a well-known monthly magazine with a small but select circulation, I argued that there was need for a shift in policy, reducing the degree of control and extent of protection from imports. The somewhat puzzling title was a hint that the economists weren't doing their job.

3

COMING HOME

Our son Pavan was born in 1977 and it brought a new focus into our lives. We could have continued in Washington DC, enjoying our cosmopolitan lives and pursuing our professional careers. But the idea of returning to India surfaced again, with renewed strength. Isher had always felt that our children — we planned to have another — should have strong Indian roots and this was only possible if we brought them up in India. She also intended to pursue policy-oriented research on the Indian economy and it was therefore logical to relocate to India. For my part, I felt I had done enough of advising developing countries from the outside. I had learnt a lot from the experience but I really wanted to make an impact on economic policies in India trying to negotiate the political constraints, which could only be done working from within.

Dr Manmohan Singh, who later became finance minister and PM, was secretary in the Department of Economic Affairs in the Ministry of Finance and I turned to him for advice. I had first met him in Delhi through Isher in the winter of 1970. I was on home leave and she was also visiting her family prior to taking up her IMF appointment. We were introduced to him by Udham Singh, who was head of the Economics Department at Khalsa College, where Isher had taught for a year before going to MIT.

Udham Singh had invited Dr Singh and the two of us to dinner at the Khyber, a well-known eatery opposite Kashmiri Gate in old Delhi, quite popular in those days among the university crowd. Dr Singh was then a professor at the Delhi School of Economics.

Udham Singh was an austere neo-Marxist with deep reservations about the influence the World Bank may have had on my views on economic policy. But he thoroughly approved of Isher's choice of a Sikh boyfriend! This was a common reaction among her Sikh friends and relatives. She kept telling everyone my religion had little to do with her choice but they were happy at the end result, and also keen to make the reason for their happiness known to her! Many years later, our good friend Surjit Bhalla, now a well-known economist, was smitten by Udham's daughter, Ravinder Kaur, who is now a professor at IIT Delhi. On checking with Ravi that the attraction was mutual, Isher promptly went to work to persuade Udham Singh that Surjit would make a worthy son-in-law, despite his World Bank connection! Having got Udham to shed his prejudice against the World Bank as far as I was concerned, she felt the least she could do was to get him to extend the same concession for his daughter's choice of life partner.

The dinner at Khyber went very well, with light conversation. Those who know Manmohan Singh know he is a man of few words with long silences between bursts of highly substantive conversation. This can be very awkward when you don't know him well. But we both felt he was very happy to meet two young economists starting out in the world and encouraged us to do our best wherever we were working. He was interested in knowing how McNamara was performing as president of the World Bank, which, as he observed, was quite a change from his previous job as US defense secretary. We did not discuss government jobs in India as I wasn't looking for one at the time. In any case, he was not in government at the time.

Shortly after that first introduction, Manmohan Singh did move to government, first as economic advisor in the Ministry of Commerce and soon thereafter as chief economic advisor in the Ministry of Finance. In some ways, he became a role model for me as he had given up an attractive job at the United Nations Conference on Trade and Development in New York to return to

India, first as an academic and moving later to government. As chief economic advisor, he used to visit Washington DC every year for the World Bank and IMF meetings and I would always meet him informally on these occasions. And when we visited Delhi on home leave, lunch with him and his wife Gursharan Kaur at their government home became a regular feature. We were both very impressed with the light touch with which he conveyed his deep understanding of the Indian economy without the slightest impression he was talking to people who knew much less. I would go back every time determined to return and work on the development challenges of India.

On one of his visits to Washington DC, shortly before Pavan was born, I asked him whether there was any chance of my working in the Ministry of Finance for some years. He told me a vacancy was coming up for the post of economic advisor. He explained that all recruitments to senior permanent positions were made through the Union Public Service Commission (UPSC), which advertised the position and then recommended a candidate chosen on a competitive basis from the applicants. He encouraged me to apply as soon as the advertisement appeared. I followed his advice and was selected.

Isher and I were delighted at the opportunity to return home. M. Narasimham, India's executive director in the World Bank, persuaded the management to let me go for a three-year leave without pay when the normal practice was to allow such leave only for two years. Isher was also granted a similar dispensation from the Fund for two years. When the time came, a few years later, we were happy to cut the links to our international jobs without a second thought, but I must admit it was much easier to make the first move knowing we had options. Many of our Indian friends in Washington DC, especially the older ones who had worked in the Government of India, were puzzled that we would leave our comfortable, well-paid jobs. I was warned I would find it difficult to work in a bureaucracy that was not known to value economic expertise. But we had made up our minds.

We relocated to India in June 1979. As the plane descended slowly into the scorching heat of a pre-monsoon Delhi evening, Isher and I were both excited, full of expectations and hope. Our son Pavan was then just short of two years, and too young to have an opinion. Isher was expecting our second child in a few months and our family would soon be complete.

SETTLING DOWN

Our first six months in India saw political instability of a high order. The Janata Party government headed by Morarji Desai fell apart a month after we returned. Chaudhary Charan Singh, who had formed Lok Dal, a party rooted in rural interests, was widely known to be unhappy at being only deputy PM. He broke away with his 64 MPs and became PM with a promise of support from the outside by the Congress party. However, three weeks later, Congress withdrew support, Parliament was dissolved, and fresh elections called in early January 1980.

The wait for a new government gave me more time to deal with the mundane aspects of settling down in Delhi. Our first concern was to find a place to live. Initially, we stayed with my parents in their small three-bedroom home in Panchsheel Enclave. We had helped them buy this house in 1978 and were happy to stay there for the first few weeks. I was entitled to government housing; at my level, this meant a three-bedroom flat at a nominal rent in one of the centrally located government residential complexes. The fine print clarified that this entitlement was 'subject to availability', and it might take a couple of years before such a flat would actually become available. We decided to rent a private accommodation near my parents' home, in good time for Isher's expected date of delivery in October 1979.

It wasn't easy to rent a flat in those days because rent control laws gave tenants so much security that landlords worried that they may not regain possession of their property at the end of the lease period. People often left their properties vacant until they could get a tenant they were comfortable with. We found a very nice first-floor flat in Panchsheel Park, very close to my parents' home. We decided to dip into our savings to allow ourselves this luxury for two years, by when my official accommodation was likely to become available.

The next major decision was acquiring a car. Young people today are used to a variety of cars on offer, with easy financing and manageable monthly payments. In 1979, there were only two choices: the bulky-looking Ambassador, an updated version of the old British Morris Oxford of the mid-1950s, produced by Hindustan Motors; and the smaller and sleeker Padmini, based on the Italian Fiat Millecento of the late 1950s, produced by Premier Automobiles. The Padmini was a much easier car to drive but there was a waiting line of about two years. I could buy a used car straightaway, which sold at a scarcity premium, or wait to buy a new car at the official price. It was my first exposure to the reality of scarcities in a controlled economy. However, there was an escape clause in the form of an 'out-of-turn allotment' that the suppliers could make from the manufacturers' quota at their discretion. Having moved to Delhi to take up what was considered a moderately senior position in government, I qualified. Evidently, the system found ways to allow the official elite to escape the rigours of the controlled economy. I did not have to pay anything for the favour although I was told that a substantial proportion of the manufacturers' quota was effectively sold for a consideration!

Our household effects had been shipped from Washington DC and arrived in Bombay after two months. The shipment was quickly released by customs—apparently, this had much to do with the fact that I was in the Ministry of Finance—and arrived in Delhi in good time for our move. By September 1979, we were comfortably ensconced in our new home in Panchsheel Park. Our second son Aman was born a month later on Diwali, which everyone regarded as extremely auspicious.

I was lucky to accomplish the task of finding a place to live and settle down while work in the ministry was at low ebb. As we all waited for a new government to be formed in January 1980 after the elections, I had time to contemplate what I should focus on when work began in earnest.

ONE OF THE BOYS

The Ministry of Finance occupied half of North Block, one of the two magnificent secretariat buildings on Raisina Hill. As an economic advisor (a joint secretary-level position), I had one of the large, high-ceiling offices on the ground floor. It was much larger than my modest office as a division chief in the World Bank but I missed the open-plan system where the personal secretaries sat on desks outside the offices. In North Block, the joint secretaries had a string of offices next to each other off the main corridor and their support staff shared every fourth room.

The extent of overstaffing was a culture shock. I had a personal assistant, or PA, who took phone calls, typed and managed my appointments, an office clerk who assisted him, and a peon who performed miscellaneous functions such as carrying files from office to office and carting my briefcase to and from my car to the office. My support staff sat in a separate room some distance away; when I needed them, I had to buzz them on the phone. The peon sat immediately outside the office on a chair in the corridor and was available on call.

Before I joined the ministry, I had expected to have frequent contact with Dr Manmohan Singh. I had called on him on my first day at work but I reported directly to the chief economic advisor, R.M. Honavar. I could walk in and out of Honavar's office at will but seeing Dr Singh was more complicated. As secretary of the department, his day was full of meetings, many outside the ministry. Realizing I may be feeling a little lost, he sent for me a couple of days after I joined to see how I was doing. One of his office staff came down to my office and said, 'Secretary sahib *aap ko yaad kar rahey hain* (the secretary is remembering you)'. I was puzzled at first but soon worked out that it was a courteous way of issuing a summons!

When he enquired how I was settling down, I told him I still had to get a hang of what was expected of me. He said that the pace of work was slow but I would soon get caught up in the flow and even have the opportunity to inject new ideas. I just had to be patient.

The Government of India, like any large bureaucracy, has its own ways of functioning and in those days, lateral entry into senior positions was rare. It took time, and some investment in building personal relationships, to become an insider.

Honavar was a mild-mannered person with a very good understanding of India's economic problems. He viewed his role as that of the kindly doctor in a small community, willing and able to help those who came to him but disinclined to push advice where it was not wanted. When I suggested we needed to be more proactive, he gently responded that one did not succeed in government by pushing. He recounted a story about a file dealing with a complex economic policy issue that was sent to him for his views. He recorded his views on the file, indicating that economic analysis suggested a different approach from that reflected in the administrative approval, and sent it forward. When he saw the file on its return journey, he found the secretary (not Dr Singh) had noted: 'This is a policy matter. It should not have gone to the Economic Division.'

Most decisions in government are taken on files in which officials, in ascending order of seniority, record their views as the file makes its way up for final approval. I was never comfortable with the file-based system of decision-making because it minimizes interaction and critical re-examination of views. In later years, when, because of seniority, I had some control over the process, I would set up meetings to discuss the issues that were complex, but the files could not be avoided entirely.

Honavar explained that the senior civil servants were IAS officers, who were all generalists. They viewed economic policy as something that required only a broad familiarity with the subject, good common sense and, above all, the capacity for quick decision-making. They did not think economists brought to the table any special understanding of how the economy would respond to different types of policy changes. Honavar had reconciled himself to this situation and decided to offer advice only when asked. Part of the problem was that there was an unstated caste division between the IAS and the Indian Economic Service (IES), the service Honavar belonged to. There was no bar to an IES officer becoming secretary although it happened only rarely.

I was a little depressed at first but soon realized the situation was not as bad as Honavar made out. Senior civil servants would resist listening to an economist if the economist was peddling specialized knowledge. However, they would happily listen if one spoke as part of the team. I concluded that if I wanted to be effective, I would have to work to be accepted as 'one of the boys' (there were hardly any 'girls' at the joint secretary level in the ministry those days). Over time, I got better at pushing my views in an unobtrusive manner and was accepted as part of the team. An approach that seemed to work particularly well was to first introduce an idea as a suggestion, explore its implications with a senior colleague, subsequently refer to the idea as one that had evolved jointly in the discussion, and finally include more and more people in that discussion and share credit for the idea. More often than not, the idea actually did evolve and got better refined through the different stages. Besides persuading my colleagues and seniors about the need for change, this approach seems to have broken down the barriers of my position vis-à-vis my IAS colleagues. Having joined government in a regular position for economists as economic advisor in the Ministry of Finance, I could have hoped to get to the position of chief economic advisor in normal course. But like Loveraj Kumar, Bimal Jalan, Vijay Kelkar and our more distinguished predecessors Dr Singh and I.G. Patel, I was fortunate to move into government positions normally reserved for the IAS.

Unlike the World Bank where people had lunch together in attractive multi-cuisine cafeterias, in the Ministry of Finance we all brought our lunch from home in insulated lunchboxes. It was common for two or three colleagues to eat together in their offices, sharing what they had brought. Most policy-related work was handled by joint secretaries responsible for different functional areas operating in verticals. Each reported directly to the additional secretary, and the secretary and did not consult their colleagues. There was no compulsion to consult the economic division but they could route the files through the economic advisor or chief economic advisor — and did so if they felt it strengthened their case. Gradually, as I got to know them better through our luncheon meetings and they understood my approach on economic policy, I found more operational work coming my way.

One of the joint secretaries I got to know well was Gopi Arora, an IAS officer from the Uttar Pradesh cadre, who went on to play a very important role in PM Rajiv Gandhi's office when we served there together. A reformed leftist, Gopi knew economic policy had to change and Indian industry needed more flexibility than the control regime allowed. But he also had a healthy scepticism about Indian capitalists. He believed they needed to be steered to a larger national perspective that would not come to them automatically from mere profit maximization. In my early days at the Ministry of Finance, I had many opportunities to discuss these issues as we rode daily in the chartered bus from Moti Bagh, where we both lived, to North Block.

The Economic Division had its own exclusive responsibilities. One of my responsibilities was to review the written answers and detailed briefs for parliamentary questions when Parliament was in session. The material was prepared by junior officers but I shared the task of clearing the final drafts with my colleague Mehfooz Ahmed, the other economic advisor. This was a demanding responsibility as any errors could get the minister into trouble in Parliament. It was hard work but a great way of learning about different aspects of the economy, especially the issues Members of Parliament (MPs) cared for.

My second major responsibility was to supervise (with Mehfooz) the preparation of the Economic Survey, which reviewed macroeconomic developments and the performance of major sectors over the previous year. It also commented on broad directions of policy for the future. As the survey was presented in Parliament a day or two before the Budget, it invariably received extensive press coverage. At first, I was excited by the prospect of being able to say something on policy but soon realized that statements made in the survey had no operational significance. Some newspaper reporters would speculate on what the Budget might contain in the light of what was said in the survey, but knowledgeable reporters knew the link was actually tenuous.

The third part of my work, participating in inter-ministerial meetings, seemed humdrum at first but, in many ways, it was the most important. In those days, the Government engaged in a great deal of micromanaging with middle-level bureaucrats translating broad objectives into specific decisions, such as whether to grant a particular import licence. Much of this took place in inter-ministerial meetings and being part of them helped me understand the system and occasionally contribute to change. One aspect of policymaking that became extremely relevant several years later was the need to bring states on board on the agenda of change. This was not in our consciousness in 1980.

Mao Tse Tung famously said that guerrillas must move among the people like fish in water, difficult to detect but working from within. It was surprisingly relevant advice for an economist in government in those days! It did not always work if strong vested interests were involved but it was an essential first step. On reflection, I think my participation in inter-ministerial committees had more impact on policy than anything I might have put into the Economic Survey.

THE PROBLEM, AS I SAW IT

It was clear to me that the central economic challenge for India was how to break out of the low-growth trajectory and ensure that higher growth would benefit lower-income groups in sufficient measure. The research work I had done at the World Bank was aimed precisely at addressing this problem. In India, there was a tendency in public debate to denigrate growth on the grounds that it did not help the poor. But our problem was not that growth did not trickle down to the poor, rather that the rate of growth itself was too low.

Prof. Raj Krishna had famously characterized India's growth rate in the 1960s and 1970s, which fluctuated around an average of 3.5 per cent per year, as the 'Hindu rate of growth'. The catchy phrase became instantly popular and was often used by critics to blame Jawaharlal Nehru and his belief in Soviet-type central planning. There is no doubt Nehru admired what the Soviet Union had achieved in transforming a feudal society into an industrial power within a few decades, but he was not alone in believing that Soviet planning could generate faster growth. In the 1961 edition of his iconic textbook *Economics*, economist and Nobel laureate Paul Samuelson had projected that if the rate of growth of GDP achieved by the Soviet Union continued, its national income would overtake that of the US possibly by 1984, but most probably by 1997. Twenty years later in the 1980 edition, the expectation of the growth of Soviet GDP relative to US GDP was moderated a little but overtaking was still projected—the dates of overtaking were pushed forward to 2002 and 2012, respectively. These projections were unceremoniously dropped from later editions. Evidently, Soviet planning was not as discredited in the 1960s as it came to be in the late 1980s.

In any case, Nehru and the Congress party never envisaged Soviet-style socialism in India. In agriculture, for example, Congress socialism extended to abolishing the zamindari system of large feudal landowners but it left land firmly in the hands of peasant proprietors operating as private farmers. For industry, it envisaged a mixed economy in which the public sector would play a dominant role, occupying what were called 'the commanding heights of the economy', with the private sector working alongside it, albeit under government control. Most economists in India viewed this 'mixed economy' approach as a reasonable way of getting the best of both worlds. Years later, at a conference on economic policy in Delhi, a visiting Russian economist who was not very fluent in English surprised the audience by describing India as a 'confused' economy, by translating 'mixed' as 'mixed up'. He may well have inadvertently hit the nail on the head in describing our system!

In fact, India's initial growth experience in the Nehruvian period from 1950 to 1965 (Nehru passed away in 1964) at 4.1 per cent per annum was much better than the 1–1.5 per cent growth experienced in pre-Independence times, although it was below the target of 5 per cent. It is during the period after Nehru, from 1965–66 to 1979–80, that growth slowed down to an average of only 2.9 per cent. This was not only lower than in the earlier period but much worse than what was being achieved by many other developing countries in the 1960s and 1970s. In retrospect, the failure to rethink policies to identify the reasons for low growth was a major mistake. China had started to rethink its policies with the agricultural reforms of 1978. We should have had a similar rethink. Mrs Gandhi did that for agriculture with great success with the Green Revolution, but not for industry.

Our system of control over domestic investment and foreign trade needed a major overhaul. Other countries also had public sector enterprises but did not view the private sector with great suspicion. They also had a much more promotional approach to exports, looking out for sectors with export potential and encouraging them to exploit export markets. While we were a large economy in terms of population, the size of our domestic market in most industrial products was quite small. Production aimed only at the domestic market would not permit economies of scale.

The domestic debate was excessively focused on the decline in the rate of investment compared to the mid-60s but there was little attention to whether the control system was promoting inefficiency, in which case, raising investment would not produce the desired results. Even though distinguished Indian economists had pointed out these problems, notably Jagdish Bhagwati, T.N. Srinivasan and Padma Desai, they had little impact on policymakers, possibly because they had all left the country to take up prestigious academic positions abroad. Economists on the left, who held more sway over policymaking, were arguing that the high growth targets were chimerical and that we should focus instead on achieving poverty reduction through intensification of anti-poverty programmes.

We also had major deficiencies in human resource development but I was less conscious of these at the time. They came to be widely recognized as a weakness from the late 1980s onwards, thanks to the energetic work of Amartya Sen. The problem had been highlighted even earlier in 1955 by Milton Friedman of Chicago University when he visited India as part of a programme in which distinguished foreign scholars came to India to advise the Government. Friedman had observed that we gave too much importance to the deficiency of capital and not enough to the deficiency of human skills. His memorandum to the Government of India emphasized that 'the fundamental problem of India is the improvement of the physical and technical quality of her people... the weakening of rigid social and economic arrangements, the introduction of flexibility of institutions and mobility of people, the opening up of the social and economic ladder to people of all kinds and classes'. All these issues came on to the policy agenda with great force only much later.

Bad policies were clearly the villain of the story and the people of India, especially the poor, were its unwitting victims. I wondered at the time whether my job as economic advisor would give me enough opportunity to make a significant contribution, especially as I was an outsider, entering the government laterally. One of my distinguished predecessors in the job, who began as economic advisor in the early 1960s and later became chief economic advisor in the Ministry of Finance, was V.K. Ramaswami. He had written extensively in well-known academic journals (including some papers jointly authored with Jagdish Bhagwati) on the inefficiency of trade policy as a means to achieve other developmental objectives. However, even as Ramaswami enlightened the rest of the world about the improper use of trade policy instruments, Indian economic policy persisted in doing just that! It taught me that mere articulation of policy directions was not enough. It would be necessary to get into the policymaking process, persuade those in senior positions that change was needed, and build a sufficient momentum for change.

The next three decades saw a gradual shift in thinking and economic policy in India and I was privileged to play a part in the process in several different capacities in government. Today, with the benefit of a broad consensus on economic reforms and policy (even if views vary on implementation and momentum), it is easy to forget that this was all highly contested when I joined the Government in 1979. The story of what happened and why it took so long is told in the chapters that follow.

Part Two

4

INDIRA GANDHI RETURNS TO POWER

The general election of January 1980 brought Indira Gandhi back to power. The electorate that had comprehensively voted her out in 1977, declaring its anger with the Emergency, brought her back with a two-thirds majority. The voters were registering their disillusionment with two years of wobbly coalition rule, full of unseemly quarrels about leadership, and the neglect of mounting economic problems.

I had never met Mrs Gandhi. She was known to favour a Leftist approach in economic policy, though many who knew her also said she was a pragmatic politician. She had certainly shown this when she launched the Green Revolution, overruling opposition from the Left, the Planning Commission and the Ministry of Finance. I hoped she would recognize the need for the new approach to policy the economy desperately needed. R. Venkataraman was appointed finance minister. He was a respected politician with a clean image but his only prior experience in the central government was as member of the Planning Commission in charge of industry, power, communications, transport and labour from 1967 to 1971 when the Licence Permit Raj was in full force.

Shortly after the Government took office, Dr Manmohan Singh was moved to the Planning Commission as member secretary. I was disappointed because I had looked forward to working under him. Ram Malhotra, an IAS officer of the Madhya Pradesh cadre, was appointed secretary. He was a civil servant of the old school: scrupulously apolitical with the conviction that incorruptibility and decency were the most important requirements for anyone in high office. He had a way of encouraging junior officers to speak frankly while leaving them in no doubt that his was the final call. It was a trait I consciously tried to emulate in my career in government.

GETTING DOWN TO BUSINESS

The new government inherited an exceptionally difficult economic situation. The Revolution in Iran and the overthrow of the Shah had disrupted oil supplies, causing the price of crude oil to shoot up from $18 per barrel in May 1979 to $39 per barrel in May 1980. This led to a sharp increase in the import bill in 1979–80. It would worsen further in 1980–81 when the full impact of higher oil prices would be felt. The failure of the monsoon in 1979 led to a fall of 13 per cent in agricultural GDP, which also contributed to a decline of 5 per cent in total GDP in 1979–80. The decline in agricultural production led to a sharp increase in food prices. Together with the impact of higher oil prices, wholesale prices increased by 17 per cent in the course of the year.

Within six months of taking over as PM, Mrs Gandhi suffered a major personal setback when her younger son and close political associate Sanjay Gandhi died in an air crash in June 1980. Sanjay was widely seen as Mrs Gandhi's political heir and she was devastated. She brought in her older son Rajiv to help her in politics. The two siblings were poles apart.

Sanjay had started assisting his mother in politics in the early 1970s and gained enormous power during the Emergency. Arrogant and intolerant of dissent, he became highly unpopular for pushing family planning via vasectomies and tubectomies. Officials adopted coercive methods to meet their targets. He also pushed slum clearance programmes in Delhi in an authoritarian fashion, uprooting large numbers of people and relocating them in distant locations.

Rajiv was the exact opposite of Sanjay. He had stayed completely aloof from politics, quietly pursuing his chosen career as a commercial pilot with Indian Airlines. His personal life revolved around his family and a very small group of friends. He had a gentle and winning manner, which he retained even after entering politics. I got an opportunity to meet him soon after he was inducted to help Mrs Gandhi because Vijay Dhar, a friend of the Nehru–Gandhi family, was asked to arrange an informal briefing on the economy for him, and Dhar asked me and Vijay Kelkar if we could do this.

Dhar had fixed a meeting at Mrs Gandhi's residential office at 1 Akbar Road. We spent close to an hour discussing different challenges facing the Indian economy. I formed a very positive impression from that first meeting. Rajiv listened attentively as we talked about how problems in infrastructure, especially in the power sector, were holding the economy back, and how we needed to pay much more attention to exports. He asked pointed questions to understand the exact nature of the problems we were highlighting. At the end, he thanked us, adding modestly that he was new to these subjects and would call us again for a fuller discussion. I had no idea that five years later, I would be working for him in the PM's Office (PMO).

The new government did not announce any big change in strategy but Mrs Gandhi began to make some changes in the old policy model. Critics later dismissed these as 'tinkering' at the margin, while others called it the start of a slow process of reforms.

FIRST STEPS TOWARDS DEREGULATION

A new Industrial Policy was announced in July 1980, which reaffirmed the Industrial Policy Resolution of 1956 and the Government's commitment to the public sector. The sense that nothing had changed was intensified by the fact that six private sector banks that had grown in size were nationalized in 1980. It looked like we were back to 1969, when 14 large private banks were nationalized.

The Industrial Policy of 1980 was essentially old wine in a new bottle but there was a subtle change in the way it was being served. There was some movement towards greater flexibility in implementing the control regime. Excess capacity that had built up in certain sectors was regularized by including the excess in the revised licenced capacity, while export production was excluded from licenced capacity. A decision was taken to allow automatic expansion of capacity every year to a larger number of industries. A licence issued for the production of certain products could now be used for producing similar products as well. These were essentially relaxations at the margin but they were welcomed by a private sector long used to tight control.

Industrial licencing was implemented with a greater willingness to allow the private sector to expand. Companies like Reliance were allowed to set up larger-scale plants, financing them from funds raised from the capital market. Dhirubhai Ambani pioneered the use of convertible debentures to attract middle-class households to invest in debt by offering significantly higher interest rates than bank deposits. The expectation that appreciation in share prices would make it attractive for shareholders to convert the debentures into equity (at the pre-announced conversion price) when the time came.

The establishment of Maruti Udyog Ltd (MUL) in the public sector was a significant — and fortuitous — development that helped change attitudes on many important aspects of industrial policy. MUL was established because Mrs Gandhi wanted to set up a public sector company to realize Sanjay's dream of producing an affordable people's car. He had started a company to produce an indigenously designed car but had made no progress. Both the Planning Commission and the Ministry of Finance opposed the idea on the grounds that automobiles were a luxury, and setting up a factory to produce them would divert resources from other priority areas. Sukhamoy Chakravarty, the doyen of Left economists, who was chairman of the PM's Economic Advisory Council (EAC-PM) at the time, wrote a note opposing the project, but it was approved nevertheless.

V. Krishnamurthy, a seasoned public sector manager, was

handpicked to head the new company. Krishnamurthy had been offered a job at the World Bank but faced with a direct request from the PM, he agreed to stay back and take up the assignment provided he was given full managerial autonomy. She assured him of this.

Several aspects of the MUL experience had implications for industrial policy as it evolved. One was the need to be realistic about the scope for indigenous design. Krishnamurthy made it plain to Mrs Gandhi that we could manufacture the car indigenously, but not design it. She accepted his advice and he began looking for collaborators. This also opened the door to a more relaxed approach to the import of foreign technology in other sectors.

Industry Minister Charanjit Chanana wanted a technology agreement with French auto company Renault. But Krishnamurthy felt the Indian market needed a smaller and cheaper car and sought Rajiv's support to help resist pressure from the minister. Rajiv advised him to stick to his belief and do the right thing. It was a good illustration of how managers in public sector undertakings (PSUs) are pressurized by politicians to act against their managerial instincts.

Krishnamurthy approached the major automakers in Japan but they were not interested. Suzuki Motors Corporation, then primarily a motorcycle producer, had just introduced a small car in Japan with an 800cc engine. They showed interest and Krishnamurthy decided they would better adapt to Indian conditions. He revealed later that this conclusion was partly based on his observation that their Tokyo offices were not air-conditioned! Suzuki initially preferred a licencing agreement with parts being supplied from Japan. Krishnamurthy insisted on 26 per cent equity, with an option to go up to 40 per cent later, because he felt that only a substantial equity stake would ensure Suzuki's long-term interest in the joint venture. The partnership agreement was also structured so that some key decisions could only be taken with the consent of the foreign partner. Krishnamurthy later told me that he did this explicitly to insulate the company from whimsical political interference, a perennial danger for a public sector company.

The MUL experience also drew attention to the importance of economies of scale. The two existing car manufacturers in India at the time had a licence to produce only 20,000 cars per year. Krishnamurthy insisted upon a licence to produce 100,000 cars because it was only at that scale that costs would be low enough to make the car affordable. This was a distinct break from the traditional practice where licencing authorities would divide the likely total domestic demand into smaller sizes to grant licences to more manufacturers. There was the case of an Indian investor who was granted a licence but was told by the machinery supplier abroad that the size of plant he was looking for was actually a pilot-scale plant, and not a commercial-scale one.

The experience with Maruti also highlighted the inflexibility of import licencing. When MUL moved from assembling cars based on completely knocked-down imports to indigenous production under a phased manufacturing programme, they needed to put equipment in place for the next stage of manufacturing. When they asked for a licence to import the equipment to machine the engine block, Hindustan Machine Tools, another public sector company, persuaded the Directorate General for Technical Development (DGTD) that the import licence should be denied as they could supply the machines needed, just as they had done for the engine block of Bajaj scooters.

The matter had to be resolved by Minister of Industries N.D. Tiwari in a meeting. R.C. Bhargava, managing director of MUL, later told me he had arranged to physically bring the engine block of a Bajaj two-wheeler and the engine block of the Maruti car into the room to let everyone see how different the two products were! MUL finally got the import licence, but the episode illustrates the arbitrariness inherent in the system. The flexibility shown here helped the case for a more relaxed administration of the regime.

MUL succeeded beyond expectations. The first car rolled out in 1983 and was an instant success, clearly out-competing the Ambassador and the Premier Padmini. It also went on to usher a revolution in component development, producing an impressive component supplier base that was later able to export auto components and meet the demands of new automobile manufacturers that entered the market in the 1990s.

A HIGHLY FLAWED SYSTEM OF IMPORT LICENCING

I represented the Department of Economic Affairs on the Import Licencing Committee in the Ministry of Commerce, which gave me a first-hand feel of how the system worked. The experience confirmed my belief that the system was extremely inefficient and radical reform was crucial.

The licencing system was as complex as could be. Imports of finished consumer goods were completely banned, except when brought in as baggage by returning travellers. It was a familiar sight to see long queues at the customs counter at the airport, of returning Indians declaring electronic goods including TVs, tape and video players, air-conditioners and even electronic calculators! The ban on imports meant domestic producers of those consumer goods enjoyed near-infinite protection. Consumers were obviously the major victims, paying high prices for low-quality consumer goods.

Machinery or capital goods not produced in India were on the 'open general licence' (OGL) list and could be freely imported without a licence, but those produced in India were on a restricted list and needed an import licence. Some raw materials (metals, ores, crude oil, petroleum products, fertilizers, etc.) could be imported only by state agencies, which then supplied the materials to the users. Other raw materials, intermediate inputs and components were either on OGL and therefore freely importable or on a 'restricted' list requiring an import licence. Further, licences were given only to 'actual users', not traders.

The Licencing Committee was chaired by the chief controller of exports and imports and included representatives of the DGTD and other ministries. The DGTD based its advice on two key considerations: the indigenous availability angle, i.e. whether the item was available from a domestic producer; and the essentiality angle, i.e. whether it was really needed.

There was a high degree of arbitrariness in the decisions. A manufacturer of electric irons wanted to import a particular grade of stainless steel. Domestically produced steel sheets were too thick and would make the iron too heavy. Import of thinner sheets would have been readily allowed if the production of electric irons was for exports, where quality was acknowledged to be paramount, but it was felt the domestic consumer could make do with a heavy iron. No one seemed bothered that the domestic producer would never gain credibility to market his product internationally if his general production line was deemed substandard!

Imports cleared from the indigenous angle could still be rejected because they were not essential. For example, import of sophisticated instrumentation equipment not produced domestically could be deemed to be not essential because the DGTD 'felt' it would not lead to much improvement in the quality of the output. The system was highly non-transparent with enormous scope for corruption to get a favourable ruling from the DGTD. Having got licences for import of raw material, many producers found it more profitable to sell the material in the black market than use it as input in their production.

Exporters were supposed to get easy access to duty-free imports but the ground reality was very different, especially for small-scale exporters. In those days, successful small-scale units often expanded by spinning off a second unit (often at the same location) as the concessions for small-scale units were withdrawn if total investment in a single unit exceeded a cut-off level. A small-scale exporter had won an export order for shoes and obtained a licence for duty-free import of compressed leather soles. The licence had been obtained in the name of one unit but the actual export of shoes had taken place in another. As transfer of duty-free imports to another user was not allowed, the exporter ran the risk of a severe penalty, including imprisonment. While he got away with a mild penalty, the incident illustrates the complexity of policy, the likelihood of unintended violations and the ever-present need to offer bribes to avoid penalties.

The system was particularly unsuitable for areas where technology was changing rapidly. N.R. Narayana Murthy, the iconic co-founder of Infosys, told me of his personal experience in 1983, when Infosys wanted to import a Data General MV/8000 computer, with three removable disk drives with a capacity of 200 MB each. They had to make several trips to New Delhi to get the import licence. By the time they got the licence, a new disk drive with a capacity of 300 MB had become available, 30 per cent cheaper. Naturally, they wanted to import the latest model. However, the original licence specified the model number and several additional visits to Delhi had to be made to modify the licence. In an area where technology was changing rapidly and timely delivery of export orders was crucial, long delays in getting equipment was fatal for exporters.

Narayana Murthy's troubles did not end there. As an exporter, Infosys was entitled to a reduction in import duty from 150 per cent to 25 per cent, provided they exported software three times the import value. They got the relevant certificate from the Department of Electronics entitling them for duty reduction but when they went to clear the consignment at the Bangalore customs, the officer hinted that he expected a bribe to clear the consignment at the reduced duty. When Infosys refused to pay, he rejected the duty reduction certificate on technical grounds and levied an extra ₹10 lakh in duty. While an appeal was possible, the duty had to be paid first. Though they were still a small company in 1983, Infosys held firm, deciding to pay and appeal. It took nine years before the Appellate Tribunal finally ruled in their favour! This is as good an example as any of what can happen when lower-level functionaries have discretionary powers and no danger of being held accountable for wrong decisions.

Having seen what licencing meant in practice, I was puzzled at the pervasive belief that we could curtail imports through a complex licencing regime without generating inefficiency and hurting growth. This belief was surprisingly widespread in academic circles in India despite enough evidence that documented the harm import controls were inflicting.[5] We were to see the worst aspect of this type of import tightening at the time of the 1990 crisis.

APPROACHING THE IMF

With oil prices remaining above $32 per barrel through 1980, it became clear that our balance of payments (BOP) would be under stress. The current account deficit of the BOP increased from 0.5 per cent of GDP in 1979–80 to 1.5 per cent in 1980–81[6], and this brought about a fall in our foreign exchange reserves. We had to either find ways of financing the deficit or cut down imports, which would hurt GDP growth. The prospects for additional external assistance from traditional bilateral donors and the World Bank were not favourable and we did not want to rely too much on commercial borrowing. The only other source of financing was the IMF, which could be approached for emergency assistance to finance the deficit while taking corrective steps that would reduce the deficit over the medium term.

Our executive director in the World Bank, M. Narasimham, advised that we should approach the IMF for a loan under the Extended Fund Facility (EFF), which had been established in 1974

---

[5]Kreuger, Anne, *The Costs and Benefits of Import Substitution: A Case Study of India*, University of Minnesota Press, 1975; Bhagwati, Jagdish and Desai, Padma, *India: Planning for Industrialisation, Industrialisation and Trade Policies Since 1951*, Oxford University Press, 1970; Bhagwati, Jagdish and Srinivasan, T.N., *Foreign Trade Regimes and Economic Development: India*, Columbia University Press, 1975.

[6]The current account deficit in the BOP is the net result of current receipts from exports of goods, services and remittances, etc; and payments for imports of goods and services such as travel, education, etc. plus interest payments. It has to be financed by net capital inflows. If the inflows are not sufficient, it leads to decline in foreign exchange reserves.

in response to demands from India and other developing countries.

Developing countries had argued that the Fund's conventional lending facilities (called standby arrangements) were ill-suited to the needs of developing countries because they viewed problems with BOP as arising from excess domestic demand spilling over into imports. This led the Fund to recommend a reduction in aggregate demand as a way to reduce the current account deficit. However, developing countries often experience BOP problems because of structural supply constraints, which force them to rely on imports. The corrective policy needed in such cases is to remove supply bottlenecks through more investment in critical supply-constrained sectors. As this takes time, financial assistance is needed for a longer period and repayment should also be stretched out over a longer period. The EFF, therefore, provided funding for three to three-and-a-half years instead of 12 to 18 months for a standby agreement.

The Ministry of Finance was reluctant to approach the IMF because the memory of the devaluation episode of 1966 was still fresh and they thought Mrs Gandhi would reject any proposal to go to the Fund (*see Chapter 2*). During a visit to Delhi, Narasimham broached the subject directly with Mrs Gandhi, explaining the need for India to approach the Fund, especially for the EFF. He also argued that as many developing countries reeling from the oil shock were likely to do the same, there was merit in putting in our application earlier, assuring her we could get funding without having to devalue. Mrs Gandhi asked him to put his ideas in a note and send it to her office.

She sent the note to Finance Minister Venkataraman with the request that he explore the possibility of EFF assistance. I was asked to prepare a note for the cabinet outlining the scale of the BOP problem and explaining the benefits of the EFF. It was my first experience of preparing a note for the cabinet on an important policy matter and I enjoyed the sense of involvement. The note was quickly approved. Commerce Minister Pranab Mukherjee cautioned Mrs Gandhi about the likely policy conditions the IMF would impose, but we were able to dispel these fears.

On the sidelines of the meeting of the IMF's Interim Committee in Libreville, Gabon, in April 1981, Jacques de Larosière, managing director of the Fund, assured Finance Minister Venkataraman that if India applied for assistance, we would have his full support. He did, however, ask whether we would accept the normal standby credit. I was present when Venkataraman was quite firm in saying we would not. De Larosière later told Narasimham that he had to fulfil this formality in case there were questions from the board.

The political sensitivity of approaching the IMF was such that the negotiations had to be conducted in secret. London was chosen as the venue and the IMF and Indian delegations checked into the Waldorf Hotel in the last week of July. The hotel was just across the street from the Indian High Commission, which made it easier to establish secure communication with Delhi if necessary. As it happened, the timing of the negotiations coincided with the wedding of Prince Charles and Lady Diana Spencer, providing a splendid backdrop of royal pageantry. The Waldorf was just a hundred yards from the Strand along which the royal procession would pass on its way to St. Paul's Cathedral. Both sides agreed to a break in the negotiations as soon as the TV showed the procession entering the Strand, so we could walk down and watch the cheering crowds wave them on. I spent £20 (a very respectable sum in 1981) on a commemorative plate with portraits of Prince Charles and Lady Diana. The plate survives even though the marriage, sadly, did not.

The EFF arrangement was the largest IMF loan ever until then, and gave India access to a total of SDR 5 billion[7] over a three-year period from 1981 to 1984. The arrangement was unusual because the corrective policies included increased public investment in key sectors such as petroleum, cement and steel to help expand

---

[7]SDR (Special Drawing Rights) is an accounting unit first created by the IMF in 1969 and used for its internal accounting purposes. It is defined as a basket of important national currencies and the weights are revised every five years.

domestic production and save on imports. We did not have to agree to any overall limit on the fiscal deficit, only on how much the Reserve Bank of India (RBI) could lend the Government.[8] There was an understanding that we would continue to liberalize import policy, a process that had already begun, albeit in a limited way. Most importantly, there was no requirement to devalue the rupee. We only agreed to ensure that the exchange rate policy would be 'appropriate', a roundabout way of saying the Government would not allow the real exchange rate of the rupee to appreciate in a way that would reduce the competitiveness of our exports.

The Fund's board approved the proposal with the US abstaining, but not opposing. Abstaining was a well-established way of the US telling its domestic constituency in the US Congress that they had not supported a loan proposal, while actually allowing it to be approved. De Larosière had fought hard against US objections to get the EFF facility established, and he wanted to have an 'India EFF' as a feather in his cap. The IMF staff naturally fell in line but I learnt later that they viewed the programme as far too soft. It was widely regarded in the Fund as a precedent never to be repeated!

Ironically, although the IMF staff thought we had got away with very little conditionality, we faced intense criticism at home for 'selling out'. The Government made public what we had agreed to do by way of corrective policies, but the actual letter of the finance minister to the managing director outlining the agreed performance criteria was not made public. This was a clear mistake that led to needless speculation about possible hidden assurances. N. Ram, then US correspondent of *The Hindu* based in Washington DC, pulled off a journalistic coup by getting a copy of the letter from the board papers circulated for the meeting and published it. It showed there were no hidden promises but such was the sensitivity that because the letter used American spelling—'labor'

---

[8]This meant that government borrowing from the market, including commercial banks, was not restricted. Only financing the fiscal deficit from the RBI was restricted.

instead of 'labour'—it was viewed as proof that the letter was drafted by the Fund! We had to explain that the Fund used American spelling in all its documents and the necessary spelling changes were made automatically in any documents distributed to the board.

The West Bengal government published a collection of articles[9] by well-known Left economists criticising different aspects of the agreement, with an introduction by Ashok Mitra, finance minister of the state. It was my first exposure to the Left view on economic policy. We were accused of 'mortgaging the whole future of the country' to imperialism and leading India into a 'debt trap'. There was criticism that the Memorandum of Understanding (MoU) allowed for policies to be discussed with the Fund! The Left even criticized an assertion in the memorandum that we would not engage in commercial borrowings as accepting a limitation on our sovereignty, ignoring the fact that the whole point of going to the IMF was that we wanted to avoid commercial borrowings! It is remarkable how deeply suspicious the Left intellectuals were of policies that have since become universally acceptable.

As it happened, the BOP improved much faster than anticipated and we were able to end the EFF arrangement a year ahead of time after drawing only SDR 3.9 billion. This happy outcome came about primarily because we struck lucky with oil production in Bombay High, which led to a decline in oil imports and an improvement in the BOP. I was later told by the Fund staff that whereas programmes in many other countries saw growth slowing significantly during the period, in our case growth in the three-year period of the programme (1981–82 to 1983–84) averaged 5.5 per cent, more than double the average in the previous three years.

Many years later, I met De Larosière in Paris and took the opportunity to thank him for his support to India. De Larosière said he was particularly proud of the India programme, as it demonstrated that adjustment in developing countries was

---

[9]*The IMF Loan Facts and Issues*, Government of West Bengal, November 1981.

possible with no damage to growth. He also told me that the US was irritated at him for having pushed to establish the EFF in the first place, and then for supporting the India programme as much as he did, with its emphasis on public investment. 'I know they referred to me as that mad French socialist!' he said.

THE SWRAJ PAUL EFFECT

R. Venkataraman moved to the Ministry of Defence in 1982 and Pranab Mukherjee moved from the Ministry of Commerce to become finance minister. He was keen to find ways of financing the current account deficit without having to depend on the IMF. He had been advised that if non-resident Indians (NRIs) were allowed to invest in Indian shares, we could attract a large inflow to help finance the deficit. In his Budget speech for 1982–83, he announced that NRIs and their overseas corporate bodies would be allowed to purchase shares in existing firms listed in the Indian stock exchanges up to a total of 40 per cent of equity. The announcement also stated that not more than 1 per cent of the shares could be bought by any one individual or company. This was clearly meant to limit any individual's ability to acquire a controlling share but careless drafting had left a loophole: there was nothing to stop an individual from acquiring additional shares operating through different companies.

Swraj Paul, a London-based NRI, used the loophole to acquire 13 per cent of the total equity in DCM and 7.5 per cent in Escorts. He also set the cat among the pigeons by announcing that he intended to press for better management of these companies and hoped the financial institutions that were large shareholders in these companies would help in this process. Indian families had for long controlled large empires by holding only small proportions of equity. The Shriram family controlled DCM with only 10 per cent of the equity and the Nandas controlled Escorts with only 5 per cent. The situation was similar in other private sector groups. There was consternation that if new entrants started mobilizing support from financial institutions for changes in management, the outcome would inevitably be politicized. Swraj Paul's perceived closeness to Mrs Gandhi only stoked this fear.

Shareholder democracy in a private company implies that if incumbent managements cannot mobilize enough shareholder support, they should give way to those who can. However, families controlling large private sector groups argued that public financial institutions had acquired large shareholdings in their companies because of the convertibility clause that was compulsorily included in loans when these companies borrowed from these institutions. They claimed they had no option but to accept this clause because the financial system was dominated by public sector institutions. They argued that institutions should either remain neutral in any takeover bid or, preferably, prevent 'established managements' from being destabilized!

The Government quickly modified the policy to limit the total direct and indirect acquisition by an NRI to no more than 5 per cent of total equity. However, these provisions did not apply to Swraj Paul's acquisitions because they were made before the new limits were put in place. The managements fought back by refusing to register the change in the ownership of the shares in his favour! In the end, the Government buckled and brokered an agreement under which Paul sold his shares back to the Nandas and the Shrirams at 'agreed prices', at which he would not incur a loss.

The episode revealed a fault line in Indian capitalism because families were controlling large industrial empires with very little equity stake. The fact that they were able to refuse to register changes in ownership of shares with impunity also revealed weakness in the regulatory framework of the capital market. These weaknesses were finally addressed 10 years later, when an independent statutory regulator of the capital markets was established and the markets opened up to foreign institutional investors (FIIs). The Swraj Paul affair also incentivized controlling families to gradually increase their stake in their companies. It was a start of a long process of moving towards better corporate governance—this remains a work in progress.

DECONTROLLING CEMENT

In 1981, I got the opportunity to get involved in the decontrol of cement when I was a member of an official committee on cement pricing. Cement at that time was under full price control. The industry was divided into low-cost, medium-cost and high-cost units of production, with different producer prices for each category. Consumers were charged a pooled price and distribution was controlled by the cement controller. Cement was allocated to the Centre for key infrastructure projects and to different states for further distribution to users. The system was guaranteed to discourage investment and perpetuate scarcities as producers were not paid the price consumers were willing to pay and the black market price for cement was four times the controlled price.

We had barely got down to work when a major scandal erupted, with Abdul Rahman Antulay, the Congress chief minister (CM) of Maharashtra, in the eye of the storm. Antulay was allegedly allocating cement from the state quota at controlled prices to individuals in return for large donations to a trust he had set up. He had also used Mrs Gandhi's name on the trust without her knowledge. The PM was extremely annoyed, and we learnt she was keen to bring in a system that would avoid such misuse.

The chairman of the committee was Arun Ghosh, a widely respected Left-leaning economist who was chairman of the Bureau of Industrial Costs and Prices at the time. He was fully aware of the irrationalities of price control as he had served as member secretary of the Dagli Committee, set up by the Morarji Desai government in 1977 to review the gamut of controls in the Indian economy. In an informal chat, Arun asked me for my views on price control. When I expressed my considered opinion to shift to decontrol and market pricing, which would give producers the incentive to invest and expand production and make Antulay-type scandals impossible, Arun felt it may be less disruptive to decontrol gradually over time. I was happy to support a phased transition. We could have a system where producers surrender a portion of their production to the cement controller for allocation to priority areas at the official price, while being allowed to sell the rest in the free market. The surrendered portion could be reduced gradually over time.

Industry representatives on the committee did not want price decontrol—they only wanted the price to be raised to reflect higher costs. Ghosh told me he would let his staff work on the cost data submitted by the industry as if we only intended to adjust controlled prices, while we quietly worked out a plan for decontrol. He had consulted other senior officials in the Ministry of Finance and the PMO to ensure this approach would be acceptable. Committees that want their advice accepted are well advised to consult those who will have to implement the recommendations!

We recommended that individual producers should be required to surrender 75 per cent (for old units) and 60 per cent (for new units) of their licenced capacity to the Government at a single retention price, and allowed to sell the rest in the free market. By specifying the amount to be surrendered as a percentage of the licenced capacity, we created an incentive to maximize production as the entire production in excess of the amount surrendered could be sold in the free market. We also recommended that the industry be fully decontrolled in five to six years. It was a classic case of gradualism, with a clear time path for reaching the end position.

The recommendations were accepted except that the retention price was lower than what we had proposed; this was offset by reducing the amount to be surrendered to the Government. The new policy was announced in February 1982 and proved to be highly effective in generating a strong investment response. The percentage to be surrendered was progressively reduced in subsequent years and we were able to achieve full decontrol by 1989. The experiment of decontrol was a great success, encouraging investment and resulting in increased production of cement.

GRADUALISM AND REFORM BY STEALTH

Sometime in 1983, I started worrying that rates of inflation in India were higher than those of our major trading partners. If this continued, it would amount to an appreciation of the 'real' exchange rate, which would have an adverse effect on our export competitiveness. I felt we should have the flexibility to manage the nominal exchange rate such that we could offset any appreciation in the real effective rate because of our higher rates of inflation.

The exchange rate of the rupee at the time was fixed with reference to a basket of five major currencies (US Dollar, Pound Sterling, Deutsche Mark, Yen and the Swiss Franc). The basket, which consisted of specified amounts of these currencies, was valued at ₹100. As the exchange rate of the pound vis-à-vis other currencies changed, the pound value of the basket changed every day. The exchange rate with respect to the pound, therefore, also changed every day and the RBI would announce the official rate vis-à-vis the pound every day at 9.00 a.m. The existing rules allowed the RBI the flexibility to fix the exchange rate within a margin of 2.5 per cent of the basket-determined exchange rate.

Flexibility of 2.5 per cent would not give enough margin to move the nominal rate to achieve a real effective exchange rate target because our inflation differentials vis-a-vis our partner countries were large. Even increasing the margin to 5 per cent would not be enough as the large inflation differentials looked likely to persist. We needed to adopt a policy whereby every time the nominal exchange rate of the rupee reached the outer edge of, say, the 5 per cent band, the RBI should recalibrate the basket by an equal proportional reduction in the amounts of the five currencies so that the rate based on the new basket would be equated with the prevailing exchange rate. This recalibration would restore the 5 per cent flexibility on either side. This amounted to devaluing the rupee against the original basket, but it would not require any public announcement on the day the change was made because the exchange rate on that day would not change.

I had discussed exchange rate issues with Dr Singh in New Delhi when he was member secretary of the Planning Commission and I knew he regarded an appreciation in the real exchange rate as an undesirable development. He had moved to the RBI as governor in 1982 and I thought I should bounce these ideas off him. I made plans to visit Bombay on some other business and arranged to call on him. It was not normal for a mere economic advisor to get a meeting with the RBI governor but our long acquaintance helped override protocol. When I outlined my proposal, he agreed this would be a better system but he pointed out that the cabinet would have to accept this as a policy. For this, the Ministry of Finance would have to take a note to the cabinet proposing the change. I suggested that if he recommended that we should examine this possibility to Ram Malhotra, economic affairs secretary, I could take it from there. He asked me to summarize my proposal in a note and leave it with him.

Shortly after I returned to Delhi, Malhotra received a letter from Governor Manmohan Singh suggesting that we consider a new system along the lines I had discussed with him and seek necessary approvals from the cabinet. Malhotra called me for a detailed discussion and I was able to convince him of the merits of the change. As the exchange rate was being announced every day, it would be possible to nudge it in a particular direction by taking small steps. He asked me to prepare an official note for the cabinet and it went through smoothly.

This was an example of both gradualism and reform by stealth. I must say it worked very well. The exchange rate was ₹9.8 to a dollar in January 1983 and it depreciated to ₹12.2 to a dollar by January 1986. The cumulative depreciation of 24.5 per cent over 36 months amounted to an average depreciation of about 0.68 percentage points per month. These small changes were absorbed without any political opposition, whereas a sudden large devaluation would almost certainly have caused a political explosion.

1984: A TERRIBLE YEAR

By the middle of 1984, I had completed five years in the Ministry of Finance. The economy had done much better than in the previous decade, but by 1984 the centre of attention had shifted away from economics to tensions building up in Punjab. In 1983, militants under the leadership of Jarnail Singh Bhindranwale moved into the Golden Temple complex and there were reports of militant activity being coordinated from the temple. Events soon spiralled out of control, culminating in the Indian Army being ordered into the Golden Temple complex to flush out the militants in Operation Blue Star. Faced with unexpectedly strong resistance, the Army ended up bringing a tank into the temple complex, causing massive damage to the Akal Takht. Other than the armed militants, the casualties included many worshippers caught inside the complex.

Sikhs in the country and outside were deeply hurt, much more than the Government had allowed for. As a Sikh, the developments were deeply disturbing for me personally. As these events were unfolding, my leave period from the World Bank came to an end and I had to make a decision.

Both Isher and I had benefitted from global exposure in the early years of our professional career but we felt totally at home in Delhi among family and friends, bringing up Pavan and Aman. Further, I had underestimated the professional satisfaction I would get from working in my own country. While there was frustration at the slow pace, I had a much better appreciation of the difficulty in bringing about change in a large and highly diverse country working within a democratic environment. It was obvious that there was a great deal to be done. And I felt there was a chance it would get done if enough people worked at it. For her part, Isher had made a successful effort at research and was about to publish a book on Indian industrial stagnation.

All these factors made the decision very simple. I wrote out a simple letter of resignation, sent it to the World Bank and settled down to continue working as economic advisor in the

Ministry of Finance. I was working under Bimal Jalan who was the chief economic advisor. He had also left the World Bank many years earlier to go to ICICI as chief economist and then to the Commonwealth Secretariat in London. I hoped that one day, when Bimal Jalan moved on to a higher position, I would have a good chance of succeeding him.

Sometime in August 1984, I was unexpectedly summoned to the office of P.C. Alexander, principal secretary to PM Indira Gandhi. He told me that Arjun Sengupta, the economic advisor and special secretary in the PMO, was being sent to Washington DC as India's representative on the executive board of the IMF, and he (Alexander) had recommended I replace Arjun. I was told Mrs Gandhi had responded favourably but a final decision would only be taken after she interviewed me, a practice she followed for all senior appointments to her staff. He told me to keep this strictly to myself until the announcement was made.

The interview with Mrs Gandhi never happened. She was assassinated on the morning of 31 October 1984 by two Sikh guards, part of her security staff, who were incensed at the attack on the Golden Temple earlier in the year. It was not until much later in the day that her death was officially announced and Rajiv Gandhi was sworn in as PM. By evening, there were reports of Sikhs being attacked on the streets of Delhi. The next three days saw murderous mobs attacking Sikhs in many parts of the city, dousing them with kerosene and setting them on fire. There was also systematic looting and burning of Sikh homes and shops. Most of the rioting and killing was concentrated in East and West Delhi, but there were scattered attacks in South Delhi, too, in which Sikhs were killed and their property looted.

We lived in Moti Bagh, a government residential complex for civil servants located right next to the heavily patrolled diplomatic area. Our particular block was also well guarded because a senior Sikh officer of the Border Security Force lived in the same block. We did not think we were in any danger but we were concerned about the safety of my parents in Panchsheel Enclave in South

Delhi. My brother Sanjeev, an Uttar Pradesh (UP) cadre IAS officer, was posted in Allahabad at the time but his wife Vidyun and their 18-month-old son Ishan were staying with my parents. My mother, who came from a Hindu family and had short hair, insisted on staying at home with Vidyun and Ishan. A Rajput from UP, Vidyun later told me that as a matter of precaution, she started applying sindoor to her hair to make her Hindu identity unmistakably visible!

My father was a turbaned Sikh and we decided he should move in with us, at least for a few days. Such was the sense of insecurity that Arun Shourie, editor of *Indian Express*, who lived close to us in West End, suggested I should not drive my father across myself, as the sight of two men with turbans might provoke an attack. He offered to drive my father over in his car and did so with great care, getting him to huddle out of sight in the back of the car, covered with a blanket. I have always felt indebted to Arun, a long-time friend from the St. Stephen's and World Bank days, for his help in those trying times.

The rioting was finally brought under control only on 4 November when the Army was called in. The full extent of the carnage became known much later and it painted a deeply disturbing picture of the fragility of communal harmony. Numerous commissions and other bodies have gone into the matter and all the reports have confirmed that the rioting was highly organized and the police clearly failed to do their duty to counter the violence that took place before their eyes. As a Sikh, I was particularly shaken by what had happened, more so because some Congress party leaders were reported to have been seen among the mobs in several places.

The fact that no politically important person, or even senior police official, was convicted for decades for the riots that took about 3,000 lives in the capital, and many more in other parts of the country as a whole, remains a blot on India's governance (one of the accused, Sajjan Kumar, was sentenced to life imprisonment by the Delhi High Court only as late as 17 December 2018). Twenty-one years later, in August 2005, Dr Singh, India's first Sikh PM, heading the Congress-led UPA government, apologized in the Lok Sabha for what happened in 1984: 'I have no hesitation in apologizing to the Sikh community. I apologize not only to the Sikh community but to the whole of the Indian nation because what took place in 1984 is the negation of the concept of nationhood enshrined in our Constitution.' Also, shortly before the 2014 elections, in an interview with news anchor Arnab Goswami, Congress Vice President Rahul Gandhi (who was a schoolboy when the riots occurred) acknowledged that some people from the party were probably involved in the riots. While the Sikhs as a community are forward-looking and large-hearted, given the scale of the violence, it is a legitimate source of grievance that hardly anyone has been punished in all these years.

The days immediately after the riots were traumatic. The loss of trust between the Hindu and Sikh communities in the capital was massive even though there were many stories of friends and neighbours from the Hindu community helping Sikhs avoid mob violence and sheltering them in their homes. Isher was then a professor at the Centre for Policy Research in Delhi. She had never experienced mob violence on this scale and was deeply disturbed by the loss of trust it caused. She decided to mobilize some of the most distinguished Sikhs in Delhi—writer Khushwant Singh, Air Chief Marshal Arjan Singh, Delhi University Vice-Chancellor Gurbaksh Singh and former Member of the Planning Commission Tarlok Singh—to draft a statement to try to rebuild bridges between the two communities.

The statement condemned Mrs Gandhi's assassination as a 'heinous crime... against all the tenets of the Sikhs and abhorrent to all who cherish the norms and values of a civilized society'. It went on to say, 'We must now act positively to combat the challenge to our society and our secular values' and called for the rehabilitation of those dispossessed, and strengthening the confidence of the Sikh community. The statement was signed by about 80 prominent Sikhs, including industrialists, retired civil servants and Army officers, lawyers, doctors and academics, and was covered by the major daily newspapers.

The general election held in December 1984 brought the Congress party, led by Rajiv, back to power with a tremendous majority. This was obviously not a normal election. An electorate shocked by the assassination of Mrs Gandhi, and swamped with fears about the rise of terrorism in Punjab, had voted for stability and the unity of the country. The year ended with the Bhopal gas tragedy, where many people died. Indeed, 1984 had been a year best forgotten and we all turned to 1985 with hope for a better future.

5

REACHING FOR THE 21st CENTURY

Rajiv Gandhi was sworn in as PM on 5 January 1985, having won an unprecedented majority in the general election. At 40, he was the youngest PM India has ever had. He had a modern outlook and his personal background was free of the socialist thinking that had influenced the older generation of Congress leaders, including his mother. In his very first speech as PM, he spoke of 'preparing India for the 21st century'. The new century was still 15 years away but the message resonated with the youth.

A few days after the new government was sworn in, I learnt that the proposal for me to move to the PMO had not been shelved and Rajiv had approved my appointment as additional secretary to the PM. I joined the PMO at the end of January. Moving from North Block to its architectural twin, South Block, where the PMO is located, was a short distance geographically — literally across the road — but very removed in its ambience. Tight security meant that only people with appointments could enter; this included cabinet ministers, CMs, visiting foreign dignitaries and other VIPs, like senior businessmen. The PM met the general public at his Race Course Road residence.

The PMO had a relatively small complement of senior officers. Arun Singh, a friend of Rajiv from their days together in Cambridge, had left the private sector to join politics. He was a Rajya Sabha MP and was named parliamentary undersecretary in the PMO. I had known Arun from our student days at St. Stephen's. Serla Grewal, an IAS officer from the Punjab cadre, was secretary to the PM, the first woman to occupy this position.

Gopi Arora, who had been a colleague at the Ministry of Finance, was additional secretary but was much more influential than his rank implied—he dealt with the most politically sensitive issues. Ronen Sen of the Foreign Service handled foreign policy issues and later went on to serve as India's ambassador to Russia and the US. We were joined a little later by Mani Shankar Aiyar whom I had known since my days at St. Stephen's. My responsibilities in the PMO spanned subjects covered by a number of different economic ministries. This broadened the range of issues I was involved in, although my engagement on each issue was not continuous.

WORKING WITH RAJIV

With a PM almost the same age as me, I had the feeling our generation had arrived and we had a chance to make a real difference. Unlike his senior cabinet colleagues who were full-time politicians and had never held a regular job, Rajiv Gandhi had worked as a commercial pilot in Indian Airlines. I thought this gave him a better understanding of how to work with professionals. He respected technical expertise and was aware of the importance of new technology and the need for training. He was licenced to fly Fokker aircraft and was about to start training to fly jets when he left his job and joined politics.

Rajiv Gandhi was comfortable with computers at a time when all ministers and almost all top government officials were computer illiterate. The difference was starkly revealed when Railways Minister Madhavrao Scindia came to the PMO to brief him on a proposal to raise passenger and freight charges to cover cost increases. The PM wanted to explore other alternatives, and every time he suggested one, the Railways officials pulled out their electronic calculators to work out the implications for total revenue. He then said, 'Madhav, this is not the way to do it. Why not get it all on a spreadsheet and we can meet again tomorrow to work in a sensible way.'

The following day, Scindia and his team walked in and one of the officials spread a large sheet of paper across the PM's desk with alternative fare combinations. The PM was genuinely surprised that the top managers of the second largest railway system in the world had no idea what 'spreadsheet' meant, three years after Lotus 1-2-3 had been commercially released. There were junior officials who were very computer-savvy but they did not get to attend meetings with the PM!

The PM then deputed someone from the computer cell in the PMO to help them install the relevant software package to enable the railway minister and his officials to conduct a spreadsheet analysis. Twenty-four hours later, the PM and the railways minister were happily exploring alternative combinations of passenger and freight rate structures, and their implications for additional revenue. They quickly agreed on what they felt was an acceptable solution. The new technology had empowered the actual decision-makers while the bureaucracy looked on passively!

Rajiv Gandhi often surprised us with his willingness to break with hierarchy. Traditionally, the finance minister calls on the President on the morning the Budget is to be presented, to inform him of its contents. When he had to perform this ritual as finance minister for the 1987–88 Budget, I had briefed him on the issues the President might raise and he asked me to come along. As I tried to move towards a car in his motorcade, he waved me into his SUV, which he drove himself to Rashtrapati Bhavan!

Quite apart from his informality, I felt Rajiv Gandhi was genuinely interested in hearing different points of view. I remember an occasion when we were reviewing a speech he was to deliver that talked about non-violence being deeply rooted in our value system. I had not said anything but he sensed my unease and asked if I wanted to comment. I said that I thought the statement was exaggerated because our history was as full of violence as other countries. He thought about it for a while and responded, 'Well, that may be true of the practice, but non-violence as a principle has been embedded in our culture and principles are important even if we don't always live up to them.' I thought that was a nice touch.

A NEW VISION

In some ways, Rajiv Gandhi was much more like his grandfather than his mother. Nehru had a distinct vision for India as a post-colonial economy going through a public sector-led process of modernization. Much of economic policy in his time was determined by that overarching vision. Mrs Gandhi shared the same vision but she was much more pragmatic and tactical — lurching to the Left in the late 1960s and '70s, and being open to reform in the 1980s when it was clear the old ways were not working. However, the fledgling reforms of the early '80s cannot be called a new vision. But Rajiv very clearly had a vision. He was the first political leader to articulate that India needed to prepare consciously for the 21st century. His reply to the President's address in the Lok Sabha in February 1985 clearly stated that 'We cannot pretend to be equal to other countries when we are operating systems that are 20 years old or 10 years out of date.'

Much of his impatience for change came intuitively because of his professional background and youth. He was fully aware of the emerging middle class in India and the reorientation it would require in many dimensions of policy: the importance of technology and telecommunications, the importance of infrastructure and the challenges of urbanization and the need to be more open and encourage FDI. He knew his background had not exposed him to conditions in rural areas but he was determined to make up for this by extensive touring.

His first rural visit as PM was in August 1985 to Kalahandi in Orissa (now Odisha), one of the poorest districts in the country that was suffering from successive droughts with reports of famine. Sonia Gandhi was with him. He had expected to see poverty and distress, but was not prepared for the utter ineffectiveness of the government programmes that were meant to help the rural poor. Public works programmes designed to create employment were often not started in time because funds were not released by the state government to the district. Where funds were released, implementation was poor, with complaints of underpayment of wages and leakages owing to corruption.

It was after the Kalahandi visit that Rajiv made his much quoted remark that out of every rupee spent by the Government to help the rural poor, only 15 paise actually reaches them. Many journalists assumed his statement was based on inputs provided by me but it was based entirely on his personal impressions. A few years later, Kirit Parikh, a distinguished economist who later served as a member of the Planning Commission, carried out an empirical study of the Public Distribution System (PDS) to work out how much actually reached the poor. His estimate was 22 paise out of every rupee spent, not far from the PM's off-the-cuff assessment!

POLITICS UNRAVELS

The political environment at the start of Rajiv Gandhi's term could not have been better. He had the largest majority ever in the Lok Sabha and his position as the leader of the Congress party was unassailable. He began well by seeking to address long-standing political problems. In July 1985, he signed the Punjab Accord with Sant Harchand Singh Longowal, president of the Akali Dal. It listed the steps the Government would take to address the many grievances that had made Punjab a troubled state and was widely seen as heralding a new era of peace. This was followed by the Assam Accord later in the year and the Mizoram Accord in 1986. Speaking at the Congress centenary celebrations in Bombay in December 1985, he talked of inner-party reform to ensure the top positions went to those with genuine support from the rank and file, and not to those he called the 'brokers of power' who 'rode on the backs of Congress workers'. Many read the speech as promising internal elections to the top positions in the party.

Had he succeeded in these efforts, he would have gained enormous political strength and would be better placed to undertake the economic reforms he had talked about, but the political environment turned very quickly. Sant Longowal was assassinated in August 1985 and the Punjab Accord disintegrated soon thereafter. The Assam Accord also ran into problems. There was a serious falling out with V.P. Singh, a key member of his economic team. Singh was moved from finance to defence in January 1987 and he resigned on 12 April 1987, exiting from the party shortly thereafter.

On 16 April 1987, Swedish radio alleged that Swedish arms manufacturer Bofors AB had made illegal payments to Swedish politicians and officials in other countries in relation to arms contracts. One of the contracts mentioned related to the purchase of the FH 77B Howitzer for the Indian Army. There was uproar in the Parliament because the payment of commissions in defence deals had been explicitly banned by Rajiv Gandhi himself. The Bofors scandal cast a very long shadow over his government. The investigations showed that some payments from Bofors were made to Ottavio Quattrocchi, who was known to the Gandhi family and represented the Italian public sector company Snamprogetti in India. No evidence was ever uncovered tracing any money actually going to Rajiv, or any member of his family, but the suspicion remained a millstone around his neck.

There were political missteps also, notably the decision to enact a law to overturn the Supreme Court judgement on the Shah Bano case[10] and the subsequent decision to concede the demands of orthodox Hindu groups to open the doors of the Babri Masjid[11].

---

[10]Supreme Court ruled that a divorced Muslim wife, unable to maintain herself, was entitled to maintenance under Section 125 of the Code of Criminal procedure. It rejected what it described as the 'extreme position' taken by some intervenors, including the All India Muslim Personal Law Board.
[11]The Masjid was built by one of the generals of Mughal Emperor Babur in 1528 on what many Hindus believe was the birthplace of Lord Rama in Ayodhya. Devout Hindus had been agitating since the 19th century for control of the site to build a new temple. In 1949, idols of Lord Rama and

By the end of 1987, V.P. Singh (his finance minister in the first two years), Arun Singh (a close friend and political associate), Arif Mohammed Khan (a young and moderate Muslim Congressman) and Arun Nehru (a cousin and political heavyweight), all viewed as key members of his core team, had resigned from the Government, each for his own reasons. The inner-party elections Rajiv Gandhi had hinted at never happened. He was soon surrounded by a coterie of the old guard, precisely the brokers of power he had attacked in his speech at the centenary celebrations.

These developments weakened Rajiv politically in the second half of his term and limited what he could do. Nevertheless, many important economic initiatives were taken during his term.

REFORMS IN TAX POLICY

My first important engagement in policymaking in the PMO came when the 1985–86 Budget was being discussed with Finance Minister V.P. Singh. Rajiv Gandhi's views on taxation had been strongly influenced by L.K. Jha, who had earlier served in many important positions in government, and was advisor to the PM on administrative reforms in the rank of a cabinet minister. LK, as he was universally known, believed revenue was best mobilized through a system with moderate rates of tax and a broad tax base. I shared this view and pushed it strongly.

It was a pleasure to see the PM and finance minister work together on a common approach to tax reform, which V.P. Singh would then implement energetically. Traditionally, the finance minister would brief the PM on the details of tax changes proposed in the Budget only a few days before its presentation to get his

---

Sita were found placed in the mosque. This was seen as a miracle and Hindu groups began to agitate to be allowed to enter the Masjid to offer prayers. The district administration had declared the Masjid a disputed structure in 1949 and locked the gates. These locks were opened in 1986, conceding the right to pray before the idols. In November 2019, the 2.77 acre land was handed over to a trust to build a temple in a landmark judgement by the Supreme Court.

final approval. Rajiv wanted a more hands-on involvement and suggested I could be included in the finance minister's internal discussions with ministry officials on the tax changes being considered, so I could keep him regularly briefed. V.P. Singh readily agreed. I knew I was being granted a very special privilege that ministry officials would view as a wholly unwarranted intrusion into their turf!

An important issue that came up in the discussions between the PM and the finance minister was the need to give businessmen a longer-term perspective for fiscal policy so they could make investment plans more easily. In his first Budget speech in March 1985, V.P. Singh announced that the Government would prepare a Long Term Fiscal Policy (LTFP), outlining the Government's intentions on tax policy over the medium term, while presenting medium-term projections of major fiscal magnitudes.

The LTFP was laid on the table of the House in December 1985. It was the first time the Government had presented a medium-term picture of what to expect on tax policy. It made a very important commitment that income tax rates would not be raised for at least five years. It also promised that central excise duties would be reformed to incorporate the value-added tax (VAT) principle of giving credit for taxes already paid on inputs, thus avoiding cascading of taxes. The LTFP also promised that import licencing would be progressively replaced by import duties in line with the traditional advice of economists that protection is best extended by import duties.

The first two Budgets of 1985–86 and 1986–87 saw significant progress in tax reforms. The maximum rate of personal income tax was reduced from 62.5 per cent (including surcharge) to 50 per cent. While the trend for reduction in tax rates had begun some years ago, the reduction was much sharper this time. The corporate tax rate had stayed at 55 per cent for many years and was now reduced to 50 per cent. These rates were still high compared to the maximum marginal rates in other countries, but they signalled a new turn.

In his second Budget, V.P. Singh introduced the VAT features in the excise duty system that was promised in the LTFP. The quick implementation of this particular reform owed much to Singh's single-minded determination. I was present at a meeting where the chairman of the Central Board of Excise and Customs (CBEC), J. Dutta, a very experienced and widely respected tax man, expressed his inability to implement such a major change so quickly, especially because the LTFP had not indicated a time horizon. V.P. Singh simply said, 'Look Dutta saheb, I am not a tax expert. I am simply telling you that politically we have decided to give credit for taxes paid on inputs. I know that if you push your people, they will find a way of getting it done.' Flattered by the confidence reposed in him, Dutta said he would do his best. He delivered and V.P. Singh was able to announce the introduction of 'Modified Vat' (later abbreviated to Modvat). It was first applied to excise duty on some of the items and extended to all in the following year.

The introduction of Modvat in 1986 was the first step in a long journey. Twenty years later, in 2006, the states introduced the VAT principle in sales tax. Its final culmination in the Goods and Services Tax (GST) covering both the Centre and the states took place in 2017. Major policy changes do take time but 31 years is certainly taking gradualism too far!

I was taken by surprise when V.P. Singh was suddenly moved from the Ministry of Finance to the Ministry of Defence in January 1987. The official explanation was that an experienced hand was needed at defence because of the rising tensions with Pakistan that had built up following the Indian Army's training exercise, 'Operation Brasstacks', which involved moving troops and equipment towards the border.[12] V.P. Singh was clearly not happy with the move and the rumour mills worked overtime

---

[12]This was also an implicit criticism of Arun Singh, who, as minister of state for defence, was in charge of the defence portfolio. Operation Brasstacks took place while Rajiv was on holiday and he was apparently not informed about the exercise.

to identify the real cause. There was much speculation that the real reason was because the tax authorities had arrested some very senior business leaders and this had led to industrialists complaining to the PM about the high-handedness of the tax department. Whatever the reason, V.P. Singh's departure meant Rajiv Gandhi lost a determined, result-oriented finance minister.

The two political leaders came from very different backgrounds but there was an easy informality between them, which made them a very effective team while it lasted. V.P. Singh had a feudal rural background. He had cut his teeth in Congress politics in UP and was familiar with manipulative ways of working. He painted, wrote poetry in Hindi and believed in astrology. He was also stubborn and known for his unpredictable and whimsical behaviour. Rajiv Gandhi, on the other hand, belonged to the modern urban elite. He was a tech-savvy professional who had shown no interest in politics until he was suddenly drafted into it after Sanjay's death. Despite these differences, I thought they shared a common perception about the need to modernize the economy to realize its full potential.

There was, however, one important difference between the two. V.P. Singh was much more naturally suspicious of businessmen. I wondered whether this reflected the feudal landed elite's traditional disdain of those engaged in trade and commerce, or that he simply shared Adam Smith's much quoted view that businessmen 'seldom meet together, even for merriment, but the conversation ends in a conspiracy against the public, or in some contrivance to raise prices'. Rajiv Gandhi was more trusting. He believed government needed to work with industry to take the country forward. In 1985, he broke with past practice and took a group of industrialists with him when he went to Moscow on his first official visit. The initiative was widely hailed by business groups as heralding a new style in government-industry interaction.

GIVING UP CONTROLS WITHOUT GIVING UP CONTROL

Many believed Rajiv Gandhi would move boldly to get rid of the controls that had long stifled the Indian economy. I thought these expectations were unrealistic. He had only just inherited the leadership of the Congress, which had an economic ideology evolved over several decades, most of it under his grandfather and then his mother. Even if he wanted to bring about radical change, he would have to prepare the party for it, especially because the mandate he had won was to hold the country together following Mrs Gandhi's assassination. Also, there was no immediate economic crisis that warranted a sudden change in economic policy. In fact, the economy had been doing reasonably well in response to the limited deregulation begun by Mrs Gandhi.

An important influence on Rajiv's thinking on industry was the emergence of what was called the 'new middle class'. India's strategy for industrialization had long been guided by the Mahalanobis strategy that assigned high priority to the capital goods industries—heavy machinery and its associated inputs such as steel—and viewed modern consumer goods as a 'non-priority' sector whose expansion needed to be controlled. However, the growing middle class wanted modern consumer goods such as refrigerators, televisions, household electric gadgets, scooters and small cars.

Though it was called the new middle class, this group comprised at most the top 15 per cent of the population and many in the Congress party felt giving too much attention to this group would undermine its image as a pro-poor party. I recall Makhan Lal Fotedar, political advisor to Rajiv, telling me I should 'explain to the PM that this new middle class is politically fickle. It is only the poor that we can rely on to be firmly with us at all times'. This elementary electoral arithmetic was not lost on Rajiv and he spent considerable energy in reaching out to the poor. But he also felt that a consumer class of 100 million, which would only grow with time, could not be ignored. Consumer goods therefore could not be discouraged and as they were generally produced by the private sector, it followed that the sector must be allowed to modernize and expand more freely.

Indian industry's attitude to liberalization was self-serving. They wanted reduced controls over private investment but were ambivalent on import liberalization. They wanted liberalization of imports of machinery and inputs for their own production but not of imports that would compete with what they produced.

There was surprisingly little support among academic economists for either domestic decontrol or external liberalization. However, empirical research was pointing to the need for a policy rethink. Isher's book, *Industrial Growth in India: Stagnation since the Mid-60s*, showed that many conventional explanations for the low rate of industrial growth in India, such as worsening income distribution and shortage of wage goods, did not stand up to empirical scrutiny.[13] The problem lay in the low rates of growth of 'total factor productivity' (low efficiency with which labour and capital were used), which suggested our policy regime was at fault.

Rajiv Gandhi was convinced that our control systems were outdated and inefficient, but he did not swing to the other extreme of putting all his faith in free markets. He would often say, 'We must give up controls without giving up control.' I understood this to mean that we must get rid of multiple and dysfunctional controls while retaining the ability to exercise strategic control. However, he never initiated the kind of systemic policy review that would reveal which strategic controls were to be retained. As a result, what happened was an accelerated processing of the incremental reforms that were already in the pipeline.

In 1984, Mrs Gandhi had appointed a committee under M. Narasimham to recommend a shift from physical to financial controls. That committee submitted its report in February 1985 to the new government, making a number of recommendations expanding the range of industries delicenced, the extent of

---

[13]Ahluwalia, Isher, *Industrial Growth in India: Stagnation since the Mid-60s*, Oxford University Press, 1984.

broadbanding[14] and the list where foreign investment was allowed, and increasing the asset level at which the Monopolies and Restrictive Trade Practices (MRTP) Act would apply.[15] Many of the recommendations were implemented in 1985. It was certainly progress but it hardly amounted to redesigning the control regime for the 21st century, which Rajiv Gandhi had spoken about.

The need to do away with controls was emphasized strongly to Rajiv by at least two knowledgeable people in my presence. In October 1985, the PM paid an official visit to London. At the reception given by the Indian high commissioner, I.G. Patel, director of the London School of Economics, who had earlier served as economic affairs secretary and RBI governor, was among the guests. I shepherded IG through the milling throng and introduced him to the PM. He used the two minutes he had very effectively, saying, 'Mr PM, there is a lot of interest in what you are doing on the economic front. If I may offer some advice, please make a bonfire of all industrial controls—you won't regret it.'

L.K. Jha had made a similar point when he was asked by the PM why the economy was not responding as much as was hoped to the policy initiatives taken. LK insightfully replied, 'Prime Minister, the Indian economy is like a vehicle with many brakes pressed fully on. Releasing one or two brakes will not make it move; you have to release many more to get results.' This exchange often came to my mind as we worked in the 1990s to define a broader reform agenda.

By the mid-1980s, it had become clear that the Indian capital market could play a major role in enabling Indian private sector companies to raise funds for their expansion. Dhirubhai Ambani had used it particularly effectively but the system was not transparent and there was far too much scope for manipulation

---

[14]Broadbanding referred to treating a licence issued for producing a particular item as valid for producing similar items within the total licenced capacity.
[15]The MRTP Act covered all units where the total assets of the investing group exceeded a specified level. Increasing this asset level reduced the scope of control under MRTP.

and insider trading. The statutory responsibility for oversight of the capital market was with the Ministry of Finance, but the Ministry focused mainly on approving the size of new capital issues and fixing their price. Supervision of trading was left to the exchanges themselves, which operated as brokers' clubs with little incentive or commitment to bring in better practices.

The Narasimham Committee had recommended that control of the capital market should be transferred from the Ministry of Finance to an independent regulatory authority. This recommendation had not been acted upon by the ministry. As Rajiv was going to deliver the Budget speech in February 1987, I suggested he announce that an independent regulator for the capital market would be set up. The Securities and Exchange Board of India (SEBI) was duly established on 12 April 1988 as a non-statutory body to begin with. As it happened, I was back in the Ministry of Finance as economic affairs secretary in 1992 when we completed the task of making SEBI a statutory body. The role of institutions in helping markets to deliver optimal results is now well recognized and we have done less of this in many areas than we should have—but for capital market reform, we acted early and it helped.

TRANSITION TO MODERNITY

When Jawaharlal Nehru spoke of the 'Temples of Modern India' he referred to dams, steel plants and heavy industry, but not infrastructure. Rajiv Gandhi was the first PM to focus on the need for high-quality infrastructure as a priority. He raised the issue at his very first meeting with the new Planning Commission, with Manmohan Singh as deputy chairman, in January 1985. I had not yet joined the PMO but I was told he urged the commission to think ambitiously about developing modern infrastructure, including electric power generation capacity, roads, highways and airports. According to C.G. Somiah, who was planning secretary, the Planning Commission members felt he was too 'urban-centric' and insufficiently aware of both the realities of rural India and the need to give priority to agriculture and rural development in allocating scarce funds.[16]

Years later, I asked Dr Manmohan Singh about his relationship with Rajiv Gandhi in view of the reports of the unsatisfactory first meeting with the Planning Commission. He did not refer to differences on infrastructure but he did say he was disappointed that the PM had not supported him on the need for larger plan funds for agriculture in the first Budget. He told me he had also offered to resign in case the PM wanted to bring in someone else, but he was categorically told that the PM did not want to make any change.

Manmohan Singh was not against modernization but he genuinely believed that India's transition to modernity could not occur without the transformation of agriculture and acceleration of non-agricultural development in rural areas. He once said publicly that you cannot take 10 per cent of the population into the 21st century leaving the remaining 90 per cent in the 19th century. This was viewed by some as a gentle rebuke to the PM but I think he was only stating something that has been a central feature of Indian planning, that growth must benefit all and not just a few.

Much was made of the fact that the PM once said to a group of reporters that the Planning Commission were 'a bunch of jokers' and this was also projected as a comment on Manmohan Singh. However, the comment seems to have been made well after Dr Singh had left to take up the position of secretary-general of the South Commission in Geneva.[17] That said, it is true that Rajiv Gandhi never used the Planning Commission for interactive exchanges to explore new ideas. A more active use of the commission to define policy priorities more precisely might have helped develop a consensus on contentious issues.

The inadequacy of funds to bring investment in modern infrastructure to the levels Rajiv had in mind was an area of

---

[16]Somiah, C.G., *The Honest Always Stand Alone*, Niyogi, 2010.

[17]Singh, Daman, *Strictly Personal: Gursharan and Manmohan*, HarperCollins, 2017.

contention. If the commission had been tasked with alternatives, it might have come up with ideas such as allowing private investment in areas otherwise reserved for the public sector, which happened in 1991. Alternatively, an aggressive strategy of asset sales might have been proposed to raise funds. Such options were never posed to the PM.

CONNECTING WITH THE WORLD

Being a part of the PMO, I was part of the PM's delegation on many visits abroad to the US, the UK, France, Japan, China, Turkey, Cuba and Jordan. These visits provided many opportunities for informal exchanges with the PM.

On a visit to the US, Rajiv Gandhi decided to finalize his speech to the US Congress as we flew over the Atlantic. It was to be the first address to the US Congress by an Indian PM since Jawaharlal Nehru in 1949. He called a few of us into the conference room attached to his bedroom on the plane and went over the draft carefully. That was when the line, 'I am young and I, too, have a dream', was added poignantly, evoking Martin Luther King Jr's words. The visit was a great success, with a confident Rajiv conveying to the Americans that our friendship with the Soviet Union was not a barrier to building a stronger relationship with the US.

The visit to Paris to inaugurate the Festival of India was memorable for many reasons. I recall the splendid reception at the Belle France restaurant on the first floor of the Eiffel Tower when the PM ceremonially presented baby elephant Kaveri to President Francois Mitterrand. She had been hauled up in a wooden cage and was cheerfully munching on bananas as the other guests sipped champagne. We also visited the air show at Le Bourget where the PM got to see the new 'fly by wire' Airbus A320, which was on static display. Being a pilot himself, he had a natural curiosity to check out the plane and sit in the cockpit. These planes were later purchased by Indian Airlines and the acquisition became controversial when one of the planes crash-landed in Bangalore in 1990, leading to a completely politically motivated effort to rake up a controversy about its purchase (*see Chapter 6*).

Although prime ministerial visits usually have predictable outcomes, there are occasional surprises. The Commonwealth Heads of Government Meeting in the Bahamas in 1985 was one such visit. Rajiv put up a strong fight to get the Commonwealth to join the struggle against apartheid. He spoke eloquently about Nelson Mandela's prolonged incarceration and urged mandatory sanctions on South Africa until it ended its abhorrent apartheid regime. I thought his determination was admirable but I doubted if we would see the end of apartheid anytime soon, given the obduracy of the South African regime and the opposition of Margaret Thatcher and other developed countries to mandatory sanctions. I was wrong. South Africa did bend to mounting international opinion; Nelson Mandela was freed in 1990 and apartheid abolished in 1991.

OTHER STEPS TOWARDS REFORM

There were other areas in which I was less directly involved where important initiatives were taken, but which led to important changes only much later. Perhaps the most important of these was the move to give panchayats and urban local bodies constitutional status to assure them of free and fair elections and greater devolution of resources. Mani Shankar Aiyar in the PMO was the point man leading this effort, ably supported by the Department of Rural Development under its secretary, Vinod Pande. After a series of regional meetings with district magistrates, the PM discussed the issues in a meeting of state CMs. A majority of them supported the move for a constitutional amendment to make elections to panchayat raj institutions mandatory.

A draft Constitution Amendment Bill was prepared and was even passed by the Lok Sabha but could not get through the Rajya Sabha before the announcement of the 1989 elections. It was left to the Congress-led government headed by Narasimha Rao in 1991 to pick up the thread. The 73rd Constitution Amendment finally became law in 1993. Sadly, Rajiv did not live to see the fruit of his efforts. It is indeed a major achievement that about 300,000 people are now regularly elected to village panchayats, with reservations for scheduled castes (SC) and scheduled tribes (ST) and one-third representation for women. However, effective empowerment requires devolution of functions, finances and functionaries, and this process has been very slow.

Telecommunications was another sector that deeply interested Rajiv. In today's digital universe, it is difficult to imagine the state of telecommunications in the mid-1980s. There were only 3 million telephone lines in India (there are 1.2 billion today) and almost all were in urban areas. Most long-distance calls had to be placed through the operator and often involved several hours of waiting to connect.

Sam Pitroda played a crucial role in pushing the telecom agenda in the Rajiv years. He had returned from the US at the invitation of Mrs Gandhi and Rajiv to set up C DoT, an autonomous society tasked with developing an indigenous digital exchange that would meet the need for smaller exchanges as the telecom network rolled out into rural areas. C DoT quickly proved itself by developing an exchange that functioned well in Indian ambient temperatures without needing air-conditioning, and which was modular and could be easily scaled up.

In 1987, Sam was appointed telecommunications secretary and tasked with increasing tele-density. The system was based on landlines, and expansion in rural areas was not easy, given the long distances and lack of electricity. Sam was able to increase tele-density from 0.39 (per hundred of population) in 1985 to 0.52 in 1989—but this was still very low. He then came up with the innovative idea of increasing access to the network by licencing privately run telephone booths where anyone could make a phone call by paying a regulated charge with the booth operator keeping a certain percentage of the charge as his commission. The STD booths, with their distinctive yellow signs, became a familiar sight in small towns and remote places. They made it possible for individuals travelling anywhere in India to call others with access to a phone. Policy at the time still treated telecom services as a state monopoly but the STD booths were a form of privatizing the last mile of telecom access.

Rajiv did not live to see the massive improvements in tele-density that occurred after mobile telephony arrived some years later. The new technology made all the difference because it bypassed the problem of stretching landlines across rural areas and the unreliability of electricity. Tele-density had reached only 1.25 in 1995 when mobile telephony was first introduced. It increased to 3.42 by 2000 and has since shot up to 93.27 in 2018. The increase has been entirely because of mobile penetration; the tele-density of landline connections has actually fallen. Interestingly, this expansion occurred not through the public sector, as Rajiv believed it would, but through the private sector, which brought in vast resources that the public sector would never have been able to mobilize.

Rajiv was also ahead of his time in recognizing the importance of urbanization. The traditional approach was that rural-urban migration should be discouraged as it puts pressure to develop high–cost infrastructure in urban areas. Rajiv realized that faster growth would lead to urbanization and we needed to be prepared for it. In 1986, he appointed the National Commission on Urbanisation with acclaimed architect Charles Correa as chairman. The commission submitted its report in 1988. It was the first detailed exploration of the nature of the urban challenge for India and proposed the abolition of the Urban Land Ceiling Act as well as changes in rent control laws, both of which were carried out some years later.

MISSED OPPORTUNITIES

Public sector reform was an area that should have been addressed, but was not. Rajiv knew the public sector was underperforming.

Instead of contributing resources towards investment, most units generated far fewer surpluses than they were expected to and many had become a drain on scarce budget funds. But there were strong vested interests among both politicians and the bureaucracy that saw the public sector as a golden goose. Not surprisingly, they were determined to hang on to it. Rajiv's soft corner for the public sector may also have been because of his personal experience at Indian Airlines, where he worked for many years.

As an experiment, top private sector managers were brought in to run public sector companies. Rajan Jetley was brought in from ITC to run Air India, and Sudhir Mulji of Great Eastern Shipping Company to run the State Trading Corporation of India. Jetley improved the financial performance of the airline but returned to the private sector after three years. Mulji resigned in two years. Mulji told me that as a businessman, he found it impossible to function given the many controls exercised by the ministries.

Gopi Arora and I persuaded the PM to announce in the Budget speech he was delivering as finance minister in 1987 that the Government would present a White Paper in Parliament that would explore all aspects of public sector policy to develop a consensus on reform that would improve performance in future. The note spelt out the need for greater management autonomy, but also proposed that public sector enterprises making persistent losses would be sold to the private sector if possible, and closed down if no buyer was available. None of the ministers was willing to endorse this approach. The most they were willing to do was to experiment with the French system of the Government entering into an MoU with the PSUs, which would specify the criteria on which they would be judged and indicate what support the Government would give. This was tried, but it had very little effect. As we could not reach agreement on any substantive issues, the promise to submit a White Paper in Parliament remained unfulfilled.

Another area of missed opportunity was FDI. Rajiv Gandhi had seen what FDI could do in the case of Maruti and wanted to replicate the experience of modernization in other sectors.

But our policy limited FDI to certain high-priority areas and put a limit on the foreign equity share at 40 per cent, except for 100 per cent export units.

However, there were at least two important projects in which the PM could create an enabling environment to attract FDI. The first was Texas Instruments, which wanted to set up its first offshore software development subsidiary in Bengaluru, with a satellite connection to its main unit in Houston. This would provide infrastructure support to the globally connected IT sector. Here, Rajiv nudged the Department of Telecommunications (DoT) to find a constructive solution to ensure satellite connectivity for the project. The facility became the company's largest centre outside the US—and a trigger for the software revolution in India. The second project was PepsiCo's proposed soft drinks venture in Punjab, with backward linkages to the rural sector and agricultural productivity. In this case, Rajiv confronted the naysayers with arguments of promoting employment and development for better security in Punjab. These cases apart, we missed the opportunity to carry out a broader-ranging reform of FDI policy. This had to wait until 1991.

BALANCE OF PAYMENTS WORSENS

The last two years of Rajiv's term saw the emergence of serious macroeconomic imbalances. The LTFP of 1985 had envisaged a reduction in borrowing to finance the fiscal deficit. This did not happen. The revenue targets were actually met but expenditure projections went off track. Subsidies ended up higher than projected because prices of subsidized items were not raised in line with rising costs. Public sector surpluses fell short of expectations, reflecting the lack of reform. The plan expenditure of the Government was also higher than projected because both 1986 and 1987 were drought years, which led to additional expenditures that were not pulled back in later years. There was also a sharp increase in defence expenditure on account of modernization of equipment, which was long overdue. All this led to an increase in the fiscal deficit, generating excess demand in the economy. This excess demand spilled over into the BOP and the current account deficit increased from 1.8 per cent of GDP in 1986–87 to 2.4 per cent in 1988–89.

The higher current account deficit was financed by an increase in short-term external borrowing and a decline in foreign exchange reserves. I recall RBI Governor Ram Malhotra calling on the PM in late 1988 to express his concern about the rising fiscal deficit and the widening current account deficit. He did not ask the PM to take any action but mentioned that he would share his concerns with the finance minister. He wrote to the finance minister on 7 January 1989, drawing attention to the worsening fiscal position of the central government and its linkage with the worsening current account deficit.[18]

The fact that nothing was done in the Ministry of Finance reflects the lack of strong leadership at the ministry after V.P. Singh's departure. Rajiv was himself the finance minister for only a few months up to July 1987, after which N.D. Tiwari took over. He was there for a year and was followed by Shankar Rao Chavan.

As the BOP came under pressure, foreign exchange reserves began to decline after 1986. The Ministry of Finance took only a few cosmetic steps, such as using balances kept with the India Supply Mission at the Indian Embassy in Washington DC. These balances were not part of the official reserves, so their use helped to hide the full extent of the reserve decline from the public. When I learnt this was being done, I set up a mechanism to get data every week from Deputy Governor Rangarajan on the extent to which such balances were being used, so I could brief the PM on the full extent of the use of reserves.

Part of the reason no effective corrective action was taken is that the Ministry of Finance feared that reducing government expenditure would hurt growth. They were also not convinced that reducing the fiscal deficit was necessary to reduce the current

---

[18]RBI, *Volume IV*, 1981–1987.

account deficit. They tended to think that the current account deficit could be managed by tightening control over imports and strengthening incentives to export. It was a convenient way of passing the buck to the Ministry of Commerce.

In March 1988, Michel Camdessus, managing director of the IMF, visited New Delhi. He called on the PM and told him that the IMF was concerned about the deteriorating BOP. He said the government needed to act quickly to reduce the fiscal deficit, but he added that he recognized that it may not be practical to introduce such a programme with general elections due at the end of 1989. He emphasized that if it was not done before the elections, it would have to be done immediately after. He added that if the Government wanted assistance from the IMF after the elections, he would do everything in his power to help.

I made a note to remind the PM of this conversation or leave a note for the successor PM, if that became necessary. As it happened, I stayed on in the PMO after the change of government and was able to brief his successor prime minster, at great length.

SOME DIFFERENCES BETWEEN INDIAN AND CHINESE REFORMS

Rajiv Gandhi began his term by articulating a vision for a new India that called for deep structural reforms. Five years is too short a period to bring about major structural reforms, especially for a new PM with very limited experience in politics. In practice, he had much less than five years because the political situation unravelled very quickly after the first two years. In a surprisingly candid interview given to Aveek Sarkar and Vir Sanghvi after demitting office, Rajiv admitted that inexperience was probably one reason why he was not able to achieve more.[19]

Although Rajiv was not able to bring about the fundamental reform that was needed, there can be no doubt that he changed the nature of the discourse on India's economic policy by legitimizing

---

[19]*Sunday*, 12–18 August 1990.

the goal of moving towards a less-controlled economy, with a much greater role for the private sector. He created a greater appreciation of the role of modern technology and its relevance for the common man. He also initiated the process of empowering the panchayats as the third tier of government. He definitely succeeded in accelerating the pace of domestic liberalization, but there were important missing elements. Very little was done to liberalize trade policy, which explains the lacklustre performance of exports at a time when world exports were booming. He sensed the potential role FDI could play and gave it a push in some areas, but did not articulate a new policy towards it. And the absence of any reform in the public sector was a missed opportunity.

India's efforts to push reforms in the 1980s were very different from the reforms in China. Deng Xiaoping, who masterminded the reforms in China, was a veteran in the Communist Party with decades of experience. He had been expelled by Mao for being a 'capitalist roader' but was rehabilitated later and rose to the top in 1978 after Mao's death. Deng was effectively in power for 15 years from 1978 to 1992. He was careful never to repudiate Mao's approach openly but gradually built a coherent team, promoting like-minded individuals within the party while gradually marginalizing others.

Time and experience aside, Rajiv was also hampered by the fact that not enough work had been done to identify the critical ingredients of reform. Here again, the contrast with China is striking. We now know from Ezra Vogel that Deng took pains to encourage internal discussion on what might be the best way to restructure the economy, including an extensive process of interaction with outside experts.[20] In 1985, the Chinese government asked the World Bank to organize a team of foreign economists with whom Chinese experts could discuss alternative approaches to the transition. The discussions took place in an environment away from the public gaze during a week's cruise on the Yangtze

[20]Vogel, Ezra, *Deng Xiaoping and The Transformation of China*, Harvard University Belknap Press, 201.1

aboard the Bashunlun from Chongqing to Wuhan, passing through the Three Gorges en route. The economists included Nobel laureate James Tobin from the US, Alec Cairncross from the UK and János Kornai from Hungary. The Chinese had initially thought that Kornai's suggestions, based on Hungary's experience as a former socialist economy, might be more relevant, but James Tobin's arguments convinced them otherwise.

Vogel also points out that the Chinese government used its bilateral contacts to learn about the Japanese experience. In 1987, they persuaded the World Bank to organize a small inter-governmental discussion on development policy issues in Bangkok, at which minister-level representatives were invited from China, Korea, India, Thailand, Indonesia and the Philippines. Dr Singh, then deputy chairman of the Planning Commission, represented India, and I was assigned to assist him. Each delegation talked about the policies in their country, while others asked questions. I recall that after the Chinese representative made a presentation of what they were planning to do, Dr Singh asked, 'Aren't you worried that this may lead to rising inequality?' Unfazed, his Chinese counterpart responded, 'Yes, it will, but we are not worried because we have too much equality in China!' The Chinese government was very clear that it was making big changes and went about doing so with a great deal of deliberation, consultation and confidence.

Years later, a friend in the World Bank told me the meeting was organized primarily to give the Chinese government an opportunity to interact informally with senior officials of South Korea. The rest of us were actually props in a carefully staged performance!

In India, frank airing of differences of opinion in an open political system was too easily politicized and therefore never took place. In China, these discussions took place outside the glare of publicity. It led to China being described as a closed society with an open mind, and India an open society with a closed mind. Principal Secretary B.G. Deshmukh recognized this problem and suggested to me that as we waited for the election to be over, we should work out a plan of action on the economic side that we could present to Rajiv if he was re-elected. I started working on such a note to keep it ready.

When the election results were announced, the Congress vote share declined from the exceptionally high 48 per cent achieved in the immediate aftermath of the assassination of Mrs Gandhi to 40 per cent. The number of seats in the Lok Sabha fell dramatically from 411 to 197, because many opposition parties had come together to oppose the Congress. The Congress was still the largest party by far and Rajiv could have tried to patch together a coalition government. To his credit, he did no such thing, accepting the verdict as a vote for the Congress to sit in opposition. He was young enough to hope he would get another chance. Tragically, fate decreed otherwise.

6

THE CRISIS OF 1990

The installation of a National Front government at the end of 1989 marked a significant change—the country went from five years under a Congress government with a large majority in Parliament to a minority government dependent on outside support from the Left and the BJP. The Front itself was a coalition of several parties, held together only by a common anti-Congress sentiment. The arrangement had all the ingredients for political instability and could certainly not handle an economy sliding towards a BOP crisis. Political developments occupied centre-stage through the year and as politics usually eats economics for breakfast, economic management was neglected. Problems that should have been tackled almost immediately were neglected. In less than a year, the Government was overwhelmed when the Gulf War in August 1990 triggered a full-blown BOP crisis.

A NEW PRIME MINISTER

The 1989 election campaign was dominated by the issue of corruption and Vishwanath Pratap Singh, better known as V.P. Singh, was seen nationally as the principal crusader. However, his ascent to the prime ministership was not a foregone conclusion. He was the leader of Janata Dal, which he had formed by merging his own Jan Morcha (started after he left the Congress) with Lok Dal and a few other parties. However, he had fought the election as part of the National Front, which was a broader anti-Congress alliance including regional parties such as the Dravida Munnetra Kazhagam (DMK), Telugu Desam and Asom Gana Parishad. There were leaders in the National Front, notably the erstwhile 'Young Turk' Chandra Shekhar of Janata Dal and Haryana strongman Devi Lal of Lok Dal who regarded themselves as senior to V.P. Singh, and with equally strong claims to leading the pack. After some devious manoeuvring, V.P. Singh was elected leader of the National Front by the MPs of all the parties that formed the Front, and was sworn in as PM on 2 December 1989.

I had got to know V.P. Singh from my years in Rajiv's PMO but I fully expected to be moved out as the new PM constituted his own team. As special secretary to the PM, I held the secondmost senior position in the PMO after Principal Secretary Deshmukh, and dealt with all economic matters. There was speculation in the press that either S.V.S. Raghavan, who had served as chairman, Metals and Minerals Trading Corporation of India and was known to V.P. Singh, or Deepak Nayyar, who was chief economic advisor in the Ministry of Finance, would replace me. As it happened, V.P. Singh brought in some officers he had worked with earlier but both Deshmukh and I remained in our old positions. The decision surprised me but Deshmukh explained it in a wonderfully self-deprecatory manner, 'Montek, *Dilli aisa shehar hai jahan cup badalte hain, lekin chamche nahin.*'[21] It was the best put-down I have heard of the much-vaunted permanency of the civil service by someone at the very top of the heap!

I got the opportunity to brief the new cabinet on the economic situation at its very first meeting and made it plain that the situation was extremely challenging. The fiscal situation was out of control and the Government was spending much more than the revenues it was able to garner. The fiscal deficit was, therefore, too high, injecting excess demand into the economy that had led

---

[21]The phrase does not lend itself easily to a literal translation in English, which would simply be, 'Delhi is such a place where cups change, but spoons do not.' However, the word 'chamcha', which means spoon, is also a quasi-derogatory reference to an acolyte or advisor in government. Deshmukh was intending to contrast the fluidity in the political class of ministers with the permanence of the civil service.

to high inflation and high imports, which were reflected in a high BOP deficit. This was leading to a continued bleeding of foreign exchange reserves. I did not mention this in my briefing but I separately told V.P. Singh what Michel Camdessus, managing director of the IMF, had said to Rajiv at the start of the year about the need for corrective action, and his offer of help.

Gopi Arora was finance secretary and present at the briefing. While complimenting me for spelling out the facts, he said I may have put my job on the line because a recommendation to keep fiscal deficit in control would not be liked by many members of the cabinet, who were hoping to reward the electorate by announcing new government schemes!

The economic situation should have been given top priority but it took a back seat because the political situation deteriorated very fast.

AN UNEASY ALLIANCE

V.P. Singh's government was politically unsteady from the very start. His leadership of the Janata Dal was not without challenge from within and his relations with the BJP were also uneasy. He was not comfortable with their long-standing campaign for building the 'Ram Mandir' on the site of the Babri Masjid.

The day after the Government was sworn in, Kashmiri militants kidnapped Rubaiya Sayeed, the daughter of Home Minister Mufti Mohammed Sayeed, and demanded the release of five jailed Jammu Kashmir Liberation Front militants in exchange for her release. The new government released the militants, which led to inevitable charges of weakness and ineffectiveness. Punjab also presented a difficult challenge. V.P. Singh had promised several times during the election campaign that President's Rule would be lifted and state elections held in February 1990. Soon after taking office, he visited the Golden Temple in Amritsar and his apparent sincerity was well received. However, he reneged on his promise of an early election and introduced legislation extending President's

Rule for another six months, thus damaging his credibility.

Deputy PM Devi Lal had his own agenda. He was determined to install his son Om Prakash Chautala as CM in Haryana even though it went against V.P. Singh's known opposition to dynastic politics. Chautala's election from Meham was marred by violence and thus countermanded. A strong public outcry forced V.P. Singh to insist Chautala stay out of government for some time. Devi Lal felt personally let down and even threatened to resign. He later went on to accuse Commerce Minister Arun Nehru of corruption and demanded action against him. V.P. Singh finally sacked Devi Lal on 2 August 1990, whereupon he promptly announced he would hold a public rally on 9 August, the anniversary of Mahatma Gandhi's Quit India Movement in 1942, to demonstrate the strength of his rural base.

Two days before the rally, V.P. Singh played a trump card by announcing that the Government would implement the recommendation of the Mandal Commission for reserving 27 per cent of the jobs in the central government (excluding the armed forces) and in the central public sector enterprises for members of the 'other backward classes' (OBCs). The commission had been set up by the Janata government of Morarji Desai in 1979 to examine the condition of the OBCs. It had estimated the OBC population as 52 per cent of the total and recommended reservation of 27 per cent for them.[22] By the time the report was submitted, Mrs Gandhi had come back to power and it was effectively shelved. The announcement of reservations two days before the Devi Lal rally looked as if it was designed to take the sting out of the event, but the decision to implement the Mandal Commission recommendation was not a sudden development. It had been part of the National Front manifesto as a commitment to social restructuring, and had been publicly reiterated by

---

[22]Backwardness was defined in terms of 11 socioeconomic criteria, and 3,743 jatis were identified as backward on this basis. The census data of 1931 – the last census to collect information on castes – showed that these jatis accounted for 52 per cent of the population.

V.P. Singh soon after he took office, and repeated several times.

The announcement made V.P. Singh an instant messiah for the OBCs. This caused concern in the BJP because it weakened its hold on the Hindu community in support of the agitation to build the Ram temple. It also produced a reaction among the 'forward castes' as it implied a significant reduction in the percentage of government jobs open for them. There were widespread protests from students across North India.

As domestic politics was unsettled by these events, the situation in the Middle East erupted with Saddam Hussein invading Kuwait on 2 August 1990, leading to the first Gulf War. The resulting sharp increase in oil prices triggered a BOP crisis for India. The fact that the oil price shock occurred precisely when the domestic political situation was getting out of control made the management of the economic crisis much more difficult.

Political tension came to a head when a group of students in Delhi University announced a self-immolation protest on campus on 19 September 1990. Of the two students who attempted self-immolation, one could be saved but the second, Rajiv Goswami, was badly hurt, with 50 per cent burns. More cases of immolation followed as did widespread incidents of rioting and police firing, resulting in many casualties and over 260 deaths. The age of multiple TV channels competing fiercely to bring 'breaking news' to viewers had not yet dawned and broadcasting was monopolized by the state-owned TV channel Doordarshan, which provided suitably muted coverage avoiding any implicit criticism of the Government. However, *India Today* had introduced a weekly video news magazine, *Newstrack*, presented by Madhu Trehan. It covered the student protests in great detail, including Rajiv Goswami's self-immolation attempt. Its reach was obviously limited to those who had access to a video recorder but it had significant viewership among upper-income urban households. Madhu Trehan boldly announced, 'This PM has the blood of students on his hands' — it certainly helped mobilize urban upper middle class opinion against V.P. Singh.

The BJP saw the introduction of reservations as an attempt to split its Hindu vote base and reacted by intensifying the Ram Mandir campaign. On 11 September 1990, BJP President L.K. Advani announced that he would set out on a Rath Yatra (chariot journey) in which he rode at the head of a motorcade in a Toyota van decked up to look like Lord Rama's chariot. Atal Bihari Vajpayee later admitted they were answering Mandal with 'kamandal', a copper vessel for drinking water carried by Hindu holy men.

Advani's rath yatra began on 25 September from Somnath in Gujarat, which was symbolically important because the ancient temple of Somnath was destroyed in 1024 CE by Mahmud of Ghazni. The yatra was to go through several states before finishing at Ayodhya on 30 October. It was extensively covered by the press and generated considerable enthusiasm among the party faithful along its route. The National Front coalition at the Centre took a political decision to stop the yatra. A youthful Lalu Prasad Yadav, CM of Bihar at the time, stopped the yatra in Samastipur on 23 October and Advani was placed under preventive detention.

The BJP promptly withdrew support and the Government lost its majority. Instead of resigning immediately, the PM chose to seek a vote of confidence in the Lok Sabha but lost. V.P. Singh resigned on 10 November 1990, a little over 11 months after he had been sworn in.

CLASHING WITH THE PLANNING COMMISSION

Shortly after being sworn in, V.P. Singh appointed former Karnataka CM Ramakrishna Hegde as deputy chairman of the Planning Commission. He also appointed a surprisingly large number of members reflecting the multiple political interests he needed to cater to. Among them were Lakshmi Chand Jain, a well-known Gandhian economist; A. Vaidyanathan, an agricultural economist who had worked in the commission earlier; political scientist Rajni Kothari; J.D. Sethi, a Gandhian and public intellectual; and Ela Bhatt, founder of NGO SEWA (Self-Employed Women's Association of India). The Seventh Five-Year Plan was scheduled to end in 1989–90 and it was time to begin preparations for the Eighth Plan.

Within a month of the Government taking over, the new Planning Commission sent a note to the PM outlining its initial thinking on the approach paper to the Eighth Plan. The note was based on a somewhat old-fashioned view of economic policy. It criticized the economic liberalization initiated under Rajiv and laid emphasis on employment creation as a central objective of policy to be achieved through a shift towards traditional employment-intensive areas such as handlooms and handicrafts. It also talked of a new Right to Work Programme, which would have added to expenditure at a time when fiscal discipline was the need of the hour. The note paid no attention to the need to modernize industry and was critical of the growth of modern consumer industries that catered to the demands of the rich and the emerging middle class.

When briefing the PM before his meeting with the commission, I expressed my reservations about the note. I reminded him that as finance minister in the Rajiv Gandhi government, he had led the effort at implementing tax reforms that had been widely applauded and produced strong economic growth in the second half of the decade. He had thereby acquired the reputation of a reformer. If his government now condemned everything that had gone before, which the Planning Commission's paper seemed to be doing, it would be seen as reversing course, which I felt was the wrong signal.

I suggested the PM ask the Commission to plan for a 6 per cent growth rate, in effect trying to do better than what had been achieved in the 1980s, while addressing the weaknesses that had emerged, including unemployment. An approach paper redrafted along these lines would give a clear signal that his government would pursue reforms.

V.P. Singh heard me out carefully but did not reveal his mind. This was actually typical of all my interactions with him during his premiership. He would tolerate a frank articulation of views but keep his own counsel. I was never sure if this was because he knew the Government was not going to last long and therefore had no interest in revealing his position on difficult economic issues. At the meeting, I was pleased to see he raised precisely the issues I had flagged, including the need for a robust growth target. V.P. Singh was fully aware of the importance of growth but also recognized it was not a sufficient condition for broad-based improvement in welfare. He was a poet and I recall him saying to me once, 'Montek, what we need is growth that falls like rain on the mountains and flows down in streams to the valleys and plains below, not growth that is like snow, which sticks to the mountain tops.' It was the most eloquent articulation I have ever heard of an acceptable version of the 'trickle-down' thesis.

The issues raised in the meeting with the Planning Commission were duly minuted in the PMO and conveyed by me in a letter to Deputy Chairman Hegde. This letter agitated the members no end. The press had a field day reporting the conflict between the Planning Commission and the PMO, drawing on numerous quotes from irate members who vented their displeasure openly. The report in *The Observer* of 22 April 1990, though a little sensational, was broadly accurate:

> The crux of what appears to be...a face off is that while Ahluwalia is propagating market economy concepts, the Commission is seeking to stick to traditional tenets of a self-reliant economy. In his letter, Ahluwalia is said to have advocated integration of the Indian economy into the global economy and progressively reducing protection to domestic industry. He has also questioned the planners' wisdom in preparing an approach paper which does not mention the 'agreed' growth rate of 6 per cent... (which is) essential to ensure a 3 per cent increase in employment.

One of the members, J.D. Sethi, was quoted as complaining about 'intolerable interference by top bureaucrats who were seeking to scuttle the very process of planning for a self-reliant economy at the behest of western powers, international monetary bodies and other vested interests'. Sethi identified the other vested interests as 'the big business lobbies, those who wish to preserve the previous government's legacy, and those who wish not to devolve powers to the states'. An unnamed Planning Commission official was reported as complaining, 'These bureaucrats (in the PMO) have not adjusted to the change in government and policies; they want to flood the market with Marutis and refrigerators, and to hell with the masses and creating jobs for the people.' Similar reports about the disagreement appeared in *The Telegraph* of 25 April 1990 and in the 6–12 May 1990 edition of *Sunday*.

I wondered whether the PM was annoyed with me for having provoked this controversy, so I sought a meeting to explain my position. I came back with a distinct impression that he did not mind the public discussion of these issues. I volunteered to meet Hegde and explain that I had raised genuine issues in good faith, with no disrespect intended. We had a very cordial meeting where I emphasized that I had spoken because I felt the PM and deputy chairman should have the benefit of an honest independent assessment, adding that I held him in very high regard as a modernizing politician. Hegde was relaxed and not nearly as angry as the other members undoubtedly were.

As I was leaving, I dropped in on T.N. Seshan, whom I had known since he was cabinet secretary in Rajiv's government. Seshan had been 'kicked upstairs' to the Planning Commission to make room for Vinod Pande whom the PM wanted. Planning Commission members had a higher rank than the cabinet secretary but much less real power. The shift was clearly not to Seshan's liking. He was sitting pugnaciously behind a desk, conspicuously free of papers or files, as if aggressively conveying to visitors that he did not have any substantive work assigned to him! Somewhat to my surprise, Seshan warmly congratulated me on my performance in raising the issues in the Planning Commission meeting and urged me to keep speaking my mind. I assured him I had every intention of doing so, but wondered why he did not himself speak up at the meeting.

The commission made some changes in the draft approach paper but these fell far short of what I had suggested. Instead of adopting a 6 per cent growth target, they proposed a lower target of 5.6 per cent, only slightly higher than the 5.3 per cent growth achieved in the 1980s according to the data then available. (However, when the full data became available, the growth rate turned out to be around 5.6 per cent.) The commission's target was clearly unambitious. The revised approach paper also took the position that it was not necessary to have high GDP growth to achieve the target of 3 per cent growth of employment, provided we could support small and tiny industries adequately and expand employment programmes.

The approach to employment creation was a major area of difference between me and the Planning Commission. L.C. Jain strongly believed the best way of expanding employment was through an expansion of the highly labour-intensive handloom sector. He favoured limiting the growth in the organized textiles sector to promote the traditional unorganized sector. I argued that while Gandhiji's focus on khadi was a brilliant political strategy to mobilize a broad base of support during the struggle for Independence, the emphasis placed by contemporary Gandhians on handloom and khadi more than four decades after Independence was highly questionable. I often argued with him that had we followed a different strategy and developed a competitive modern textile and garment industry as East Asia had done, we would have been able to expand exports and generate much more employment at higher wages. I pointed out that there would always be a niche for traditional handlooms as items consumed by the rich, but the notion that handloom products would meet the demands of the masses was simply unrealistic.

The interaction with the Planning Commission drove home to me that our system did not encourage frank and critical discussion of contentious issues. Criticism was typically papered over and differences smoothed out rather than resolved. In this particular case, it did not matter as the commission's approach paper was never translated into a Plan.

THE M DOCUMENT

In June 1990, I got an opportunity to present my views on economic policy to an inter-ministerial forum. It started with an informal exchange with V.P. Singh during his visit to Malaysia. He observed that he had visited the country as deputy minister of commerce in the 1970s and was impressed at the progress the country had made since. I responded that I had the same impression based on my visits on World Bank missions in the early 1970s. Kuala Lumpur had a distinctly provincial character in those days with a lone Hilton Hotel as the only visible link with the global economy, but had transformed itself into a much more modern city over the years. When the PM asked me what I thought was the reason, I replied, perhaps a little cheekily, that they had been much more forthright in undertaking economic reforms whereas we seemed to lack the will. He reflected for a moment and then asked me to prepare a note indicating the kind of reforms we needed to consider.

Deshmukh had earlier asked me to prepare a paper on policy issues that we could submit to Rajiv if he was re-elected. I quickly dug out my working notes and prepared a 34-page paper for V.P. Singh titled 'Restructuring India's Industrial, Trade and Fiscal Policies'. It put together some key changes I felt were needed in the interrelated areas of macroeconomic, industrial, trade and foreign investment policy.

Many of these ideas had been discussed informally at official levels but had never been put together as an internally consistent set of specific policy changes. I sent the note to the PM, wondering what he would do. He directed it be submitted formally for inter-ministerial discussion in the Committee of Secretaries chaired by the cabinet secretary. Vinod Pande congratulated me on the note and the discussions in the Cabinet Secretariat took place over two days, 13 and 14 June. They were among the most stimulating discussions I have had in government.

The note did not indicate authorship but all recipients knew it had come from the PMO, which ensured serious attention even though there was no indication the PM had approved its proposals. Many journalists speculated it came from me. A leaked copy of the note was published in *The Indian Express* of 11 July 1990 and this led to a spate of articles by leading economists, including C.T. Kurien, R.M. Honavar, Manu Shroff, B.S. Minhas and P.R. Brahmananda. Ashok Desai, writing on 8 August 1990 in *The Indian Express*, said the paper was widely attributed to me, but as I neither accepted nor denied authorship, he had decided to call it the 'M Document'. The name stuck and many commentaries of the period have referred to the paper as such.

At the risk of appearing unduly self-indulgent, it is worth summarizing the contents of my note, if only to set the stage for the controversy that followed. The note began by pointing out that although a gradual process of liberalization had been under way for some time, most other developing countries had gone much further, and even the former Communist countries of Eastern Europe had started adopting market economy concepts. We could not expect to compete internationally if our industry continued to operate in an environment that was much more restrictive and less congenial for various types of international linkages. This echoed what Rajiv Gandhi had said in Parliament in 1985.

The note also emphasized that we needed to articulate a clear medium-term strategy in which the different but interconnected components of the reforms are identified, and the extent of change needed in each clearly stated. This was in some ways the most important feature of the note. Typically, policy changes were discussed based on notes circulated by the individual ministry concerned, which meant the focus was on the policies controlled by the ministry, with little attention to either the supportive steps needed by other ministries or the adverse consequences of the policy on other sectors.

A five-year agenda for reform in five major interrelated areas was spelt out. The first priority was to reverse the deterioration in the fiscal position that had occurred over several years. As this had happened because of excessive expansion in expenditures rather than a shortfall in revenues, corrective policies needed to focus more on containing expenditure. It recommended containment of defence expenditure and food and fertilizer subsidies, and restructuring of ministries to bring about a reduction in government staff by at least 10 per cent. The note also urged that new expenditure commitments such as the Right to Work should not be undertaken until the resources position improved. This proposal was much criticized by the Planning Commission.

On public sector reforms, the note recognized that although privatization was being adopted all over the world, it may not be acceptable in India. It recommended six specific reforms I thought could make a significant difference: (i) Partial privatization by sale of minority equity in selected PSUs would help to bring in capital and change the management culture. We could also experiment with a possible induction of a strategic partner in some cases, such as the India Tourism Development Corporation, Indian Airlines and Air India; (ii) Amend the law to exclude PSUs from the definition of 'state' under Article 12 of the Constitution to increase the flexibility available to public sector managers; (iii) PSUs that were demonstrably unviable should be closed down. The National Textile Corporation Limited had identified as unviable a number of textile mills under itself; (iv) The policy of reserving certain areas for the public sector should continue only where security considerations or mineral resources were involved; (v) The system of PSUs giving preference to public sector suppliers in their purchases should be ended and the public sector should be free to source their requirements from the most cost-effective source, whether public or private; (vi) Wage negotiations in the public sector should be based on the ability of the enterprise to pay, rather than uniform wage negotiations across all PSUs.

On industrial decontrol, I was constrained by the fact that only a few days earlier, on 31 May, the Ministry of Industry had announced a new Industrial Policy in Parliament, which liberalized industrial controls to a limited extent by removing industrial licencing for all investments of less than ₹25 crore (₹75 crore in backward areas) for a defined list of industries (to be announced later). I did not want to undermine what had just been done by the Government; so the note sought only to expand the coverage of liberalization and raise the threshold below which licencing would be dispensed with.

On trade liberalization, the note laid out a phased process of gradually replacing import licences with tariffs for capital goods and intermediate goods, which would increase revenues initially; lowering import tariffs progressively, beginning with high-end tariffs and avoiding duty inversions in the process; cushioning the effect of lowering tariffs on domestic industry by allowing the exchange rate to depreciate; managing the pressure on the BOP by reducing the fiscal deficit; and offsetting the revenue loss from lowering tariffs by raising domestic indirect taxes. Some of these proposals, such as the replacement of import licencing by tariffs, had been mentioned in expert committees but without recognizing the need to act on all the other fronts indicated.

As all this would take time, the note suggested, as an interim measure, that a broad range of imports currently under licencing of one sort or the other could be made freely importable against replenishment licences given to exporters as a percentage of export earnings. These licences could be sold to anyone wanting to use them for imports. This was the first articulation of an idea that subsequently developed into Eximscrips, which were the centrepiece of the Trade Policy Reforms of 1991. A similar proposal had been made in an op-ed by Prakash Hebalkar in *Business India*, and I had also discussed it with Rangarajan, deputy governor, RBI.

Finally, the M Document outlined a more positive approach to FDI. In addition to the list of industries where 40 per cent FDI was allowed, it proposed a second list where 51 per cent foreign equity would be allowed automatically. It also recommended that some large public and private sector units should be encouraged to seek joint venture collaborations in attractive areas. Reputed international companies should be proactively approached to look at India as an investment destination.

The trade policy proposals in the note illustrated the problem of having to coordinate across different agencies. The Ministry of Commerce was in charge of import licencing, but the Ministry of Industry had to accept that the interest of domestic industry would be sufficiently protected by the new system, including the proposed exchange rate depreciation. The Department of Revenue had to accept that while reduction in customs duties would reduce revenue, this could be made good by an increase in domestic indirect taxes. The Department of Economic Affairs and the RBI had to accept that exchange rates would have to be calibrated to play the role envisaged in supporting the change.

When the note was discussed in the cabinet secretary's meeting, it revealed interesting differences across ministries. Amarnath Verma, industries secretary, was strongly supportive. He later became principal secretary to the PM in the Narasimha Rao government and played a critical role in implementing the 1991 reforms. I learnt later that Verma, ably supported by Rakesh Mohan (whom I knew well from my days at the World Bank), economic advisor in the ministry, had actually persuaded Minister of Industry Ajit Singh that major liberalization of industrial policy was needed, but they faced opposition from Finance Minister Madhu Dandavate as well as the officials of the ministry.[23] The Industrial Policy announced on 31 May 1990 was therefore a scaled-down version of what Ajit Singh had initially approved and Verma was happy to support the proposal in the M Document to push industrial liberalization further.

The Ministry of Finance was represented by Finance Secretary Bimal Jalan and Chief Economic Advisor Nitin Desai. They had

---

[23]Mohan R., ed., *India Transformed: 25 Years of Economic Reforms*, Penguin Random House, 2017.

reservations about the trade liberalization measures proposed in the note in view of the BOP position. I had a strong feeling their position was constrained by the views of Dandavate. It may also have reflected the traditional unwillingness of the Ministry of Finance to give up import licencing, which was viewed as an instrument for controlling the BOP.

Members of the Planning Commission who had earlier clashed with me on the draft approach paper were particularly unhappy that the PM had sent my note to the Committee of Secretaries just a few days before the approach paper was sent to the National Development Council (NDC). Writing in *The Times of India* on 24 June, Bharat Bhushan described the M Document as a 'counter approach paper to planning' and quoted unnamed senior officials of the Planning Commission as saying that 'if the policies argued for are adopted by the Government, the NDC's efforts would then seem to be sheer waste in retrospect'. Bhushan also stated that several secretaries objected to the proposals in the M Document on the grounds that 'this was what several multilateral lending institutions like the World Bank and IMF wanted India to do'.

Damning an idea by putting an IMF or World Bank label on it was common practice. I would not have minded criticism of the substance of my proposals because these could be examined rationally, but being criticized just because what I was saying had some resemblance to what the World Bank was also saying was both irrational and irritating.

The Planning Commission was especially unhappy at the recommendation that new commitments such as the Right to Work should be avoided until the finance position improved. Jain was quoted by the press as saying, 'The suggestion can only come from a mind which wants the government to be scuttled.' Another member (unidentified) took a more nuanced view, saying, 'There was a need for modernization of Indian industry and competition to make industry more efficient, but this should not be at the cost of self-reliance in certain crucial sectors.'

Chandra Shekhar, ever eager to criticize the V.P. Singh

government, called a press conference on 1 July and used the occasion to criticize the changes in industrial policy that the Ministry of Industry had announced a month earlier, especially the provision allowing FDI freely up to 40 per cent of equity in a defined list of high-priority industries. I was puzzled that he had not criticized the industrial policy when it was announced on 31 May but decided to do so a month later. I wondered whether he considered the M Document, with its bolder suggestions for liberalizing FDI, as a 'trial balloon' from the PMO signalling further changes. In any case, he waxed eloquent, proclaiming, 'I do not want multinational corporations to be allowed in unless absolutely necessary in some areas. They should certainly not be allowed in the area of consumer goods,' and further that 'the need of the hour was for some austerity measures and a pursuit of the swadeshi experiment'.

The debate showed general support for the call for macroeconomic discipline. This was common ground for all economists, though there were differences on how this objective should be achieved. There were different views on the proposals for industrial liberalization and opening of the economy, but the majority opinion seemed to favour greater liberalization. My former boss, Honavar, who was chief economic advisor when I had just joined the Ministry of Finance, did not question the logic of the proposals but asked whether there was any political will.

Ashok Desai was broadly supportive, but felt it should have gone even further. He concluded with the words, 'M has been a model bureaucrat for long enough: self-effacing, press-avoiding, conciliatory, well behaved and sedate—in short, studiously colourless. In this paper, he is seen with his grey suit off, almost losing his shirt so to speak. Maybe the Government should leak its discussion papers more often; they are not all that bad.'

The PM maintained a studied silence as the controversy continued. He never discussed the issue with me in the PMO, so I cannot say how far he would really have been willing to go if circumstances were more propitious. In my judgement, he knew perfectly well that we needed to move in this direction but he had other worries. He gave some indication of his thinking on 28 June 1990 at the National Convention on Growth with Employment, when he spoke about the need for India to adapt to changes taking place in the world economy, and the need to welcome competition. This reinforced my feeling that his views were not very different from those of Rajiv Gandhi, with whom he had worked very closely and effectively as finance minister.

In July 1990, V.P. Singh visited Moscow and I was part of the official delegation. During the discussions with Mikhail Gorbachev in the Kremlin, the issue of economic reforms came up. The PM explained to Gorbachev that we had to undertake reforms but needed to proceed slowly so as not to disrupt the economy too much. Gorbachev responded somewhat firmly that there was a momentum in reforms that had to be maintained. He then used a military analogy: 'Mr Prime Minister, you cannot stop in the middle of a cavalry charge.' I could see V.P. Singh was not convinced. Eighteen months later, in December 1991, the Soviet Union collapsed and Gorbachev was forced out of office. He had not done much by way of economic reform (perestroika), concentrating instead on political reform (glasnost), and it had not worked. V.P. Singh had gone out of office a year earlier. He, too, fell not because of any economic reforms but political failures.

BALANCE OF PAYMENTS COLLAPSES

The BOP crisis in the second half of 1990 was truly a crisis foretold. The current account deficit in the BOP had averaged 1.5 per cent of GDP in the first half of the 1980s and increased in the second half, reaching 2 per cent in 1989–90. However, while the Government inherited a festering problem, it was squarely its responsibility to take corrective action and it failed to do so. Import control was tightened, but that by itself was unlikely to achieve much in the absence of serious efforts at curbing domestic demand. This meant the fiscal deficit had to be reduced. Instead, the high current account deficit was financed by increased resort to external borrowings, combined with a decline in reserves.

I had apprised V.P. Singh of the BOP problem on several occasions. He was also separately briefed by the Ministry of Finance. The RBI was also coming around to the view that a loan from the IMF might have to be negotiated. However, given the views of some of the prominent ministers at the time, notably George Fernandes and Madhu Dandavate, it would not have been easy for the National Front government to reach an acceptable agreement with the IMF.

On one occasion, in the course of a debate in the Lok Sabha that extended late into the evening, V.P. Singh came out of the House to his office in Parliament for a cup of tea. Finding me in the outer office, he asked me to join him. He then pointedly asked whether I thought we would have to go for an IMF loan. I told him frankly that with reserves running very low, the IMF was the only possible source of getting the necessary funding to keep going a little longer while taking corrective steps. If IMF funding was ruled out for political reasons, we needed to act immediately and more or less in the same direction as the IMF would want. My advice was that there was merit in approaching the IMF, but he would have to defend the policy package with the Fund as in the country's interest. He heard me out patiently, did not question what I had said, finished his tea, and returned to the House without further comment.

Saddam Hussein invaded Kuwait on 2 August 1990—this was the immediate trigger that precipitated the crisis. Crude oil prices doubled from around $17 per barrel in July 1990 to $34 per barrel by November 1990. The current account deficit in the BOP was also badly hit by the fall in remittances from the Gulf and the uncertainty about their future. Worse, there were 150,000 Indian citizens stranded in Kuwait who had to be evacuated. This was successfully carried out in what became the largest airlift of people ever, an event subsequently dramatized in the Bollywood film, *Airlift*.

All these momentous developments occurred at a time when the domestic political situation was going awry. Moody's downgraded India a notch. Foreign banks ceased to extend loans and the inflows of NRI deposits, which were an important source of support for the BOP, providing $2.4 billion in 1989–90, turned into outflows in October 1990. The Government drew $682 million from the so-called reserve tranche at the IMF, effectively our own reserves deposited in the IMF. However, this was the equivalent of applying band aid to a deep wound!

V.P. Singh resigned in November 1990 after losing the vote of confidence. He had inherited a problematic BOP but had made no attempt to introduce corrective steps despite ample advance warning. He came into government when the foreign exchange reserves were $3.6 billion, or about eight weeks of imports of that year. This was very low by any standards. By the time he left in November 1990, the reserves had dropped to $1.9 billion, just over three weeks' worth of imports!

V.P. Singh understood the complexities of modern economics but as a politician I think he was excessively focused on short-term political gains. This was to some extent a reflection of his weak political position. Dr Singh once said, 'Politicians have to be in power long enough to act like statesmen', and V.P. Singh was very aware of the limited time he had. His preoccupation with short-term objectives was most evident when one of the fourteen A320 aircraft newly purchased by Indian Airlines crashed in Bangalore airport in February 1990. All the new planes were grounded, pending the outcome of an enquiry to be conducted by the Directorate General of Civil Aviation (DGCA). The enquiry revealed that the crash was caused by pilot error and there was nothing wrong with the aircraft.

The order grounding the planes should have been promptly lifted but it was not. I happened to be present when Minister of Civil Aviation Arif Mohammed Khan told V.P. Singh that the DGCA enquiry had established that there was no reason to keep the A320s grounded, especially as these planes were being used by many airlines internationally. The decision imposed a huge financial loss on Indian Airlines, which had to pay interest costs on the purchase, while earning no revenue. The PM said he would think it over, but the clearance was not given and the aircraft remained grounded for several more months.

The decision to keep the planes grounded was obviously linked to the fact that a CBI enquiry had been ordered on whether the original purchase in 1986 was improperly influenced by Rajiv Gandhi. He had seen the plane at the Le Bourget Air Show in 1985 and visited the cockpit. Indian Airlines had earlier planned to buy the Boeing 757, but shortly after the Paris visit, the decision was changed to buy the A320, which was a next-generation aircraft. The CBI investigation never led to any charges.

V.P. Singh was a complex personality. There were not many people he was close to. Vinod Pande was perhaps the only exception. Pande had served under him as revenue secretary and was brought in as cabinet secretary by pushing T.N. Seshan out. Both men believed in astrology; Vinod was actually an amateur astrologer. He once told me that when V.P. Singh was elected PM, he had told him that the stars were very favourably aligned when he was sworn in and it augured well for a long innings. When I asked Pande how his prediction squared with what actually happened, he replied, 'You know, I checked later and found my stars were not well aligned for astrological predictions on that day.'

I recall bidding goodbye to V.P. Singh as he left the PMO after handing in his resignation. He knew my doubts about the merits of his decision to implement the Mandal Commission recommendations and said to me in good humour, 'Well, Montek, you may think I have broken my leg, but you will have to admit I scored a goal!'

THE CHANDRA SHEKHAR INTERLUDE

The Chandra Shekhar government, which came into office in November 1990, was even more fragile than the one it replaced.

It had only 64 MPs and was totally dependent on the support of the Congress. President R. Venkataraman, before swearing in the Government, was reported to have extracted a promise from the Congress party that it would not withdraw support for at least a year—but this was obviously an empty promise.

Almost immediately after taking over, PM Chandra Shekhar told me he would be reconstituting the PMO and sending me to some other ministry. He then very graciously asked where I would like to go. I knew Commerce Secretary S.P. Shukla was being moved to the Ministry of Finance in place of Bimal Jalan, who was appointed chairman of the EAC-PM. I cheekily replied that ideally I would have wanted finance, but knowing that was not available, would he consider sending me to commerce? He thought about it for a minute and agreed. He had already announced that Subramanian Swamy would be the new commerce minister. Dr Singh had been appointed economic advisor to the PM and he later told me Chandra Shekhar had asked him for his advice on where I should go—he had recommended the Ministry of Commerce.

I moved to my new position as commerce secretary on 14 December 1990. Swamy, my new minister, had the reputation of being pro-market. He had given up a teaching position at Harvard University to return to India in the 1970s to teach, and then joined politics. Isher and I had met him briefly when he visited Washington DC in 1976. This was just after he became famous for having walked into the Rajya Sabha during the Emergency when there was an arrest warrant against him, stayed there long enough to register his presence, and then left unobstructed to go underground and resurface abroad! Although he was well known because of this dramatic escapade, very few people in government knew he was a trained economist who had taught at Harvard and also co-authored a paper, 'Invariant Economic Index Numbers and Canonical Duality: Survey and Synthesis' with Paul Samuelson, which was published in the prestigious *American Economic Review* in 1974.

I briefed Swamy about the nature of the BOP crisis the Government had inherited. The Ministry of Commerce had started to compress imports in the last months of the V.P. Singh government as the Ministry of Finance sounded the alarm on the scarcity of foreign exchange, but the method of import compression was entirely arbitrary. At times, compression was achieved by the simple expedient of delaying the issuing of licences, a phenomenon that hurt smaller producers much more.

Those producing import substitutes for the domestic market actually benefited from the tightening of imports as domestic customers were forced to shift to domestic sources of supply, irrespective of cost or quality. Exporters were operating in world markets where customers could source supplies from anywhere in the world and would not accept lower quality or delays.

I felt we could avoid these problems if we implemented the proposal in the M Document to get rid of import licencing for a very wide range of imports and allow these items to be imported freely against tradeable replenishment licences earned by exporters. The Ministry of Commerce could not initiate policy changes on the exchange rate—that was a subject jealously guarded by the Ministry of Finance—but the proposal I had in mind would have a similar effect as the premium on the tradeable replenishment licence would vary with excess demand for imports. Swamy agreed that we should build it into the Trade Policy for 1991–92, to be announced in April 1991. However, the Government was pulled down much earlier and my chance to push the idea had to wait until after the general election in 1991.

The Chandra Shekhar government faced an almost impossible situation. It had run out of foreign exchange reserves and did its best to mobilize extra financing. Finance Minister Yashwant Sinha made a special effort to obtain bilateral assistance from Japan, and even visited Tokyo for this purpose, but to no avail.

In January 1991, the Government borrowed (or 'drew' in IMF parlance) $777 million from the IMF for three months through the first credit tranche facility that had minimal conditionality. An additional drawing of $1,009 million was made from another low-conditionality Compensatory and Contingency Financing Facility of the Fund. But reserves continued to decline. We needed a much larger loan to meet our financing needs for a few years, but that would involve conditionalities. The Government felt it could only negotiate with the IMF after presenting the Budget.

As the time for the Budget approached, the Congress became worried that if the Government opted for a 'hard Budget' to deal with the crisis, the party would be blamed because it was keeping the Government in power. The Government was thus persuaded not to present a regular Budget on 28 February and make do with presenting only a 'vote on account' on 4 March that would enable it to continue spending for the first three months of the financial year, starting on 1 April 1991. This was a clear signal that its days were numbered; a few days later, the Congress withdrew support. A general election was called, which would be conducted in stages through different parts of the country in May and June 1991.

The announcement of the election shifted public attention to the political arena, but the Ministry of Finance and the RBI were hard at work trying to stave off default in the face of a continuing erosion of reserves. Foreign exchange reserves dropped to an all-time low of $1.1 billion in June 1991, barely sufficient for two weeks of imports! In fact, some of this amount was not readily available for making payments if needed. In the absence of a credible adjustment strategy with assured financing, the expectation of devaluation grew stronger by the day. Exporters began to delay remitting export receipts while importers began to accelerate payments for imports. These leads and lags could easily produce heavy pressure on the BOP in the short term, much like speculative capital outflows.

In May 1991, Finance Minister Yashwant Sinha authorized the State Bank of India to sell 20 tonnes of gold from the Government's stock of confiscated gold to the Union Bank of Switzerland with a provision for repurchase within six months. He also authorized negotiations for pledging 47 tonnes of gold from the gold reserves as collateral for a loan of $600 million from the Bank of England and the Bank of Japan. The actual transaction, however, was completed after the new government took office. Though the Chandra Shekhar government was criticized for 'selling the family jewels', these were actually bold decisions indicating that the Government was willing to take unpopular steps to stave off default. Dr Singh later went out of his way to praise Sinha for this action because it created credibility that India could take tough action if necessary.

The Bank of England and the Bank of Japan, somewhat humiliatingly, insisted that the gold pledged with them should be physically shipped to the Bank of England vaults in London! The RBI was one of the authorized depositories for holding some of the IMF's gold. Years later, Camdessus told me he was advised that perhaps the small part of the IMF's gold that was held with the RBI should be withdrawn. To his credit, he turned down the suggestion as he felt it would send the wrong signal.

The physical transfer of gold to London had its lighter moments. It had to be done in strict secrecy and security arrangements were made for an armoured truck to transport the gold from the vaults of the RBI in Bombay to a chartered Air India plane waiting for it at Santa Cruz airport. As there were no cell phones in those days, Deputy Governor Rangarajan (who later became RBI governor) was following the truck's progress by radio. Rangarajan has written that he had a nerve-wracking moment when he was informed that the motorcade was halted because one of the vehicles in the convoy developed a flat tyre! Fortunately, they were able to change the wheel without incident and the valuable cargo was soon on its way to the airport, and thence to London.

The Congress fought the election vigorously under the leadership of Rajiv, hoping to come back into government. Its manifesto focused on the economic problems caused by the National Front government, promising an early return to normalcy and renewed economic dynamism. Tragically, just before the campaign was to end, Rajiv was assassinated by a female suicide bomber of the Liberation Tigers of Tamil Eelam (LTTE), who blew herself up as she bent to touch his feet. Late in the evening of 21 May, Suman Dubey, an old friend of mine who is also a close friend of the Gandhi family, telephoned to give me the news. Suman sounded completely devastated — and so was I. The body was brought to Delhi and lay in state at the Nehru Memorial. Dr Singh, Isher and I went together to pay our respects. I was deeply saddened to see Sonia Gandhi and their two children, Rahul and Priyanka, sitting just behind where the body was kept. I could not help recalling the many occasions I had seen them together as a happy family. It was a truly tragic end to a life that held so much promise for the future.

The assassination led to the postponement of the last stages of the election by a few weeks, and the process was completed in June. When the votes were counted, the Congress had won 244 seats, making it the single largest party, though still short of a majority.

Part Three

7

1991: SEIZING THE OPPORTUNITY

The Congress was able to form a government with support from the Jharkhand Mukti Morcha and a few independent MPs. The leadership tried to persuade Sonia Gandhi to head the new government but she firmly refused. They then chose P.V. Narasimha Rao, a 70-year-old veteran Congressman who was a former CM of Andhra Pradesh and had served as cabinet minister under both Mrs Gandhi and Rajiv Gandhi. Rao had not contested the elections; he had planned to retire and was packing to move back to Andhra Pradesh when he was suddenly drafted to be the leader of the party.

When the Government took over in 1991, foreign exchange reserves were at rock bottom, default seemed imminent, and crisis management was the need of the hour. Managing the crisis without implementing reforms would have been achievement enough. However, the Government used the crisis to implement far-reaching structural reforms. It started the process of dismantling one of the most rigidly controlled policy regimes in the world and integrating the Indian economy with the rest of the world.

I was commerce secretary through most of that momentous year, at the end of which I moved back to the Ministry of Finance as secretary, economic affairs.

The new government was to be sworn in on 21 June and I was pleasantly surprised to be called to a meeting at the PMO before the ceremony. Among those present was Dr Manmohan Singh, who had recently returned to India after spending three years at the South Commission in Geneva. He had been appointed chairman of the University Grants Commission and economic advisor to

PM Chandra Shekhar. Others at the meeting included Cabinet Secretary Naresh Chandra, Finance Secretary S.P. Shukla and Chief Economic Advisor Deepak Nayyar. The PM designate had called us to discuss what he should say in his first broadcast to the nation, scheduled for the next day. With the economic crisis still raging, he had to give some indication of how it would be addressed.

Rao was very much of the old school as far as economic policy is concerned and many of us wondered how he would handle the crisis. Cabinet Secretary Naresh Chandra had already given him a detailed briefing, leaving him in no doubt about the seriousness of the economic crisis. He also told Rao that we would need to seek assistance from the IMF and the World Bank and should think about the policy reforms they would inevitably insist upon. In his opening remarks, Rao made it plain that the Government would have to take difficult decisions and come up with innovative solutions. 'We must get rid of the cobwebs in our mind,' he said. This raised the hope that the Government may be willing to go beyond merely cutting the fiscal deficit and take bolder steps that I thought were long overdue, including decontrol of industry and liberalization of trade policy. Rao ended the meeting by saying, 'Manmohan, you know what needs to be done. Why don't you work on this in your office in North Block and send me a draft text later in the day about what I should say on TV.'

That's when I first realized Manmohan Singh would be the new finance minister! I had known him for over 15 years by then. Isher and I had even taken our children to stay with his family in Mumbai when he was RBI governor. He and his wife Gursharan Kaur had gone out of their way to make the stay memorable for our boys.

The fact that he was going to work on the draft speech greatly raised my expectations. Only a few weeks earlier, he had delivered the convocation address at the Indian Institute of Management (IIM) in Bangalore, where he had outlined a reform agenda for the future. He had touched on many of the points I had raised a year earlier in the M Document, including the need to reduce the fiscal deficit and get rid of controls over industrial investment that came in the way of domestic competition. He had highlighted the negative effects of the import control regime and called for tariffs to replace import restrictions, and eventually to be reduced over time. He had also said that the exchange rate should reflect the scarcity value of foreign exchange and called for making the rupee a convertible currency in 'a reasonable period of time, in any case before the end of a decade'. He was more cautious on the public sector, admitting privatization may not be feasible, but called for rethinking the policy of reserving areas of economic activity exclusively for the public sector. The address received very little publicity at the time because no one thought the speaker delivering it would soon become the finance minister!

The PM's speech the next day did not come up to my expectations. It promised a time-bound programme to streamline our industrial policies and programmes, but that was a very general statement. A reference to 'creativity, enterprise and innovativeness' could be seen as a signal of a larger role for the private sector, but it was hardly a clarion call for a new direction in policy. There were just four weeks to go before the Budget. Foreign exchange reserves were only a little over $1 billion and the markets were awash with speculation on whether India might be forced to default on payments. It was known that the Ministry of Finance had been negotiating with the IMF for a programme to provide financing to manage the BOP deficit, subject to corrective policies being put in place. I had hoped the PM's speech would be a vehicle to prepare the public on what we needed to do, but it said almost nothing.

Some years earlier, Rajiv Gandhi had asked me to show the draft of his foreword to the Seventh Plan to Rao because, as he put it, 'Narasimha Rao ji is a master at spotting what might have political implications.' I wondered if this instinct explained why the speech only hinted at changes without saying anything that might pose political problems! It made me think whether he would be willing to take some of the tough decisions needed. I was proved wrong.

The next few weeks saw a virtual blizzard of action. The rupee was devalued, trade policy was liberalized, domestic investment controls were dismantled, and a new policy towards FDI was articulated. All this was bound to face major resistance from several quarters at home, including sections of the Congress.

PM Rao could not have made a better choice of finance minister. Manmohan Singh was widely respected in financial circles internationally as well as at home. He knew he had to untie the multiple knots that bound the economy, and he knew better than most about how the system functioned and which critical levers to pull.

DEVALUATION IN TWO STEPS: HOP, SKIP AND JUMP

The first step in responding to the crisis was the announcement on 1 July 1991 that the rupee was devalued by 9 per cent. As commerce secretary, I was not in the loop about the decision. But I had no doubt it was the right step, though 9 per cent seemed too little. Two days later, a second devaluation took the cumulative depreciation to about 19 per cent—a much more reasonable adjustment to deal with the BOP crisis.

Dr Manmohan Singh later told me that the two-step process was adopted at the insistence of PM Rao. He had advised the PM that devaluation was unavoidable as we needed an exchange rate that markets would regard as credible. He also advised him not to take the matter to the cabinet, where it might lead to interminable and inconclusive discussions. He recommended that the PM decide the matter on his own authority, which the rules allowed him to do. Knowing the move would be politically sensitive, Rao decided to first administer a small dose to gauge public reaction, followed by a second step later.

Dr Singh also later told me that he had quickly prepared a handwritten note outlining the two-step process and obtained the PM's signature of approval. The decision was conveyed to RBI Governor S. Venkitaramanan and Deputy Governor

C. Rangarajan, who was actually the official in charge of exchange rate management. They were, of course, aware of the impending devaluation and supported the idea. The procedure was informally codenamed 'Hop, Skip and Jump' so they could refer to it on the telephone while maintaining secrecy.

Devaluation was a politically sensitive decision in most countries in the days of fixed exchange rates because the value of the currency in foreign exchange was often confused in the public mind with national honour. This was particularly so in India, given the unhappy experience of 1966. The situation in 1991 was very different. For one thing, unlike in 1966, when the exchange rate had been rigidly fixed for many years, the rupee had been depreciating gradually year after year. Between 1988 and 1991, for example, it had depreciated by 48 per cent against the dollar. However, a gradual depreciation is one thing, a sudden large devaluation quite another.

The first devaluation provoked strong criticism from many quarters. Nikhil Chakravarthy, editor of Communist Party of India (Marxist) [CPI(M)] journal *Mainstream* and a confidant of the PM, was sharply critical. He had been told by some economists that the Government could easily get large sums of money on loan from a variety of sources, including the Sultan of Brunei, without any conditionality; he felt this option should have been explored. Dr Singh later confirmed that some senior officials were keen to do so but he was able to dissuade Rao on the grounds that it would convey the impression of a government clutching at straws and unwilling to take decisive action.

When Dr Manmohan Singh briefed President Venkataraman on the need for devaluation, the President was not at all happy. He was proud of having successfully negotiated an EFF arrangement with the IMF in 1981 when he was finance minister without having to devalue and felt we should have done the same. He was also not happy that the Government had taken this step before proving its majority in Parliament. The President also conveyed his unhappiness to the PM, who was sufficiently alarmed that he actually asked the finance minister to hold back the second devaluation! As it happened, Manmohan Singh had already instructed the RBI to take the second step before markets opened on 3 July. When he called Rangarajan again at the PM's request to check whether it was possible to hold back the second step, Rangarajan said, in the code they had agreed, 'But I have already jumped.'

Manmohan Singh later explained that the reason he had advanced the second step was because *The Economic Times* on that day wrongly reported that the SBI had defaulted on a payment due in the US. As finance minister, he felt that given the nervousness in the markets, any anticipation of a second devaluation could trigger large speculative outflow. It was to forestall this possibility that he had instructed that the second devaluation be advanced to 3 July.

One of the reasons devaluation was highly controversial was that most people did not understand the role it played in dealing with an external payments crisis. They understood that the problem arose because the country was 'living beyond its means'. With more demand in the system than available supply, the excess demand spilt over to create a current account deficit in the BOP. They also understood that to reduce the current account deficit, it was necessary to curtail total demand in the economy and this involved some 'belt-tightening'. This justified reducing the fiscal deficit, which involved either cutting government expenditure or increasing taxes. Cutting government expenditure cuts demand directly. And raising taxes reduces income in the hands of the consumers, thereby reducing private consumption.

However, it was not immediately obvious to most people why devaluation had to be part of the package of reducing the current account deficit. Devaluation raises the price of tradeables (exports and imports) relative to non-tradeables. This shifts domestic demand away from tradeables towards non-tradeables, and this 'expenditure switching effect' increases exports and reduces imports. The effect of this relative price change on the composition of demand reduces the extent of the belt-tightening that might otherwise be needed to bring the current account deficit under control.

Those who realized that devaluation made our exports cheaper in dollar terms and, therefore, more competitive often saw it as a policy that only helped exporters, including high-profile software exporters like Infosys, Wipro and TCS. It was not sufficiently appreciated that all domestic producers competing with imports would also benefit because the higher price of imports would make their products more competitive. Many also did not realize that a large part of the higher incomes earned in the export sector would be spent on domestically produced commodities and services, hotels, restaurants, domestic tourism, etc., thereby adding to employment.

Devaluation had another major advantage. It made it much easier to abolish import licencing without having to levy high tariffs because the price of imports increased automatically with devaluation. The two-step devaluation of 1991 was crucial to the success of the trade policy reforms that followed.

SOARING IN THE HIGH SKIES OF TRADE

I was working on a trade policy package in the Ministry of Commerce that would have come up for consideration in April 1991 if the elections had not intervened. In the new government, P. Chidambaram was appointed minister of state for commerce (independent charge). He was one of the young ministers brought in by Rajiv Gandhi in 1985, and had served as minister of state for personnel and, later, internal security. I never got to know him during the Rajiv years as he did not deal with economic issues at that time, but it was a pleasure to work with him in the Ministry of Commerce. A lawyer by profession , with an MBA from Harvard, he was comfortable dealing with practical economic issues and was a completely hands-on minister. He was able to master the details of highly complex issues quickly and was very decisive.

I briefed Chidambaram on how the import licencing system was hurting the economy, especially exports, and made the case for shifting to a more liberal trade policy. A key element was a proposal, originally outlined in the M Document, for a new licence called Eximscrip that would replace the replenishment licences issued to exporters to meet their import requirements. Whereas replenishment licences were given to cover the actual import requirement of each export, Eximscrips would be earned by exporters at a uniform rate of 30 per cent of the value of exports. These could be freely traded in the market and used by anyone even to import items that otherwise needed a licence. If the demand for imports exceeded the supply of Eximscrips, the premium on the licence would increase, thereby making imports more expensive and reducing import demand. By increasing the profitability of exports, it would also increase exports. As the value of imports allowed through this route would be limited to the total value of Eximscrips earned by exporters, it would automatically restrict imports to an acceptable level. Items such as crude oil and petroleum products, fertilizers and metals and ores importable only by specified government agencies would continue to be imported under the old regime. Consumer goods were banned and would remain banned.

These moves to liberalize trade policy were a radical change from anything the Ministry of Commerce had done thus far. The Trade Policy Division of the ministry would earlier spend most of its energy defending our import licencing policies at the General Agreement on Tariffs and Trade in Geneva. Chief Controller for Exports and Imports D.R. Mehta, an IAS officer of the Rajasthan cadre, was persuaded of the need to liberalize. Economic Advisor Jayanta Roy was also very supportive of trade liberalization. Few others were involved in the reformulation of trade policy. Chidambaram appreciated the logic of what I was proposing and gave the go-ahead to work out the details of a radically new trade policy that could be announced in August 1991.

Action on trade policy was precipitated when the second

devaluation was announced on the morning of 3 July. Finance Minister Manmohan Singh telephoned me to say that as the rupee had been devalued by a cumulative 19 per cent over the past two days, there was no longer any justification for continuing with the cash compensatory support (CCS), which was a subsidy for exports. The devaluation had done much more to incentivize exports than this subsidy and as he had to take steps to reduce the fiscal deficit as part of the policies agreed with the IMF, he wanted to announce the abolition of the CCS with immediate effect. He asked me to brief Chidambaram on the logic of the move, after which he would talk to the minister himself.

I briefed Chidambaram, saying the proposed abolition was absolutely the right thing to do in the aftermath of the devaluation. However, I also warned him that exporters would fear that their buyers abroad would renegotiate the price downwards for all exports in the pipeline to reflect the benefit of devaluation and the exporters would be in a weak position to resist such demands. While they would benefit in future when competing for fresh export orders based on the new exchange rate, they feared they would be forced to accept a discount on exports in the pipeline. I suggested to Chidambaram that exporters would be much happier if the abolition of the CCS was announced simultaneously with the introduction of Eximscrips, which would be a new incentive, thus reassuring them that their interests had not been forgotten.

In those days, changes in trade policy required consultation with the Ministry of Finance at the official level and the final proposal was then sent on a file for approval of the finance minister and PM. If we followed this procedure, it would not have been possible to announce the new trade policy on that day. I was also concerned that officials in the Ministry of Finance would end up diluting the proposal considerably and getting the finance minister to approve the modified version. I therefore suggested we approach the finance minister directly and persuade him to agree.

Chidambaram and I went to meet Dr Singh with this plan. S.P. Shukla and Deepak Nayyar were also in the meeting. While the finance minister responded favourably, both Shukla and Nayyar were not in favour of immediate announcement of Eximscrips. They suggested the proposal be examined in the normal course along with other proposals in the trade policy. I explained that what was being proposed was a major trade policy reform that would get rid of an important set of 'cobwebs', as the PM had put it. I particularly emphasized that the replacement of import licencing with imports through Eximscrips would be a major efficiency-enhancing reform that would be self-balancing as far as the BOP was concerned.

Manmohan Singh heard out both sides and overruled the objections of his officials. He asked how quickly we could get the proposals on a file to take to the PM for his approval, as he wanted to announce the abolition of CCS by the end of the day. I prepared a note in two hours outlining the proposal, which Chidambaram approved. We then took the file to Dr Singh's office by late afternoon, he promptly signed it, and all three of us went straight to the PM's residence to obtain his approval.

Chidambaram explained the proposal to the PM, emphasizing that it would represent a major liberalization of import policy in line with the objectives he had outlined in his address to the nation. After Dr Singh confirmed his agreement to the proposal, Narasimha Rao signed the file without further ado. A major step in liberalizing trade policy was completed in the space of about eight hours!

The finance minister was able to issue a statement later in the day about the abolition of CCS for exports with effect from midnight of 3 July. He also said the commerce minister would announce other important changes in trade policy. On 4 July, Chidambaram held a press conference to explain the main elements of the Eximscrip proposal, highlighting that it would effectively eliminate licencing for a wide range of imports. The premium on the tradable Eximscrips would directly increase export profitability. He also stated that it was the intention of the Government to reduce tariffs over time and move to 'full convertibility of the rupee on trade account' in three to five years.

The announcement was extremely well received by the press. In its editorial on 5 July, *The Times of India* described it as a commendable example of thinking big: 'Instead of being a scratch here and a fiddle there, it outlines a strategy to make the rupee convertible in three to five years. Its importance lies not in its many individual clauses but in the vision of a new India that stands on its own feet and pays for its imports through exports that do not need artificial props and never-ending subsidies.' The editorial went on to quote Chidambaram, 'We have always had wings but suffered a fear of flying.' Building on Chidambaram's evocation of Jonathan Livingston Seagull[24], the editorial concluded with a flourish: 'We should now soar in the high skies of trade.' It was a refreshing change from the defensive stance of the press about our export prospects.

The speed with which trade policy reforms were approved in July 1991 throws up some important lessons for the future. First, the response to a crisis must be speedy, but well considered. Second, it is not always possible to get everyone to agree. The reforms we proposed did not have the support of the senior bureaucracy in the Ministry of Finance but this was not allowed to lead to interminable inter-ministerial consultations. Finance Minister Manmohan Singh understood the issue and was willing to overrule his officials. And PM Rao trusted his finance minister!

THE LEFT CRITIQUE

The Left was not comfortable with the direction that economic policy was taking and the first salvo was fired by the West Bengal government: it produced an alternative strategy paper that reflected the Left position. The paper was issued on 4 July 1991 and sent to the finance minister and the PM—the same day we announced the Eximscrip reform. It was widely covered in }the press and found resonance in some quarters, especially among academics.

---

[24]The eponymous hero of a novel by Richard Bach.

The Left Strategy Paper (LSP) attributed the crisis of the economy to what it called the 'indiscriminate rush towards import liberalization' in the earlier years. This was supposed to have encouraged a pattern of production that was more capital-intensive and produced an unequal distribution of income and was also viewed as generating a demand for luxury consumer goods that were import-intensive.

The LSP argued that there was no need for devaluation because the BOP could be handled by resorting to strict control of imports, 'going through each item of the import bill...to reduce a significant quantum of imports of all items unless they are connected with mass consumption goods, essential production, infrastructural requirements or exports'. I had basic differences with this approach. The faith reposed in the ability of administrators to make decisions on which imports were necessary and which were not, and to act speedily without breeding inefficiency and corruption, was a common misconception of the Left. Interestingly, the LSP suggested there should be a strong appeal to NRIs so that NRI capital outflow could be reversed.

The LSP acknowledged the need to reduce the fiscal deficit but emphasized that this must be done by increasing revenues from income taxes, unearthing the black money held abroad, and cutting non-priority expenditure without affecting the interests of the poor. This was a reasonable proposition with which I agreed. The paper rejected any notion of dismantling the public sector and relaxing restrictions on monopoly houses.

I was struck by how little the Left in India was affected by the remarkable changes Deng Xiaoping had brought about in China by opening the economy. They were also unaffected by the abandonment of statist policies in East Europe following the collapse of Communism after the fall of the Berlin Wall in 1989. Of course, the Soviet Union was still intact, though its economic weakness was by then known to most knowledgeable people. It collapsed once and for all a few months later in December 1991.

Finance ministers traditionally stop speaking on policy issues as Budget day approaches for fear of revealing any secrets. I have always felt that the fetish of Budget secrecy actually prevents full consideration of alternatives. I was happy Dr Manmohan Singh consciously departed from this tradition of silence because leaving the Left critique unanswered for two weeks until Budget day would have only allowed fear of loss of sovereignty to gain weight. In an interview given to Paranjoy Thakurta published in *Sunday* on 14 July, he responded on many critical issues.

He pointed out that the exchange rate was just another price and if we wanted our exports to be competitive, a weaker exchange rate (through devaluation) would help achieve this objective. Countries such as South Korea and China had used this mechanism aggressively, but it was the first time an Indian finance minister was saying so. He also pointed out that as the exchange rate was seen as unsustainable by markets, it was better to adjust it to a more credible level than take the risk of a run on the currency, which could provoke a payments default. He strongly differed with the argument that the BOP problem could be solved by carefully cutting non-priority imports. This approach had been tried by previous governments and produced visibly poor results. On industrial policy, he said we had to create an environment in which investment, technical change and modernization become profitable propositions.

This was Manmohan Singh's first shot as a politician, countering criticism and trying to build public opinion in favour of reforms. In his previous incarnations as a civil servant, he had spoken in much more guarded terms. He was now openly taking on the Left, although his gentle academic persona came through, more interested in converting people to his point of view than castigating them for criticizing him.

He also reached out to senior officials to explain the necessity of reforms. A few days before the Budget, he called all the secretaries of the economic ministries to a meeting. As commerce secretary, I was part of the group. He told us he needed the active cooperation of the senior bureaucracy to get the Government's new policy changes implemented. This initiative was particularly important because not all members of the cabinet were on his side. If the secretaries were also not fully on board, the reform effort could get scuttled. We were all more than a little flattered at the importance assigned to our cooperation.

He concluded the meeting with an offer that if anyone had any reservations about implementing the new approach, he would ensure they would get alternative assignments acceptable to them. It was a good example of political leadership trying to bring the bureaucracy on board while respecting the fact that there may be individuals who genuinely disagreed with the direction being taken and offering them a workable alternative.

THE NEW INDUSTRIAL POLICY: LIBERALIZING FDI

As the PM had specifically mentioned the need to streamline industrial policies in his address to the nation, and he was the cabinet minister in charge of industry, the preparation of a new policy went into overdrive. Amarnath Verma, then secretary, industrial development, was a strong advocate of industrial liberalization.

Proposals for industrial liberalization by Verma had earlier been rejected by Finance Minister Madhu Dandavate in the National Front government (*see Chapter 6*). Now, he had a freer rein and made full use of it. The new Industrial Policy of 1991 departed radically from past proposals. Industrial licencing was abolished for all but a handful of industries and the rules affecting FDI were greatly liberalized. The MRTP Act was effectively abolished and the list of industries reserved for the public sector reduced from 18 to eight.

A new Foreign Investment Promotion Board (FIPB) was created and located in the PMO. Cabinet Secretary Naresh Chandra told me that he felt strongly that the PMO should be kept out of decisions on individual cases. He was probably right in principle but I felt that locating the FIPB in the PMO was the right decision to signal a more supportive attitude towards foreign investment, and Verma was a consummate player in guiding the bureaucracy.

The new Industrial Policy, while bold in totality, was timid in one important dimension. It did not change the policy of reserving the production of a large number of items exclusively for small-scale industries (SSIs). Small was defined in terms of investment in plant and machinery below a stated level. There were 740 items reserved for production by SSIs in 1991, including garments, toys and other consumer goods. These items had tremendous export potential, but because of the reservation policy, Indian producers of these items were effectively prevented from upgrading technology and achieving the scale of production needed for export orders. The SSI producers were seen as a politically important constituency that could not be disturbed. The process of de-reservation began only in 1997 and was stretched out over almost two decades, the last item being removed from the list only in 2015.

The new policy faced political resistance from within the cabinet. It was first put before the Cabinet Committee on Economic Affairs (CCEA) on 15 July, shortly after the PM won a vote of confidence in Parliament. Several ministers said it looked like an abandonment of Congress ideology. In accordance with normal practice when there is a divergence of opinion, a GoM was constituted to consider the issues. Jairam Ramesh attended the GoM meeting as a PMO official and reported that only Dr Singh and Chidambaram supported the proposals.[25] It was decided that the policy should be revised, taking account of the views expressed by different ministers, and Jairam Ramesh was asked to prepare a second draft after consulting Dr Singh and Chidambaram.

Jairam solved the problem by the simple expedient of adding a lengthy preamble that talked of the way policy had evolved since Jawaharlal Nehru. He mentioned that both Mrs Gandhi and Rajiv Gandi had moved it forward and then added firmly, 'Government's policy will be continuity with change.' With the

---

[25]Ramesh, J., *To the Brink and Back: India's 1991 Story*, Rupa Publications, 2015.

addition of this preamble, the CCEA approved the policy with no change in any of the substantive proposals!

I was disappointed that instead of wanting to take credit for introducing new directions that were truly historic, the party was happiest claiming that it was simply continuing to do what it had always done! I was told later that economists in the IMF, reading these genuflections to continuity, concluded that the reforms would not amount to much in practice. They later acknowledged that they had greatly underestimated the scope of what was done. The dissonance in the CCEA put the PM's well-known instinct for caution on high alert. He wanted the proposals cleared by the full cabinet and discussed in the Congress Working Committee—he obviously had no intention of leaving himself open to the charge of pushing through a new policy without consulting all concerned!

This process took time and, as a result, the policy was finally cleared for announcement only on the very day the Budget was to be presented. The Industrial Policy statement was formally laid on the table in Parliament by Minister of State for Industries P.K. Thungon a few hours before the Budget speech. Ironically, Thungon, according to Jairam Ramesh, was personally not in favour of the changes!

THE BUDGET OF 1991-92: A NEW VISION

The 1991-92 Budget has often been described as ushering in the economic reforms, but actually much of the action had been taken before the Budget. The devaluation of the rupee and trade policy reforms had already been announced two weeks earlier in July 1991. The Industrial Policy reforms were also tabled in Parliament just before the Budget.

Manmohan Singh announced in his Budget speech that the fiscal deficit would be reduced from 8.4 per cent in 1990-91 to 6.5 per cent in 1991-92. This was a much awaited signal of belt-tightening, but the speech also announced that it would not be at the expense of critical programmes for the poor, such as food subsidies. The corporate tax rate was raised from 40 per cent to 45 per cent, while the excise duty rates on items such as air-conditioners and refrigerators were also raised, both designed to signal that the Government did not want the burden of adjustment to fall on the poor. The Budget also signalled the need for a gradual reduction in customs duty over time and took the first step by reducing the maximum rate of customs duties from 300 per cent to 150 per cent.

Further, the speech announced the establishment of two committees to lay out an agenda for reforms in taxation and the financial system. The Tax Reforms Committee was set up under the chairmanship of Raja Chelliah, widely regarded as the doyen of tax economists in India. He had served as the head of the Tax Policy Division of the IMF and had wide knowledge of tax policy and practice in developing countries. The Committee on the Financial System to make recommendations on reform of the banking system was set up under the chairmanship of M. Narasimham. The decision to set up committees with experts reflected Manmohan Singh's style of bringing the best expertise in the country to look at complex problems and prepare a multi-year road map of reforms that would be made public to invite comment and then steadily implemented.

The Budget proposed raising the price of fertilizers by 40 per cent to reduce the fertilizer subsidy but this faced stiff opposition from MPs, including those from the Congress. Rao asked him to convince members of the Congress Parliamentary Party and even advised withdrawal of the proposal. Dr Singh held his ground, spoke to the MPs, and finally agreed on a compromise, rolling back the price increase from 40 per cent to 30 per cent. He later told me he had anticipated the protest and had left room to allow for a partial rollback so the final reduction in fertilizer subsidy would still be substantial.

A major capital market reform announced in the Budget was that SEBI would be converted into a statutory body for regulating the functioning of the capital market. It was also announced that private sector mutual funds would be allowed to compete with

Unit Trust of India (UTI), which until then enjoyed a monopoly.

What made Manmohan Singh's Budget speech of 1991–92 historic was that he used it to present a masterly explanation of why the wide-ranging reforms were being attempted and how the various components fitted together. He explained that we needed to go beyond crisis management towards structural reforms, including liberalization of both industrial policy and trade policy as a means of unleashing the animal spirits of India's private sector. The opening to imports and foreign investment was necessary to subject the economy to competitive pressure.

The public sector was meant to be an engine of growth but had become an 'absorber of national savings'; this problem needed to be addressed. While there was to be no privatization—the 'P' word was politically unacceptable—20 per cent of equity in selected PSUs would be offered to mutual funds. Further, loss-making PSUs would be referred to the Board for Industrial and Financial Reconstruction to see if they could be revived; if not, they would be closed. The interests of workers would be fully protected. In this context, a National Renewal Fund would be established to finance programmes to support training and rehabilitation of retrenched workers.

Liberalization was often seen in India as responding to the interests of the rich and the privileged. Manmohan Singh took this head-on by declaring that the reforms were not meant to 'give a fillip to the mindless and heartless consumerism' we see in affluent societies. He said we must 'combine efficiency with austerity'. However, he clarified that by austerity he did not mean 'a negation of life, or a dry creed that casts a baleful eye on joy and laughter', but a way of 'holding our society together'. He went on to say, 'The basic challenge of our times is to ensure that wealth creation is not only tempered by equity and justice, but is harnessed to the goal of removing poverty, ignorance and disease.' He also invoked Gandhi's notion of trusteeship to make great wealth acceptable. This was vintage Dr Singh. The words were not spoken just for effect but sincerely felt.

Left intellectuals accused him of selling the country to foreign interests—harsh words for a man who had devoted his life to public service and always conducted himself with impeccable integrity. His wife confided to Isher that in the mornings, as he went about getting ready for work, he would often hum his favourite shabad (hymn) from the Tenth Guru:

> *Deh shiva bar mohe ihe, shubh karman te kabhoon na taroon;*
> *na daroon ari se jab jaye ladoon, nishchay kar apani jeet karoon.*

> Grant me this boon Oh God, from Thy Greatness. May I never refrain from righteous acts. May I fight without fear all foes in life's battle, with confidence and determination, claiming the victory!

For Manmohan Singh, his religion is an intensely personal matter. But Isher, who has observed him closely and enjoys singing Gurbani herself, tells me that behind that gentle exterior is a Sikh who derives tremendous strength from Gurbani.

Both Isher and I went to see the finance minister deliver the Budget speech live in the House. He concluded on a distinctly upbeat note, which has been much quoted: 'As Victor Hugo once said, "No power on earth can stop an idea whose time has come." I suggest to this august House that the emergence of India as a major economic power in the world happens to be one such idea. Let the whole world hear it loud and clear. India is now wide awake. We shall prevail. We shall overcome.'

Manmohan Singh's upbeat conclusion has turned out to be remarkably prescient. Exactly 10 years later, in 2001, a Goldman Sachs research team led by Jim O'Neill identified India as one of the BRIC countries (Brazil, Russia, India, China) likely to be the main source of global growth in future. (The acronym was later expanded to BRICS with the addition of South Africa.)

In the years that followed, Russia and Brazil wobbled quite a bit. China, after growing at over 10 per cent for 30 years, has now slowed down as expected. India's overall growth has varied but it has remained relatively robust, averaging 7.5 per cent per year over the past 15 years.

Abid Husain, former commerce secretary who had been a member of the Planning Commission when Dr Singh was deputy chairman, was then serving as India's ambassador to the US. He telephoned us excitedly from Washington DC to say that Manmohan Singh had struck absolutely the right notes in his Budget speech, especially the self-denying and Gandhian touches. He then asked Isher to give the finance minister a hug on his behalf and convey his personal congratulations with a verse from a song in the 1956 film *Jagriti*, referring to Mahatma Gandhi's success in delivering Independence without violence. Abid sang out the verse in tune, over the transcontinental telephone call:

De di hame azadi, bina kharag bina dhal,
Sabarmati ke sant, tu ne kar diya kamaal.

You won for us independence without sword or shield
Oh saint of Sabarmati, what a wonder you achieved!

Abid had caught an important point. It was the simplicity and austerity of Dr Singh's personal lifestyle that enabled him to push liberalization without any danger of being accused of having any personal love of consumerism or luxurious living. Nothing illustrates this self-denial better than the fact that when he remitted his savings from his stint with the South Commission in Geneva, he calculated the gain in rupee value of his savings because of the devaluation he had ordered and donated the calculated gain to the Prime Minister's Relief Fund.

The public reaction to the Budget was broadly positive, but the Left was critical and many of Dr Singh's political colleagues were clearly unconvinced. Jairam has reported that PM Rao organized a number of meetings of the Congress Parliamentary Party in August 1991 at which MPs grilled the finance minister on various aspects of the Budget.[26] Only two members supported him: Ram Niwas Mirdha, who was convinced of Dr Singh's good intentions, and Mani Shankar Aiyar, who approved of the fact that he had given

[26]Ramesh, J., *To the Brink and Back: India's 1991 Story*, Rupa Publications, 2015.

credit to Rajiv as an early reformer! There was no overt revolt but it was clear that many Congressmen had doubts. They were only holding their powder dry to see if the reform programme ran into difficulties.

The reaction of Indian business to a Budget is always difficult to assess as business leaders have a compulsion to say positive things, especially when a new government has just taken over. Looking beneath the surface, it would be fair to say that businessmen were enthusiastic about domestic liberalization, but less so about liberalization of imports. However, their resistance to import liberalization was softened because of the additional cushion provided by the devaluation and premium on Eximscrips. Besides, the duty reduction was only applied to the very high-peak level of 300 per cent. As for FDI, Indian industry was not sure how foreign investors would respond. It was two years later that the first murmuring from the Bombay Club was heard (*see Chapter 8*).

In the weeks following the presentation of the Budget, we worked overtime in the Ministry of Commerce to finalize the details of the new trade policy, the main elements of which had already been announced on 4 July.

Shortly before leaving the Ministry of Commerce, I had an interesting exchange with a young lady officer from the Indian Trade Service (ITS). She said she would like to continue in the ITS if she felt it had a future, but she realized that if we liberalized, licencing would become largely irrelevant, in which case she would rather do something else. She had a good offer from one of the export houses and wanted my advice on whether to leave. I told her I could not possibly advise her on whether she should leave. But I admitted that, in my view, the licencing function needed to be drastically reduced rather than expanded. She thanked me and resigned shortly thereafter. It showed that younger people are much more willing to adjust to change and take up new opportunities. Politicians all too often underestimate this willingness to change. There are many, like the young lady, for whom reforms opened up new careers in a new India.

8

THE ROAD TO REFORMS

Shortly after the trade policy was announced, Manmohan Singh offered me the position of secretary, economic affairs, in the Ministry of Finance, in place of S.P. Shukla. It was well known that Shukla was not on the same wavelength as the finance minister. He was uncomfortable with the new directions of policy and I was told he was offered an attractive assignment as India's executive director in the Asian Development Bank (ADB). He turned it down and took premature retirement.

I was delighted to return to the Ministry of Finance, where I had started my government career. Dr Singh had brought me into the ministry as economic advisor 12 years earlier and the idea of returning as secretary to work with him at a time when the economy was passing through difficult times was both deeply satisfying and challenging. Over the years, I had developed tremendous respect for his knowledge of the economy and his judgement on how to push for economic reforms in an environment of obdurate mindsets.

Amar Nath Verma, principal secretary to the PM at the time, later told me that when the proposal for my appointment came for the PM's approval, he had strongly endorsed my professional credentials but felt it was his duty to draw the PM's attention to the fact that both Manmohan Singh and I were Sikhs. Rao's response was, 'Well, you and I are both Hindus; so why should it matter that they are both Sikhs?'

The IMF deal had been signed by the time I arrived in the Ministry of Finance but the structural adjustment loan of $500 million from the World Bank was yet to be approved. I had no doubt it would be approved as it would rely on the same policy promises made to the IMF. The task before us was to ensure that the performance of the economy came up to expectations, and the policies on which the IMF programme was based were implemented. I also strongly felt that we needed to define a medium-term reform agenda going beyond the policy conditionalities agreed with the IMF. The next two years saw intense activity on all these fronts. Looking back, I am struck by how quickly we were able to overcome the crisis. The current account deficit had ballooned to 3 per cent of GDP in 1990–91. It was brought down to 0.4 per cent in 1991–92 but this was mainly because growth had come down to 1.4 per cent in 1991–92 and import curbs were still in place for the first half of the year. Growth recovered to 5.6 per cent in 1992–93 and the current account deficit also expanded to 1.4 per cent of GDP—but this was quite manageable. By 1994, the crisis was over but we kept pushing for the longer-term objective of structural reform.

TAKING THE REFORMS AGENDA FORWARD

Putting the Budget together was the responsibility of the Budget Division, which was part of the Department of Economic Affairs in the Ministry of Finance. The division interacted with the Department of Expenditure, which put together the expenditure side of the Budget, and the Department of Revenue, which produced the tax revenue projections. The most significant part of the Budget was the tax changes; these were worked out by a select 'Budget Group', which consisted of the three secretaries in the Ministry of Finance from the departments of economic affairs, revenue and expenditure, and the chief economic advisor. This group would work with the chairmen of the Central Board of Direct Taxes (CBDT) and the CBEC to prepare a package of tax proposals for the finance minister. The process was shrouded in secrecy because we had adopted the British tradition that any 'leak' of a tax proposal would be a breach of privilege and could lead to demands for the finance minister's resignation. The proposals emerging from this group would be first approved by the finance minister and then by the PM before being incorporated in the Budget documents.

Well before the Budget was presented, Deepak Nayyar informed me of his intention to resign from his position as chief economic advisor. He candidly told me he simply did not agree with the direction in which policy was moving and would prefer to return to his academic position at Jawaharlal Nehru University. Dr Manmohan Singh wanted to bring Ashok Desai in his position. As the UPSC had to formally appoint Ashok, which would take time, he was appointed chief consultant immediately and performed the role of chief economic advisor.

The Budget group meetings became an annual ritual for me in the next six years, and one I looked forward to. We would meet in my room in North Block in the second half of January, in the afternoons. This was the time military bands would be rehearsing for the Beating Retreat ceremony traditionally held on 29 January at Vijay Chowk, the main square at the foot of Raisina Hill where the North Block and South Block stand. We would typically have military music wafting in through the windows as we discussed tax changes.

At sunset, when the bands marched back up Raisina Hill, playing 'Saare jahan se accha, Hindustan hamara', the music would get steadily louder as they reached the flat ground between the two blocks. When they arrived directly in front of my window, they would no longer be visible to the audience from Vijay Chowk; that's when the decorative lights on North Block, South Block and Rashtrapati Bhavan would be switched on. Exactly at that moment, red and green flares would be shot into the air, landing moments later on the open ground where the bands had arrived. As the flares shot up, the bandsmen, marching in perfect step until a moment ago, would run helter-skelter to escape them. This very unmilitary scramble was a view only we were privileged to observe.

The insistence on secrecy meant all the Budget documents had to be printed in an internal press located in the basement of the

Ministry of Finance. Some 80-odd individuals were locked in for seven days and let out only after the speech was over. They were provided dormitory-style accommodation and their meals were provided by caterers and served inside. Only a few senior officers of the ministry had special passes to go in and out to make last-minute changes. Spirits in the basement were generally high as those present felt they were performing a very special function.

As Finance Minister Manmohan Singh rose to present the Budget in the Lok Sabha on the last day of February 1992, MPs from the Left Front and the Janata Dal started protesting that it had been leaked to the World Bank and the IMF! The memorandum of policies we had submitted to the president of the World Bank in connection with the structural adjustment loan had mentioned that we intended to reduce customs duties, and decisions would be taken in the Budget for 1992–93 on the basis of the Chelliah Committee report. The opposition alleged, without any basis, that the contents of the report were leaked to the World Bank. Interestingly, the MPs did not criticize the intention to reduce duties that had already been announced in the 1991–92 Budget, only that the decision had been leaked!

At one stage, it looked as if the opposition would stage a walkout. It would not have prevented the Budget from being passed but would certainly have been embarrassing for the finance minister. Fortunately, the BJP, while thoroughly enjoying the discomfiture of the Government, took a less confrontational stand and the finance minister was allowed to present the Budget after a delay of about half an hour. Later in the course of the debate, Atal Bihari Vajpayee, while being mildly critical of the Budget as was expected of an opposition leader, advised Manmohan Singh, in a very avuncular style, to develop a thick skin. He said he had grown old listening to insults and abuses!

The recommendations of the Chelliah Committee helped shape the tax reforms that began in 1992–93 and continued over the next several years. I had known Raja Chelliah from our Washington days, and soon after taking charge as economic affairs secretary,

I had an informal discussion with him on key issues in tax reforms. I urged him to submit an interim report early enough to serve as an input into the 1992–93 Budget. He obliged and the recommendations of his interim report were reflected in the Budget (*see Box*).

Highlights of Tax Measures: 1992–93

- Reduce number of tax slabs of personal income tax from four to three
- Abolish wealth tax on financial assets
- Reduce maximum customs duty from 150 per cent to 110 per cent
- Reduce customs duty for new projects and general machinery from 80 per cent to 55 per cent

---

Reduction in import duties was a priority and Manmohan Singh had signalled this in his first Budget when he reduced the maximum duty rate from 300 per cent to 150 per cent. The Budget for 1992–93 continued this thrust. At my suggestion, he also stated that duties would be progressively lowered in future to reach levels comparable to those of other developing countries.

The final reports of the Chelliah Committee became available later in 1992 and helped guide tax reform in subsequent years. In his Budget speech of 1993–94, Finance Minister Manmohan Singh stated that he broadly accepted the approach of moving to a regime of moderate rates of direct taxation, broadening the tax base, low to moderate customs duties, a simpler system of excise duties with fewer rates, and a long-term aim of a VAT system. Much was done in this direction in the following three years.

The maximum rate of personal income tax (including surcharge) was reduced from 56 per cent in 1990–91 to 44.8 per cent in 1992–93, and then to 40 per cent by 1994–95. Corporate tax rates had been raised to 45 per cent in the first Budget but were brought down to 40 per cent in 1994–95.

Reducing import duties was part of the strategy of opening up the economy and increasing its competitiveness and we were able to reduce duty rates faster than envisaged by the Chelliah Committee. By 1995–96, the last year of the Rao government, the maximum rate of duty was down to 50 per cent and the duty on capital goods and machinery was lowered to 25 per cent. This brought India's average import duties down to 36.6 per cent by 1995–96, but it was still much higher than 20.4 per cent for Indonesia, 13.7 per cent for the Philippines, 7.8 per cent for Malaysia and 6.9 per cent for Thailand.

Domestic industry often complained that we were lowering import duties much below the 'bound rates' negotiated with the World Trade Organization (WTO) (i.e. the rates we had promised not to exceed). We would explain that we had negotiated high bound rates to give ourselves more flexibility but it was not in our interest to retain such high duties as they made the economy uncompetitive. The debate on import duties was often conducted on the assumption that high import duties helped Indian producers and hurt only foreign producers who were seeking to compete with our producers in the domestic market. There was little recognition that high duties also hurt Indian consumers and made exporters uncompetitive.

An important start in 1994–95 was to bring services within the indirect tax net by levying a services tax on three services: telephones, non-life insurance and stockbrokers. The list was steadily expanded in subsequent years and the tax on services proved to be a buoyant source of revenue. General acceptability of a tax on services was an important precondition for switching to a generalized GST, which came many years later.

FINANCIAL SECTOR REFORMS

Financial sector reforms formed an important part of the reform agenda, largely owing to Manmohan Singh. He had closely followed developments in Latin America in the 1980s where liberalization of the capital account in the presence of financial weaknesses had led to serious banking crises, and he was determined we should not suffer the same fate.

The Narasimham Committee on Financial Sector Reforms submitted its report in 1991 and Dr Singh announced the acceptance of many of its recommendations in the Budget speech of 1992–93. This included reduction in statutory liquidity ratio (SLR) and cash reserve ratio (CRR) in a phased manner from their very high levels. Banks were also given greater freedom to fix interest rates on loans on the basis of risk perception. Banking licences were opened up for new private sector banks and 10 new banks were licenced.

The committee also recommended aligning prudential norms in Indian banking with the Basel I Norms, which had been put in place internationally in 1988. The RBI should have done this on its own earlier but it now prescribed that Basel I Norms would be reached by 1997. As tighter provisioning requirements under the new norms would erode the capital of public sector banks, the committee recommended that bank capital could be enhanced by attracting fresh equity from the market. This would lead to dilution of government equity to 51 per cent. This recommendation was accepted, and the Bank Nationalization Act 1969 and State Bank of India Act 1955 were amended to allow the dilution. Many banks accessed capital markets in the following years.

A potentially important recommendation that was not accepted was that supervision of the banks should be taken out of the RBI and entrusted to a separate quasi-autonomous Banking Supervisory Board. The Harshad Mehta scam had just broken out and the RBI felt taking supervision out of its purview would look like an expression of lack of confidence in the RBI. A new department for supervision of banks was created within the RBI, presided over by a Board of Financial Supervision chaired by the governor and including all deputy governors. Had we created a separate Banking Supervisory Board at that time, we might have avoided some of the problems with bank lending that surfaced much later.

Another recommendation that was not accepted was to create a four-tier structure for the public sector with the top tier consisting of banks that would have an international presence, a second tier operating nationally, and lower tiers for more constrained operations.

A significant reform implemented in 1994 was to end the practice of automatic financing of the fiscal deficit by the RBI. This practice, first introduced in 1955, ensured that every time the Government's cash balance with the RBI went below a certain level, the RBI would top it up by issuing 'ad hoc' Treasury Bills at artificially low rates of interest. Governor Rangarajan had been arguing that this practice made monetary policy a hostage to fiscal policy and should be ended. There was resistance at the official level in the ministry because automatic financing made it easier for the officials to manage the fiscal deficit. I felt Rangarajan was right and backed him fully. We were happy when the finance minister decided the practice should stop. The Government would have to finance its deficit through open market borrowing at market interest rates.

In 1994, Governor Rangarajan, on behalf of the RBI, and I, on behalf of the Ministry of Finance, signed the agreement that ended an arrangement that had been in place for over 40 years. The issuance of ad hoc Treasury Bills would be capped at declining levels for the next two years and completely eliminated in 1997–98. I was pleased to have played a role in this important structural reform that, for the first time, allowed monetary policy to operate independently of fiscal policy.

In his very first Budget in 1991–92, Manmohan Singh had announced that SEBI would be given statutory status as a regulator of the stock markets. I wanted to make sure it was done before the 1992–93 Budget. We issued an Ordinance in January 1992, followed by legislation in April 1992. The Capital Issues (Control) Act 1947, which provided the statutory basis for approving the pricing of new issues, was repealed, and the office of the Controller of Capital Issues in the Ministry of Finance was abolished. I recall that SEBI Chairman G.V. Ramakrishna suggested that control over pricing of issues should not be abolished immediately, but perhaps retained with SEBI at least for a while. We decided to act boldly instead and prior approval of pricing of capital issues became history.

Just as we were congratulating ourselves on having completed a major reform, we were hit by what came to be known as the Harshad Mehta[27] scam. The Sensex had risen strongly after the new government took over in 1991. While the increase from around 1,200 in April 1991 before the election to about 1,900 in the second half of December 1991 could reasonably be attributed to the establishment of a stable government, the continued rise of the Sensex, reaching a peak of 4,467 on 22 April 1992, was worrying. There was concern whether prices were being manipulated, perhaps by inflows of illegal funds from abroad.

We soon learnt the problem arose because interbank transactions in government securities were being manipulated by brokers to siphon money out of the banking system, and used for speculation in the stock market. In the absence of an electronic exchange, a bank wanting to buy government securities either to maintain its SLR or deploy surplus funds would be approached by brokers who would find banks willing to sell government securities. The buying bank would issue a cheque and the bank selling the securities would issue a banker's receipt (BR) indicating that funds had been received for the securities sold. The buying bank would record the securities in its books for purposes of compliance with the SLR.

As records of ownership of government securities in the Public Debt Office of the RBI were manually maintained, any transaction of buying or selling securities would take time to record. As many of the transactions were short term, to be reversed within 15 days (the so-called ready forward deals), a practice had evolved whereby many transactions went unrecorded. BRs were issued first

---

[27]An Indian stockbroker who had 27 criminal charges brought against him; he was only convicted of four before he died at the age of 47 in 2011.

and then cancelled when the transaction was reversed. This was against RBI rules but was not the underlying cause of the scam.

The real cause of the scam was that <u>cheques issued by the bank buying the securities were credited not to the account of the bank selling them but to the account of the broker</u>! The broker would then use these funds for speculation and return the money due at the end of the period to the bank that had bought the securities and issued the cheque. Officials of smaller banks even issued BRs for securities <u>the bank did not</u> have, helping brokers siphon money out for short periods.

The RBI set up a committee under Deputy Governor R. Janakiraman that submitted a number of reports detailing what had gone wrong. There was uproar in Parliament and a joint parliamentary committee (JPC) was appointed in August 1992 with 30 members from all parties. The committee held several meetings at which I, along with other colleagues, testified. As the Department of Economic Affairs dealt with the RBI and the public sector banks, I had to do most of the talking.

We were criticized for describing the crisis as a 'system failure', which many MPs saw as an attempt to shield individuals. I stated categorically that we had no doubt there had been wrongdoing, which is why the CBI was brought in and action would be taken against those found responsible. However, there were also systemic weaknesses that created an environment which encouraged fraud, and these weaknesses needed to be addressed. For example, if electronic trading of government securities between banks had been put in place, there would be no need for brokers to bring buying and selling banks together. The failure to computerize the records of the Public Debt Office encouraged the use of BRs, which were then misused. Labour unions resisting computerization in the banking system were part of the problem. The RBI's imposition of ceilings on interest rates in the call money market pushed cash-surplus banks to look for better returns by parking surplus funds in repo transactions (purchase and repurchase of government securities).

The MPs suspected that while those directly involved would be indicted, there were bank officials at higher levels who must have been aware of the dubious practices and turned a blind eye. They also suspected the role of corporate interests that were keen to ramp up share prices to support forthcoming public issues. We could only hope the investigative agencies would get to the bottom of all this.

At the end of the gruelling questioning by the JPC, I felt pleased I had answered all questions. I realized later I had probably overdone it when the chairman of the JPC, Ram Niwas Mirdha, with whom I had a very good personal equation, was reported by the press to have said, *'Sardarji bahut bolte hain'* (The sardar speaks a lot). I never quite worked out whether he felt I took too long to say what needed to be said, or whether he thought my effort to explain complexities was simply too exhausting!

The JPC report was submitted in December 1993. We were happy it did not recommend any rollback of the policy of financial liberalization. This was an important gain. However, it criticized the functioning of Indian and foreign banks, the supervisory authorities and the Ministry of Finance. No individual in either the RBI or ministry was named but Dr Manmohan Singh promptly tendered his resignation and we went through a couple of anxious days. I have no doubt that if the PM had accepted the resignation, it would have been a major setback to the reform effort. Fortunately, it was not accepted and Dr Singh was back at work. This not only strengthened his position but signalled that the Government was not going to back down on economic reform.

A favourable spill-over effect from the thorough exposure of problems by the JPC was that union leaders in public sector banks moderated their opposition to computerization. This was prompted to some extent by the fact that the RBI, reacting to the JPC report, accelerated its pace of computerization. I recall when a delegation of union leaders came to meet Dr Singh to protest against computerization. He knew them all personally from his days as governor, and patiently explained that with foreign and private sector banks computerizing rapidly, it was necessary for public sector banks to accelerate computerization in order to compete effectively. At the end of the meeting, in his typical courteous manner, he went to the door of his office to shake hands with each union leader as they left. Perhaps touched by this courtesy, one leader said, 'Mr Finance Minister, I don't agree with you at all, but I don't mind telling you that my son agrees with you.' Shortly thereafter, in 1993, the unions signed an agreement allowing a phased process of computerization.

UNIFIED MARKET–DETERMINED EXCHANGE RATE

One of the most important reforms we were able to achieve was the shift to a flexible exchange rate. This was actually critical for the liberalization of industrial licencing to work, although this linkage was not well understood. If imports were not liberalized, investors freed from industrial licencing would have to queue up at the other end of Udyog Bhawan in the Ministry of Commerce to get import licences. Import liberalization, in turn, needed a mechanism to ensure that the foreign exchange required for the additional imports would be available.

The Eximscrip mechanism had provided some flexibility by incentivizing exports, which increased the supply of foreign exchange. However, Eximscrips were issued only against exports of goods. Other forms of foreign exchange earnings, including tourism, were not covered by them. Also, as Eximscrips were issued on proof of remittance of export earnings, the system was prone to delays. I discussed these problems with Rangarajan, former deputy governor of the RBI, who was then a Planning Commission member. We agreed it was time to move on by abolishing Eximscrips and introducing a flexible exchange rate in two stages.

In the first stage, Eximscrips would be replaced by a dual exchange rate system, in which all earners of foreign exchange would have to surrender a portion of their receipts to the RBI at an official exchange rate. This would be used by state agencies to import essential items such as crude oil, petroleum products, fertilizers, etc., at the official exchange rate. The rest of the foreign exchange could be sold in the free market and used to pay for all other permissible imports of goods, services and remittances. Excess demand for foreign exchange would lead to a change in the free market exchange rate, discouraging imports and encouraging exports. Once the dual exchange rate system stabilized, we could move to the second stage of unifying the market. It would be an extension of the dual pricing we had tried in other areas, notably cement and sugar.

I discussed this approach with the finance minister, reminding him that he had mentioned in his Bangalore convocation address that the exchange rate should reflect the scarcity value of foreign exchange. I suggested we set up a committee under the chairmanship of Rangarajan to look at the medium-term prospects for the BOP, going beyond the period covered by the IMF programme. The committee could also examine the dual exchange rate idea and work out the modalities of the proposed shift.

The Rangarajan Committee included all the senior officers in the Ministry of Finance and the RBI who would have to implement the proposal if finally approved. The first draft was prepared by Y.V. Reddy, joint secretary in the Department of Economic Affairs, who was the member secretary of the committee. He went on to become deputy governor and later governor of the RBI. The draft was reviewed and modified in the RBI. Commerce Secretary A.V. Ganesan was also a member. He not only agreed to get rid of the Eximscrips but was able to persuade Chidambaram, who was still minister of state for commerce, to accept. The proposal was cumbersomely christened 'Liberalized Exchange Rate Management System (LERMS)' and outlined in an Interim Report, which was submitted to the finance minister just before the Budget for 1992–93.

With the RBI and the Ministry of Commerce on board, the finance minister announced the shift to a dual exchange rate regime in the Budget. All earners of foreign exchange, including exporters, would surrender 40 per cent of their earnings at the official rate, leaving 60 per cent for free sale. The new system came into effect on 1 March 1992 and worked extremely well, with the market exchange rate ruling about 20 per cent higher than the official rate and very little volatility during the year.

Rangarajan had become governor of the RBI at the end of December 1992 and we discussed the prospect of unifying the two exchange markets. Some officials in the RBI and the ministry favoured a phased unification over time, as they worried that a sudden unification could send the rupee into a free fall. Both Rangarajan and I thought it unlikely, especially as the overall economic situation looked good and we felt the market would accept the unification in one go. The fact that Rangarajan was willing to take the plunge clinched the issue for the finance minister. The shift to a unified exchange rate was announced in the Budget speech for 1993–94 and the new system came into effect on 1 March 1993.

The exchange rate behaved exactly as we had expected. Just before unification, the exchange rate of the rupee in the free market was around ₹32.6 = US$1, whereas the official rate was ₹26.2 = US$1. In March 1993, the first month of the unified rate, the market exchange rate settled at ₹31 = US$1 and stayed at about that level through the next 12 months! It is to the credit of the RBI team under Rangarajan that they managed the transition smoothly, with no undue volatility in the foreign exchange market. A year later, we were able to inform the IMF that the rupee was fully convertible on the current account.

A direct consequence of this declaration was that Indian credit cards could now be used to cover sundry expenditures when checking into hotels abroad. Until then, whenever an official team visited overseas, a member of the Indian Embassy would have to be present at the time of check-in to offer their credit card to get us into the hotel!

Generations of Indian administrators and economists had come to believe that import licencing was necessary to manage the shortage of foreign exchange. The ease with which we were able to shed these controls and let the exchange rate handle the shortage of foreign exchange showed that these fears were unwarranted. This particular reform went well beyond what the IMF had insisted upon as a condition for its assistance. It was a purely homegrown component of the reform programme.

I often met informally with journalists on visits abroad to brief them on policy changes under way in India. On one such occasion, when Isher and I happened to be in London together, we met our old friend Martin Wolf of the *Financial Times* (*FT*). Martin had started his career in the World Bank in the Fiscal Policy Division, where I was the deputy division chief, and he then left the Bank to return to London and join the *FT* at about the same time we returned to India. Isher had read Martin's book, *India's Exports*[28], which was a devastating critique of our licencing system, and she asked him whether he had ever imagined that India's trade policy regime would change as much as it did. Martin said no, but he added that he had also not thought that the Soviet Union would collapse as it did! He clearly viewed both as what would today be called 'black swan' events[29], although he did not say whether he thought they were connected.

THE CRISIS ENDS

One of the enjoyable rituals of the Ministry of Finance was the meeting of the Aid India Consortium in Paris in June. Organized by the World Bank to review India's economic performance and our need for development assistance, it was attended by bilateral aid donors and representatives of international financial institutions (the IMF, World Bank and ADB). At the end of the meeting, the donors would make a pledge of the level of official assistance for the next year.

---

[28]Wolf, M., *India's Exports*, Oxford University Press, 1983.
[29]A black swan is an unpredictable event that is beyond the normal limits of probability. Because of their extreme rarity, such events are often used to explain failure in hindsight.

My first consortium meeting was in June 1992. I led the Indian delegation, which included chief consultant Ashok Desai and N.K. Singh, then joint secretary in the ministry dealing with the IMF and the World Bank. I had known NK from our days together in Delhi University when we used to debate against each other. We were to work closely together in many capacities in the years ahead.

The 1992 consortium meeting was the first review after we had signed the loan agreements for crisis management with the IMF and World Bank. In his concluding remarks, World Bank Vice President Joseph Wood, who chaired the meeting, said, 'If this pace of reforms is maintained over the next three to four years, India could become one of the most dynamic economies of the world in the second half of the 1990s and beyond.' I felt that expecting the reforms to continue at the same pace as in the first year was asking for too much, and I was right. But we certainly lived up to the expectation of becoming one of the most dynamic economies. The meeting ended well and the donors pledged a total of $7.2 billion, an improvement over the $6.7 billion pledged in the previous year. This was widely reported in the Indian press as a signal of international support.

We had thought at first that we may need assistance from the IMF beyond the period of the first loan. As it turned out, we did not. Exports grew strongly in 1993–94 and our effort to attract private foreign capital began to show some results. In the post-Budget press conference in New Delhi in March 1994, I was able to announce that we were no longer considering assistance. In a way, this marked the formal end of the BOP crisis.

I discussed with NK the strategy we should adopt for the consortium meeting in June 1994. I felt it was time to break out of the traditional 'donor-recipient' relationship and convert it into a two-day meeting: the first to be devoted to official donors, and the second to an interaction with private investors, in which the official donors would also join. The new format amounted to a formal recognition of our willingness to attract private capital flows. I asked NK to get the World Bank on board and to agree to rename the meeting 'The India Development Forum'.

The first meeting of the India Development Forum was held in Paris on 30 June and 1 July 1994. The official part went well, with the World Bank noting the improvement in the external situation but warning about the deterioration in the fiscal deficit in 1993–94. It concluded with a pledge of $6 billion in assistance, significantly lower than in 1993; but as the World Bank clarified, the lower amount only reflected lower need.

The meeting with the private sector the next day was a great success. Representatives of the international private sector included General Electric, Mitsubishi, Sony, the Hindujas, Morgan Stanley and Merrill Lynch. On the Indian side, we had the crème de la crème of Indian industry, including Ratan Tata, Mukesh Ambani and Aditya Birla. Indian Ambassador to France Ranjit Sethi hosted a reception for the participants at his official residence, close to the Eiffel Tower. Many bilateral aid officials from the smaller European countries commented to me that a structural change was underway, and it looked as if their role would diminish. This was indeed true, and a welcome development. India's focus would shift increasingly to private capital flows.

The Indian press applauded the replacement of the Aid India Consortium by the India Development Forum. In an editorial on 2 July 1994 titled 'Towards Self Reliance', *The Economic Times* proclaimed that 'for the first time in this annual gathering, India's representatives could play a role other than that of supplicants'. At the end of the formal meeting, NK, Shankar Acharya (chief economic advisor and an old friend) and I decided to walk back to our hotel. Somewhere on the Champs-Élysées, I said that it was a nice feeling to be able to tell the IMF and the other donors that we would not need further IMF assistance. We had gone to the IMF in 1981 and had to do it again in 1991, but we had a very good chance, if we persisted on the path of reform, that we wouldn't have to do it again in 2001! Shankar, ever ready to puncture any over-optimistic claim, offered to bet that we would be back in the court of the Fund well before 2001. Not being a betting man, I did not nail down the specific terms of the wager. I would have won big time if I had—we have not had to go to the IMF for 27 years after the programme ended in 1993!

MOBILIZING FOREIGN CAPITAL FLOWS

Although we began the reforms with an IMF umbrella, we were intent on preparing for the period when we would do without the IMF and start repaying what we had borrowed. The Rangarajan Committee on Balance of Payments had suggested that a current account deficit of around 1.6 per cent of GDP was sustainable. To be safe, we set ourselves the target of evolving a financing strategy that would attract net capital flows equal to 2 per cent of GDP, or about $6 billion per year.

Our normal foreign aid flows (excluding emergency assistance) were about $3 billion per year but this was likely to decrease as India's eligibility for IDA was being questioned. Our objective was to mobilize $3–4 billion per year in other flows. The potential sources were external commercial borrowing, portfolio flows and FDI. We evolved a new policy towards each of these.

External commercial borrowing was a potentially volatile source of capital and we therefore put in place relatively tight controls on such flows. Total permissions for external commercial borrowing were limited to about $2 billion per year. Actual disbursements would be lower and, allowing for repayments of earlier borrowings, the net inflow would be even lower. Within this total, short-term debt was discouraged. Interest rate caps were also introduced to ensure that Indian firms would not borrow abroad at an unduly high cost. Antoine van Agtmael—the man who originally coined the phrase 'emerging markets'—pointed out to me that imposing interest rate caps discriminates against smaller firms even though they are possibly more innovative and would use the capital more efficiently. He was probably right, but one often has to use blunt instruments that have unavoidable side-effects.

Long-term borrowing (more than 10 years) was exempted from any cap in the belief that very few Indian firms would be able to raise long-term debt. As it happened, some years later in 1997, Reliance Industries sought permission to float a 100-year bond for $100 million. It was successful, making it the first Asian company to have a 100-year bond in the market. We had really come a long way from a situation where, seven years earlier, the Government could not get a loan without dispatching its gold abroad, to one where a private Indian company could issue a 100-year bond for $100 million!

Portfolio flows were a source of capital we had not utilized in the past. They were also potentially volatile but we felt they would be relatively less unstable than short-term external debt because they have an element of self-correction. Any large outflow of portfolio capital would depress equity prices, which would make Indian equities more desirable, attracting other inflows. Liberalization of portfolio investment would also give Indian companies with a reputation for good corporate governance an opportunity to raise foreign capital through new issues. We announced a new policy in September 1992, allowing qualified FIIs registered with SEBI to invest in listed companies in the stock market. We restricted such opening to institutional investors managing large funds to avoid the kind of problems posed by the Swraj Paul affair in 1983. Institutional investors were not likely to attempt management takeovers. The total investment from all FIIs in any one company was also limited to 24 per cent. In a parallel move, Indian companies were allowed to issue fresh capital abroad through Global Depository Receipts (GDRs).

The establishment of the National Stock Exchange (NSE) in 1993 was an important development that helped attract institutional investors. The NSE was the first exchange in India to introduce electronic trading, allowing brokers who met the qualifications to trade on the exchange from anywhere in the country using

VSATs (very small aperture terminals) and leased lines. It greatly increased transparency, with electronic matching of buy and sell orders and prices of all trades being displayed on the screen. The NSE also put competitive pressure on the 120-year-old Bombay Stock Exchange, forcing it to reform its ways.

FDI was the most stable form of capital inflow and, therefore, the most preferred. The Industrial Policy announced in 1991 had signalled a new approach to FDI. Automatic approval of FDI up to 51 per cent of equity was allowed in selected industries, and a higher percentage was allowed subject to permission.

We needed to identify the many constraints that came in the way of FDI inflow. There were a surprising number of them. On one occasion, a visiting group of Japanese businessmen called on Finance Minister Manmohan Singh. They raised an issue none of us had thought about. They said Japanese companies found it difficult to send executives with their families to India because the prohibition of consumer goods imports made it impossible to get the basic Japanese ingredients they needed for cooking! They would have happily paid a high import duty, but the import ban created real problems. I later discovered that some Japanese companies actually paid their Japanese employees to visit Bangkok periodically to pick up essential supplies! We tried to introduce some flexibility in the import policy that would allow such imports.

We also tried to involve the PM directly in the effort to attract FDI. We got an opportunity when Narasimha Rao visited Japan in June 1992. I suggested that we allow some time for meetings with important Japanese investors individually, so that business leaders would open up about their concerns and get a sense of the PM's personal commitment to promoting FDI. The Ministry of External Affairs was not happy with my proposal as one-on-one meetings would take up a lot of time. Fortunately, Verma agreed with me and we were able to arrange for half-a-dozen top Japanese businessmen to call on the PM.

Akio Morita, chairman of Sony, was the first. In the briefing meeting before the call, I suggested that the PM might consider inviting Morita to set up a Sony TV manufacturing unit in India; if Morita raised the issue of 100 per cent foreign equity, he could agree to make an exception. Rao listened carefully and produced his famous pout—an indication that he was weighing things—but said nothing.

At the meeting with Morita, the PM was at his disarming best. After the usual pleasantries, he leaned across and said, 'Mr Morita, every Indian I know wants a Sony TV but you don't have a factory in India. Don't you think you are missing out on a huge demand?' Morita was taken aback at Rao's directness and, as predicted, brought up 100 per cent FDI. Rao then smiled and said, 'I suggest you apply and we will see what we can do.' Sony did apply, was allowed to invest, and started producing TVs a few years later.

As we had expected, it took time for FDI flows to build up—from $129 million in 1991–92, to $315 million in 1992–93, and $586 million in 1993–94. Thereafter, FDI flows averaged over $2.5 billion per year over the four-year period from 1994–95 to 1997–98. The total private capital inflow from FDI, FIIs and GDRs together averaged about $5 billion per year in the second half of the 1990s, a little more than what we felt was necessary to manage the BOP in a world of declining aid flows. Opening the window for GDRs enabled some of our leading companies to raise funds abroad. In 1997, Infosys applied for an American Depository Receipt (ADR) issue of up to $75 million when they listed the company in NASDAQ. Infosys was the first Indian IT company to list on NASDAQ.

FDI flows built up gradually. But they exploded after 2005 to an average of $33 billion per year over the next 10 years. The opening up to foreign capital flows was criticized at the time in many quarters as succumbing to pressure from the IMF, even though we had no IMF programme in place after 1993. In fact, the criticism was completely misplaced as the policy we followed was completely different from the free movement of capital recommended by the Washington Consensus.[30] We retained tight control over commercial borrowing, encouraged portfolio investment in equity and gave top priority to FDI flows. Our approach was vindicated many years later when the IMF itself changed its position on capital flows, shifting away from its earlier general endorsement of completely open capital accounts to a cautious approach.

THE BOMBAY CLUB

The liberalization of policy towards FDI was not without opposition. The Left had always opposed FDI because they believed it focused on producing high-end luxury consumer goods for the upper classes with high import content. The Swadeshi Jagran Manch formed in November 1991 began to articulate protectionist views on both trade and foreign investment. The opposition to FDI was often based on the fear of a latter-day East India Company, destabilizing Indian business and perhaps even politics. Congress politicians did not openly oppose the policy but I felt many of them had not quite abandoned the anti-FDI policy of the earlier Congress governments.

The reaction of business was also negative. In November 1993, a group of distinguished businessmen, including stalwarts such as Lala Bharat Ram, L.M. Thapar, Hari Shankar Singhania, Rahul Bajaj, M.V. Arunachalam, C.K. Birla and Jamshyd Godrej, met in Bombay to discuss the issue. The press promptly dubbed them the 'Bombay Club' and described them as a new protectionist lobby. As many of the individuals were familiar faces representing India abroad in pro-globalization forums such as the Davos meetings, they were uncomfortable being portrayed as protectionists. Only Rahul Bajaj, never one to hide his views, enjoyed saying publicly that he was not afraid to admit he had genuine concerns about liberalizing policy for FDI.

[30]Jagdish Bhagwati's celebrated article 'The Capital Myth: The Difference between Trade in Widgets and Free Capital Flows', published in 1998, spelt out the theoretical case for not treating free movement of capital the same as free trade in goods.

The group submitted a memorandum to Manmohan Singh arguing that Indian business needed a 'level playing field' before they could be exposed to foreign competition, whether from imports or FDI. Some of their concerns were entirely valid, such as the concern about 'duty inversion', which arose when customs duties on inputs were higher than on outputs. We tried to correct these anomalies, but we should have done more and done it faster. However, many of their arguments were not valid. For example, when they argued that interest rates in India were higher than abroad, making them uncompetitive, they did not take account of the fact that inflation in India was also higher, which meant that the real rate of interest was not very high. In any case, competitiveness does not depend on equalizing all costs as labour costs are much lower in India.

Not all business groups reacted defensively. Years later, Naushad Forbes of Forbes Marshall in Pune told me that after the 1991 Budget speech, he and his brother Farhad called a meeting of their top management to review their product portfolio to work out which products they could produce competitively if they allowed for import free of duty, providing they could also get the raw materials and components free of duty. They found half their product range to be uncompetitive on this basis and decided to work only on developing products that were competitive internationally. They also decided to quadruple R&D. In 1991, Forbes Marshall exported only 1 per cent of their turnover. By 2007, they had reached 20 per cent. They are now at 25 per cent and targeting 50 per cent by 2025. Other businesses may not have taken such a clear strategic decision quite so early, but they moved in that direction gradually.

Tarun Das, director-general of the Confederation of Indian Industry (CII), was regarded by many of us as the moving force behind Indian industries' push for bold liberalization. Just before the elections of 1996, Tarun wrote a discussion paper for the CII board criticizing the behaviour of foreign investors. The paper acquired notoriety for referring to foreign investors adopting a 'cowboy-like' approach, not viewing the partnerships as long-term relationships to be nurtured. It also criticized them for bringing in foreign managers when perfectly competent Indian managers were available. The paper provoked speculation that perhaps CII was anticipating that the 1996 election might bring in a BJP government, which would be less friendly to FDI. This was of course hotly denied by CII. I personally thought Tarun reflected some of the genuine, if unspoken, concerns of Indian managements at the changed world they faced. It was a symptom of growing pains for Indian business, but it suggested that the issues needed to be sympathetically addressed.

PUBLIC SECTOR REFORM: A DAMP SQUIB

The Congress party's long-standing commitment to the public sector ruled out any privatization but the reforms of 1991 included a very important decision to reduce the list of industries reserved for the public sector from 18 to eight. This unleashed private investment in sectors such as steel, aviation, telecommunications and petroleum refining, increasing the private sector share in these sectors without privatizing any PSUs.

Reform of existing PSUs remained a distant dream. The Government initiated a process of selling minority stakes (less than 20 per cent) in the equity of PSUs to mutual funds and public financial institutions, but this was driven primarily by the need to mobilize resources for the Budget. As long as the Government retains 51 per cent of equity and the power to appoint the management, no PSU management can afford to ignore the ministry controlling it. Besides, as long as the Government has 51 per cent equity, the legal position of the PSU remains identical to the state and subject to all the restraints on decision-making that would normally apply to the government. This makes it impossible for public sector managers to act with the flexibility and commercial orientation available to private sector managers.

Manmohan Singh had indicated that PSUs deemed to be irretrievably sick should be closed down, but this too remained a dead letter. No unit was closed down.

A missing link in the Indian financial system was the absence of a market for long-term funds for financing infrastructure development. Insurance companies and pension funds are the principal source of long-term debt in developed markets but this subsector was not covered in the terms of reference of the Narasimham Committee. To fill this gap, we set up a committee in 1993 under the chairmanship of R.N. Malhotra, former economic affairs secretary and RBI governor, to recommend reforms in the insurance sector. The Malhotra Committee submitted its report in 1994 and recommended a two-stage reform process. A statutory regulator for insurance had to be set up first so that both the Life Insurance Corporation (LIC) and the General Insurance Corporation (GIC), which operated as unregulated government monopolies, subject only to oversight by the Ministry of Finance, could come under it. Once the regulator was in place, the sector could be opened for new private sector insurance companies. The committee also recommended that foreign insurance companies could be allowed to enter in partnership with Indian promoters, but no limit was specified for the extent of FDI in this sector.

The Left was known to be opposed to private investment in insurance and it was not clear what stance the BJP would take. The Government therefore avoided the legislative route to begin with and decided to set up a non-statutory insurance regulatory authority to undertake the consultations required to frame the necessary legislation and rules. It was set up in 1996 under N. Rangachary, former chairman, CBDT, who did an excellent job of preparing the groundwork. It was converted into a statutory authority, following legislation in 1999, when the name was changed to Insurance Regulatory and Development Authority of India (IRDAI). The heavy lifting of passing the legislation to set up the IRDAI and opening the sector for private participation was left for the next government after the election.

'REAL' ARCHITECT OF THE REFORMS

It is clear that the reforms of 1991 initiated a truly historic change. A highly inefficient system of controls had held back the Indian economy for several decades. This was dismantled and gradually replaced with a system more suitable for an open and market-driven economy. Consumers benefited because of the large increase in the choice of products available and their quality. Businessmen benefited because they were freed from innumerable micro controls and were able to expand freely and upgrade technology. Farmers benefitted because reduced protection for industry led to an improvement in the terms of trade for agriculture. The fear that opening up would send the economy into a tailspin was put to rest.

Interestingly, the GDP growth rate in the decade of the 1990s (1990–91 to 1999–2000) averaged only 5.8 per cent, which is only marginally higher than the average of 5.6 per cent in the 1980s. However, the decade includes the crisis year of 1991–92, when growth collapsed to 1.4 per cent, as well as the year 1997–98, when the East Asian crisis lowered growth to 4.3 per cent. If these two years are excluded, the average growth rate was 6.6 per cent, much better than for any eight-year period in the past. Moreover, the gradualist nature of the reforms meant that many of the measures had not begun to have their full impact. The impact was seen only in the next decade, when average growth reached 7.2 per cent.

It is natural to ask how the credit for the reforms should be apportioned between Narasimha Rao and Manmohan Singh. The answer is not easy. Rao deserves full credit for choosing Manmohan Singh because of his acknowledged expertise to manage the economy and backing him throughout. Without that, there would have been no reforms.

Rao also recognized that changes were necessary if India were to realize her full potential. Unlike most senior Congress politicians who were locked into old mindsets, he was pragmatic and willing to change. He was convinced of the need for reducing controls over private sector investment decisions and he led this process as minister for industry. However, I do not think he realized the importance of the full gamut of change needed to unleash the economy's potential. Trade liberalization, the shift to a flexible exchange rate and reforms in the financial sector occurred largely because of Manmohan Singh's expertise and wisdom. He knew the interdependence of these reforms and orchestrated them skilfully. He had been in government for 20 years as a senior civil servant, most of that time under Congress governments. This made him in many ways an ideal person to explain to Congress politicians why the changes were necessary.

Rao's claim to be the real father of India's economic reforms would have been unassailable if he had led from the front and pushed the Congress party and the public to think afresh on the policies needed to meet contemporary challenges. This he did not do. He fully backed the economic policy changes while the crisis was raging and spoke in defence of the reforms as essential for managing the crisis. Once the crisis was over, Rao did little to educate the public on the need for continued reform. That required upfront political leadership, which always comes with attendant risks. Rao was not inclined to take those risks. Perhaps this was because he was not a leader with a mass base of his own. He had been chosen as a consensus candidate and his position in the party had become vulnerable after the demolition of the Babri Masjid in December 1992.

Rao was once asked by a journalist how he had managed to make a 180° turn on economic policies. He replied, 'I have not turned at all. I am facing in the same direction. It is the world that has turned 180° under me.' It was a clever remark but it also illustrates his reluctance to be identified as a change agent. He left it to Manmohan Singh to make the case for continuing the reforms to bring about a longer-term transformation of the economy. Dr Singh once told me that Rao had been very frank, telling him, 'Manmohan, go ahead and do what is needed and make a case for reforms both within the party and to the public. If the reforms succeed, I will claim my share of the credit. If they fail, you will be blamed.'

Dr Singh understood and accepted this bargain and played his part brilliantly. His public statements are crystal clear about the reforms needed to realize India's productive potential. And the gentle manner in which he made his case and his personal integrity and austerity persuaded many people who had doubts about the reforms to reconsider their views.

Rao's was clearly a strategy of 'reform by stealth', which is sometimes confused with gradualism, but is actually quite different. Gradualism implies a clear indication of where we are heading, but with an acceptance that the pace of change will be tailored to make it more acceptable. Reform by stealth is essentially opportunistic. You point in a broad direction without committing to any particular pace of change and then take a step forward whenever it is politically opportune to do so! The trouble with such an approach is that it can never create a broader constituency for reforms looking ahead. Dr Singh was a genuine gradualist. He conceptualized a complex and multidimensional structure of reform and consistently articulated the need for it, while acknowledging that change must be made slowly to be digestible. We owe it to Dr Singh's clarity in advocating the reforms and delivering their positive results in a manner that the process could continue as it did through succeeding governments.

A few years after stepping down as PM, Rao was speaking at a book release function in New Delhi when he was asked to comment on the relationship between a PM and a finance minister. He said the finance minister is in charge of designing and implementing economic policy, but he can be effective only with the backing of the PM. 'Without the prime minister's backing, the finance minister would be a zero,' he said. 'It is the prime minister's backing that puts a one before the zero, making it a 10.'

It was neatly put. I had the distinct feeling that Rao had no desire to be recognized as the 'architect of the reforms' in the sense of formulating the details, certifying their technical soundness and publicly defending their need. Dr Singh did all that with great aplomb, which made him the true architect of the reforms. But none of this would have happened if Rao had not backed Dr Singh and that is what Rao wanted acknowledged. It is an acknowledgement Rao fully deserves.

9

UNITED POLICIES, DIVIDED POLITICS

There were many reasons why the economic successes of the Rao government could not be translated into political gains in 1996. The Congress went into the elections debilitated by several adverse political developments.

The failure to prevent the demolition of the Babri Masjid in Ayodhya on 6 December 1992 alienated Muslim voters all over the country. There was little unity within the party, especially because it was widely speculated that Rao had encouraged the CBI to unleash investigations of suspected bribery of politicians in the infamous Jain diaries, primarily to keep his rivals in the party on a short leash. Just before the election, N.D. Tiwari left the party along with Arjun Singh to form the All India Indira Congress (Tiwari). Rao's last-minute decision to have an alliance with J. Jayalalithaa of the AIADMK to fight the 1996 election, despite strong opposition from the Tamil Nadu wing of the Congress under G.K. Moopanar, was a political blunder. It led to the Moopanar group (which included Chidambaram) breaking away to form a separate Tamil Maanila Congress and fighting the election in alliance with the DMK. The alliance swept the polls and the Congress seats from Tamil Nadu dropped from 28 in 1991 to zero in 1996.

For all these reasons, the Congress went into the elections divided and somewhat directionless. It would also be fair to say that the party never positioned itself to take credit for the far-reaching economic reforms that were carried out.

ENTER THE UNITED FRONT

As the leader of the BJP, the largest party, Vajpayee was invited to form a government and prove his majority in Parliament. However, most parties were unwilling to embrace the BJP and he resigned within 13 days before facing a vote of confidence. The non-Congress opposition parties used this time to stitch together a post-poll alliance of parties, small and large, into what they called the United Front (UF). The UF had only 192 seats but with outside support of the Congress (140 seats), they could comfortably form a government. However, they had to find a prime ministerial candidate behind whom all the parties could unite.

Haradanahalli Doddegowda Deve Gowda of the Janata Dal, who was CM of Karnataka, emerged as the consensus candidate. The son of a farmer, and a former Congressman, he had no national exposure and spoke no Hindi. But he was an intensely practical man with no ideological predispositions. As soon as Vajpayee resigned, the UF staked its claim and the new government was sworn in with Deve Gowda as PM on 1 June 1996.

The UF was such a disparate group that they sensibly decided to prepare a Common Minimum Programme (CMP) to define a consensus on policy. The involvement of Chidambaram in its preparation ensured a substantial reformist tone.

PM Deve Gowda released the CMP on 4 June 1996. It declared a commitment to growth with social justice, targeting a GDP growth of 7 per cent per year over the next 10 years, and 12 per cent growth in industry. The PM's pro-farmer stance was reflected in the promise that reforms would be extended to agriculture. The CMP promised large investment in infrastructure ($200 billion over the next five years), taking it from 3.5 per cent of GDP to 6 per cent. The recognition of a private sector role in infrastructure development was an important signal considering that the coalition included the Left parties.

The CMP also sent a strong positive signal on FDI by stating that India needed at least $10 billion of FDI annually, a threefold increase from the average of the previous three years, although FDI in 'low-priority' areas would be discouraged. The disinvestment initiatives of the previous government were taken a step forward by announcing the establishment of a Disinvestment Commission to make recommendations on privatization of PSUs in 'non-core' and 'non-strategic' areas. The CMP also contained a specific statement that insurance would be opened to the private sector.

On 6 June 1996, *The Times of India* certified editorially, 'Continuity is the hallmark of the United Front Government's economic policy as enumerated in the Front's Common Minimum Programme.' The title of the editorial, 'Good Script: Act on It' urged the Government to follow up its intentions with implementation. But no one could be sure how long the Government would last.

Deve Gowda's decision to appoint Chidambaram as finance minister turned out to be the best call he made to ensure economic policy was insulated from multiple political pulls. It sent a message of continuity with the reform initiatives of the previous government. I asked Chidambaram later whether he knew he was going to be finance minister, and whether Moopanar had pushed for it. He told me there were no such discussions and the appointment, when it came, was a pleasant surprise.

I had worked with Chidambaram in 1991 when he was commerce minister and looked forward to working with him again. In keeping with tradition, the joint secretary, administration, went to Chidambaram's residence in the official white Ambassador car designated for the finance minister to escort him to the office. Chidambaram refused to ride in the official car with the flashing red VIP light mounted on the roof, and insisted on driving his white Premier Padmini to North Block, saying he was entitled to use the official car only after signing the papers to take official charge!

Chidambaram told me he wanted to bring in Jairam Ramesh as his chief economic advisor. I explained we already had an excellent incumbent, Shankar Acharya. Chidambaram clarified that he had absolutely no reservations about Shankar's professional excellence but surely he could bring in his own advisor! Jairam came in as a consultant with the title 'advisor to the finance minister'. The arrangement worked very well. We would send official files directly to Chidambaram and he could consult Jairam on any issue he wanted or bring him into meetings.

The UF government under Deve Gowda as PM lasted for just under 11 months, but included two Budgets for 1996–97 and 1997–98. Other than his concern about farmer interests, he allowed Chidambaram full freedom to push the tax reform agenda.

During the few occasions I personally interacted with PM Deve Gowda, I found that he fully realized the need for broad-based reforms and was aware that farmers would only prosper if the economy did. I was part of his delegation to Davos in 1998 and he used the opportunity to interact with foreign investors to convey the message, very convincingly, that India welcomed foreign investment.

On one occasion in the cabinet, I witnessed his well-known habit of appearing to doze off while others were speaking but keeping an ear open for anything important. One of the ministers was saying we could not raise the price of cooking gas cylinders because it would hurt the poor. Deve Gowda, who seemed to have slid into a comfortable slumber, suddenly sat up and said forcefully, 'I can assure you these cylinders are not being consumed by the poor. If you don't believe me, come with me for a drive tomorrow and I will show you how many rich people are having garden parties in their lawns, and using cooking gas to cook seekh kebabs and chicken tikkas!'

Shortly after the second UF Budget was presented, the Congress withdrew its support and Deve Gowda lost a vote of confidence on 21 April 1997. It was widely rumoured that this was a manoeuvre planned by Sitaram Kesri, Congress president, who hoped he might be able to form a government himself by destabilizing Deve Gowda. But the constituents of the UF were not willing to line up behind Kesri. Instead, they quickly zeroed in on Inder Kumar Gujral of the Janata Dal as the next PM.

Gujral was in many ways the opposite of Deve Gowda. He, too, was originally from the Congress and had joined the Janata Dal only in the 1980s. However, there was nothing agricultural about this Punjabi. He was a Delhi-based politician who epitomized the Nehruvian ideals of secularism, a soft form of socialism, commitment to liberal values and non-alignment in foreign policy. As Information and Broadcasting minister during the Emergency, he had the courage to say no to Sanjay Gandhi's demand that he be shown the texts of news broadcasts from All India Radio before they were aired; he paid the price by being sent off as ambassador to Moscow.

CONTINUITY IN REFORMS

Throughout the two years of the UF government, Chidambaram continued as finance minister and I as finance secretary. And continuity in tax reforms was the hallmark of the two UF Budgets (*see Box*).

An attempt was made to widen the tax base through a provision whereby anyone living in a large metropolitan area and meeting two of the specified criteria—owning a four-wheeled vehicle, occupying immovable property with certain conditions, foreign travel in the previous year and owning a telephone (still rare enough at the end of the 1990s)—would have to file an income tax return. This provision was steadily expanded in subsequent years to cover a larger number of cities, adding more criteria.

In 1993–94, Manmohan Singh had stated in his Budget speech that our customs duty rates should be aligned to the levels prevailing in other developing countries. I suggested to Chidambaram that he could make the objective more precise by announcing the intention to align duty rates with those of the Association of Southeast Asian Nations (ASEAN) countries. He used the phrase 'Asian developing countries' and added that we would do so 'by the turn of the century'. As that was only three years away, it conveyed a sense of imminence to the goal.

Tax measures in the 1996–97 and 1997–98 Budgets

- The maximum rate of personal income tax was lowered from 40 per cent to 30 per cent in 1997–98, making the rate fairly comparable with most countries. A three-slab system was put in place, with tax rates of 10, 20 and 30 per cent, respectively.
- The corporate tax rate for domestic companies was reduced from 40 per cent plus surcharge of 15 per cent in 1996–97 to 35 per cent with no surcharge in 1997–98.
- A minimum alternate tax (MAT) was introduced in 1996–97 to counter the practice whereby companies were able to reduce their tax liability to zero by claiming investment-related incentives.
- The rate of tax on long-term capital gains for domestic companies was reduced from 30 per cent to 20 per cent.
- Dividends were exempted from tax in the hands of the recipient but a flat 10 per cent tax was levied on dividends to be paid by the company before distribution.
- Reduction of import duties was continued in the 1997–98 Budget with the peak duty reduced from 50 per cent to 40 per cent and the duties on capital goods from 25 per cent to 20 per cent. The 1996–97 Budget had made a commitment to move to four rates of excise duties over a period of three years. The 1997–98 Budget indicated that the four rates would be 8, 13, 15 and 18 per cent in 1997–98, but several items remained outside the four-rate structure.

A new voluntary disclosure scheme (VDS) was introduced in 1997 under which individuals and corporations were allowed to declare past undisclosed income and pay the new maximum tax rates for individuals or corporate taxpayers. I have never favoured tax disclosure schemes because they are ultimately unfair to honest taxpayers. That said, it certainly proved to be much more successful than other such schemes earlier.

The 1997–98 Budget with its tax cuts and VDS was much applauded by the business community and the financial press as the 'Dream Budget'. We were pleased with the applause but I kept my fingers crossed. Extensive coverage of Budgets on television had become a standard feature such that leading industrialists would be asked to rate the budget on TV on a score of one to 10. I never felt these assessments could be taken seriously because no industrialist would ever want to openly criticize any budget. In any case, the performance of the economy depends on a number of factors beyond the Budget, including the state of the monsoon and its impact on agriculture and conditions in the world economy.

As it happened, economic growth did not live up to the expectations raised by the Dream Budget. Poor rains led to a 3 per cent decline in agricultural GDP. The East Asian financial crisis in the middle of the year also took its toll on the growth of industry and services. GDP growth slowed down sharply from almost 8 per cent in 1996–97 to 4.3 per cent in 1997–98.

The reforms in the banking system were also taken forward by the UF. There was further progress in decontrolling some interest rates, a gradual reduction in the SLR and a tightening of prudential norms.

Another example of continuity was the establishment of the National Securities Depository Limited (NSDL) in 1996. The Depositories Ordinance, promulgated in 1995, was converted into an Act by the Government in August 1996. The NSDL was set up by IDBI, UTI and NSE, and was inaugurated by Chidambaram in Mumbai in September 1996. I was present on the occasion and privy to the efforts of two successive governments steering this major reform. I could sense the excitement among the senior members of Mumbai's financial community. Indeed, many people from the financial sector had played a critical role in bringing NSE and NSDL about. Notable among them were S.S. Nadkarni and R.H. Patil. The detailed architecture of both was worked out in Mumbai.

The NSDL made it possible to dematerialize paper securities and maintain all records of ownership electronically in the depository. The NSE introduced a fully automated trading system in India ahead of major exchanges in America, where open outcry was still prevalent. The NSDL succeeded in rapidly increasing the percentage of securities dematerialized. SEBI played an important role by making it mandatory for mutual funds and other institutional holders of securities to hold them in dematerialized form. The net result was that the percentage of dematerialized trades in India was soon higher than in the US!

Investments by FIIs were further liberalized. They were allowed to invest up to 10 per cent in the equity of any company, including unlisted companies and debt instruments. The class of eligible FIIs was expanded significantly. These steps were consistent with the policy followed thus far of gradually opening the capital account to inflows. This increased our vulnerability to negative reactions in global capital markets but it was early days yet and the opening was small.

The permission given in 1992 to Indian companies to raise funds abroad through GDRs led Infosys, in 1997, to apply for permission to raise $75 million through ADRs. They also sought permission to issue Employee Stock Ownership Plans for their foreign-based employees in the form of ADRs since foreign individuals were not eligible to invest in Indian shares. Infosys became the first Indian IT company to list in NASDAQ in 1999. I recall Narayana Murthy telling me that the merchant bankers advised them that there would be ample demand at $34 per share but he decided to price the share a few dollars lower, because he wanted the investors to see the ADR price rise immediately after the issue. I thought it was very good marketing, but I also told him that government officials facing the same situation when disinvesting PSU shares would be loath to recommend a lower price than advised by the merchant bankers for fear of being accused of having caused a loss to the exchequer!

OPENING UP INSURANCE: A TOUGH NUT TO CRACK

Progress on insurance reform proved surprisingly difficult. There was political resistance to allowing the private sector in insurance, which was completely illogical considering that private banks, including foreign banks, were operating in competition with public sector banks and there was no reason why this principle should not apply to insurance. Interestingly, the Left parties had gone along with the idea in the CMP, although they were clearly not enthusiastic. The real opposition was from the BJP. Their opposition was not to private insurance companies but foreign equity in insurance. However, such objections had become completely obsolete. Even China had allowed foreign insurance companies to operate for many years and the only countries that did not allow foreign insurance companies were Myanmar, Cuba and North Korea!

Chidambaram tried to navigate a course through these choppy waters. He stated categorically that LIC's monopoly on life insurance and GIC's monopoly on general insurance would not be touched. He proposed to recognize pension funds as a distinct sector from life insurance that would open up a new space. UTI had been operating a retirement scheme similar to a pension fund. He proposed to make changes in the law that would allow UTI to set up a proper pension fund. Implicitly, other private entities would be allowed to do the same. There was a similar reference to medical insurance as an unexploited area. GIC would be allowed to form joint ventures in medical insurance; this would also be allowed for other private entities with majority Indian ownership.

Opening the insurance sector to private companies could only happen after a statutory regulator was put in place and a Bill seeking to set up an insurance regulatory authority was introduced. But the BJP was not willing to come on board. At one stage, Chidambaram even offered to include a limit of 20 per cent on foreign equity in the Insurance Bill. Although Vajpayee initially assured him this might be acceptable, he later backed out because some important senior members of the party were not willing to agree.

Ironically, a near identical Bill was passed 18 months later in 1999 by the NDA government under PM Vajpayee, with foreign equity capped at 26 per cent. It was an example of parties opposing a move when in opposition but implementing the same when in power. The same thing happened a few years later when the Indian partners in the new insurance joint ventures wanted the foreign equity limit increased to 49 per cent. The UPA government tried to make the change but the BJP would not agree. It was the NDA government under PM Narendra Modi that finally amended the legislation in 2016 to allow the foreign equity percentage to be increased to 49 per cent.

EAST ASIAN CRISIS

The year 1997 is remembered globally as the year of the East Asian crisis. It began with the Thai baht coming under pressure in May and finally collapsing on 2 July, depreciating 50 per cent against the US dollar. Contagion spread quickly to other countries in the region including Malaysia, Indonesia and finally even Korea, all of whom were regarded as the success stories of development. Weak regulatory institutions allowed vulnerabilities to build up unchecked and the open capital account made it possible for private capital to leave the country in large quantities—and suddenly—once economic weakness surfaced.

Indian industry had been putting pressure on the Government to liberalize the capital account for access to cheaper capital in global markets, but the Government had deliberately adopted a cautious approach. Earlier in the year, I had suggested to Governor Rangarajan that the RBI should set up a Committee on Capital Account Convertibility to propose a suitable roadmap for liberalization of the capital account. Rangarajan set up the committee under former deputy governor Savak S. Tarapore. It submitted its report in May 1997, recommending a process of step-by-step liberalization, parallel with progress in reducing fiscal deficits, building reserves and strengthening the financial system, especially the banks. We were in the process of considering the report when the crisis erupted in Thailand.

The annual meetings of the IMF and the World Bank for 1997 were scheduled to be held in Hong Kong in September. With the crisis in full blast in Thailand, with spillover effects in Malaysia, our participation in these meetings provided an ideal opportunity to get a feel of the crisis and how it was perceived by the countries most affected. The meetings got off to an unexpectedly colourful start with PM Mahathir Mohamad of Malaysia pronouncing in a public lecture in Hong Kong, 'Currency trading is unnecessary, unproductive and totally immoral... It should be stopped. It should be made illegal.' He topped it by calling currency traders 'morons'. He never mentioned investor George Soros by name in Hong Kong but he had done so a few days earlier in Malaysia when talking to the press. Soros was also scheduled to speak during the meetings and he responded spiritedly, if somewhat rudely, 'Dr Mahathir is a menace to his own country.' He went on to say, 'Interfering with the convertibility of capital at a moment like this is a recipe for disaster.' Ironically, years later, following the 2008 banking crisis in the US and Europe, Soros himself began to warn that financial markets were especially vulnerable to panic because of actions in the market that could produce self-reinforcing destabilization.

The East Asian crisis effectively derailed a proposal to amend the IMF Articles of Agreement to make the liberalization of the capital account one of the 'purposes' of the Fund. The Fund had a clear mandate to promote liberalization of the current account but it had no mandate at all on the capital account, which meant countries were free to impose whatever restrictions they wanted on capital flows. The top management of the Fund and many industrialized countries had been arguing that the Articles of Agreement should be amended to give the Fund a suitable mandate to cover the capital account as well. Developing countries feared that such an amendment would lead to greater pressure from the Fund to liberalize the capital account as a condition for accessing assistance. With the crisis still unfolding, the resistance of developing countries hardened and the insistence of the industrialized countries also weakened. The proposal was effectively consigned to a limbo, where it remains.

The crisis prompted the Japanese to float the idea of an Asian Monetary Fund (AMF). The idea originated with Haruhiko Kuroda, then a middle-level official in the Japanese Ministry of Finance (he became president of the ADB and later governor of the Bank of Japan, a position he currently holds). Kuroda knew that in the Mexican crisis of 1994, the limited IMF resources had to be supplemented by US support of about $12 billion from the Exchange Stabilization Fund managed by the US Treasury but he judged that East Asia could not count on similar large US support. He therefore floated a proposal for the creation of a regional facility to help countries in the region in the event of a panic attack. His fears were borne out when the rescue package for Thailand was discussed at a meeting convened by the IMF in Tokyo in August 1997. The US said it could not contribute more than $250 million because Congress had closed the Exchange Stabilization Fund window that was used for Mexico. Japan ended up having to contribute $4 billion, about the same as the contribution of the IMF, and the balance of the $17.6 billion package was made up by smaller contributions from other countries as well as Japanese banks.

The Japanese delegation pushed the proposal to establish a regional financing facility at the meeting of East Asian finance ministers held in Bangkok just before the Hong Kong meetings. All the participants, including Korea and China, supported the proposal, which was also discussed informally on the sidelines of the Hong Kong meetings. The AMF was designed to cover only 10 members—China, Hong Kong, Japan, South Korea, Australia, Indonesia, Malaysia, Singapore, Thailand and the Philippines—but not India. This was because these countries had much larger Japanese investments and exposure to Japanese banks. Japan had a deep interest in financial stability in the region because a crisis in these countries, with the risk of contagion to others, could have potentially serious repercussions on the Japanese economy, especially banks.

It was an interesting example of how intensity of economic engagement determines geo-economic interests, which in turn have geopolitical implications. We had traditionally taken the view that we preferred multilateral arrangements and did not favour the growth of regional arrangements. But if the multilateral institutional framework was not likely to be strengthened sufficiently, we would lose out by not being part of regional arrangements. As it happened, the US strongly opposed the idea of an AMF. It clearly did not want an institution that would become a possible substitute for the IMF, which it effectively controlled. This strong opposition also led to Australia and China backing off. The idea of an AMF faded out, although it was reincarnated later in a much weaker form as the Chiang Mai Initiative.

Although I did not know it then, the East Asian crisis was to impinge on my life in two different ways in the years ahead. As the Fund was strongly criticized for imposing an excessively stringent conditionality on Indonesia, which proved to be ineffective during the crisis, there was pressure from member countries that IMF activities should be subjected to independent evaluation. An IEO was set up to review IMF programmes, acting independently of the management and reporting only to the board. I was selected to be the first director of the IEO and one of the evaluations we conducted in my time was of the East Asian crisis.

The crisis also led to the creation, in 1999, of a permanent Group of 20 (G20) finance ministers, which included all the members of the Interim Committee who had a permanent seat on the board of the IMF, plus some other important countries.[31] Unlike the Interim

---

[31]The Interim Committee was a committee of all the finance ministers of the countries represented on the IMF board. The larger countries had permanent seats on the board of the IMF while others represented constituencies of smaller countries and took turns on the board. The membership of the committee was therefore not permanent.

Committee, which included some rotating members, the G20 was a permanent grouping. In 2008, after the global financial crisis, the G20 became a summit-level group and I was designated the Indian 'Sherpa', in which capacity I assisted PM Manmohan Singh for all the summits from 2008 to 2013.

CONTAGION FROM EAST ASIA

On return to Delhi from the meetings, I discussed with Finance Minister Chidambaram the lessons we could learn from the crisis in our neighbourhood. I pointed out that adherence to a fixed exchange rate is potentially dangerous because it invites a speculative attack. We were in a reasonably good position on this score, having moved to a flexible exchange rate in 1993. A second lesson was recognizing the importance of avoiding excessive exposure to short-term foreign debt. We had suffered on this front in 1991 and had consciously acted to reduce short-term debt exposure. As a result, our short-term debt as a percentage of GDP was much smaller than of the East Asian countries. A broader lesson was the need to strengthen the banking system, especially in its ability to cope with foreign exchange exposure. We had taken some steps, but I felt we needed to do much more. The Tarapore Committee had also emphasized the need to strengthen the banking system as a precondition for a gradual opening of the capital account, but had not made any specific suggestions. I suggested we set up a second committee under former RBI governor, Narasimham, to review the status of banking reforms. Chidambaram readily agreed and the Narasimham Committee II was set up in December 1997.

We had our first taste of contagion soon after the Hong Kong meetings. There was pressure on the rupee and although the exchange rate was supposed to be market-determined, the RBI adopted a policy of 'leaning against the wind' to avoid excessive volatility. As a result, foreign exchange reserves declined in September 1997 for the first time in several months and the RBI also intervened in forward markets. All this was happening when the domestic political situation was unravelling. The Jain Commission, investigating the assassination of Rajiv, asserted that the DMK had colluded with the LTTE and the Congress demanded that the DMK ministers be dismissed. Gujral refused to do so and the Congress withdrew support.

PM Gujral resigned in November and it was not clear for a while whether we would have another shaky coalition or elections. He was to stay as caretaker PM until the next election was called in February 1998. This was also the time Governor Rangarajan's term at the RBI came to an end and Bimal Jalan was appointed in his place on 22 November 1997.

Jalan had a baptism of fire, coping with pressure on the rupee at a time when there was a political vacuum with a caretaker government. The rupee was at ₹36.4 to a dollar at the end of October 1997. It depreciated steadily in the course of November, reaching ₹38.8 to a dollar by the end of the month. Some of this depreciation was actually desirable, because the rupee had appreciated in real terms over the previous year. The depreciation was also gradual because the RBI was able to cushion the fall in the rupee by using reserves we had built up earlier. However, the reserves dropped about $2 billion in November and there was also a build-up in the forward position of about $3 billion.

The rupee continued to depreciate and on 14 January 1998, it broke the psychological mark of ₹40 to a dollar. Sushma Swaraj of the BJP blamed the fall of the rupee on the policies of the Government and was quoted as saying that if the BJP were voted to power, it would take immediate measures to halt the decline.[32] I was mobbed by a group of reporters as I left the Ministry of Finance at the time; one of them pointedly asked me whether I was worried about the rupee. I said I was not as I got into my car, and this was prominently quoted in the press the next day. Chidambaram, who read the major papers very carefully, chided

---

[32]*Indian Express*, 16 January 1998.

me gently on whether the remark was really necessary. When I explained that I was caught by reporters, and did not think I should have refused to comment or say I was worried, he saw my point but couldn't help suggesting, 'Couldn't you have anticipated this and gone out by the back entrance?'

It was clear some action was necessary to avoid a self-fulfilling panic setting in. Fiscal action was not possible as we had a caretaker government and a new one would not be in place until sometime in March. The interest rate was the only instrument available. The RBI had reduced the bank rate in a series of steps from 12 per cent in April 1997 to 9 per cent by August 1997. This would now need to be reversed. Shankar and I discussed the situation with Bimal and we agreed we needed more than just a token increase. Bimal moved boldly and decisively to raise the bank rate by 2 percentage points on 17 January 1998. The CRR, which had been lowered a few months earlier from 10 per cent to 9.5 per cent, was raised to 10.5 per cent, and the interest rate charged on bank credit for imports was also raised.

The NDA government was sworn in on 19 March 1998 and some of the new ministers could not resist asserting that the Government would ensure the rupee would soon be strengthened. Bimal later told me that he requested PM Vajpayee to dissuade his ministers from making any pronouncements on the rupee as it would only provoke speculation that would make management of the situation more difficult. His intervention was obviously successful because the subject did not surface in political statements thereafter. The rupee soon stabilized at around ₹39.5 to a dollar, without any further depletion of reserves. The situation was sufficiently normalized by April 1998 to allow the bank rate to be reduced to 10 per cent; the CRR was also reduced to 10 per cent.

NEW INITIATIVES

The UF government took early initiatives to attract private investment into road projects. S. Sundar, surface transport secretary, had served in the Commonwealth Secretariat in London and was familiar with the UK's effort to attract private investment in infrastructure. He was keen to promote private investment in roads—an interesting example of a senior bureaucrat exploring new opportunities. For this, it was necessary to be able to levy tolls and the National Highways Act was amended in 1995 for this purpose. Until then, the law allowed tolling of bridges, but not roads. A start was made by seeking private investment for relatively small road bypasses around cities. The tolls charged were calibrated to cover costs and provide a reasonable return. This worked for bypasses because commercial traffic was willing to pay the toll charges as considerable time was saved from not having to go through the cities.

Sundar wanted to extend the bypass initiative to invite private investment in intercity highways. He consulted Gajendra Haldea in my department, who had experience with PPP projects in power generation. Haldea pointed out that a cost-based approach to fix tolls for large stretches of highways would produce a toll that would be too high and unacceptable to motorists. Instead, they should fix a 'reasonable' toll per kilometre reflecting willingness to pay, and index it over time to reflect inflation. Investors could be invited to bid competitively for the subsidy they would need and the concession would be awarded to the investor bidding the lowest. The capital subsidy would be a fiscal burden but it would be much lower than if the road had to be built in the public sector.

The first PPP in road development was a 550-km highway between Jaipur and Kishenganj in Rajasthan, upgrading an existing two-lane National Highway into India's first six-lane highway. It was based on a build-operate-transfer (BOT) concession for a period of 20 years. The concession agreement for the project was finalized in the last years of the UF government but awarded during the succeeding NDA government. The highway was finally completed in 2005, when the Congress-led UPA government was back in power!

The UF made some progress on disinvestment. The CMP had promised the establishment of a Disinvestment Commission and this was quickly established in August 1996 under the chairmanship of G.V. Ramakrishna, with whom I had worked when he was SEBI chairman. Forty PSUs were referred to the commission in September 1996, followed by another 10 in March 1997. The commission submitted a series of reports beginning in February 1997. The initial reports only recommended conventional disinvestment through sale of part of the equity in some selected units as had been done earlier, but later reports recommended strategic sales. However, the sale of anything other than minority stakes in public sector enterprises remained controversial during the life of the UF and there was little progress in this area.

An effort was also made by the UF to increase the degree of autonomy given to public sector enterprises. Nine PSUs were designated as 'Navratnas' and given a higher degree of autonomy but this did not amount to making the enterprises effectively board-managed. As long as the appointment of senior management remains with the Government and not an independent board, the notion of managerial autonomy will remain fanciful.

Another initiative to modernize the system of foreign exchange controls was the decision to abolish the Foreign Exchange Regulation Act (FERA) and replace it with a modern legislation, more consistent with the objective of progressive liberalization of the external sector. FERA was a somewhat draconian control-oriented legislation with the explicit objective of 'conserving' foreign exchange. It needed to be replaced by legislation that reflected the liberalization in the current account that had occurred, and the gradual liberalization of the capital account expected in future. While presenting the Budget for 1997–98, Chidambaram announced that modern legislation to replace FERA was being drafted by the RBI and would be introduced later in the year. It was ultimately passed in 1999 by the NDA government under Vajpayee, a reassuring demonstration of continuity across different governments.

A LESSON FROM THE MAHABHARATA

The two UF governments were in power for a total of less than two years, too short a time to make a definitive impact on policy or performance, especially as the second year was dominated by domestic political instability and the impact of the East Asian crisis. The most important achievement of the UF was to signal continuity in the reform process. This was particularly important because the coalition included the Left parties.

Much of the credit for continuity must go to Chidambaram as finance minister. Part of the previous government that had launched the reforms, he was convinced these policies would deliver the high growth necessary for India to achieve her full potential, and he made his case eloquently. At an event in Bangalore where he was addressing a group of businessmen and other professionals, Chidambaram firmly announced that achieving high growth was possible, but only if government concentrated on the objective the way Dronacharya had taught Arjuna to concentrate all his attention on the 'eye' of the wooden bird he was using as a target. Invoking the Mahabharata to make a contemporary point about economic policy was a rhetorical device that drove the point home much more effectively than the dry terminology routinely used in the Ministry of Finance's Economic Surveys and the Planning Commission's documents!

10

CONTINUITY WITH CHANGE

The BJP fought the general election of 1998 as part of the NDA, a pre-election coalition of 14 parties including regional parties such as AIADMK from Tamil Nadu and Shiv Sena from Maharashtra. It fared slightly worse than in 1996 but the other parties in the alliance did much better and the NDA emerged with a slim majority. Vajpayee was sworn in as PM on 19 March 1998. A year later, the AIADMK withdrew support, leading to another general election. This time, the NDA came back with a stable majority that saw them through a full five-year term.

I had been in the Ministry of Finance for six-and-a-half years by the time the new government took over and expected to be moved out. A few days after the Government was sworn in, Brajesh Mishra, the new principal secretary to the PM, called me to his office to inform me that there would be changes of key officials, but only after the regular Budget was presented in June. He also mentioned that I would be told in advance and he would discuss with me where I would like to go. It was a gracious gesture and certainly not the norm when senior officials are transferred, either before or since.

REFORMS WITH A SWADESHI THRUST

The transition from the Congress-led government to the UF had been accomplished with a high degree of continuity in economic policy but it was not clear that this would continue. The BJP was known to favour less controls on the domestic private sector and was also expected to be more flexible on privatization. However, the RSS and the Swadeshi Jagran Manch were opposed to subjecting domestic producers to competition from imports and opening the economy to foreign investment. The BJP also had a strong base among small business and this group often worried that the expansion of large Indian business may be at its expense. Everyone waited to see how these differences would be reconciled in policy.

The NDA quickly produced a National Agenda for Governance (NAG) to define a common approach to keep the coalition together. Controversial issues such as the Ram temple, abolition of Article 370 (which gave special status to Jammu & Kashmir [J&K]) and the Uniform Civil Code, which were important elements of the BJP's electoral campaign, were not mentioned in the NAG. Much of what was said on the economic front suggested continuity: GDP growth at 7–8 per cent per year; removal of unemployment and total elimination of poverty; and emphasis on infrastructure, agriculture, education and housing. The new twist lay in the promise that reforms would have a strong 'swadeshi thrust'. No one knew quite what that meant and everyone waited to find out.

Yashwant Sinha, the new finance minister, had joined the BJP only recently, having earlier served as finance minister in the Chandra Shekhar government. He had retired prematurely from the IAS in 1984 to join politics; having been a civil servant himself, he knew that civil servants and technocrats looked at things differently from politicians. I felt he recognized the value of non-political advice even when he disagreed with that advice or was simply unable to put it into practice.

From the very beginning, the Vajpayee government went out of its way to reassure foreign investors that it was not anti-FDI. Shortly after the Government was formed, a group of American businessmen called on the new PM in his office in Parliament House. Vajpayee was pointedly asked if his government would continue the path of economic reforms and whether foreign investment would be welcome. He assured them that as a democracy we believed government could change without disruptive changes in policy. I was sitting a few places away on his side of the table and was startled to hear him say, 'Montek Ahluwalia sitting there represents continuity, and I represent change.' I was more than slightly embarrassed but I realized he knew that many of the businessmen on the delegation would meet me later and was encouraging them to pursue their doubts with me, while also giving me a signal on the new government's line.

In April 1998, Sinha, on his way back from the IMF and World Bank meetings in Washington DC, stopped in New York to meet a large group of investors to explain the policies of the new government. He reassured them that swadeshi meant the ability to deal with the BOP without having to rely on external aid. This meant developing a strong industrial sector with export capability, and foreign investment was welcome because it would increase our competitiveness. He repeated the Vajpayee line, pointing to me as continuity and himself as change.

Hank Greenberg, the CEO of the American International Group, asked Sinha about prospects for further liberalization in the financial sector, especially FDI in insurance. It was a difficult question as it was known that the BJP had prevented Chidambaram from opening insurance a year earlier. But Sinha, making no reference to the BJP's earlier opposition, simply said the Government would consider the issue very carefully. The audience gave him credit for not claiming too much while showing an open mind. Insurance was opened to the private sector two years later, subject to a cap of 26 per cent on foreign equity.

INDIA GOES NUCLEAR: OPERATION SHAKTI

On 11 May 1998, barely two months after the new government was sworn in, we got the news that three simultaneous nuclear tests (one large thermonuclear fission device and two smaller devices) had been successfully carried out at the testing facility at Pokhran. I was not entirely surprised as the BJP had said that they would undertake a nuclear test if they came to power.

India had refused to sign the Treaty on the Non-Proliferation of Nuclear Weapons (NPT) because it was discriminatory, allowing some countries to have nuclear weapons but denying them to others. While campaigning vigorously for universal nuclear disarmament, PM Rajiv Gandhi had offered that India would be willing to give up the nuclear option, provided all those who had nuclear weapons agreed to eliminate them totally in a phased process. Until such an agreement was in place, we would not rule out the nuclear option. In fact, we had refused to sign the Comprehensive Test Ban Treaty (CTBT) precisely to keep our options open.

I knew Rajiv Gandhi had given the go-ahead to develop a nuclear weapon in 1987 when it was clear that Pakistan was working towards the same objective clandestinely.[33] Preparations had continued under Narasimha Rao and in 1994 I came to the conclusion that a test could occur at any time because I was asked by the cabinet secretary for a confidential note on the reactions of the international community if we were to conduct a nuclear test. Our note indicated that the reaction would be highly negative. We were no longer dependent on IMF aid flows and the BOP had turned comfortable but we could not rule out an interruption in external assistance flows. I learnt later that US satellites had picked up unusual activity at the Pokhran site and the US ambassador had called on Amarnath Verma to confront him with satellite images of the site, which suggested preparations were being made for a test. Years later, speaking on the occasion of Narasimha Rao's death in 2006, Vajpayee paid him a tribute by revealing that when he took over from Rao in 1996, for what turned out to be a 13-day tenure, Rao had told him that everything was ready for a nuclear test and he should go ahead and do it.

Codenamed Operation Shakti, the tests were an instant political success for the BJP. A poll conducted by *India Today* showed

---

[33]Naresh Chandra, who was defence secretary at the time, told me this years later.

that 87 per cent of those sampled were in favour of the tests.[34] Opposition leaders Sonia Gandhi and Sharad Pawar also supported the tests. The reaction in New Delhi was very positive. This was not misplaced jingoism but pride that the country had ended its self-imposed nuclear ambivalence and stepped forth as a nuclear power.

The day after, on 12 May, the PM chaired a meeting with a select group of ministers and key officials to review the global reaction. I was invited, as was Dr A.P.J. Abdul Kalam, then secretary in charge of the Defence Research and Development Organisation (DRDO). Kalam, who later became President of India, gave a very detailed presentation of the reactions of individual scientists in major Western countries, including their assessment of the success of the tests based on what different monitoring stations around the world had picked up. I was impressed by his informative presentation and as he was sitting next to me, I whispered to ask how he was able to get so much information in such a short time. He replied that he had got most of it from the Internet!

When it was my turn, I said governments in industrialized countries had already been critical of the test and would now be under pressure from non-proliferation lobbies to take punitive action. Access to technology in crucial areas was already tightly controlled and we could assume it would be further tightened. I did not think we would face trade sanctions against our exports but we should expect restrictions on aid, especially from the US and Japan (which was traditionally sensitive about nuclear proliferation), and possibly some of the European countries. However, I pointed out that bilateral aid had shrunk considerably and we were already planning for a reduction in bilateral flows. A faster pace of reduction in these flows would not be very damaging. The flows that really mattered were those from the World Bank and the ADB. The actual inflows in any given year were largely on account of loans approved earlier, which I did not think would be interrupted.

---

[34]*India Today*, 25 May 1998.

The US could start opposing new loans but it did not have a veto. As long as it did not launch a concerted campaign to pressurize the managements of these institutions to delay bringing new loans to the board, we would not face serious problems.

I went on to say that as long as we continued with our openness to trade and investment, US companies could be persuaded to lobby their government to avoid taking punitive action. The PM went out of his way to voice his agreement with what I had said. It got me thinking that the special effort by the Government to send a positive signal on FDI to US investors in its early days may have been in anticipation of the likely strain on the relationship following the nuclear tests. The meeting concluded with Vajpayee telling Kalam and R. Chidambaram, chairman of the Atomic Energy Commission (AEC), that they could leave because they had 'important things to attend to'.

The following day, I went to see the finance minister in his office around 11.30 a.m. to discuss a minor issue connected with the forthcoming Budget and found him unusually preoccupied, constantly glancing at the television screen. Seeing I had noticed this, he volunteered, 'In another seven minutes, we will have conducted two more atomic tests.' I realized those were the 'important things' R. Chidambaram and Kalam had to attend to. We waited together for confirmation from the TV, which came soon enough. Operation Shakti had produced five successful tests; with that, the Government announced that no more tests were planned.

Two weeks later, on 28 May, Pakistan conducted its nuclear test. There was much discussion internationally about the implications of two new nuclear powers with a long tradition of hostility and suspicion confronting each other in South Asia. International security analysts viewed the development with alarm as it increased the possibility of nuclear conflict, but domestic perception was much more sanguine.

NDA'S FIRST BUDGET

The first regular budget of the NDA was presented on 1 June 1998. The central government's fiscal deficit in the previous year, 1997–98, had increased to 5.7 per cent. Revenues had fallen short of targets partly because of the tax concessions in the 'Dream Budget' but also because growth had decelerated to 4.3 per cent. Expenditures had ballooned because of the implementation of the Pay Commission recommendations to raise government salaries.

Sinha had to present a Budget that would build market confidence in an environment of uncertainty created by the reaction to the nuclear tests. He did what finance ministers have often done. He listed a large number of ambitious objectives, such as reversing the decline in agricultural production, restoring the momentum of industrial growth, ensuring macroeconomic stability, raising domestic savings to achieve higher levels of investment, providing impetus to social sector development, and calibrating the pace and character of integration with the world economy. To his credit, he managed to avoid committing to new and profligate programmes aimed at achieving these objectives.

The Budget sent important signals of continuity in tax reforms, FDI policy and reforms in the financial sector. The maximum rate of personal income tax had been reduced in the previous year to 30 per cent and the corporate tax rate to 35 per cent. These were left untouched through the six years of the NDA government, though surcharges were added at varying rates. There was a declaration that the indirect tax system would be simplified around a mean cenvat rate of 18 per cent, with one lower rate and another higher one for luxury products. This was a modification of the four-rate structure Chidambaram had announced earlier. Some commodities were grouped into the new rate structure but many other rates continued to exist outside the structure and the full consolidation of rates into a three-rate structure was left for later years.

Action on import duties was mixed. Industrial growth had fallen to about 4 per cent in 1997–98 with no sign of an early reversal and this led to many demands for increased levels of protection through import duties. Business interests also felt that the BJP-led government would be sympathetic to demands for higher import duties. Sinha resisted the pressures for sector-specific increases in duties but he did introduce a new 4 per cent tax on imports to equalize the burden imposed by state sales taxes. This was a belated response to the complaint of domestic producers that whereas a countervailing duty was levied on imports at the same rate as central excise duty to ensure that the import duty was actually the effective protective duty, there was no comparable duty to offset the effects of the sales tax. This was a valid point and I tried to explain this to the press but I was criticized for defending what appeared to be indefensible. The introduction of GST in 2017 finally made it possible for imports to bear the same rate of duty as the central and state duty in addition to the purely protective import duty.

OVERTURNING SEBI ON INSIDER TRADING

In the summer of 1998, I had to deal with the consequences of SEBI finding Hindustan Lever Ltd (HLL) guilty of insider trading and ordering criminal prosecution of the top management. HLL had appealed against the order, and the Appellate Tribunal that heard such appeals was located in the Ministry of Finance. I was chairman and C.M. Vasudev, special secretary, banking, was the other member.

It was a high-profile case as it involved India's largest multinational corporation (MNC). The case arose out of a complex transaction. London-based MNC Unilever owned 51 per cent of HLL and 50.27 per cent of Brooke Bond. The parent company decided to merge these two subsidiaries in India but also wanted a 51 per cent holding in the merged company. This was achieved by getting HLL to buy a small proportion of Brooke Bond shares from UTI, and then cancelling the shares. The reduction in the total number of shares of Brooke Bond raised Unilever's shareholding in

Brooke Bond to 51 per cent, which meant Unilever's shareholding in the merged company would also be 51 per cent. UTI had complained that in buying Brooke Bond shares from it, HLL had engaged in insider trading as it had inside knowledge of the proposed merger. SEBI found HLL guilty and ordered that its top management be prosecuted and UTI compensated. UTI also appealed against the order on the grounds that the compensation awarded was inadequate.

The different parties were represented by extraordinarily distinguished lawyers. The counsel for SEBI was Mukul Rohatgi, who later became attorney general. HLL was represented by Harish Salve, who became one of our most distinguished senior advocates in the Supreme Court and India's best-known lawyer in international arbitrations. UTI was represented by Arun Jaitley, who became a minister in the second Vajpayee government a year later and finance minister in PM Narendra Modi's government in 2014. Hearing these legal luminaries addressing us as 'My Lord' made me understand why judges begin to think of themselves as a class apart!

We overturned SEBI's ruling. We agreed that HLL's top management had knowledge of the merger but insider trading also required proof that HLL acted on the basis of information that was not known to the general public and was price-sensitive. SEBI had not established either of these requirements. As far as public knowledge was concerned, a large number of stories had been published in the business press speculating about the merger and it could reasonably be assumed that the market had priced this in. UTI was a major investing institution and its contention that it was not aware of these stories was simply not credible. As the two companies were already under common control, there was no reason why a merger of the two would make a difference to the Brooke Bond share price. The only potentially price-sensitive information was the swap ratio. A high swap ratio in which Brooke Bond shareholders acquired more shares of HLL would have raised the Brooke Bond share price in the market, and advance information on the ratio could be said to be price-sensitive information. However, it was clearly established that the swap ratio was not known when the share purchase was made; it was decided later, based on the recommendations of consulting firms presented to the boards of the two companies.

We also faulted SEBI for not prosecuting under Section 15, which contained specific provisions to penalize insider trading. It opted instead to act under Section 11, which dealt with undefined violations and included imprisonment as a punishment. SEBI's decision to invoke Section 11 may have been prompted by the fact that the penalty provided under Section 15 was too small but the solution lay in amending the law to impose a larger penalty rather than take recourse to a broader section that allowed a larger penalty. We also set aside SEBI's order of compensation to UTI because there was no provision in the SEBI Act that empowered it to order compensation.

Although we had decided the case strictly on its merits, it clearly raised issues of conflict of interest. Criminal prosecution of the top officials of an MNC at that stage would have had a severe adverse effect on investor sentiment. The Government was new, its stance on foreign investment was not yet known, and it was dealing with sanctions after Pokhran. We were fortunate that SEBI's case was weak on merits — had it gone the other way, it may have been read as a signal of government intent. It convinced me that the Appellate Tribunal should be completely independent of the ministry. We acted quickly on that front and, shortly thereafter, an independent quasi-judicial tribunal was established.

Our order was issued on 14 July 1998. It was challenged by SEBI in the Bombay High Court and also in some respects by both HLL and UTI. The court directed that all the writ petitions be listed together. It is a sad reflection of the speed of the judicial process that the case is still pending 21 years later!

IMPORTS OF CONSUMER GOODS: THE LAST BASTION

The trade reforms of 1991 had liberalized imports of machinery and intermediate inputs but imports of all final consumer goods remained banned. The WTO allows countries to resort to bans or quantitative restrictions (QRs) only on BOP grounds. The industrialized countries protested in the course of the WTO Trade Policy Review that our BOP had improved considerably and the QRs on consumer goods imports were therefore no longer justifiable.

The commerce secretary had written to me to say that they intended to make a case for continuing with QRs on consumer goods for BOP reasons, and he wanted confirmation of support from the Ministry of Finance. I promptly wrote back to say that it would be against our national interest because it painted a picture of helplessness that was completely contrary to what we in the Ministry of Finance were projecting to foreign investors.

The Ministry of Commerce persisted in defending the QRs on consumer goods at the WTO. The European countries agreed to the QRs being phased out by 2003. The US did not accept this compromise and took the issue to the WTO dispute resolution panel.

In an internal meeting with the PM, I had argued that the ban on consumer goods was not in our interest and we should remove it on our own. Vajpayee decided that as the matter was in dispute, it would be best to wait for the outcome. The WTO panel ruled against India and pronounced that we should remove the QRs in two steps: the first by 1 April 2000 and the second by 1 April 2001. The NDA government complied with the ruling. It is worth noting that when imports of consumer goods were finally allowed in 2001, we did not find it necessary to raise tariffs as there was no unmanageable surge in imports. It illustrated how many of our positions taken in trade negotiations are based on irrational fears of a surge in imports with little acknowledgement of the capacity of domestic producers to adjust to competition.

A BACKWARD STEP ON FDI

In 1998, the Vajpayee government took a step back in liberalization of FDI in response to pressure from Indian investors in joint-venture (JV) partnerships with foreign companies. When FDI limits were raised from 40 per cent of equity to 51 per cent in 1991, many foreign investors who had earlier accepted the 40 per cent limit, now wanted to increase their share to 51 per cent. If this was resisted by their Indian JV partners, the foreign partner would set up a new JV with other Indian partners willing to accept a minority stake. The Indian partners in the existing JVs lobbied that foreign investors should not be allowed to abandon existing partners to set up new JVs in the same sector. The Government conceded to this demand and introduced a condition that foreign investors with existing JVs would need a 'no-objection certificate' from their existing partners before they could set up another venture in the same sector.

Foreign investors saw this as patently unfair as companies that had not entered India earlier when policies were more restrictive were now being allowed to set up majority-owned JVs, while those who had invested earlier were denied the same flexibility. In many cases, the need for a no-objection certificate only led to existing domestic partners extracting a price for the no objection, vitiating the atmosphere. The no-objection requirement was finally removed in 2005 by the UPA government under Dr Manmohan Singh.

FROM DISINVESTMENT TO PRIVATIZATION

An area where the Vajpayee government broke new ground was in divesting government equity in public sector enterprises. The Disinvestment Commission, which was set up by the UF government, had advised going below a 51 per cent stake for some enterprises. The NDA government enunciated a new principle that while the Government could retain a majority holding in PSUs in strategic areas, 'in the generality of cases' government holdings would be brought down to 26 per cent. This was clearly a big step forward.

I recall a meeting of the EAC-PM in 2001 when I pointed out that we essentially had three ways of managing the fiscal situation: cut government expenditure, raise tax revenues, or raise funds by selling controlling stakes in PSUs such as Maruti, Ashoka Hotel, Bharat Aluminium Company, Hindustan Zinc, etc. PM Vajpayee thought about it for a while, and then said, '*Montek, Maruti mein government stake kam kiya toh bawaal khada ho jayega* (Montek, if you lessen government stake in Maruti, it'll lead to a ruckus).' I had invited Ashok Gulati who was also in the meeting to have lunch with me at home, and on the way we discussed whether the country would ever be ready to face the 'bawaal'. A few weeks later, the government vacated the co-driver's seat in Maruti Udyog Limited, ceding total control in favour of its joint venture partner Suzuki Motor Corp of Japan. PM Vajpayee had obviously decided to take the political plunge and face the 'bawaal'.

The NDA government managed to offload several PSUs to private managements, including VSNL to Tatas, CMC to Tata Consultancy Services (TCS), and Balco and Hindustan Zinc to Vedanta. Several public sector hotels were also privatized. These were not easy decisions and Arun Shourie, who was then disinvestment minister, has documented in great detail the extraordinary procedural complexities he had to face when trying to sell PSUs to private buyers.

The privatization/strategic sale effort soon ran aground owing to allegations of impropriety levelled against Arun Shourie and Pradeep Baijal, disinvestment secretary, in the sale of hotels. These allegations were ultimately found to be baseless and the charges dropped, but they disrupted the momentum. As a result, less was done in the six years of the NDA on privatization than might otherwise have been possible.

PRIVATE INVESTMENT IN POWER GENERATION: DABHOL AND OTHER PROJECTS

Power generation was opened up for private investment in 1992 as part of the reforms, and both the central government and state governments were keen to invite foreign investors to set up electricity-generation plants to sell electricity to state-owned electricity distribution boards. Enron International was one of the first to respond, entering into an agreement with the Maharashtra State Electricity Board to set up a naphtha/gas-based power plant at Dabhol.

The Enron project became a symbol of everything that can go wrong. The power purchase agreement signed by the Congress government in Maharashtra in 1993 had to be renegotiated when the state government changed, and a BJP-Shiv Sena government came to power in 1995. Even when the Congress came back to power in 1999, they cancelled the project because the cost of power had increased massively as the price of imported naphtha had shot up and the rupee had also depreciated. It was clear that the Maharashtra state government had failed to assess some of the risks involved, especially of the fuel price and rupee depreciation.

The experience with Dabhol showed that the complexity of moving from the public sector-based system in the electricity sector, to one that involved private sector generators was underestimated. For example, the power tariff was criticized because it was not competitively determined but was based on negotiating a cost-plus formula. This was not seen as problematic when public sector projects were involved, but became highly controversial in the case of a negotiated price for the private sector. There were also several complaints of corruption in getting regulatory clearances and unfair practices in land acquisition.

Enron and other joint venture partners invoked arbitration in London, but before the arbitration proceedings could be finished, Enron itself collapsed because of fraudulent activity in other areas. The project was ultimately taken over by a combination of NTPC,

GAIL, and Indian banks that had lent to the project. Both Indian and foreign lenders took some haircuts.

Dabhol was not the only problem project. The Narasimha Rao government had decided to extend counter-guarantees for seven 'fast-track' private sector power projects to backstop the primary guarantee given by state governments. This was to cover situations where the arrangement to buy electricity at an agreed price from the private sector producer was terminated prematurely by the distribution companies that were owned by state governments. The cabinet had approved that the counter-guarantee should only be offered if tariffs fixed in the Power Purchase Agreement (PPA) conformed strictly with the tariff notifications in force, and it was the responsibility of the ministry to certify compliance with the provisions.[35] We found that state distribution companies/ electricity boards (SEBs) uncritically accepted PPAs drafted by power producers, which often contained many provisions giving the producers a better deal than was strictly allowed in the power tariff guidelines in force. Gajendra Haldea in the Ministry of Finance diligently dug out these provisions and insisted that the promoters modify the PPAs to bring them in conformity with the guidelines if they wanted a counter-guarantee from the Government of India.

This made Haldea highly unpopular with the investors, which was understandable, but it also made him unpopular with officials in the Ministry of Power. They felt that it created delays in reaching the internal targets they had set for private investment! Minister of State for Power, Rangarajan Kumaramangalam, a former Congress politician who had subsequently joined the BJP, asked for a meeting with Finance Minister Yashwant Sinha to see if the approval of counter-guarantees could be speeded up. On Haldea's

---

[35]Dabhol was not one of the fast-track projects but they got a counter-guarantee to establish a level playing field with the other projects that came up later. Since the Maharashtra state government had already signed the PPA, we did not have the opportunity to examine it. We concentrated only on limiting the extent of the counter-guarantee.

advice, I suggested at the meeting that if the Ministry of Power requested the cabinet to modify its earlier decision and designate it as the certifying agency, it could move as fast as it wished. Kumaramangalam reacted immediately, 'You see Yashwant, Montek is trying to trap me!' He knew perfectly well that the issues being raised by us were valid and would also be raised by officers of his ministry if they had to take the responsibility for providing the certification.

Private power projects faced many other problems that illustrated the difficulty in facilitating private investment in the sector. Coal India, the public sector monopoly supplier, was not willing to enter into a legally binding coal supply agreement with penalties for delayed delivery and shortfalls in quality. In any case, Coal India would only take responsibility for delivering coal to the railhead, after which the Railways would have to take responsibility. The Railways was also a monopoly with no tradition of accepting any penalty for non-performance.

For all these reasons, only three counter-guarantees could be signed before I left the Ministry of Finance in 1998. The experience demonstrated that bringing private investment into the power sector was not a simple matter of 'allowing' it, as many politicians and civil servants thought. It was also necessary to create an environment in which private investors could expect to be able to finance the project, service the debt and make a reasonable return on their equity, while generating electricity. It was important to ensure that the Centre was not burdened with risks that should have been borne by the private sector or the state governments.

Very little thought had been given to these issues. One reason was that we were striking out into untested waters and learning as we went along.

MY MOVE TO THE PLANNING COMMISSION

Sometime in August 1998, Brajesh Mishra informed me that the Government was ready to make changes at the secretary level, and asked me where I would like to go. I asked if I could be sent to the Planning Commission as a member. I had become increasingly interested in problems of infrastructure development and knew that if we wanted a large programme of investment in infrastructure, we would have to attract PPPs. This required careful policy design and coordination across ministries and I thought the Planning Commission would give me an opportunity to help shape policy in this area. Two days later, my move to the Planning Commission was formally announced; N.K. Singh, who was revenue secretary in the Ministry of Finance, would move to the PMO as secretary to the PM. Shortly thereafter, I was also made a member of the EAC-PM.

I called on Deputy Chairman Jaswant Singh to report for duty and when I expressed my interest in working on infrastructure, I was officially designated as member, infrastructure. I was the only member at the time as Jaswant Singh had not agreed to take on any others. A former cavalry officer with a deep interest in military history and strategy, he was intellectually oriented and easy to interact with. But he had limited interest in the work of the commission and made no secret of it. He had expected to be finance minister but it was apparently scuttled because of opposition from some circles within the broader Sangh Parivar. He had accepted the deputy chairmanship of the Planning Commission with the expectation that the PM would soon give him another assignment.

Soon after I joined the commission, PM Vajpayee, in a public speech delivered at the Associated Chambers of Commerce and Industry of India (ASSOCHAM), announced a new pair of four- to six-lane highways, one running North to South, connecting Srinagar with Kanyakumari at the extreme southern tip, and the other running East to West, connecting Silchar in Assam with Porbandar in Gujarat. The proposed highways were over 7,500 km in length and the idea was particularly ambitious considering most existing National Highways had only two lanes!

B.N. Puri was in charge of the transport division of the commission. He immediately brought to my attention that as there was no budgetary provision for the new programme, there was a serious danger that resources would be diverted from the ongoing upgradation of the so-called Golden Quadrilateral, i.e. the National Highways connecting Delhi, Kolkata, Chennai and Mumbai. This quadrilateral carried the bulk of the road traffic in the country and was much more important than the proposed new alignments, which would have much less traffic for quite some time. The priority should be to upgrade the Golden Quadrilateral to four lanes, with six lanes in certain stretches. I raised this with Jaswant Singh but he was reluctant to take it up with the PM as it would look like he was questioning his announcement.

I offered to try and resolve the issue at the official level and promptly explained the problem to NK, who acted quickly and effectively. A few weeks later, the PM, speaking at an International Congress on Highways in India, clarified that the programme of North-South and East-West highways as well as the proposed four- and six-laning would be part of a new National Highway Development Programme, with the Golden Quadrangle as the centrepiece. A task force was set up under the deputy chairman of the Planning Commission to work out the details. As a result, we ended up with a well-defined plan in which the Golden Quadrilateral was given priority and the North-South and East-West 'spurs' were added, along with 'spines' connecting each state capital to the quadrilateral. It was also announced that funds would be allocated as the programme was rolled out.

Sometime in December 1998, Jaswant Singh was appointed minister of external affairs. He moved out of Yojana Bhavan with undisguised joy and K.C. Pant took over as deputy chairman. A former Congressman, Pant believed in planning and set about producing the Ninth Five-Year Plan in right earnest. S.P. Gupta, S.R. Hashim and D.N. Tiwari were appointed as members.

THE TELECOM TANGLE

Towards the end of 1998, I got involved in the effort to untangle the serious problems that had arisen in the telecom sector. The

1991 reforms had opened telecommunications to the private sector, and the National Telecom Policy (NTP) 1994 was the first step in this direction. Several licences were given for cellular and basic services in the four major metros and the various 'circles' into which the rest of the country was divided. However, the policy was riddled with problems that surfaced soon enough.

The policy was not based on an adequate appreciation of the conditions needed for private operators to function. There was no independent telecom regulator. The DoT, which was administratively in charge of the public sector service providers, also doubled up as the regulator. This undermined its credibility with private sector providers. New entrants were not assured adequate points of interconnection with the incumbent network, without which they could not possibly compete. Another set of problems arose from the failure to anticipate that technology was changing rapidly and the policy needed to allow participants to adopt whatever technologies were most efficient. The differences between different types of services—fixed line, mobile, Internet, broadcasting—were getting blurred. It was likely that these services may be delivered by the same supplier in future, calling for a shift to universal licencing.

These problems were partly a consequence of unavoidable 'learning by doing' but they also arose because the policy had been formulated without adequate input from knowledgeable experts outside the Government. As there were no private sector players in the industry, many practical problems were not anticipated. An official group on telecom was set up under the chairmanship of Jaswant Singh to suggest corrections. I represented the Planning Commission. We prepared a new Telecom Policy, NTP 1999, which was accepted by the cabinet in March 1999, just before the Government lost its majority.

NTP 1999 recognized that competition should be encouraged and the regulatory system should ensure a level playing field among different service providers in the public and private sectors. The Telecom Regulatory Authority of India (TRAI), which had been set up by the UF government in 1997, was split into two. TRAI become a policy advisory body the Government had to consult on issues, such as the entry of new licencees and the pricing of spectrum, before taking decisions. A separate Telecom Disputes Settlement and Appellate Tribunal was established, presided over by a retired Supreme Court judge or chief justice of a high court, to deal with disputes between the Government and service providers, and between competing service providers.

Public sector service providers Bharat Sanchar Nigam Limited (BSNL) and Mahanagar Telephone Nigam Limited (MTNL) were separated from DoT and made into public sector corporations. A new Department of Telecommunications Services was created, which became a policymaking body with no direct control over the public sector service providers. The new policy allowed new entrants into existing circles but instead of the earlier system of licence fees payable upfront, there was to be a shift to a revenue-sharing principle—the share to be fixed on the basis of recommendations of TRAI. The licence period was also proposed to be extended from 10 years to 20.

Incumbent players were keen to migrate to revenue sharing because their revenues were much lower than anticipated and they were unable to pay the licence fees they had committed to. Telecommunications Minister Jagmohan stoutly opposed any post-bid relaxation on the grounds that bidders who had lost out could argue that the incumbents had deliberately submitted high bids to get the licences, with a view to negotiating better terms subsequently. In his view, the appropriate course of action was to cancel the licences and invite fresh applicants as well as existing incumbents to bid for them.

Jagmohan was technically correct but there were additional aspects to consider. First, under the NTP 1999, new entrants were being allowed to enter on more favourable terms (mainly revenue sharing and a longer concession period). As the Government itself was changing the goalposts and increasing the degree of competitive pressure, some compensating concession to earlier entrants could be justified. Second, cancellation of the licences in a situation where incumbents had undertaken substantial investments was bound to be challenged in court, which could tie the Government down in litigation for a long time. I was reliably told such litigation could take 10 years or more to resolve; during this period, telecom services would definitely be interrupted.

As Jagmohan was not willing to change his position, PM Vajpayee moved him to the Ministry of Urban Development, took charge of the Ministry of Telecom himself in June 1999, and implemented the migration proposal. The opposition complained that the migration involved a large loss to the Government in terms of the waiver of the amounts due under the old licence regime. The decision was also challenged through PIL in the Delhi High Court. The propriety of the Government taking the decision was also questioned because it had lost the vote of confidence and was only a caretaker government. The Government argued that it was only implementing the Telecom Policy 1999, which had been accepted before the vote of confidence. The court upheld the Government's decision subject to ratification by the new cabinet to be formed after the elections. PM Vajpayee returned to power in the general election in October 1999, and the cabinet ratified the decision within the month.

Subsequent developments have vindicated the migration decision as there was a veritable explosion in telecom connectivity (mainly mobile) in the decade that followed, most of it under the UPA government. It is remarkable that the Government was able to make post-bid changes in the terms of the licences without an outburst of protest. The comptroller and auditor general (CAG) submitted a report on the migration decision and pointed out that there was loss of revenue (though he did not quantify it). But there was no outcry about cronyism and undue favouritism of the kind that erupted 10 years later (*see Chapter 17*).

Y2K: THE MILLENNIUM BUG

The Y2K problem, also known as the Millennium Bug, arose because computer software typically used a two-digit field to indicate the year, which meant that 1999 was written as '99'. But when 1999 turned into 2000, the New Year would appear as '00', which would be indistinguishable from 1900! This could create serious problems in a wide range of industries, especially banking and finance, all process industries where computers were involved in process controls, and also in transport (railways, airlines and air traffic control).

The US and many of the developed countries were taking preparatory action well in advance and Indian software companies were benefitting from the demand for companies that could undertake large-scale rewriting of software. We were late in getting off the ground, but towards the end of 1998, a Y2K Action Force was set up under my chairmanship, which included as members, key secretaries of the government and public sector banks, as well as representatives of industry associations. Our task was to identify the critical sectors that needed to be protected and get a sector-specific action plan prepared by the relevant organizations, monitor its implementation, and also have plans ready to deal with post-1999 problems, should any arise. We quickly identified 11 sectors as critical: banking and finance, insurance, telecommunications, power, civil aviation, railways, petroleum and natural gas, ports, space, atomic energy and defence. Remedial plans were prepared for each of these and widely publicized.

We would be ruining a brand image if we failed to ensure Y2K compliance within India. We also needed to publicize our efforts and the well-known advertising firm Lintas helped to design a slick publicity campaign based on a series of catchy ads featuring well-known faces proclaiming 'India is winning the fight against the Millennium Bug', with a few additional sentences of punchy text. Having become a spokesman for Y2K compliance, I had to agree to be featured in some of the ads, but I was in very good company. The other ads featured informally posed photos of A.P.J. Abdul Kalam; fashion designer Ritu Beri; Chairman Hindustan Lever, Keki Dadiseth; and cricketer Ajay Jadeja.

I was holidaying with my family in Goa on New Year's Eve, and I confess I had a twinge of anxiety, hoping that all would go well. We were not the only ones nervous. British Airways announced that their chairman would board a flight before midnight on 31 December, to be in the air when the millennium turned. This was to reassure passengers that there was no danger of airplanes falling off the sky because of some malfunction in the software or in an embedded chip!

As things turned out, we (and indeed other countries) passed the test with flying colours. The millennium dawned with no disasters. Inevitably, people wondered whether the whole thing was overblown, and there was never a problem anyway. However, it could equally be argued that the reason nothing happened is because of all the precautions that were taken. I recall a story I had read in the newspapers about a Swiss pharmaceutical unit that, before it undertook corrective action, forwarded its clocks to the year 2000 to see what would happen. It was reported that the plant came to a grinding halt in 90 seconds. Whatever the truth about the extent of the real danger, Y2K proved to be a boon to Indian software, exposing Indian companies in this sector to world markets.

All things considered, the Vajpayee government made a major contribution in endorsing the message of continuity in India's economic reforms. The BJP was expected to favour a lowering of direct taxes, reducing control over the Indian private sector and building better quality infrastructure, and to be more proactive in privatizing the public sector. However, it was not expected to endorse the opening of the economy to foreign trade and investment. By doing so, it succeeded in convincing most observers that India's democratic polity had evolved a new consensus on economic policy. I have often described this as a strong consensus on weak reforms!

11

THE IMF INTERLUDE

Towards the end of 2000, I received a phone call from an international headhunting firm asking if I would consider applying for the position of director of the new Independent Evaluation Office (IEO) of the IMF. The IEO was being set up as part of the reform of the Fund prompted by the criticism of its handling of the East Asian Crisis of 1997. The new office was expected to conduct an evaluation of the actions of the IMF to increase transparency of its functioning and improve future performance by learning from the past. They said my name had cropped up in their consultations from many sources. I told them that while I thought the establishment of an independent IEO was indeed an important institutional reform, I was not looking for a new job.

Several weeks later, early in 2001, the same firm contacted me again to say that they had narrowed the applicants down to a shortlist of half a dozen, but they had been advised to approach me again to see if I would agree to be added to the shortlist. This was a very different proposition. I was not being asked to apply but whether I would be willing to be interviewed at the last stage of a selection process. I was told that the shortlist included a former finance minister as well as a former PM of one of the smaller member countries. This was meant to convince me of the prestige associated with the assignment.

Isher had overheard my side of the conversation and before I could ask for her views, she pronounced, 'I think you should say yes.' I was a little surprised because I knew she was thoroughly enjoying her job as director and chief executive of the Indian

Council for Research on International Economic Relations (ICRIER), a premier think tank in Delhi. Explaining her reaction, she said, 'This does not look like a normal international job. Reviewing the performance of the IMF in handling crises in emerging market economies would involve tremendous learning and may even come in handy if India ever faces such an eventuality,' adding immediately, 'God forbid!' She promised that if I got the job, she would join me a year later after completing her four-year term at ICRIER and giving them time to find a good successor.

I asked Brajesh Mishra for his advice. He said he liked the idea of having an Indian as the first head of the new office and that I should agree to be interviewed. He also said he would inform the PM. I told him that though it was a professional and not a government assignment, it would still be necessary for the Government of India to give full support to my candidature. He assured me of this.

The selection committee decided against personal interviews in Washington DC for fear of the names going public. They decided to interview everyone by video link, including the one candidate who happened to be in Washington DC, to ensure a level playing field. I told them we had an excellent facility in the Planning Commission but they said it would have to be in a private facility to ensure secrecy, and had made arrangements with one in Safdarjung Enclave in South Delhi. When I went across to take a look, I was surprised to find only a modest-sized private residence. I telephoned the Fund board secretariat to ask whether they were sure it was good enough. They assured me that it had been recommended by Microsoft; Bill Gates had used it when he needed a discreet video link in Delhi. I had to concede that if it was good enough for Gates, it was good enough for me!

The interview was conducted by a committee of the IMF board and other board members were free to sit in, albeit outside the range of the camera as they would all have to vote on the recommendation of the committee. Soon after I reached home, I got a call from a reporter from *The Economic Times* about being interviewed for the job. I could not deny the report and, sure enough, it was splashed on the front page of the paper the next day. I wondered how it would all turn out if I did not get the job. As it happened, the offer came through shortly thereafter.

Before leaving Delhi, I paid a farewell call on PM Vajpayee. I thanked him for appointing me as a member of the Planning Commission and the EAC-PM. I told him I had enjoyed my stint in the commission and learnt a lot, but that I had a suggestion: to change the name of the institution. The name 'Planning Commission' gave the impression of a Soviet-style central planning institution, micromanaging every aspect of the economy. With the collapse of Communism, there were no planning commissions left in the world; even the Chinese had changed the name of their Planning Commission to the National Development and Reforms Commission. I suggested we rename it the National Commission for Restructuring and Reform. He listened carefully and, after a long pause, said, 'You have a point but how does the name matter? Our planners can always do what they think is necessary, while leaving the name the same.' Then, relapsing into Hindi, he said, 'Arre bhai, naam badalne se Left aise hi naaraz ho jayegi (If we change the name, the Left will be unnecessarily annoyed).'

SETTING UP THE IEO

I arrived in Washington DC in June 2001 and got down to the business of setting up the IEO from scratch. The most remarkable thing about the experience was the flexibility to choose my team. In the Government of India, whenever a vacancy arose, I had to select a suitable candidate from a panel of eligible names prepared by the Department of Personnel. I had now moved to the other extreme in recruitment, where I had the flexibility to approach anyone, anywhere in the world! And salaries at the Fund were attractive enough to get the best.

My first substantive decision was to have a deputy director from within the Fund. I thought if the IEO was going to criticize the functioning of the institution, its credibility would be enhanced if the No. 2 position was filled by an insider. I got in touch with David Goldsbrough, a British national who was chief of the India division at the time of the 1991 IMF India programme and was deputy director of the Latin America and Caribbean Department. David knew the Fund very well but also had empathy for the country point of view. I wasn't sure he would be willing to leave his position in a large and important operational department to move sideways into a new but small department. He asked for some time to think it over, but a few hours later he phoned back to say he would be happy to come. It was the best administrative decision I made in the IEO. We quickly moved to recruit the rest of the staff, a majority of whom were from outside the Fund.

The board had already decided that the director of the IEO would be completely independent from the Fund management and report directly to the board. In the spirit of infusing transparency in working, we worked out a modus operandi to decide the subjects for evaluation. We began by posting online a set of possible subjects to review each year, inviting comments and suggestions for new subjects. Based on feedback from stakeholders, the director would choose the work programme for the year, which would then be submitted to the board for approval. The Fund management would have no say, though we agreed we would not review any ongoing programme.

I also proposed—and the board agreed—that in addition to interviewing Fund staff, the IEO would have access to all internal files, including minutes of meetings of staff relevant to a programme being reviewed. However, we agreed that minutes of meetings between the managing director and representatives of borrowing countries would not be automatically made available, as this might compromise the confidentiality essential for the Fund's functioning. I made it clear from the very start that the focus of our reviews would not be to pin responsibility for mistakes made by the Fund on individuals. Rather, we would look at how the Fund conducted itself in the specific operation being reviewed, with a view to identifying weaknesses and drawing lessons for the future.

Isher joined me in Washington DC by the start of the second year and took up a teaching assignment as a visiting professor at Maryland University, teaching development economics at its School of Public Policy. We bought a house for a down payment of only 10 per cent, with mortgage financing covering the rest. Credit for home purchases was to become even more readily available in the US a few years later when anyone, not just well-paid international civil servants, would get mortgages practically thrown at them. I recall I was confidently told by the real-estate agent that I simply couldn't lose money on buying a house, provided I held it for three years. It was this kind of irrational exuberance that fed the property boom that produced the subprime crisis of 2007, which led to the financial collapse in 2008. At that time, I thought we would be in Washington DC for the next five years and did not think twice about purchasing a house on a loan.

EVALUATIONS FOR THE FUND

The main function of the IEO was to subject Fund programmes, including the underlying thinking that guided these programmes, to critical review. The principal audience for our reports was the Fund board, which could be said to represent the member countries, both developed and developing. However, we also had to carry credibility with a larger community of stakeholders. This included the Fund management and staff, the broader economic policy community, and the very vocal critics of the Fund that had come up in the wake of the Asian crisis. Many of them believed the Fund was using economic principles derived from developed country experiences that did not work in developing countries in quite the same way.

We completed five independent evaluations during my period in the IMF. Of these, I found two to be particularly instructive because they had lessons for India: a study of recent capital account crises that evaluated the Fund's role in Korea and Indonesia in 1997 and in Brazil in 1998; and the evaluation of Argentina's currency crisis of 2001–2002.

An important point to note is that each country's policy response had a major influence on the outcome. Korea was badly hit initially, with GDP falling by 6.7 per cent in 1998, but it rebounded quickly to record 10.9 per cent growth in 1999. External financial support mobilized by the Fund clearly helped but the speed of recovery had much to do with Korea's own policy response. Korea sought IMF assistance in December 1997 when a presidential election was underway. The Korean people resented the IMF laying down conditions for funding and viewed it as a loss of national sovereignty and prestige. Kim Jae Dung, the opposition candidate in the election, had campaigned to end cronyism among the chaebols (large family-owned business conglomerates), which was widely viewed as one of the underlying causes of the excessive lending that led to the crisis. He won the election and was able to get the Korean people to rally behind the new government and accept temporary pain as the economy adjusted. Steps were taken to control the chaebols, declaring many of them bankrupt. The government clearly communicated what it intended to do in the area of bank restructuring, and was rewarded with an early return to normalcy.

In sharp contrast, the Indonesian response was much less surefooted. The country suffered a bigger decline in GDP (a fall of 13 per cent in 1998) and had a much slower recovery thereafter, with poverty increasing in the post-crisis period. There was an unwillingness to recognize the scale of the problem in the banking system, partly because some of the private banks were owned by politically connected elites, including members of President Suharto's family. Corruption scandals involving the president's family made the situation worse. The associated political uncertainty and domestic social tension contributed to the delay in recovery of investor confidence. This was only achieved when Suharto resigned in May 1998, several months after the crisis erupted.

The IMF also misjudged the Indonesian situation by putting too much emphasis on pushing microeconomic reforms in various parts of the economy aimed at getting rid of market distortions. The primary focus in the middle of the crisis should have been on macroeconomic stabilization, including cleaning up the banking system. The multiple interventions provoked resistance from many vested interests.

The Brazilian crisis of 1998 was very different. It arose from weaknesses in the public sector that were reflected in rising fiscal deficits. The government attempted to offset the deficits by a tight monetary policy, but this only raised interest rates and further weakened the fiscal position because of high debt ratios. It was in some ways a classic case for fiscal correction, which was the IMF's usual remedy. A common wisecrack at the time in Latin America was that IMF stood for 'It's Mainly Fiscal'. In Brazil in 1998, it was indeed mainly fiscal! The fiscal tightening recommended by the Fund was the right remedy and it was administered well. The currency was also allowed to depreciate to a more credible level. Both the IMF and the Brazilian government acquitted themselves well in the crisis.

The Argentina crisis in 2001/2002 was among the most severe currency crises of any. I watched it unfold live while I was at the IEO. In 1991, Argentina had put in place a currency board-type regime meant to counter inflationary expectations by pegging its currency, the peso, at a 1:1 parity with the US dollar, while capital flows were freely allowed. In a properly functioning currency board, the domestic currency is supposed to be fully backed by an equivalent amount of reserves in US dollars, which gives the fixed exchange rate credibility. The Argentine system did not observe this discipline and soon ran into problems. When interest rates for emerging market countries increased in the wake of the East Asian crisis of 1997, Argentina's interest payments on its sovereign debt increased. Its fiscal deficit increased and so did its debt-to-GDP ratio. Soon thereafter, the devaluation of the currency of Brazil, its main competitor, in the wake of the Brazilian crisis of 1999, presented another external challenge. Argentina did not have the option of devaluing its own currency to maintain the competitiveness of its exports because it was committed to the hard peg under the currency board arrangement.

The 1:1 parity with the dollar made the exchange rate highly overvalued leading to a widening current account deficit. Argentina kept borrowing to pay for imports. Mounting requirements of servicing its debt led the country to declare a default on its sovereign debt. To prevent an outflow from accounts in Argentinian banks under the free capital mobility regime, these accounts were frozen. This led to an immediate loss of confidence and the collapse of the currency regime. After having been at 1:1 parity with the US dollar for 10 years, the exchange rate collapsed to 1.4 peso for $1 in January 2002 and to 4 pesos for $1, four months later.

The IEO evaluation of the Argentina crisis was completed by June 2004. I approved it as director in 2004 but could not be present in the board when the report was discussed because I had returned to India by then. The IEO faulted the IMF for not warning the Argentine government clearly during its regular surveillance activity that its fiscal policy was inconsistent with the hard peg. Had it done so, Argentina might have been encouraged to plan for an earlier exit from the currency board arrangement instead of the highly disorderly and disruptive collapse it actually experienced.

The collapse was relevant to the larger debate on whether developing countries aiming at free mobility of capital should allow the exchange rate to float freely or aim for some degree of exchange rate stability through central bank intervention. The conventional wisdom at the time—much endorsed by leading US economists and the IMF—was that countries wanting full mobility of capital must either choose a clean float (i.e. no central bank intervention) or a currency board-type hard peg.

From India's perspective, the Argentinian collapse showed that hard peg arrangements do not work if the implicit discipline they require in fiscal policy is unlikely to be achieved. I thought the

Argentina experience made respectable the 'mixed strategies' that we and most other developing countries were following, in which capital mobility was not completely free and the exchange rate was flexible, but not a completely free float. The central bank would intervene when necessary. It also pointed to the fact that fiscal imbalances in the face of high debt ratios can lead to a sudden loss of confidence. This lesson for India is as relevant today as it was 10 years ago.

INDIA ON OUR MINDS

Although my work in Washington DC had nothing to do with India, India was always on our minds. There was a large community of Indian professionals in the World Bank, International Finance Corporation and IMF and we all followed developments at home very closely. The image of India had changed considerably from the last time we were in Washington DC in the 1970s. In those days, India was seen to be lagging behind other developing countries in economic growth. As mentioned before, thirty years later, we had begun to be seen as an economy showing the results of the reforms introduced in 1991, with Goldman Sachs identifying India among the 'BRIC' countries best placed to grow rapidly and contribute significantly to global growth.

The extraordinary success of the IT and software industry in India had much to do with the change in image. A friend visiting from New Delhi was surprised when I told him there was more interest in India in the development community than before but India rarely made it to the US newspapers — and when it did, Bangalore was mentioned more often than Delhi! The city had even contributed a new verb to the English language: when someone's job was outsourced, he/she was described as having been 'bangalored'. The scale of outsourcing at that time was still modest and the overall employment position in the US was much better, so there was none of the public antipathy towards outsourcing that emerged later.

UNEXPECTED ELECTION RESULTS

As the general election of 2004 approached, we started following events at home more closely, greatly aided by the Internet that provided ready access to Indian TV channels. The NDA campaigned under the slogan 'India Shining', which seemed quite reasonable from afar and was consistent with the country's changing image.

Most Indian analysts and opinion polls predicted an NDA victory but the results were a surprise. Unlike in the past, the Congress had entered into a number of seat-sharing alliances with regional parties to consolidate the anti-BJP vote. The strategy paid off handsomely. When the results were declared, the NDA dropped from 270 seats in the Lok Sabha to 181 in 2004. The Congress and its multiple allies—the DMK, Nationalist Congress Party (NCP), Rashtriya Janata Dal, All India Trinamool Congress (TMC) and other smaller parties—won 218 seats. They formed a post-poll alliance, the UPA, which included the Left Front as part of the Alliance although not participating in the Government. There was also a promise of support from the Bahujan Samaj Party, led by Mayawati, in the event of a no-confidence motion moved by the BJP. Evidently, the UPA was comfortably placed to form a government.

Sonia Gandhi had led the election campaign as Congress president and we all assumed she would become PM. The BJP was quick to raise the issue of her foreign origin. Uma Bharati, Madhya Pradesh CM, called on all political parties to rally against a person of foreign origin becoming PM. A day later, Sushma Swaraj proclaimed that she and her husband would rather resign their seats in Parliament than address Sonia Gandhi as 'Madam Prime Minister'. A few days later, K.N. Govindacharya of the RSS launched a nationwide Swabhiman (self-respect) Movement.

Isher and I watched the drama unfold via the Internet. The time difference was very convenient. We would watch Indian TV in the morning while sipping our tea to get an update on the events of the day just ending in New Delhi, and watch again at night to catch the early morning news of the next day in India. Contrary to expectations, Sonia Gandhi declared she would not take up the prime ministership, attributing the decision to what she called her 'inner voice'. Like other Indians overseas, we watched online the pandemonium in the Congress party, with MPs and party workers repeatedly appealing to her to reconsider. One former MP in the crowd outside her residence was reported to have climbed atop the roof of a car with a pistol, threatening to blow his brains out in protest! Sonia Gandhi stood her ground. She would remain the chairperson of the UPA and therefore the political head of the ruling coalition. On 18 May, she announced that Dr Manmohan Singh would be the PM and head of the UPA government.

As soon as the news was confirmed, we telephoned Dr Singh in New Delhi to offer our congratulations. He thanked us and said I should come back and help him. I told him he could count on my return whenever he wanted. I was scheduled to visit Beijing in a few days to deliver a lecture to a group of investors on the state of the global economy and India. Isher was travelling with me as we had planned a short holiday in Xian to see the famous clay warriors. We decided to route ourselves via Delhi and call on our new PM.

I left the IEO and the US a couple of weeks later to join the new government. I had the satisfaction of successfully setting up an organization within the IMF that has grown from strength to strength. In my view, the IEO has contributed to an understanding of the weaknesses in various Fund policies and practices. Most important, it convinced me that the establishment of such independent evaluation offices can richly contribute to the work of governmental and official bodies.

With my mother Pushp at the age of 2

*With my father Jagmohan Singh,
in 1962*

*With my sister Anjali and brother Sanjeev
in Dehradun, 1961*

The Delhi University contingent for the Youth Festival of 1962 with PM Jawaharlal Nehru; I am standing on the extreme right

Queen Elizabeth II visited the Oxford Union in 1968 during the presidency of William Waldegrave (seated centre). The photo includes current and past officers of the Union. I was a former president of the Union, and am standing fourth from the left. Former PM Harold Macmillan, who was then Chancellor of the University, is seated on Waldegrave's left

*With Isher on our
wedding day in 1971
in Washington DC*

*Relaxing on vacation in the woods outside Mussoorie
in 1982*

*Isher and I holidaying in Gulmarg with our sons Aman and Pavan in the summer
of 1986*

Isher and I, with PM Rajiv Gandhi and Smt. Sonia Gandhi at his residence in 1986. The occasion was a get-together for him to meet his staff

On board PM Rajiv Gandhi's airplane during his visit to the US in 1985. Natwar Singh, Ronen Sen, Suman Dubey, Abid Hussain and I are standing. Seated with the PM are Foreign Secretary K.P.S. Menon, Sarla Grewal and Sharada Prasad

Backstage – Behind PM V.P. Singh and Mikhail Gorbachev, president of the Soviet Union, in the Kremlin on the PM's first visit to Moscow in July 1990. I.K. Gujral, foreign minister, who later became PM, is to V.P. Singh's left.

Signing an India-France Bilateral Agreement in the presence of the respective countries' PMs, Narasimha Rao and Pierre Bérégovoy, in 1992

With Finance Minister Manmohan Singh and members of the Budget Group in 1994. Expenditure Secretary K. Venkatesan; Minister of State, Finance, Chandrasekhara Murthy; and Revenue Secretary B. Sivaraman are to the right of the PM. I was the finance secretary and am standing to his left, along with Chief Economic Advisor Shankar Acharya

The Budget group with Finance Minister Chidambaram, just before the Dream Budget of 1997. Standing behind are Revenue Secretary Sivaraman, Expenditure Secretary N.K. Singh, I and Chief Economic Advisor Shankar Acharya

At the release of the report of the EAC-PM, by PM Vajpayee in 2001. Some of the others in the picture are Amaresh Bagchi, Rakesh Mohan, Ashok Gulati, Bimal Jalan, I.G. Patel, K.C. Pant, Kirit Parekh and Yashwant Sinha. N.K. Singh can be seen between the PM and Kirit Parikh

At the IEO, with my deputy David Goldsbrough and Raghuram Rajan, chief economist of the IMF, 2003

PM Manmohan Singh administering the oath of office to me as deputy chairman, Planning Commission, 2004

With Shri Narendra Modi, then CM Gujarat, at the Planning Commission

With CM Punjab, Amarinder Singh, at the Planning Commission

With Lord Patten of Barnes, Chancellor of the University of Oxford, just before receiving an honorary doctorate in Civil Laws, in 2008. When I complimented him on his splendid regalia, complete with a liveried page to hold up the trailing gown, he responded, 'My position as Chancellor is best described as impotence assuaged by grandeur.'

At the India–China border at Nathula with Isher

At Pakhiralaya in the Sundarbans, pedalling a cycle thela, with Isher sitting behind, in March 2008

In Kohima, Nagaland, with Isher and CM Nagaland, Neiphiu Rio

With Isher, Amartya Sen, PM Manmohan Singh and Gursharan Kaur at the PM's residence, 2008

With Dilip Kumar, Isher and others celebrating our honorary PhD degrees from Guru Nanak Dev University, Amritsar, 1997

With US President George W. Bush at the White House in September 2008, shortly before the signing of the US-India Nuclear Deal

At the reception given by Queen Elizabeth II at Buckingham Palace for the G20 Summit in London, in April 2009

Members of the India-US CEO Forum with US President Barack Obama and PM Manmohan Singh at the White House during the PM's state visit to the US in 2009. I am standing second from the right

Being introduced to Chinese President Xi Jinping by PM Manmohan Singh during an official visit to China in 2013

Speaking at the High Level Thematic Debate on 'State of the World Economy and Finance in 2012' at the United Nations headquarters in New York

With the PM of Japan, Shinzō Abe

Receiving the Padma Vibhushan Award from President Pratibha Devisingh Patil in 2011

Part Four

12

THE UPA: AN UNUSUAL COALITION

The UPA government was a coalition, but that was not particularly remarkable. All Indian governments after 1989 had been coalitions and two—under Narasimha Rao and Atal Bihari Vajpayee—had actually served a full term. But the UPA was different. The Congress had only 145 seats in the Lok Sabha and the UPA coalition had only 218 of the 272 needed for a simple majority. It was the outside support of the Left parties with 59 MPs that gave it a majority. This was an inherently more fragile arrangement with no spoils of office binding the parties providing support from outside.

The biggest difference, however, was that PM Manmohan Singh was a technocrat with no political base of his own. Sonia Gandhi had led the Congress to victory and had chosen him over other Congressmen who felt they had stronger claims. Questions were raised about how this arrangement would work. Party spokesmen said there would be no problem: she would run the party; and the PM, the Government. This was clearly an oversimplification because she was not just the head of the Congress party organization. She was its undisputed political leader and the final decision-maker on cabinet positions. As chairperson of the UPA, the allies saw her as the final authority for resolving any differences that might arise with the Congress. She also chaired the UPA-Left Coordination Committee, which made her the focal point for reconciling differences between the Government and the Left.

Manmohan Singh was fully aware of the constraints this imposed on him and even described himself once as an 'appointed'

PM. It limited his authority, not only among the allies but his senior Congress colleagues. It was a situation without precedence but it reflected political reality. We all hoped it would work in practice.

A SECOND CHANCE IN GOVERNMENT

As I had promised, Isher and I called on PM Manmohan Singh in Delhi on our way to Beijing and he asked once again if I would be willing to resign my position in the IMF and join his government. I reiterated that I would be delighted to do so. He had in mind either a senior advisory position in his office or the post of deputy chairman of the Planning Commission. I felt I would be more useful to him at the Planning Commission because I could use the position to try and push policy changes in different ministries while building productive relationships with the states. He said he would consult Sonia Gandhi and get back to me soon. Isher and I flew off to Beijing for my talk with investors.

The next day, in the course of the dinner following my address, I received a phone call from the PMO in Delhi to say my appointment as deputy chairman was being announced that very evening and that I should return as soon as possible. Impressed at the speed at which decisions were being taken, we cancelled our planned visit to Xian and booked a flight to Delhi instead.

Journalist Pallavi Aiyar, daughter of my old friend Swaminathan Aiyar, was posted in Beijing at the time and had got the news of my appointment. She traced me to the hotel and asked for an interview—a scoop for her as the first TV interview of the deputy chairman designate! I agreed, but other than expressing my happiness at the opportunity, I avoided any specific statements that might suggest preconceived notions about what needed to be done before I had even talked to the PM. At the end of the interview, Pallavi charmingly asked whether I would be willing to carry the videotape back with me for telecast as they didn't have satellite connectivity from China. I consented to act as a courier though it did strike me that I could be accused of egregious self-promotion by carrying the footage of my own interview for airing in Delhi! However, I was impressed by her dedication in tracking me down and felt she deserved the scoop.

Back in Delhi, I called on the PM to thank him for the announcement. He said to me, half-teasing, 'You know this is a coalition government and it may last only a few months. Are you sure you would like to give up a highly paid job for this?' I did not rise to the bait and said emphatically, 'It would be worth giving up the highly paid job even if it were only for a few weeks.' I informed the PM that I had already conveyed to the IMF board my intention to resign. The board had understood the exceptional nature of the request and agreed. I only had to return to Washington DC to fulfil the formalities.

To my surprise, many of our older Indian friends in Washington DC discouraged me, expressing doubts about how long the Government would last. I think they perceived the election results as a rejection of the India Shining campaign and were fearful that economic policy would shift away from reforms. None of these doubts worried me. I knew I was being given a chance to make a contribution, working under someone I greatly admired. I could not possibly pass up this opportunity. As Anne Krueger, an old friend who then held the No.2 position in the IMF, had said, 'It is not just an opportunity of a lifetime but an opportunity of several lifetimes.' We quickly arranged to put the house we had bought barely two years ago up on sale. I left for Delhi within a few days; Isher stayed behind to take care of all the arrangements for the return and joined me in Delhi a month later.

One of the first things I did was to call on Sonia Gandhi. I had met her earlier on a few occasions when I was a member of the Rajiv Gandhi PMO, but she was not in politics then. Now, she was the most important political personality in the ruling coalition. I thanked her for the confidence she had reposed in me by agreeing to appoint me deputy chairman. I did not refer to it but I knew the Left had wanted another candidate for the post, and by agreeing to my appointment she must have used up some political capital.

Before the meeting ended, she said I would often be told by people that some government project that had come to the Planning Commission was of special interest to her, in the hope that I would expedite its clearance. I was to ignore all such requests. If there was anything she wanted to communicate to me on a policy issue or otherwise, she would do so herself. It was a very useful communication. In the 10 years I was deputy chairman, she never spoke to me about any project. But people would often drop her name in connection with a project we had to clear. It was much easier to let the system work as it should because of what she had told me.

Before taking over, I also called on K.C. Pant, the outgoing deputy chairman, with whom I had worked as Planning Commission member before I left for the IEO. He said he had no specific advice for me as I knew what the commission did, but was happy I was back.

I mentioned to the PM that I planned to call on all the cabinet ministers but asked if there was anyone else he would like me to meet. He suggested I call on Harkishan Singh Surjeet, general secretary of the CPI(M). It was the dominant party in the Left Front and its support was critical for the stability of the Government. Unlike the Chinese Communist Party, which had accepted the logic of market-oriented economic reforms, the CPI(M) remained suspicious of economic liberalization, viewing it as a neo-colonial idea imposed by organizations such as the World Bank and the IMF acting on behalf of their major shareholders. I had seen reports in the press that the Left parties were unhappy with my appointment as I had come 'straight from the International Monetary Fund'.[36] I felt a meeting with Surjeet would give me an opportunity to clarify my position on economic policy.

Harkishan Singh Surjeet, or Comrade Surjeet as he was commonly called, was 88 years old and had been in politics for over seven decades. He offered me tea and biscuits. He was visibly

---

[36]*The Hindu*, 18 June 2004.

frail but I knew that he exercised undisputed control over the CPI(M) politburo. I began by saying that I was aware that many of the ideas I had pushed in my earlier stint had been opposed by his colleagues but explained that they had been adopted by most developing countries, including China. All these countries were encouraging private investment and greater integration with the global economy, and India could not afford to be left behind. Addressing the assumption of the Left that these policies do little for the poor, I gently contended that it was perfectly possible to design growth-promoting policies that would reduce the extent of poverty and produce widespread benefits. In fact, a strategy to improve the living conditions of the masses could only succeed in the context of rapid overall economic growth and I hoped to combine both objectives in our plan strategy.

The grand old man of the CPI(M) heard me out patiently. While he did not endorse my point of view, he did not express his disagreement or disapproval either. Somehow, the fact that I had made my position clear to the most important political personality on the Left, and had not been rebuked for doing so, was a source of comfort in the years that followed when I had to face younger representatives of his party adopting a much more aggressive and confrontationist line.

THE NATIONAL COMMON MINIMUM PROGRAMME

The parties that formed the UPA had campaigned against the NDA's India Shining slogan on the grounds that it was too elitist and urban-centric, and were expected to come up with an alternative strategy. This was outlined in a National Common Minimum Programme (NCMP) that was adopted shortly after the Government was sworn in. The Left had declared that it would support the Government only as long as it adhered to the NCMP. The Government also set up a National Advisory Council chaired by Sonia Gandhi, which would monitor progress in implementing the NCMP.

The NCMP was adopted before I returned to India. I read it very carefully because I knew that any initiatives I would take in the Planning Commission would have to be consistent with it. There was much in the NCMP with which I fully agreed. It called for strengthening performance in agriculture, which had slowed down under the NDA, and I also thought this should be a priority. It emphasized the need to do more on education and health. These areas had indeed been neglected, and I felt better performance in these sectors would not only improve welfare directly but serve as preconditions for rapid growth.

The NCMP also identified a number of pro-poor programmes to achieve inclusiveness. I thought there was definitely a role for such programmes; however, their effectiveness critically depended upon the implementation capacity of states. And the scale on which they could be rolled out depended on our ability to raise tax revenues, which in turn crucially depended on the rate of GDP growth, a linkage often ignored by those who advocated these programmes.

The NCMP did not neglect growth. In fact, it set a target of 7 to 8 per cent growth in GDP, which was significantly higher than the 6 per cent achieved under the NDA. The problem was that it said little about the policies needed to encourage this growth. This was a weakness but I felt there were at least three signals that were clearly reformist. The NCMP endorsed macroeconomic stability by reiterating the targets laid down in the Fiscal Responsibility and Budget Management (FRBM) Act 2003. It rightly emphasized the importance of infrastructure such as roads, ports, power and railways for economic growth, stating the need to attract private investment in infrastructure. Finally, it sent a positive signal by declaring that the country could easily absorb FDI 'two to three times the present level'. There were many more issues relevant for a full-blown growth agenda but I thought serious progress on these three would constitute a significant step forward.

GRAPPLING WITH POLITICS

Our first task in the Planning Commission was to prepare a mid-term appraisal of the Tenth Plan (2002–03 to 2006–07), which would become the basis for our approach to the Eleventh Plan (2007–08 to 2011–12). Over the years, the commission had evolved a practice whereby the mid-term appraisal was prepared largely by officials in the commission and various ministries with some economists from outside the Government. I felt we needed wider consultation with professionals and domain experts.

We set up 19 consultative groups, each chaired by a member of the Planning Commission. A total of 450 experts from different segments of society, including academics, representatives of industry organizations, trade unions and NGOs, were included in these groups. Among them were 15 experts from UN agencies such as the World Bank, ADB and United Nations Development Programme (UNDP), as well as international management consulting firms such as McKinsey and Boston Consulting Group. The inclusion of experts associated with 'foreign organizations' evoked a strong protest from the Left. Four top leaders—Prakash Karat of the CPI(M), A.B. Bardhan of the CPI, Abani Roy of the Revolutionary Socialist Party and Debabrata Biswas of the All India Forward Bloc—issued a joint statement on 8 September 2004 complaining that the inclusion of these individuals was a breach of sovereignty.

Fourteen of the 15 were actually Indian citizens and there was only one foreign national, who had done a great deal of work on water in India. Among the 14 was Feroza Mehrotra, who had only recently retired as advisor in the Planning Commission and joined the UNDP after retirement! I wrote to each of the four Left leaders explaining there was no loss of sovereignty as we were not outsourcing the preparation of the mid-term appraisal to these groups. They would only provide inputs for the Planning Commission to consider before we prepared the appraisal.

I received no response to my letter and some prominent Left-leaning economists in the consultative groups threatened to withdraw unless the individuals being objected to were removed. They said we could consult them separately if we wished but they should not be part of the groups. I pointed out that it was much more transparent to include them so everyone could hear what they had to say. But this argument cut no ice.

It was clear that the Left criticism was part of a broader signal of unhappiness about the functioning of the UPA government. A few days earlier, A.B. Bardhan had expressed disappointment that the UPA government was formulating policies without consulting the Left.[37] He referred specifically to the announcement in the Budget speech of the intention to raise the foreign equity cap in telecom, civil aviation and insurance, and the announcement of the Foreign Trade Policy on 31 August. The idea that all policies would be discussed with the Left before they were announced was clearly not practical, and I wondered what it meant for the future.

The response of the Right was mixed. BJP spokesperson Yashwant Sinha attacked the Left for its criticism but the *Organiser*, a mouthpiece of the RSS, echoed the Left by describing the decision to invite foreign experts as a 'blow to India's sovereign status.' When some journalists asked me to comment, I quoted Mahatma Gandhi: 'I want the culture of all lands to be blown about my house as freely as possible but I refuse to be blown off my feet by any.' Arun Shourie telephoned me to say that I shouldn't take the protest as a personal attack as I was only being used to get at the PM. As he put it in his inimitable way, '*Raje ki jaan totey mein hai, iss liye totey ki gardan maroro*' (The king's life is in the royal parrot, so twist the neck of the parrot). It was not a very flattering description of my role but I got the point.

Looking for a way to end the deadlock without expelling people we had consciously invited, I suggested to the PM that the best course would be to disband all the groups and revert to

---

[37]*Indian Express*, 6 September 2004.

separate consultations with different individuals or groups as was the practice earlier. He agreed, and that is what we did.

I was very encouraged to find many young MPs taking a keen interest in policy challenges. Milind Deora, a young, first-time Congress MP from Mumbai whom I knew personally, told me that several younger MPs cutting across party lines were keen to have a discussion on policy issues. He hosted a lunch at his residence for me to meet them. The group included Jitin Prasada, Jyotiraditya Scindia, Madhu Yaskhi and Lagadapati Rajagopal from the Congress; Manvendra Singh and Dushyant Singh of the BJP; and two MPs from J&K: Mehbooba Mufti of the People's Democratic Party and Omar Abdullah of the National Conference.

The MPs asked a range of pertinent questions to which I gave frank answers, trying to avoid formula responses. The next day, *Business Standard* reported one of the MPs as saying, 'We felt we were talking to someone who was an expert but did not talk down to us.' It was the best compliment I could get. It was particularly reassuring that MPs who would inevitably take confrontational positions in Parliament determined by party whips wanted to meet and discuss issues in a professional manner. I have always told the various think tanks in Delhi that they should do more to involve interested MPs across parties in public discussions on policies.

We busied ourselves with preparing the mid-term appraisal, which was completed in April 2005, and then got down to preparing the Eleventh Plan. By the end of 2006, we had completed extensive consultations on the draft approach to the Plan and got it approved by the NDC. As the economy had been growing robustly, we raised the growth target range from 7 to 8 per cent indicated in the NCMP to 8 to 9 per cent. When the Plan was finally approved, the target was set at 9 per cent.

13

INDIA HITS PEAK GROWTH UNDER UPA

U PA saw India hit a high growth path with GDP growth averaging 8.4 per cent in the five years from 2004–05 to 2008–09. This was much faster than ever in the past and especially commendable because the global slowdown had lowered growth to 6.7 per cent in 2008–09. We managed the impact of the global crisis fairly well and the economy experienced robust growth in both 2009–10 and 2010–11. Thereafter, it ran into a bump in 2011–12 and slowed down in the last two years.[38]

PRIVATE INVESTMENT: A DRIVING FORCE

The investment boom was led by the private corporate sector. Private investment is largely affected by government policies, expectations about future policies and the prevailing global economic environment. The global environment was, of course, very positive but the sharp acceleration in economic growth during this period went well beyond what could be explained by the global tide. The presence of Dr Singh as PM was a strong confidence-building factor. He had initiated the economic reforms in 1991 and it was natural for the business community to believe that the economy was in safe hands.

---

[38]The Central Statistical Organization revised the national accounts series in 2015 and issued a new series with base 2011–12. GDP growth rates used in this book are based on the old series up to 2011–12 and the new series for the years 2012–13 and 2013–14. The growth estimates (based on the new series) for the two years 2012–13 and 2013–14 are higher than those from the old series. There are many problems with the new series, which are mentioned in the epilogue.

The rate of private corporate investment more than doubled from 6 per cent of GDP in 2003–04 to 14.3 per cent in 2007–08, the year before the crisis. It dipped to 10.3 per cent in 2008–09 but this decline was offset by a rise in investment by the informal sector, farmers and households (largely investment in housing). Total domestic fixed investment increased from 24.5 per cent of GDP in 2003–04 to 32.3 per cent in 2008–09 (*see Table 1*).

Table 1: Macroeconomic indicators (UPA–1)

	Per cent per annum					
	2003–04	2004–05	2005–06	2006–07	2007–08	2008–09
GDP Growth (factor cost)	8.0	7.1	9.5	9.6	9.3	6.7
Inflation (WPI*)	5.5	6.5	4.5	6.6	4.7	8.1
Exports of goods & services (in US$)	25.2	29.2	25.9	24.9	29.4	13.3
	Per cent of GDP					
Gross Domestic Savings	29.0	32.4	33.4	34.6	36.8	32.0
Gross Capital Formation	26.8	32.8	34.7	35.7	38.1	34.3
Gross Fixed Investment	24.5	28.7	30.3	31.3	32.9	32.3
of which						
Private Corporate	(6.0)	(9.1)	(11.8)	(12.5)	(14.3)	(10.3)
Private Households	(11.8)	(12.7)	(11.2)	(10.9)	(10.6)	(13.5)
Public	(6.7)	(6.9)	(7.3)	(7.9)	(8.0)	(8.5)
Foreign Direct Investment	0.7	0.8	1.1	2.4	2.8	3.4
Gross Fiscal Deficit						
Centre	4.3	3.9	4.0	3.3	2.5	6.0
Centre + States	8.3	7.2	6.5	5.1	4.0	8.3
Current Account Deficit	+2.3	–0.4	–1.2	–1.0	–1.3	–2.3

Source: Ministry of Statistics and Programme Implementation, National Accounts Statistics (2014–19) and RBI, Handbook of Statistics (RBI; 2013, 2019)

*wholesale price index

Fiscal discipline, which had been explicitly endorsed by the NCMP, was an important achievement in the first four years of the UPA.

Table 1 says it all. The central government's fiscal deficit declined from 4.3 per cent of GDP in 2003–04 to 2.5 per cent in 2007–08, the lowest it has ever been. The combined deficit of the Centre and states fell by 4.3 percentage points of GDP, which meant funds that were earlier used to finance the central and state government fiscal deficits were now available to finance private investment. All this happened in a period when domestic savings were also buoyant, increasing from 29 per cent in 2003–04 to 36.8 per cent of GDP in 2007–08, the highest ever, before falling to 32 per cent but still high in the crisis year.

A positive attitude towards FDI was another factor boosting investor confidence. The very first Budget speech of UPA 1 announced that the ceilings on foreign equity holdings would be increased from 49 per cent to 74 per cent in telecommunications, from 40 per cent to 49 per cent in civil aviation, and from 26 per cent to 49 per cent in insurance. The increases in the telecommunications and civil aviation sectors were implemented within a few months and attracted significant inflows. Raising the FDI limit to 49 per cent in insurance presented a problem because it required a change in legislation. Both the BJP and the Left opposed the necessary change in legislation. The BJP changed its position when the NDA came to power in 2014 and the Bill was passed in 2015. In effect, the reform to allow larger FDI in insurance was delayed for 10 years for purely political reasons.

Manmohan Singh was keen to signal that the UPA government welcomed FDI. When he first visited New York as PM in September 2004, he met with a group of businessmen of Indian origin and invited Victor Menezes, then vice chairman, Citibank, to put together a group of Indian American businessmen to make recommendations on what we should do to attract investment from the US. Victor collected an impressive group including Indra Nooyi, Gururaj 'Desh' Deshpande, Vinod Khosla, Anshu Jain, Romesh Wadhwani, Vikram Pandit and Parag Saxena, and they submitted a very practical report containing a number of important suggestions, many of which were incorporated into policy.

A year later, we set up the India-US CEO Forum co-chaired by Ratan Tata on our side and Bill Harrison, chairman, J.P. Morgan, on the US side. This proved to be a very useful forum for exchange of ideas primarily between the two business groups, but with each government also having a co-chair. I was the government co-chair for the next 10 years and my counterpart was Al Hubbard, assistant to the US president for Economic Policy. The forum was continued by the Obama administration and my counterpart was Mike Froman, deputy national security advisor who later became the US trade representative. The forum provided a mechanism for the private sector on both sides to exchange views, with the governments listening in. Convergence of views among the businessmen helped to identify areas of mutual interest where the government needed to act more forcefully. The forum helped throw up ideas such as the need to have a policy to facilitate the establishment of debt funds to make long-term debt available for infrastructure. The US members of the forum also played an important role in lobbying support for India on the India-US Nuclear Deal (see Chapter 14).

Indian business became decidedly upbeat as the economy clocked high growth rates in the first two years. In October 2006, *The Economic Times* decided to use its annual business awards function in Mumbai to celebrate the 15th anniversary of India's economic reforms. Everyone who was anyone in the business world was there. PM Manmohan Singh was the chief guest. He gave away awards to a distinguished group of business leaders, starting with Mukesh Ambani receiving the Business Leader of the Year award.

The PM used the occasion to share his thoughts on the future course of the economy. Going well beyond what was said in the NCMP, he promised to work towards a more open and efficient economic system with the long-term goal of full convertibility of the rupee. In the interactive session that followed, Anand Mahindra asked the PM what he considered the most important reforms needed in the present circumstances. He responded that for the next 10 to 15 years, we needed to concentrate on infrastructure, labour laws and financial sector reforms. He also said better performance in agriculture was critical for inclusiveness. He added that if growth could be accelerated to 8–10 per cent, the resulting expansion in employment opportunities would create an environment in which labour would be more willing to accept changes in labour laws. All this was music to the ears of his audience.

A HUNDRED SMALL STEPS

I was deeply interested in financial sector reform from my days in the Ministry of Finance. Things looked quite calm on the financial front in 2006 and central bankers were widely celebrated as 'Masters of the Universe', having ensured a long period of steady growth with very low inflation. There was much praise for financial innovations that were said to increase efficiency and reduce risks, and developing countries were constantly advised to allow such innovations more freely in their financial systems.

The only contrarian note was sounded by Raghuram Rajan, then chief economist of the IMF, who delivered a paper at the Jackson Hole Conference[39] in 2005. He warned that much of the financial innovation was increasing rather than reducing the risk in the system. Larry Summers famously described him as a Luddite and the IMF more or less ignored its chief economist's 'warning'.

I was greatly impressed with Raghu's understanding of the working of the financial system. He had returned to his academic position at the University of Chicago by 2007 and I suggested to the PM that the Planning Commission could set up a committee under him to suggest an agenda of financial sector reforms for the next several years. Almost 10 years had passed since the Narasimham-II Committee had set out an agenda for the financial sector and it was time to take another look. The new committee was asked to look at financial sector reform not just narrowly

---

[39]The Jackson Hole Conference is an exclusive annual conference for central bankers, finance ministers, finance experts and academics, sponsored by the Federal Reserve Bank of Kansas and held at Jackson Hole in Wyoming.

in terms of regulation and supervision but more broadly in the context of other macroeconomic developments, including policies on the interest rate, exchange rate and capital mobility. Raghu agreed to chair the committee and submitted a report a year later, in 2008, modestly titled 'A Hundred Small Steps'. It proposed an action agenda that could be adopted one step at a time, which was ideal given the political compulsion to be gradualist. I briefed the PM on the main points in the report. However, the global financial crisis exploded almost immediately thereafter, and the report received less attention than it should have. Nevertheless, the proposed agenda of reform proved extremely useful some years later, particularly when Raghu was appointed governor of the RBI in September 2013, and was able to start acting on some steps.

THE GLOBAL FINANCIAL CRISIS

The global financial crisis exploded in mid-September 2008 when Lehman Brothers, the fourth largest investment bank, filed for bankruptcy. Problems in mortgage-based lending in the US were building up for some time but the collapse of Lehman Brothers was a major event. It sent a ripple of fear through the financial markets. No one knew which bank would collapse next, putting a freeze on inter-bank lending and a general tightening of credit. The New York Stock Exchange nosedived and, for a few weeks, the Dow mirrored its behaviour after the market crash of 1929, which had led to the Great Depression.

This ended the hitherto benign global economic environment we had enjoyed. The change was particularly worrying because India had become much more integrated with the world economy. Our capital account was not fully open, which meant funds could not flow out freely, but we had received substantial volumes of portfolio capital that could, in principle, flow out. We were also dependent on external commercial borrowing and this was an area where new flows could stop suddenly while repayments on past debt would continue.

We had a moment of anxiety when the credit default swap rate (a derivative instrument pricing the probability of a default on bank paper) for both SBI and ICICI quoted in the Singapore market increased substantially. We were worried that if these signals were interpreted by domestic depositors as signalling financial weakness, they might start withdrawing money. It was not a serious danger for SBI, because depositors would assume that the Government would back the public sector bank fully, but the same could not be assumed for a private bank. I was told ICICI had some exposure to Lehman Brothers through its UK subsidiary, but it was small. Nevertheless, there were reports of unusual withdrawals of cash and rumours of some large corporations shifting their deposits from ICICI to SBI.

The Finance Ministry prodded the RBI to announce that any bank experiencing liquidity pressure would receive support. K.V. Kamath, chairman, ICICI, was persuaded to make a public statement reassuring depositors that their money was safe. We avoided a bank run but it made us aware that while internationalization of financial markets brought many benefits, it also increased risks and vulnerabilities.

In October 2008, Finance Minister Chidambaram, RBI Governor D. Subbarao and I participated in a meeting called by the PM to discuss our possible response to the new global uncertainties. It was not normal for a PM to call a meeting on such issues, but the circumstances were exceptional and Manmohan Singh was no ordinary PM. He had a long experience of dealing with the international economy and had also dealt with the 1991 crisis as finance minister. Chidambaram was the commerce minister in 1991 and I was economic affairs secretary. It looked a little bit like old times, except we were not battling a crisis that had exploded, as in 1991. We were only preparing to avoid one.

Both Chidambaram and I argued for fiscal and monetary stimulus to counteract the contractionary impact of the global crisis. The RBI had been steadily tightening monetary policy, which was the right thing to do earlier when GDP growth exceeded 9 per cent, credit was growing rapidly and inflation was edging up. It was now time to change course. The great advantage of monetary policy, unlike fiscal policy, is that it can change course quickly. Subbarao had only recently taken over as governor but I knew him well from his days as finance secretary. I did not want to impinge in any way on the independence of the central bank on monetary policy, but I gave him my assessment as an input.

I said I could understand that the RBI would be reluctant to change policies but the situation had changed completely and a more expansionary stance was necessary to assure markets that we would not allow recessionary trends to gather ground. } I particularly emphasized that while there would be much attention on the repo rate, lowering the CRR may be as important to inject liquidity into the banking system. Subbarao acted quickly and, on 20 October 2008, the repo rate was lowered from 9 per cent to 8 per cent and the CRR dropped from 9 per cent to 5.5 per cent over a month. A series of further reductions in the repo rate brought it to a low of 4.75 per cent in 2009.

The PM set up an Apex Group under his chairmanship to keep the situation under review and ensure a coordinated policy response. It included Chidambaram; Commerce Minister Kamal Nath; C. Rangarajan, chairman of the EAC-PM; and me. Governor Subbarao also participated in some of the meetings. PM Manmohan Singh asked me to contact Raghuram Rajan for his assessment. It was typical of Dr Singh that despite his own expertise and experience, and the presence of many knowledgeable people in his team, he wanted to consult experts beyond the normal government circle for the widest possible advice.

Raghu sent us a note within a couple of days, warning that the negative impact on growth could be worse than what official sources were projecting and there could be a substantial widening of the current account deficit, putting pressure on the rupee. He favoured a lowering of interest rates as growth had decelerated sharply and inflation was not too high. He was not supportive of fiscal expansion, arguing that the underlying fiscal deficit was actually higher than it seemed.[40] He also suggested that the RBI should draw up a contingency plan in case of a run on any financial institution and should try to anticipate stress in particular sectors, notably airlines and real estate. I agreed with most of the note except I felt there was a role for fiscal policy in our situation as the mechanism for transmission of monetary policy was not nearly as smooth in India as in the US. Raghu's note and my comments on it were sent to the Ministry of Finance and the RBI governor.

In mid-November 2008, growing international concern about the potential dangers of the crisis led US President George W. Bush to convene a meeting of the G20 countries at the summit level in Washington DC to discuss ways of limiting the impact of the crisis.[41] The PM attended the meeting accompanied by Chidambaram and me. I was later designated the 'sherpa' assisting the PM in all the G20 summits that followed.

The G20 summit in Washington DC was the first-ever summit-level meeting of the major economies of the world going beyond the G7, which used to meet regularly. It was especially important because it was convened to deal with an ongoing crisis. There was general recognition that the system faced an existential threat and corrective action was urgently needed. However, there were subtle differences in perception across G7 countries. The European members seemed to feel that the problem had arisen primarily because of poor financial regulation in the US. The French, in particular, had strong views that hedge funds and derivatives had added to the instability of the system, and there was need to tighten regulation in this area.

---

[40]This was due to unpaid subsidies because petroleum product marketing companies and fertilizer companies were paid via bonds to be held by the companies, which were not shown as part of the fiscal deficit.

[41]The G20 was a group of important economies constituted in 1999 in the aftermath of the East Asian crisis of 1997, which met regularly at the level of finance ministers and central bank governors to review the world economy. This was the first time it was convened at the head-of-government level, reflecting recognition of the seriousness of the crisis.

The PM used the occasion to get the message across that although developing countries had not caused the crisis, they were likely to be its worst victims, and the global community should ensure they were suitably protected. He emphasized the need to provide additional resources for the IMF as well as the need for the major economies to expand aggregate demand. Along with other developing countries, we were able to get the summit to acknowledge that international financial institutions needed to be reformed to reflect the changing economic weights of the world economy, giving greater voice and representation to emerging market economies.

The meeting ended with a broad consensus that strong action was needed to strengthen the international financial system along with domestic action to stimulate each economy using both fiscal and monetary means. The finance ministers of the G20 were tasked with working out the details.

When we got back to New Delhi, the PM asked me to prepare a note on what we should do, taking account of the discussions at the Washington summit, which could then be taken up in the Apex Group. My note recommended further steps to loosen monetary policy along the lines outlined in Raghu's note, but also some fiscal stimulus in the form of expanded government expenditure on infrastructure. China had introduced a very large stimulus package and I was convinced that a monetary stimulus alone would not suffice. The note also proposed measures to relax some restrictions that existed on external commercial borrowing to ease access to external funds and help finance the current account deficit.

As we grappled with these problems, the country was rocked by a terrorist attack in Mumbai on 26 November 2008. Ten Pakistani terrorists of the Lashkar-e-Taiba group, having slipped into Mumbai from the sea, went on a rampage, opening fire indiscriminately at a number of places using automatic weapons and causing heavy casualties. Some of them also entered the iconic Taj Mahal Palace Hotel where they holed up. It was painful to watch innocent lives held hostage as the siege of the hotel, with smoke billowing out of its windows, continued for three days and was watched live on TV. The total number of deaths (including some foreigners) was 174, while 300 people were wounded. Our security forces were not only caught unawares by the terrorist attack, their response was highly unsatisfactory. Home Minister Shivraj Patil had to resign and Chidambaram was moved to the Ministry of Home Affairs (MHA).

Chidambaram's departure was a loss to the PM's economic team. Manmohan Singh himself took charge of the Ministry of Finance, which swung into action to introduce a stimulus package along the lines discussed in the Apex Group earlier. This included seeking parliamentary approval for additional spending of ₹20,000 crore. Cenvat duties (central government indirect taxes) were reduced by 4 per cent on all items other than petroleum products.

As the PM was holding the finance portfolio, he asked me to take a press conference on 7 December, along with Cabinet Secretary K.M. Chandrasekhar and Finance Secretary Arun Ramanathan, to explain the rationale of the fiscal and monetary steps being taken to counter the slowdown. This was a conscious decision to convey to the market that the Government was acting in close coordination with the RBI. The RBI governor had made a statement on the previous day, reviewing the steps taken since September to relax monetary policy and announcing a further reduction in the repo rate by 100 basis points and other relaxations on credit, including for exporters. The apparent coordination with the RBI was well received by markets. Independence of the monetary authority is an excellent practice for normal times but, in a crisis, markets feel much more comfortable if all relevant wings of the Government are seen to be acting in concert.

RESCUING SATYAM

Barely six weeks after the terrorist attack, the new year brought another shocker. On 7 January 2009, B. Ramalinga Raju, chairman of Satyam Computer Services, wrote a letter to investors, employees and regulatory agencies, confessing to manipulating the company's accounts and siphoning off over ₹7,000 crore. Raju and other senior executives were held for questioning and later charged with a number of criminal offences. The Company Law Board moved to bar the members of the Satyam board from functioning and the Ministry of Company Affairs announced that the Government would appoint a new board to run the company.

I was concerned that we might end up with a board of serving civil servants who would be in no position to handle the problem. I urged the PM that while the investigative agencies must get on with the task of charging those responsible, we should launch a parallel effort to save the company. Satyam was one of the better-known Indian software companies with an extensive global clientele. Its collapse would create a great deal of disruption for clients worldwide and seriously damage India's reputation as a reliable source of software services. Our best bet was to appoint a group of distinguished individuals of impeccable integrity who understood the private sector and ask them to organize a quick takeover by a reputable new buyer, who would move quickly to restart the company. Until that could be done, the new board should make a special effort to reach out to Satyam's clients and reassure them that the company would survive. I suggested we appoint Deepak Parekh, HDFC chairman and one of the most respected figures in the Indian business scene, as chairman of the new board.

The PM agreed and personally told Deepak that he viewed the assignment as very important for India's reputation in the IT sector and that I would explain our concerns to him in detail. He also explained to Minister for Company Affairs Prem Chand Gupta his decision to have a board consisting of individuals from the private sector. It included Kiran Karnik, former NASSCOM (National Association of Software and Services Companies) chairman; Tarun Das of CII; T.N. Manoharan, a well-known chartered accountant from Chennai; and C. Achuthan, former SEBI member. There were no serving civil servants on the board.

All these unconventional decisions were taken by the PM a few days before he heard he would have to undergo heart surgery. In fact, Deepak told me that before going in for the surgery, the PM telephoned him again to say he had appointed Pranab Mukherjee as finance minister and spoken to him about the Satyam rescue effort. As it happened, Deepak had to go to the finance minister because the income tax authorities, suspecting tax evasion by Satyam, had attached the bank accounts of the company, making it difficult for the company to make routine payments. Mukherjee was extremely helpful and advised the income tax authorities not to do anything that would jeopardize the rescue effort under way.

Parekh, Karnik and Das spent the next few days on the telephone talking to Satyam's global clients to inform them that while Raju had confessed to massive wrongdoing and would be dealt with under the law, Satyam would soon have new private management. Their personal credibility must have played a large part in convincing the clients to stay on. The same message was conveyed discreetly to the technical people in the company to ensure they did not leave. Four months later, based on a transparent public auction, Tech Mahindra, a subsidiary of Mahindra and Mahindra, acquired Satyam. It was a satisfactory resolution of what could have been a very damaging development. The PM's willingness to follow an unconventional approach helped to protect India's reputation in the IT world. The rescue of Satyam through an effort led by the private sector was a signal achievement of UPA 1. It created a template that was later used by the NDA government to handle the IL&FS (Infrastructure Leasing & Financial Services) fiasco.

A MANDATE RENEWED

Pranab Mukherjee was the most experienced senior Congress minister in the cabinet and he was instinctively more in favour of an expanded fiscal stimulus than Chidambaram. He announced a third stimulus package in February 2009, which involved further tax cuts. Had I been consulted on this initiative, I would have suggested that any additional stimulus should take the form of expanded investment expenditure rather than stimulating consumption by a tax cut. I knew increases in investment take time to be felt on the ground whereas tax concessions are easily implemented and more quickly reflected in increased consumption expenditure. However, tax cuts are also notoriously difficult to reverse. I must confess I also wondered whether the tax concession was initiated more with the coming elections in mind than the compulsions of macroeconomic management.

The stimulus measures of 2008–09 led to the Centre's fiscal deficit in that year shooting up to 6 per cent of GDP. The states were allowed to increase their borrowing by about 1 per cent of GDP in that year, which meant that the combined fiscal deficit of the Centre and the states more than doubled to 8.3 per cent in 2008–09. Monetary policy was also loosened and the repo rate lowered in a series of steps to reach 4.75 per cent on 21 April 2009, staying at that level for the next 11 months. It was a massive stimulus, but the circumstances were utterly without precedent and China was doing much more.

By March 2009, the PM was back in harness after his surgery. He was deeply concerned about the macroeconomic challenge the Government might have to face if re-elected and asked me to have a note prepared in the Planning Commission with our assessment of what the Government should do in the full Budget if re-elected. Kirit Parikh got down to work, using our in-house model as well as other models developed by research institutions with which we were in touch. We came to the conclusion that we could aim at 7.5 per cent growth if plan expenditure could be raised by ₹50,000 crore (about 1 per cent of GDP) in the regular Budget for 2009–10.

The general election of May 2009 gave the UPA a renewed mandate, with the Congress party increasing its strength in the Lok Sabha from 144 to 206 seats. The news channels were full of PM Manmohan Singh flashing the 'V' sign, with slogans of 'Singh is King', echoing the hit Bollywood movie of the previous year. I was asked to continue as deputy chairman. Unlike the situation with UPA 1, when I took some time to define my agenda, this time the priorities were quite clear. The global crisis was continuing and the immediate task was to counter its impact on GDP growth.

Mukherjee continued the fiscal stimulus for 2009–10 by providing for a sharp increase in plan expenditure but also retaining the substantial cuts in indirect taxes that were announced in December 2008, and again in February 2009. The fiscal deficits of the states were also allowed to widen. As a result, the combined deficit of the Centre and states increased from 8.2 per cent of GDP in 2008–09 to 9.3 per cent in 2009–10.

The Government was criticized in later years for continuing the fiscal expansion in 2009–10 and many of the problems of later years were often traced to this decision. However, I think the circumstances at the time the Budget was prepared justified a continuing stimulus. GDP growth for the last quarter of 2008–09 was down to 3.5 per cent and most observers expected the pace of recovery to be very slow. The IMF projected GDP growth in 2009–10 at 5.25 per cent. Analysts in international investment banks were more pessimistic, putting India's growth at somewhere between 4.5 per cent and 5 per cent. Inflation as measured by the WPI did not appear to be a problem. It had declined sharply in the months preceding the Budget and the 12-month rate of inflation in June 2009 was actually negative at –0.4 per cent. The prospects for global growth were also highly uncertain. The second G20 Summit in London in April 2009 had signalled a resolve on the part of the major economies to provide a stimulus to aggregate demand, but it was not clear how successful they would be.

I thought the finance minister's decision to go for a continued stimulus was justified under the circumstances, especially as he had also requested the Thirteenth Finance Commission to recommend a new fiscal consolidation roadmap. The commission recommended that the central government's fiscal deficit be reduced to 5.7 per cent in 2010–11, with further reductions to 4.8 per cent, 4.2 per cent and 3 per cent, respectively, in the subsequent three years. The actual deficit in 2010–11 was much lower at 4.8 per cent, thanks to the one-time gain from the 3G auction that year. However, fiscal performance went off-track after 2010–11.

The decision to continue with the stimulus in 2009–10 was amply vindicated by the results. GDP grew robustly at 8.6 per cent in 2009–10 and 8.9 per cent in 2010–11 before slowing down. It is reasonable to conclude that our problems arose not because of the decision to continue the stimulus in 2009–10, but the failure to stick to the consolidation path recommended thereafter by the Finance Commission. The fiscal deficit from 2011–12 onwards was much above the path recommended by the commission (*see Table 2*).

Table 2: Macroeconomic indicators (UPA 2)[42]

	Per cent per annum				
	2009–10	2010–11	2011–12	2012–13	2013–14
GDP Growth	8.6	8.9	6.7	5.4	6.1
Inflation (WPI*)	3.8	9.6	8.9	6.9	5.2
Exports of goods & services (in US$)	–3.1	29.1	18.4	0.3	4.1
	Per cent of GDP				
Gross Domestic Savings	33.7	33.7	34.6	33.9	32.1
Gross Capital Formation	36.5	36.5	39.0	38.7	33.8
Gross Fixed Investment *of which*	31.7	30.9	34.3	33.4	31.3
Private Corporate	(10.2)	(10.4)	(11.2)	(11.8)	(11.7)
Private Households	(13.2)	(12.7)	(15.7)	(14.6)	(12.5)
Public	(8.4)	(7.8)	(7.3)	(7.0)	(7.1)
Foreign Direct Investment	2.4	1.7	1.8	1.5	1.7
Gross Fiscal Deficit					
Centre	6.5	4.8	5.9	4.9	4.5
Centre + States	9.3	6.9	7.8	6.9	6.7
Current Account Deficit	–2.8	–2.9	–4.3	–4.8	–1.7

Source: Ministry of Statistics and Programme Implementation, National Accounts Statistics (2014–19) and RBI, Handbook of Statistics (RBI; 2013, 2019) *wholesale price index

---

[42]Growth rates up to 2011–12 are based on the old GDP at factor cost series with base year 2004-05. Growth rates for subsequent years are based on the new series with base year 2011-12. In the new series, the CSO switched from GDP at factor cost to a closely related concept of GVA at basic prices.

Given the many demands to expand developmental expenditure, the key to achieving fiscal discipline was mobilizing more tax revenue. The Vajpayee government had set up a committee chaired by Vijay Kelkar to advise on how the fiscal targets laid down in the FRBM Act (2003) were best met. The Committee's report was submitted to the UPA government in 2004 and it recommended that shifting to the GST would modernize the tax system and ensure revenue buoyancy. The intention of moving to the GST was formally announced by Chidambaram in 2006. The GST was widely regarded by economists, tax experts and business groups as a potential game-changer, which would increase revenues and also generate efficiencies that could raise the GDP by up to 2 percentage points.

Introducing the GST required a constitutional amendment because the taxation powers of the Centre on goods were limited to the production stage and did not extend to subsequent sale. The states also did not have the power to levy a tax on services. The Committee of State Finance Ministers, chaired by Asim Dasgupta, West Bengal finance minister, was tasked with evolving a consensus. A Constitution Amendment Bill was introduced in the lower house by Mukherjee in March 2011 and referred to the Standing Committee, which recommended some changes.

There was strong opposition from the BJP. Gujarat CM Narendra Modi and Madhya Pradesh CM Shivraj Singh Chouhan opposed the Bill on the grounds that it would hurt the interest of states and limit the sovereignty of the state because the tax rates would be left to the GST Council consisting of the union finance minister and the finance ministers of the states. The Bill lapsed with the end of the Lok Sabha term.

As it happened, the BJP changed its tune when it came to power in 2014 and the Amendment was finally passed in 2016 with support from all parties. The GST finally became operational in July 2017. It has experienced many difficulties because of faulty design (see epilogue) but if the BJP had cooperated in passing the necessary legislation in 2011, it would have been in place much earlier, and the fiscal situation could have been brought under control.

THE BOOM-BUST PHENOMENON

The decline of inflation in the middle of 2009 proved to be temporary and inflation picked up in the second half to reach 10.9 per cent in April 2010. The major drivers of this resurgence from mid-2009 were a sharp increase in domestic food prices and increase in international oil prices.

The rise in food prices was not on account of the prices of foodgrains but because the prices of fruits, vegetables, eggs, meat and edible oils increased. High growth had created rising demand for these items. But because of poor marketing arrangements and logistics, high prices paid by consumers were not reflected adequately in higher prices received by farmers, so there was insufficient supply response. I felt we could have offloaded 5–10 million tonnes of foodgrains in the market, which would have softened foodgrain prices, offsetting to some extent the rise in prices of other food items. The publicly held stocks of foodgrains had increased from 35.8 million tonnes in January 2009 to 47.4 million tonnes in January 2010, which was 90 per cent above the recommended buffer stocks. This build-up of excess stocks was the combined result of the production response to the National Food Security Mission and the continuing ban on exports.

The Ministry of Food and Civil Supplies was comfortable releasing stocks of foodgrains at very low prices through 'fair price' shops in the PDS because the loss on that account was covered by a subsidy from the Budget. They were unwilling to incur any loss on account of releasing the stocks in the open market. In internal meetings, I argued that if the objective was to lower the market price, the best course would be to organize auctions at various places, while fixing the reserve price below the market price. This might nudge traders to lower their prices as they would fear aggressive offloading of public sector stocks. Chidambaram, who took over as finance minister in 2012, even offered to cover the loss arising from such market operations from the Budget. But the officials remained reluctant for fear that selling foodgrains below market prices in open auctions might make them vulnerable to the charge of favouring traders. The result was mounting levels of public stocks. I recall commenting at a meeting of the Cabinet Committee on Prices that the public often simplistically attributes inflation to hoarders but we were actually in a situation where the biggest hoarder, and therefore the source of inflation, was the Government of India!

Rising oil prices was the second factor responsible for the upsurge in inflation. Crude oil prices increased from $41 per barrel in December 2008 to $69 per barrel in June 2009 and further to $111 by March 2011. They stayed at that level for the next four years. We could not do much to mitigate the inflationary impact of this global phenomenon. In fact, in December 2008, the cabinet had approved a policy of linking domestic petroleum product prices to world prices but this could not be implemented because, facing an election in May 2009, the Government did not want to pass on the price increase resulting from the heavy surge in international price of crude oil. Prices of domestic petroleum products were raised in June 2009 after the election but the adjustment was much smaller than what was necessary.

I was a consistent advocate of adjusting petroleum prices in line with world prices and was often criticized in the press because it was felt that this would only increase inflation. I tried to explain that while raising the prices of petroleum products would contribute directly to a rise in the price index, it would also reduce purchasing power in the hands of the consumers, thereby reducing the demand for other commodities, which would moderate the rise in those prices. Besides, not raising petroleum prices was only leading to a build-up of unpaid subsidies that would have to be cleared sooner or later, generating inflationary pressure via the Budget. This argument found few takers.

Inflation remained a problem through the end of UPA 2 and

the Government was pilloried on this issue in the months before the general election in 2014. The Raghuram Rajan committee had recommended an institutional response to improve our ability to control inflation by setting an explicit inflation target, but this took time to implement as explained later in this chapter.

The fact that growth in real GDP (i.e. GDP adjusted for inflation) averaged 8.5 per cent in the first seven years of UPA meant that job opportunities expanded. The poor were not hit as hard as might have happened otherwise. The combined effect of better agricultural performance, the boom in construction and the support provided by the Mahatma Gandhi National Rural Employment Guarantee Act (MGNREGA) ensured that the real wage of rural labour grew at about 6 per cent per year between 2004–05 and 2011–12, much faster than earlier, helping to reduce poverty in this period (*see Chapter 15*).

Critics of the UPA sometimes downplayed the high growth of the UPA years by saying much of it was due to favourable global conditions fanned by excess bank lending. This criticism has little merit. Global conditions were indeed favourable but only a well-managed economy could benefit from favourable global conditions. Rapid growth in bank lending is not unusual in a boom. The important point is that it fuelled real growth. The Index of Industrial Production showed an average growth rate of 9.3 per cent per annum between 2004–05 and 2010–11 and many segments such as electrical machinery, communications equipment and the automotive industry showed even faster growth.

Some of the lending turned into non-performing assets (NPAs) later, but the extent of NPAs was fully known by 2015. The NDA government should have taken faster action to resolve the problem by recapitalizing and reforming the banks. This did not happen.

Growth fell to 6.7 per cent in 2011–12 and decelerated further to 5.4 per cent in 2012–13, before turning around modestly to 6.1 per cent in 2012–13[43]. A slowdown after a long period of

---

[43]The growth rates for these years in the old national accounts series (base 2004–05) were 4.5 per cent and 4.7 per cent for 2012–13 and 2013–14 respectively.

high growth is not abnormal. A string of good years generates irrational exuberance, leading to overambitious investment plans and a build-up of excess capacity. This then leads to a slowdown or even a decline in new investment. Once the excess capacity has been 'worked out', investment revives again, getting the economy back on the rails.

Some aspects of this 'boom-bust' phenomenon were almost certainly at work after 2011, but there was more to it. Many attributed the slowdown to the tightening of monetary policy by the RBI beginning in 2010. I did not agree with this view. The RBI had greatly loosened monetary policy after the global crisis in October 2008, which was the right thing to do. It reversed course only in March 2010 after inflation had touched double-digit levels. The repo rate was raised from 4.75 per cent in March 2010, through a series of 25 basis point increases, to 8.5 per cent in October 2011. But as inflation was at 10 per cent, the real interest rate (i.e. nominal interest rate after adjusting for inflation) was actually quite low.

The external environment definitely contributed to the problem. The sovereign debt crisis in Europe that surfaced in 2011 led to a slowdown in global growth and world trade. India's export growth (in US$) decelerated from 29.1 per cent in 2010–11 to 18.4 per cent in 2011–12. Export growth collapsed to 0.3 per cent in 2012–13 and then picked up marginally to 4.1 per cent in 2013–14. Poor export performance at a time when investment was also slowing down was bound to lead to a deceleration in GDP growth.

An important factor contributing in a major way to the slowdown was the emergence of delays in getting environmental and forest clearances, as well as land acquisition for large investment projects. Businessmen complained that civil society activists were intimidating administrators from granting clearances, often going to courts to obtain stays. For their part, civil society activists complained that a culture had evolved whereby project authorities in both the public and the private sectors managed to get environmental clearances that should never have been given.

Companies implementing projects would accept environmental protection conditions they had no intention of complying with once the project was cleared. There was a pervasive belief among civil society activists that environmental regulations could be flouted with impunity, aided by corruption.

Two examples of high-visibility projects that ran into serious implementation constraints illustrate the nature of the problem. Sterlite Industries (India) Ltd, owned by NRI businessman Anil Agarwal, had entered into an agreement with the state-owned Odisha Mining Corporation to mine bauxite on top of a hill in Niyamgiri, to be refined at its refinery at Lanjigarh in Odisha. The Dongria Kondhs, a tribal group living in that area, were opposed to the mining because they believed that the hill symbolized their deity, Niyam Raja. Environmental activists also raised concerns about damage from mining and disposal of waste from the refinery. The Ministry of Environment and Forests (MoEF) sent a team to look into the complaints and withdrew the initial clearance that had been given in 2009. Sterlite appealed against the cancellation, first in the high court and then Supreme Court. The Supreme Court found that the gram panchayats in the area had not been consulted, which was a requirement under the new Forest Rights Act of 2006. Twelve gram panchayats were selected for the consultation and all of them rejected the project in 2013. Evidently, clearances were given initially without full regard to the rules for environmental protection. However, from the investors' perspective, the fact that a clearance given in 2009 could be negated four years later indicated a high degree of uncertainty in the system. The economic basis for locating the refinery in Lanjigarh was that bauxite would be available nearby. The refinery has since been functioning based on bauxite brought in from other places, which has meant higher costs.

The construction of Lavasa town in the Western Ghats by the Lavasa Corporation Ltd, a subsidiary of Hindustan Construction Company Ltd, one of the leading construction companies in the private sector, provides a second example. The town was modelled on the Italian town of Portofino and it had been cleared by the Maharashtra government as a 'tourism' project. It ran into opposition from civil society activists who complained of unacceptable violations of environmental regulations in a highly eco-sensitive region. The MoEF ordered a halt on project activity in November 2010 and sent an expert team to report on the situation. The team found numerous violations and concluded that the promoters and the Maharashtra government had wrongly proceeded on the assumption that central government clearances were not needed. The ministry finally allowed work to be resumed a year later, but only on the condition that certain steps would be taken to remedy the environmental damage. The project promoters claimed the remediation costs imposed were much higher than in other similar cases. The long delay led to an increase in costs and created uncertainty about the project's future, disrupting the marketing effort. The project collapsed and the Lavasa Corporation declared bankruptcy.

Unlike the case of Niyamgiri where the local population was strongly opposed to the project, the local population in Lavasa actually supported the project because of the employment it was expected to generate. The opposition came from NGOs alleging violation of environmental norms and corruption in granting permissions. Indian law permits anyone to approach the courts and seek a stay on a project on grounds of public interest. Heightened public sensitivity to environmental concerns encouraged the courts to be more responsive.

These examples show that we did not have a sufficiently robust system of granting environmental clearances that would stand up to subsequent scrutiny. For their part, regulatory authorities had become hesitant to grant clearances for private sector projects because these were much more likely to lead to accusations of corruption than similar permissions given to public sector projects.

A NEW LAND ACQUISITION ACT

A well-intentioned initiative of the UPA, which became highly controversial, was the attempt to amend the Land Acquisition Act of 1894. This colonial legislation, which governed compulsory acquisition of land by the Government for public purposes, was widely seen as providing inadequate compensation for land compulsorily acquired, with no provision for resettlement of displaced persons. It also did not recognize the customary rights on land by tribal groups living in forests. The term 'public purpose' was also not well defined and could be used to include acquisition for handing over the land to private industry. The West Bengal government under Buddhadeb Bhattacharya ran into fierce opposition when it tried to acquire 1,000 acres of land in Singur district for the Tatas to build an automobile plant to produce the Nano, and again in Nandigram when it tried to acquire 10,000 acres for the Salim Group of Indonesia to build a chemicals export zone. Civil society activists had long pushed for a major change in the law and a Bill was introduced in 2011, which was finally passed in 2013.

There were several provisions in the new legislation that created apprehension. The provision for a social impact assessment before land acquisition was seen as potentially adding to delay. The compensation level was set at a multiple of the officially recorded price based on recent transactions (up to twice the recorded price for urban land and four times for rural land) on the ground that prices were typically understated in the official records. It also provided generous resettlement and transportation allowances, not just for those who lost their livelihood because of the acquisition but also for non-landholders, including those whose livelihood was disrupted. The compensation provisions were also made applicable for 'large' projects, even when land for the project was acquired by project developers in a voluntary sale.

Representatives of industry complained that the new law would increase the cost of land to financially unsustainable levels.

It would also make it easier for anyone wanting to stop a project to use the various consultative processes required under the new law to delay matters. Some of them pointed out that NGOs were at times fronts for other interested parties, including competitors, who wanted to delay the project. ı arranged a meeting in the Planning Commission between industry representatives and Jairam Ramesh, the minister for rural development who was piloting the Bill. Several suggestions were made to introduce some flexibility. Some of these were accepted but business representatives remained unconvinced about the merits of the Bill.

After coming to power in 2014, the NDA initially promised to amend the Bill to remove some of the more onerous provisions, but failed because of political resistance within the BJP.

When the Twelfth Five-Year Plan document came up for approval by the cabinet towards the end of 2012, we highlighted the fact that many large projects were experiencing difficulties getting clearances and this was leading to a slowdown in investment and therefore growth. I suggested we set up a special mechanism to resolve inter-ministerial problems. Accordingly, a Cabinet Committee on Investment chaired by the PM was set up in early January 2013 to review projects of over ₹1,000 crore, which were stuck for want of clearances. In the meeting of the committee in June 2013, the finance minister presented a list of 215 projects. The committee was able to resolve some problems but could not possibly deal with the large number of projects, especially as many of the clearances needed were from state-level authorities.

FDI IN RETAIL

As the economy slowed down in 2011, the Government tried to improve investor sentiment by liberalizing the policy for FDI in retail. Major international retailers such as Walmart, Carrefour, Target and Metro were keen to enter India, in JVs with Indian companies if necessary, but this was a sensitive area that was dominated by small retailers. Business groups such as CII favoured allowing FDI in multi-brand retail as did farmer groups as they felt the entry of multinationals would encourage investment in cold chains and logistics. The Planning Commission had supported FDI in retail as early as the mid-term appraisal of the Tenth Plan in 2005. However, both the Left and the Right (in the form of the Swadeshi Jagran Manch) were strongly opposed. They argued that the entry of multinational giants would hurt small retailers and reduce employment.

UPA had taken some small steps at opening up retail to FDI, such as allowing 100 per cent FDI on an automatic approval basis for B2B operations and allowing foreign equity up to 51 per cent in single-brand retail, subject to sourcing 30 per cent of the turnover domestically. B2B operations helped small retailers by improving their supply facilities and single-brand retail was not a sensitive area for small retailers as they were not selling high-end, single-brand products. It was multi-brand retail (department stores) that small retailers worried about and here the door had remained firmly shut.

In November 2011, the Government made two important announcements. The earlier 51 per cent FDI limit on single-brand retail was raised to 100 per cent. This allowed iconic Swedish retailer IKEA to enter India. IKEA's willingness to accept a domestic sourcing requirement created a window for Indian products to access customers all over the world. The Government also announced that 51 per cent equity would be allowed in multi-brand retail in cities with population above 1 million. The multi-brand initiative evoked strong protest. Uma Bharti said she would burn any stores Walmart would put up in UP. West Bengal CM Mamata Banerjee, an ally of the UPA with 19 MPs in the Lok Sabha, said she was against the move. Tamil Nadu CM J. Jayalalithaa also opposed the move.

In response, the Government modified the policy so that it would be applicable only for those states that volunteered to accept it. This created new problems. Delhi CM Sheila Dixit, from the Congress party, asked for the policy to be notified as applicable in Delhi. However, when the Aam Aadmi Party (AAP) won the election in Delhi in 2013, Arvind Kejriwal, the new CM, asked the central government to de-notify Delhi. The same thing happened in Rajasthan when Vasundhara Raje, the new CM from the BJP, declared that she wanted the state de-notified. The Centre took the view that once a policy was notified as applicable, it could not be reversed by a successor government. The NDA government, which came to power after the 2014 elections, put the policy on multi-brand retail on hold, and no further approvals have been given.

The UPA also opened up real-estate development for FDI, allowing investors to come in and develop entirely new industrial and residential complexes. The initial conditions were relaxed gradually over time and this led to a new type of FDI flow.

THE SHOCK OF THE VODAFONE AMENDMENT

Investor sentiment suffered a major blow in 2012 from Pranab Mukherjee's decision to amend the Income Tax Act retroactively to overcome a ruling by the Supreme Court in favour of Vodafone International. The Indian Income Tax Act 1961 provided that when an Indian asset is acquired from a foreign resident, the buyer (whether Indian or foreign) is liable to pay the capital gains tax that would normally be paid by the seller. The buyer was expected to factor in this liability when settling the price of the transaction. Vodafone International, incorporated in the Netherlands, had bought Hutchison Telecommunications International Limited based in the Cayman Islands, which was a subsidiary of Hutchison Telecommunications Hong Kong and owned 67 per cent shares in the Indian telephone company Hutchison Essar. Vodafone International had not bought any Indian asset directly but it had bought a shell company whose only asset was the shareholding in Hutchison Essar. The Department of Revenue viewed the purchase of Hutchison Telecommunications International as an 'indirect' transfer of the shares of Hutchison Essar to Vodafone, and held the buyer Vodafone liable to pay tax on the capital gains made by Hutchison Telecommunications Hong Kong. The Income

Tax Department won its case in the Bombay High Court but the Supreme Court reversed the decision on 20 January 2012.

The finance minister had invited me to give suggestions for the 2012–13 Budget, and I used the opportunity to convey to him that if we wanted to impose capital gains tax on indirect transfers, we should amend the law prospectively. A retroactive amendment to overcome a Supreme Court judgement would have very negative effects. I was disappointed when I learnt that the ministry had gone ahead with the amendment. The Department of Revenue no doubt felt that a very large amount of tax revenue could be mobilized. The finance minister made what was called a 'clarificatory amendment' to establish that this was the intention of the law all along. The amendment became applicable not only to Vodafone but also a number of other cases in the pipeline, and led to the reopening of several other cases. All these are being arbitrated under bilateral investment treaties and it remains to be seen how it will turn out for net revenue mobilization.

In July 2012, Pranab Mukherjee became President of India and Chidambaram returned as finance minister. Shortly thereafter, Raghuram Rajan joined the Ministry of Finance as chief economic advisor. I was delighted at Raghu's induction into the system. I knew he was keen to return to India but the job he was really interested in was that of the governor of the RBI. This was indeed the logical position for him, given his background and expertise, but I had pointed out to him that it was highly unlikely in our system that a complete outsider would be considered for that position. However, if he came in as chief economic advisor, he would be an insider by the time the job opened up in 2013, at the end of Subbarao's term.

COPING WITH THE TAPER TANTRUM

The new team in the Ministry of Finance had to deal with a difficult situation as the current account deficit had increased from 2.9 per cent of GDP in 2010–11 to 4.3 per cent in 2011–12 and 4.8 per cent in 2012–13. This was much above what was regarded as reasonable and it was financed mainly by larger commercial borrowings and NRI deposits. Loose monetary policy in the industrialized countries had made capital easily available, but there was an obvious danger that a reversal of these policies could lead to outflows that could be very destabilizing. This is precisely what happened in May 2013 when Chairman of the Federal Reserve, Ben Bernanke, testifying before the US Congress, said quantitative easing (QE)[44], which the Fed had been following for some time, would soon be tapered off. The markets read Bernanke's statement to mean tapering was imminent and capital began to flow out from emerging markets including India, precipitating what came to be called the 'taper tantrum'.

Morgan Stanley identified India as one of the 'fragile five' that were vulnerable to a change in market sentiment because of a weak macroeconomic situation. The other four were Indonesia, Brazil, South Africa and Turkey. As capital inflows reversed in May, our fragility became evident. The exchange rate depreciated sharply, crossing ₹60 in early August. This was despite the fact that foreign exchange reserves of almost $20 billion were used up to support the currency in those months. India's credit rating was only one notch above junk status at the time and both S&P and Moody's put the country on watch with a negative outlook.

No finance minister wants a currency crisis on his watch and Chidambaram was understandably concerned. He invited me to a meeting with his officials to discuss the situation. Everyone agreed that some depreciation in the exchange rate was desirable given that the current account deficit had widened considerably and the real effective exchange rate index had appreciated in the past few years. However, it was also important to avoid a loss of confidence leading to a currency collapse.

Chidambaram felt an exchange rate of a little below ₹60 to the dollar reflected sufficient depreciation and the RBI should be

---

[44]A process of increasing liquidity in the system by the central bank buying government securities and, at times, even other securities.

able to hold it at that level. My view was that if we wanted to stabilize the currency, we could not just rely on RBI intervention in the forex market. We had to put in place policies to reduce the underlying current account deficit to a more reasonable level, which meant some fiscal tightening. I also pointed out that in a market-determined exchange rate system, the market was likely to cause the rate to overshoot first, and only then return to a 'reasonable' level. Intervening too early in this cycle risked losing reserves to little effect.

Raghuram Rajan pointed out that much of the widening of the current account deficit reflected a large increase in gold imports, which was really a disguised form of capital outflow. High inflation had made domestic financial assets unattractive and as capital outflows were not freely permitted, there was increased demand for gold as an asset. However, even after adjusting for the effect of gold imports, the underlying current account deficit was well over 3 per cent of GDP, which was unsustainable.

Steps had already been taken to restrict gold imports as a temporary measure by imposing a customs duty and linking gold imports to gold exports. We also recognized that it would be necessary to show credible reduction in the fiscal deficit by cutting expenditure wherever possible. The Ministry of Finance could do this very effectively by simply holding back release of funds. I knew that in practice this meant cutting funds for plan expenditure and I wondered whether, as deputy chairman, I should insist that this not be done. However, faced with a threat of a currency crisis spinning out of control, I felt stabilization had to take top priority. The brunt of the contraction was eventually borne by plan expenditure, with actual plan expenditure in 2013–14 ending up about 18 per cent below Budget estimates.

The rupee continued to depreciate to a low of $1 = ₹67 in late August but then started to improve. RBI also took some actions to ease restrictions on foreign borrowing by corporations and encourage Indian banks to attract NRI deposits as a form of foreign exchange mobilization. Raghuram moved to the RBI in September 2013 at the height of the crisis and his credibility in international financial markets had a lot to do with the fact that the situation stabilized very quickly. The RBI offered swap arrangements to the banks under which it would take the exchange risk beyond a point. By the end of March 2014, the exchange rate recovered to below ₹60 to a dollar as Chidambaram was hoping for, and the current account deficit, which had expanded to 4.8 per cent of GDP in 2012–13, narrowed sharply to 1.7 per cent in 2013–14. It was a good demonstration of the linkage between fiscal policy and the BOP.

The fact that we were able to manage without having to call in the IMF, as we had to in 1991, was an important achievement. The current account deficit in 1990–91 was only 3 per cent of GDP but we had to go to the IMF because our reserves were very low (less than $2 billion) and the Chandra Shekhar government was seen as too weak to take any corrective steps on its own. In 2013, we were in a much stronger position. The flexible exchange rate achieved a significant part of the adjustment that was necessary without provoking any immediate outcry. Foreign exchange reserves at almost $300 billion gave us plenty of time to take corrective steps. The UPA was a coalition, it was under attack politically on corruption issues (*see Chapter 17*), and there was a general election approaching. Nevertheless, markets were willing to believe that the Government was capable of taking corrective action.

It was a lesson in the importance of building buffers that provide time to handle a crisis. I was also reminded of an aphorism often heard during the East Asian Crisis of 1997: 'Confidence grows at the rate a coconut tree grows, but falls at the rate a coconut falls.' In 2013, we were able to prevent this particular coconut from falling by taking corrective action in time.

Raghuram's appointment as RBI governor represented an important innovation in personnel policy because it exemplified a willingness to bring in world-class expertise in senior positions. He moved quickly to implement some of the ideas from the report of the Rajan Committee. Steps within the power of the RBI were implemented early, such as opening entry to small finance banks, liberalizing banking correspondent regulations that allowed for much greater financial inclusion, and freeing banks to set up branches and ATMs anywhere. Others took a little longer.

An important idea proposed by the Committee was the adoption of inflation targeting for the RBI. As RBI Governor, Raghuram promptly set up a committee under Deputy Governor Urjit Patel to work out the modalities. The committee recommended a six-member Monetary Policy Committee (MPC), with the governor having a casting vote. The proposal was approved by Chidambaram just before the end of the term of UPA 2, but he left the final decision to agree with the incoming government after the general election. Finance Minister Arun Jaitley signed off on the proposal and the MPC was set up in June 2016 with the mandate to fix the interest rate within the framework of flexible inflation targeting. It has succeeded in keeping inflation within the target zone.

The introduction of an Insolvency and Bankruptcy Code (IBC) was another extremely important proposal of the Rajan Committee, but work on this started only after the general election. The IBC Bill was introduced by the NDA government in December 2015 and passed in 2016. It is going through the usual teething problems, but is expected to fill an important gap in the financial system, strengthening the rights of secured creditors. Both the establishment of the MPC and the IBC demonstrate the importance of continuity in pushing economic reforms.

14

THE END OF NUCLEAR APARTHEID

One of the most significant achievements of Manmohan Singh was the conclusion of the Indo-US nuclear agreement in UPA 1. It was a critical breakthrough, the importance of which was not well understood in India. Our decision to stay out of the NPT had imposed restrictions not only on the transfer of nuclear technology to India but on a wide range of other critical technologies that constrained us in many dimensions. PM Manmohan Singh rightly believed that the non-proliferation regime had imposed a 'nuclear apartheid' on India and it would be a major long-term gain for our economy if we could get these restrictions lifted.

The Vajpayee government had taken a number of steps to get back to normalcy with the US, following the sanctions imposed after the nuclear test in 1998; that effort had yielded good results. PM Manmohan Singh met President George W. Bush on the sidelines of the UN General Assembly meeting in September 2004 and they discussed the progress of the ongoing talks under what was called 'Next Steps in Strategic Partnership'. There was no hint in those meetings that a breakthrough in civil nuclear cooperation was possible.

TOWARDS A NEW DEAL

The first signal that a deal may be possible came when Secretary of State Condoleezza (Condi) Rice visited New Delhi in March 2005 to convey an invitation from President Bush for the PM to visit the US. She suggested that the US may be willing to explore ways of relaxing the restrictions imposed on India without us having to give up our nuclear weapons capability.[45]

In April 2005, External Affairs Minister K. Natwar Singh led a delegation to Washington DC to prepare for the PM's visit. As Indian co-chair for the Energy Dialogue and chair of a separate Economic Dialogue we were going to launch with the US, I was part of the delegation. The visit began with a call on the US president on 14 April. I had been to the White House 20 years earlier when PM Rajiv Gandhi visited in 1985 and again when PM Narasimha Rao visited in the 1990s but this was my first entry into the sanctum sanctorum of the Oval Office in the West Wing. It was also my first exposure to President Bush.

I was impressed by the President, who spoke clearly without any notes on many aspects of the India-US relationship through the half hour or so of the meeting. He seemed genuinely impressed by India as a functioning democracy and said he was determined to use his second term to build a strong Indo-US relationship. He mentioned that he found it particularly impressive that we had a Muslim population of 120 million and, as he put it, 'not a single one of them has joined Al Qaeda'.

In the course of the meeting, he specifically mentioned nuclear cooperation with India. He said the world needed to move away from coal to cleaner energy to combat climate change, but as public opinion in the US had turned against nuclear plants, he couldn't make the switch. However, he could make a major contribution to reducing emissions by helping India develop nuclear energy as an alternative to coal. He said he would like to remove the restrictions that prevented cooperation between our two countries in this area. He never mentioned the possibility that this might generate business for the US nuclear industry, though it may well have been at the back of his mind.

PM Manmohan Singh's visit was scheduled for mid-July. Foreign Secretary Shyam Saran went to Washington DC in advance

---

[45]Saran, S. *How India Sees the World: Kautilya in the 21st Century*, Juggernaut Books, 2017.

to negotiate the text of a joint statement that would be issued during the visit. Other members of the team were Joint Secretary (Americas) S. Jaishankar, who was to serve as foreign secretary, and is our current external affairs minister in the Narendra Modi government. Our ambassador to the US, Ronen Sen, whom I knew well from our days in Rajiv Gandhi's PMO, was part of the negotiating team.

The PM arrived in Washington DC with the rest of us on 17 July and was given the draft prepared by the team and cleared by Natwar Singh and Secretary Rice. The PM immediately called a meeting of the senior members of the delegation to review the draft. It mentioned that President Bush would seek agreement from Congress to adjust US laws and policies to enable full civil nuclear energy cooperation and trade with India. It also mentioned that the PM agreed to separate India's nuclear reactors into civil and military, and place the civilian reactors under International Atomic Energy Agency (IAEA) safeguards. This meant that fuel, equipment and technology obtained from outside could be transferred to the safeguarded civilian reactors. The military reactors would be completely free of any scrutiny and could produce weapons-grade plutonium for nuclear weapons based on indigenous technology and domestically produced uranium, but could not use imported fuel, equipment or technology.

We knew the agreement would be criticized at home. The Left parties were opposed to any closeness to the US and would oppose the agreement on principle. The BJP would criticize the Government for accepting too many conditions. Our Department of Atomic Energy (DAE) had legitimate concerns. They had successfully developed an entirely indigenous nuclear energy capability despite severe restrictions on technology and trade, and did not feel we needed imported reactors. There was an understandable suspicion that the US may be entering into an agreement only because they wanted to sell us their equipment. There was a historical trust deficit arising from the fact that the US had reneged on fuel supply for Tarapur after India's atomic test in 1974, even though there was nothing in the original agreement on Tarapur that called for such a reaction. On the other hand, the DAE was aware that we could not have scaled up our nuclear effort without the deal as we did not have enough domestic uranium and could not import it as long as the technology restrictions were in place.

The PM understood that no deal would be acceptable at home if it did not have the DAE fully on board. Dr Anil Kakodkar, chairman of the AEC, was a member of the delegation and the PM had made it clear that he would not accept any draft unless Kakodkar was fully satisfied. When we met to discuss the draft, both Natwar Singh and Saran indicated it was fully in line with the mandate they had received and the details would be worked out later. However, Kakodkar felt some of the wording could be interpreted to our disadvantage in the course of negotiations. Dr Singh stood firm on his decision not to accept any formulation that was not fully acceptable to the DAE. As the US negotiating team had dispersed after the draft was cleared at the foreign minister level, Saran was instructed to inform his counterpart, Under Secretary Nick Burns, that the paragraphs on nuclear issues were not acceptable and the draft statement would have to contain only a bland statement that the two sides would work together to reach a suitable agreement in future.

CONDI SAVES THE DAY

I was disappointed that the visit would not produce a major breakthrough. However, the next morning, as we assembled to go to the White House, I learnt Condi Rice had mounted a successful last-minute rescue effort. Rice reports in her memoirs that when she was informed by Burns, late the previous evening, that the PM could not accept the agreed paragraphs, which would have to be replaced by a bland statement, she promptly informed President Bush who accepted the outcome philosophically. Rice records that she thought, 'If they don't want to get out of the nuclear ghetto, I can't do anything about it.' But she woke up at 4.30 a.m. on that fateful morning, determined not to let go.

She first tried to see PM Manmohan Singh in the morning but failed. She then called on Natwar at the Willard Hotel, who persuaded Dr Singh to see her. At the meeting, she requested one more chance to work out an agreement. The PM agreed and Saran was told to get the changes that would make the draft acceptable to Kakodkar. Armed with these specific demands, Saran went off to a last-minute negotiating session with Burns in a room in the White House while the formal talks proceeded in the Oval Office.

Saran and Burns came up with a satisfactory formulation just as the main talks came to a conclusion. At the press briefing after the talks were over, Burns apologized for a delay in distributing the text of the joint statement because, as he put it, 'some last-minute changes were being included'. Little did the press realize what a hit-and-almost-miss drama had gone on behind the stage!

President Bush moved swiftly to get the US Congress to amend the US Atomic Energy Act (the Hyde Amendment) that would allow nuclear cooperation with India even though we were not a signatory to NPT and had resorted to tests after the NPT was signed. The non-proliferation lobby worked hard against the amendment but it was passed in July 2006. Senator Barack Obama voted against the amendment though later, as president, he supported nuclear cooperation with India. The non-proliferation lobby was also able to build in some provisions in the Hyde Act aimed at penalizing India if it undertook future tests, which were to fuel controversy in India.

The two sides then had to negotiate an agreement under Section 123 of the US Atomic Energy Act (the 123 Agreement). This was the critical operational part of the Indo-US agreement that would indicate the exact nature and terms of the cooperation envisaged. The negotiated text was released by both governments in August 2007. It provided that eight of the 22 reactors would be deemed to be military and not subject to any safeguards. The non-proliferation lobby wanted to allow a much smaller number of military reactors to limit India's capacity to scale up weapons production. Our negotiators ensured that the fast-breeder reactor at Kalpakkam was not in the safeguarded group as it was still a research project, well short of commercial application. The agreement included provisions to deal with situations where the supply of nuclear fuel promised for safeguarded civilian reactors was interrupted. For our part, we agreed to improve the safety standards for our nuclear assets and prevent any transfer of nuclear technology or materials to other countries, which was only an endorsement of the existing position. We also committed to continue the voluntary moratorium on nuclear testing, which had been announced by the Vajpayee government, but were careful not to make this a legal undertaking.

REACTION AT HOME

A few former chairmen of the AEC and other scientists wrote to all MPs, opposing the deal on the grounds that the Hyde Act contained provisions that were much more intrusive than envisaged in the 123 Agreement. The government explained that we were only bound by the 123 Agreement. In any case, President Bush had declared that he viewed the Hyde Act's intrusive provisions as recommendatory and not mandatory. Fortunately, the official scientific establishment supported the deal. I then realized the wisdom of the PM's decision to give Anil Kakodkar a virtual veto on the terms of the agreement.

The next steps in finalizing the nuclear deal was to get an India-specific safeguards agreement with the IAEA to put our civilian reactors under international safeguards, and get a waiver from the Nuclear Suppliers Group (NSG), allowing countries to engage in nuclear trade with India despite India not having signed the NPT. Both were necessary as preconditions for the US Congress to approve the 123 Agreement.

In October 2007, Sonia Gandhi asked me to come and see her. She had never done this before, so I was naturally curious. She said

Prakash Karat had told her categorically that if we proceeded with the deal, the Left would withdraw support. She also said the PM had told her that the Left would keep badgering the Government and if we were to be pushed to the polls in any case, it was better if it happened earlier rather than later. The PM was concerned that if we had a bad monsoon next year, the economic situation could deteriorate, reducing the scope for manoeuvre, and it was best to move quickly. She also told me that he had offered to resign and let her reshuffle the leadership at the top if she wanted. She wanted me to urge the PM not to resign. He had the full weight of her support and that of the party, but neither the party nor the allies wanted an early election.

Sonia Gandhi said she did not think the nuclear deal was an issue on which to risk an early election. I agreed with her that this was not the time for the PM to force an election. In fact, I pointed out that in the course of the Hindustan Times Leadership Summit in Delhi a few weeks earlier, an aggressive questioner, referring to the opposition to the nuclear deal, asked whether the deal was being abandoned. The PM himself had responded by saying we were not a 'one-issue' government. She asked me to brief the PM on our conversation and convey to him that this was not the time to resign.

I reported the conversation to the PM, including my view, and pointed out that the public did not fully understand the benefits of the nuclear deal and a much stronger effort was needed to educate public opinion. I felt we had not adequately emphasized that the waiver from the NSG, which prohibited members from engaging in nuclear trade with any country that was not a signatory of the NPT, would not just open the door for the US to collaborate with India but allow such collaboration with other countries. In effect, by helping us obtain an NSG waiver, the US would be opening many doors for us that would otherwise remain completely closed. He did not reveal his mind in our conversation but I was happy to find that he did not resign at that time.

Meanwhile, the Left hardened its position. In August 2007, Karat said the honeymoon with the UPA may be over but the marriage can go on. By February, the Left parties said the Government would have to choose between the nuclear deal and its own stability, setting a deadline of 15 March for the Government to indicate its intentions. The Left knew the IAEA safeguards agreement was an essential step before the US Congress could approve the 123 Agreement, so it concentrated its efforts on preventing the Government from going to the IAEA.

On 25 June 2008, Sonia Gandhi again asked me to come and see her. She said she had been told by many people that the PM was thinking of resigning and it would be a disaster for the party if he did, as none of the allies were keen on an early election. My response on this occasion was different from a year earlier. I had agreed then that it was premature to risk an election on this issue but now felt the situation had changed. The issues involved had been adequately explained in public and we had reached a point where the credibility of the Government would be affected if we appeared paralysed by a Left veto. I informed her that I had already told the PM that the right course, in my view, was to go to the IAEA and take the risk of the Left pulling out. She heard me out and asked me to convey the gist of our conversation and her views to the PM, which I did that very day.

I have no idea whether they discussed the issue further but we know that the PM stood firm and sent the draft agreement to the IAEA shortly before leaving for a G8 meeting in Japan in early July.

THE GOVERNMENT SURVIVES

True to its word, the Left withdrew support on 8 July. The PM sought a vote of confidence in the House on 10 July. It was tense as both the Left and the BJP were on the same side. The opposition from the Left was not a surprise but the opposition from the BJP was mystifying. Brajesh Mishra, former principal secretary and national security advisor to PM Vajpayee, had supported the deal. The PM told me that he had also spoken to former PM Vajpayee explaining that what the Government had done was the logical culmination of the efforts at rapprochement begun by him. He said Vajpayee seemed to agree but expressed helplessness. The BJP's opposition could only be explained by unhappiness that the Manmohan Singh government had pulled off an agreement that brought India out of the nuclear wilderness—an agreement the BJP would have loved to sign had it been in power.

Fortunately, the Samajwadi Party, led by Mulayam Singh, came to the rescue. Manmohan Singh told me later that he had asked former president A.P.J. Abdul Kalam, one of the team of scientists that had supervised the nuclear test in 1998, to speak to Mulayam and persuade him of the merits of the nuclear deal. Kalam's support was critical in getting the Samajwadi Party to support the Government on this occasion.

DIPLOMACY AT WORK

The IAEA agreement presented no problems. It was India-specific because we, unlike other non-weapon NPT signatories, would also have military reactors that would be completely free from IAEA scrutiny. Chairman Mohamed ElBaradei was extremely well disposed towards India and very helpful, a beneficial consequence of the excellent relationship the AEC had developed with the IAEA.

The next step was getting a waiver from the 45-member NSG, which was necessary to be able to get the US Congress to approve the 123 Agreement. A 'clean waiver' (without qualifying conditions) was of great value as it would allow any other country to engage in nuclear trade with India subject to its own laws.

Our diplomats fanned out to lobby individual governments extensively, but this was an area where the US played a critical role. In the first meeting of the NSG, in early September 2008, there was opposition from some smaller countries (Austria, New Zealand, Ireland). Many others were willing to support a waiver but with conditions that were unacceptable to us. The NSG agreed to meet again a few days later. By then, President Bush had personally spoken to many of the leaders, indicating his interest in the waiver and the recalcitrants came around. He also personally called President Hu Jintao of China to make the same point. China informed us at the last minute that it would not oppose the waiver and a clean waiver was granted on 6 September 2008. I have no doubt that this would not have happened without American arm-twisting.

President Bush sent the text of the 123 Agreement to the US Congress on 11 September. US Congressional rules required a notice of 120 legislative days for such a legislation to be taken up. Had these rules been insisted upon, there was no way the legislation could have passed, as there were only 40 legislative days left before the end of the session. The Bush administration managed to get the rules waived. The Indian Embassy also did its bit to marshal support. The Indian diaspora, admirably mobilized by Ronen, played an important role in lobbying Congress. American members of the Indo-US CEOs Forum, set up under the Economic Dialogue, also lobbied both Houses to support the agreement.

The 123 Agreement was passed by the House of Representatives on September 2008 with a vote of 298 to 117 and by the Senate with a vote of 86 to 13. Senator Obama, then readying for his presidential bid, voted for the agreement but only after moving a few amendments that would have been unacceptable in India. I mention this only to point out that the non-proliferation lobby had much stronger roots in the Democratic Party than among Republicans.

MAKING HISTORY

The 123 Agreement was finally signed in Washington DC on 10 October 2008 by Secretary of State Condoleeza Rice and External

Affairs Minister Pranab Mukherjee[46]. The importance of this achievement remains unappreciated. The Government of India never projected it domestically as a major achievement as it was controversial to begin with. Critics in the US made much of the fact that the US was not able to sell nuclear reactors to India because India's nuclear liability regime did not come up to American expectations. However, getting nuclear reactors from the US was never our prime objective. It was to remove restrictions on trade in nuclear materials to allow us to import uranium, which was in short supply. It also allowed us to import reactors from France and Russia, potential suppliers who were less demanding on nuclear liability. The real importance of the nuclear deal was that it paved the way for lifting a number of these restrictions and opened the door to a much wider range of cooperation in defence. The expansion of our defence purchases from the US, with possibilities of manufacturing in India, which are now being explored under the 'Make in India' policy, would not have been possible if the technology restriction had not been removed.

Manmohan Singh's quiet leadership was the critical driving force that made the nuclear agreement a success. He put together a team of key players and got them to cooperate and be part of the consensus that evolved. Leading from the front was particularly important because many in the Congress party were ambivalent about the deal. They worried about the political consequences of seeming to get too close to the US, because they feared loss of support from the Left and were also concerned that closeness to the US would alienate Muslim voters. At critical points, the PM had to mobilize political support from outside the party, such as from Dr Kalam who spoke to Mulayam to support the Government. The PM was able to navigate the choppy political waters with skill and patience and keep his party on board. He certainly could not

---

[46]Mukherjee took over following Natwar Singh's resignation in 2006, after the latter was named by an Independent Inquiry Committee set up by the UN Secretary General and headed by Paul Volcker to report on possible improprieties in the Oil for Food programme.

have achieved this without the support of Sonia Gandhi who was fully aware of the party's ambivalence.

The PM's excellent personal rapport with President Bush also helped. It must have been difficult for the US president to appreciate the many constraints on PM Manmohan Singh when he was himself taking bold initiatives disliked by the non-proliferation lobby in the US. I saw a glimpse of Bush's personal regard for Dr Singh when he was in Washington DC on a working visit in September 2008. The Troubled Asset Relief Program (TARP), a key US Treasury initiative to deal with the financial crisis, was being piloted through a reluctant Congress. President Bush invited the PM and a few members of his delegation to a small working lunch at the White House. The PM began the discussion by thanking the president for meeting us at a time when he was greatly preoccupied by the efforts to persuade Congress to approve TARP. Bush paid him a charming compliment: 'Mr Prime Minister, I cannot think of anyone else I would rather meet at a time of crisis. You have a very calming effect on people!' I thought it was a very perceptive remark.

One must also acknowledge the significance of Rice's personal intervention on the morning of the talks. If she had behaved as most other foreign ministers, the matter would have been left to senior officials who would have found it impossible to get to the PM. While one could argue that the agreement would have happened later anyway, this assumption is questionable. The next meeting of the PM and the president would have probably taken place only a year later. As it is, the process of negotiation was prolonged and the approval of Congress to the 123 Agreement was only obtained in the last three weeks of the Bush administration. A delay would have pushed the culmination of the deal into the next administration and the Democrats had many more committed non-proliferationists. Rice was responsible for the initial shift in policy by Bush to build a stronger relationship with India. And her determination to have one more go to save the agreement in the early morning of 18 July was critical in bringing it to a historically important conclusion.

15

INCLUSIVE GROWTH

The UPA was committed to achieving high growth that was also inclusive. The strategy for ensuring inclusiveness included a special focus on agriculture, which had earlier been neglected, combined with a parallel thrust at helping the poor through a number of programmes. The pro-poor programmes received much more political attention than faster growth in agriculture. This was because these were seen as directly helping the target group, whereas the benefits from better agricultural performance were indirect.

PRO-POOR PROGRAMMES

In early 2005, the PMO announced Bharat Nirman, a four-year programme to develop rural infrastructure based on repackaging existing schemes. By the time the Eleventh Plan was approved in 2007, there were eight flagship schemes to promote inclusiveness: Sarva Shiksha Abhiyan (primary education); Mid-Day Meal Scheme; Mahatma Gandhi National Rural Employment Guarantee Scheme (MGNREGS); Rajiv Gandhi Rural Drinking Water Mission; Total Sanitation Campaign to provide toilets in rural areas; National Rural Health Mission; universalizing Integrated Child Development Services; and the Jawaharlal Nehru National Urban Renewal Mission (JNNURM). All these schemes, except JNNURM, were a continuation or restructuring of schemes that existed earlier.

JNNURM was a new initiative aimed at upgrading city infrastructure and improving service delivery. It was the first time the central government put urban development on the planning agenda. The mission was aimed at improving and augmenting the economic and social infrastructure of cities; e.g. upgrading road and transport infrastructure, drinking water, waste management, slum rehabilitation and public parks, as well as affordable housing and basic services for the poor. It was launched in 2005 with partial funding from the Government of India, linking such support to specific reforms at the state and local government level. To ensure holistic city development, projects had to be part of a city development plan and state governments had to share in the financing of the projects.

The pressure to provide funds for the flagship schemes limited the financial resources available for investing in infrastructure, which was crucial for growth. We therefore turned to PPPs to take on some of the burden. The importance given to PPPs was often criticized by NGOs as the state's abdication of its responsibility, but it was the logical consequence of responding to the demands for increased funding for pro-poor and social-sector schemes.

A distinctive feature of the UPA's strategy was to anchor pro-poor programmes in a 'rights-based approach', which converted the benefits from pro-poor programmes into legal guarantees. The National Employment Guarantee Act 2005 and the Forest Rights Act 2006 under UPA 1 were followed in UPA 2 by the Right to Education Act (RTE) 2009 and the Food Security Act (FSA) 2013. The establishment of legal entitlements was expected to strengthen the ability of intended beneficiaries to demand the benefit as a right. I had my doubts about how effective this would be in practice.

For example, the RTE would enable a child from a poor family to demand admission to a government school. This demand could be enforced, but it would not guarantee good quality education. That required wide-ranging reform to improve the system of schooling, which cannot be enforced through the courts. The legal right would be more effective when it came to preventing government from acting in a manner inconsistent with guaranteed rights. For example, the Forest Rights Act, which prescribed a procedure before granting environmental or forest clearances, could be effectively enforced by the courts, as was done in the Niyamgiri and Lavasa projects.

The Right to Information (RTI) Act 2005 was a game changer, making it much easier for anyone working for the interests of the poor to access information that would reveal how decisions are taken. It continues to be widely used, though some recent changes made by the NDA government to the terms of appointment of the information commissioners have created apprehension that this critical institution may be weakened.

A STRATEGY FOR AGRICULTURE

The importance of agriculture for inclusiveness followed from the fact that just over half the population at that time (now down to 45 per cent) derived most of their income from agriculture and the percentage was even higher if the lower income groups were included. Faster growth in agriculture could be expected to lead to faster growth in the income of small farmers as well as real wages of agricultural labour. I found it disappointing that none of the NGOs that were strong supporters of pro-poor programmes were equally supportive of policies to enhance agricultural growth. They tended to think that these would benefit only large farmers, leaving the poor unaffected.

When the approach to the Eleventh Plan was approved at the NDC meeting in December 2006, with a target GDP growth of 8 to 9 per cent, the PM also announced the objective of doubling the growth rate in agriculture from about 2 per cent in the past to at least 4 per cent in the Eleventh Plan period. A strategy paper for agriculture was presented at a special NDC meeting in May 2007. It highlighted the fact that growth of productivity per acre in agriculture had slowed down in many crops and many states were not realizing their full potential.

The strategy paper pointed out that planning for agriculture had traditionally been dominated by the objective of increasing the production of foodgrains to ensure food security. However, demand for foodgrains was unlikely to exceed 2 per cent per year. The target growth of 4 per cent for agriculture could only be achieved through faster growth in non-foodgrain items like vegetables, fruits, eggs, dairy, meat and floriculture. Demand for these products was much more income-elastic and could be expected to increase much faster.

The NDC decided that the Centre would introduce a new Food Security Mission in states where there was potential to increase the productivity of foodgrains. It also decided that states must evolve district-specific programmes for agricultural development in the non-foodgrains area. A new centrally sponsored scheme (CSS) would be launched to provide enough flexibility in implementing these programmes.

Abhijit Sen, the planning commission member in charge of agriculture, and I decided that we should initially club different existing CSS in agriculture into one umbrella scheme and let the states have a greater say in the implementation of this scheme. Instead of guidelines set by the Centre, the choice and approval of projects would be left to a committee chaired by the chief secretary of the state, in which representatives of the Ministry of Agriculture and Planning Commission would participate as members. The share of each state would be determined transparently on the basis of a formula based on area of land cultivated. After discussing the matter with senior officials in the Ministry of Agriculture, Abhijit and I called on Agriculture Minister Sharad Pawar to seek his support. We explained that the new scheme would give the states much more flexibility. As the Budget for 2007–08 had already been approved, the total allocation for the new scheme for the current year would be the total of the individual schemes. But if it worked well, we would ensure large increases in allocations in later years. Pawar readily agreed with the proposal and the Rashtriya Krishi Vikas Yojana (RKVY) was born.

The scheme proved very popular with state governments. The simple change from senior state government officers coming to Delhi to get their projects approved to the new procedure of officials from Delhi going to the state capital to attend the meetings chaired by the chief secretary shifted the balance of decision-making in favour of the states. The new RKVY began with an allocation of ₹1,000 crore in 2007–08 (13 per cent of the total allocation for agriculture) and increased to ₹7,053 crore by 2013–14 (37 per cent of the allocation). We kept our promise to Pawar.

MGNREGS was conceived as an employment-generating programme in rural areas but I felt that with proper project selection, it could help increase land productivity and contribute to faster agricultural growth. As water was a major constraint for land productivity, I felt we should work towards giving priority to projects dealing with water conservation and management. In 2007–08, the programme had a budget of ₹12,000 crore, which was more than the total central plan allocation for agriculture of about ₹8,000 crore in that year. These funds were also likely to be expanded considerably in future.

NGOs were strong supporters of MGNREGS but not happy with our approach of directing the programme towards enhancement of land productivity. They viewed it as a rights-based programme that needed to be 'people-driven' with the choice of projects left entirely to the gram sabhas and panchayats. I could see the merit of local-level decision-making, but I also felt that a strong nudge in the direction of water conservation projects would have a lasting impact on rural incomes and employment. Some activists believed MGNREGS should not be used to construct assets on privately owned land as that amounted to an implicit subsidy to landowners. However, if we wanted to increase land productivity we had to include projects on privately owned land for land levelling to improve irrigation flow or digging small ponds and shallow wells on private farms.

Mihir Shah, who joined us as a member in 2009, had run an NGO in Madhya Pradesh and had great credibility with NGO activists, who otherwise viewed the Planning Commission as too 'growth-fixated'. He managed to first get an agreement to allow such projects only on land owned by farmers from SCs and STs. Later, we were able to extend this to all small farmers, which effectively made half the land under cultivation eligible for coverage under the programme.

Increasing agricultural production was one side of the story but assuring farmers of remunerative prices was also important. The central government influenced prices received by farmers by fixing minimum support prices (MSPs) for several crops and also by controlling their exports and imports. Decisions on agricultural prices have to strike a balance between consumer interests that favour lower prices with farmer interests, which typically call for higher prices. Governments had traditionally given high priority to consumer interests and allowed only very modest increases in MSPs. The UPA increased MSPs significantly in 2007 and again in 2008 to incentivize production. This was especially justifiable because international wheat and rice prices began to rise in 2007. However, the UPA was also swayed by consumer interests in banning the export of wheat in 2007 and rice in 2008.

I argued consistently against bans on exports on the grounds that Indian farmers should be allowed to benefit from high world prices. If we want to provide food at a cheaper price to a target group, we should do so by providing a larger subsidy from the Budget rather than keeping MSPs low. Unfortunately, this argument had very few takers and governments of all political stripes have regularly banned exports when domestic prices are high. As it happened, the policy of extending a remunerative MSP for foodgrains evoked a very positive response and the production of foodgrains increased by 40 million tonnes between 2006–07 and 2011–12, twice the target for this period under the National Food Mission.

MSPs were not the answer for perishable crops such as fruits and vegetables. Farmers producing these crops needed modern agricultural markets to reduce the gap between what the consumer pays and what the farmer gets. This calls for policy changes in several areas, including amendments of the Agricultural Produce Market Committee (APMC) Acts in various states to allow private markets to develop and encourage the private corporate sector to buy from the farmers directly. We urged the states to take action along these lines. I also felt the Essential Commodities Act, a central legislation that allows imposition of stock limits, should be abolished, because the power to introduce stock limits discourages the entry of large traders. We also argued for allowing FDI in modern retail to encourage the development of supply chains. Despite our efforts, there was very little progress in this area.

Expanding credit to farmers was another instrument to facilitate agricultural growth. Public sector banks were exhorted to expand lending to agriculture; as a result, credit to agriculture doubled in the first two years of the UPA and continued to grow rapidly. Ironically, having first expanded credit to farmers, the Government subsequently faced demands for a generalized waiver of agricultural loans following the poor monsoon of 2007. I have always argued against general loan waivers as they damage the credit culture, but the political clamour could not be resisted, least of all in a pre-election year. In the Budget for 2008–09, Chidambaram announced a write-off of all loans for small farmers (up to 2 hectares) that were overdue as of 31 March 2007, plus a one-time settlement of other overdue loans, with a 25 per cent rebate on the amount outstanding. The loan waiver cost about ₹60,000 crore, or a little over 1 per cent of GDP, spread over a two-year period.

A major problem with agricultural policy was that input subsidies had grown to unsustainable levels. I have no doubt that we needed to reduce input subsidies and use the funds saved to increase public investment, especially in minor irrigation and water resource management. Subsidies were not part of plan expenditure and the Planning Commission was not involved in determining the scale of subsidies. The central government fertilizer subsidy was ₹15,789 crore in 2004–05 when the total allocation for agriculture was only ₹4,573 crore, a ratio of 3.4:1. By 2013–14, the fertilizer subsidy had increased to ₹67,971 crore when the allocation for agriculture was ₹17,693 crore, a ratio of 3.8:1. The subsidy was also concentrated on urea, leading to massive under-pricing of urea and unbalanced use of urea compared to phosphate and potassium, to say nothing of encouraging large-scale smuggling of urea into Nepal and Bangladesh.

At one stage, I even suggested that we shift the provision for fertilizer subsidy out of the Ministry of Fertilizers to the Ministry of Agriculture and let the latter determine how much of the funds should be used to subsidize fertilizers and how much for investment in agriculture. A 25 per cent cut in the subsidy would have allowed a doubling of plan expenditure on agriculture and a substantial improvement in agricultural production. But this suggestion also had no takers.

In the end, the actions taken by the Centre and states raised the growth rate of the agricultural sector from only 2.2 per cent in the previous five years to 3.1 per cent in UPA 1. However, as changes in agricultural policy take time to show results, the real impact was felt during UPA 2 when the growth rate of agriculture increased to an average of 4.3 per cent. This was driven largely by allowing agricultural prices to reflect rising world prices, which increased farm profitability and encouraged a boom in private investment in agriculture.

POVERTY REDUCTION: A BIG STEP FORWARD

Poverty reduction was a key element in our inclusiveness agenda. The percentage of the population in poverty had declined at an annual rate of 0.8 per cent in the pre-UPA period between 1993–94 and 2004–05. However, this decline was not enough to offset the growth of population, so the absolute number of the poor actually increased by 7 million in that period. We therefore adopted an ambitious target of reducing the percentage of the population below the poverty line by 10 percentage points over the Eleventh Plan period, or 2 per cent per year, which was two-and-a-half times the rate observed in the pre-UPA period.

Many politicians who used to doubt whether market-oriented reforms would raise the rate of growth had come around to accept that proposition, but they remained deeply sceptical that this growth would trickle down to the poor. Mani Shankar Aiyar, one of the most articulate members of the UPA cabinet, was a self-proclaimed sceptic. He would often say in public, 'All that Montek's reforms have given us is 8 per cent growth per year but only 0.8 per cent decline in poverty.' I would point out to him that he was cleverly juxtaposing the growth rate the UPA had achieved during its first term with the poverty reduction record of previous governments. I urged him to hold back judgement until data on poverty reduction during the UPA 1 period became available.

When the estimates for 2009–10 finally became available in 2011, they brought very good news. The percentage of the population in poverty had declined at an annual rate of 1.5 per cent (from 37.2 per cent in 2004–05 to 29.8 per cent in 2009–10) — almost twice as fast as in the pre-UPA period. While it was short of the ambitious target of the 2 percentage point decline per year that we had set for the Eleventh Plan, it was fast enough to bring about a decline in the absolute numbers of the poor — the first time this had happened.

These results vindicated our three-pronged strategy to reduce poverty. Faster growth of GDP, or the pure trickle-down phenomenon, was one part of the strategy. A pattern of growth that emphasized agriculture was the second, and the adoption of pro-poor programmes the third. The reduction in poverty was clearly the combined outcome of all these factors. We achieved GDP growth of 8.4 per cent per year, which was much faster than earlier. It generated a construction boom, which created many low-skilled jobs that helped to shift labour away from agriculture, thereby raising rural wages. The growth rate of agricultural GDP increased from 2.5 per cent between 1993–94 and 2004–05 to 3.2 per cent between 2004–05 and 2009–10, boosting income in rural areas. We also stepped up a number of pro-poor programmes, notably MGNREGS. The relative importance of these three factors varied across states and I felt this aspect needed to be studied more closely. I also felt NGOs needed to appreciate that it was the high growth and the revenues it generated that enabled us to finance pro-poor programmes.

Estimating Poverty

The Planning Commission estimated poverty in rural and urban areas using official poverty lines drawn at a basic minimum level of consumption per capita for rural and urban areas separately. Consumption data was taken from the large sample surveys of household consumption expenditure carried out by the NSSO every five years. Applying the poverty line to the consumption distribution gave us an estimate of the number of persons with per capita consumption below the poverty line, who could therefore be called poor.

Up to 2004–05, the poverty line used was the one recommended by the Lakdawala Committee in 1993. In 2005, the Planning Commission decided to update this line and a high-level committee was set up under Suresh Tendulkar. This committee significantly raised the poverty line for rural areas but left the urban poverty line more or less the same. As a result, the proportion of the poor in rural population in 2004–05 increased from 28.3 per cent according to the Lakdawala poverty line to 41.8 per cent according to the Tendulkar line. The combined (rural and urban) proportion of population below the poverty line in 2004–05 increased from 27.5 per cent based on the old Lakdawala poverty line to 37.2 per cent based on the new Tendulkar line.

From 2004–05 onward, the new Tendulkar line was used to estimate poverty. The percentage of the poor in the total population fell to 29.8 per cent in 2009–10 and 21.9 per cent in 2011–12. The absolute numbers of the poor declined from 407 million in 2004–05 to 355 million in 2009–10 and 269 million in 2011–2012.

I had hoped that the news of sharp reduction in poverty would be widely welcomed but I was in for a surprise. Opposition MPs described our estimates of poverty as a hoax on the people. Mulayam Singh said Planning Commission members 'do not have any idea of village or rural life. They live in air-conditioned rooms and make their reports on the basis of reading some papers.'[47] He went on to assert that 65 per cent of the population was poor, which was more than twice the all-India number shown by the survey data. For good measure, he added that I should be removed as deputy chairman!

I could understand opposition MPs refusing to admit a reduction in poverty as it would allow the Government to claim credit, but Congress MPs were also not happy. I wondered whether they were worried that any claim that poverty was falling would be interpreted by the electorate as a prelude to shifting attention away from the problems of the poor. Some probably also worried that households deemed to have graduated above the poverty line may be denied benefits, such as supply of highly subsidized foodgrains through the PDS.

In September 2011, the Supreme Court was hearing a petition from the Right to Food campaign, which complained that state governments were not giving below poverty line cards to many who needed them. The Court asked us to indicate what the Tendulkar poverty line would amount to in 2011 prices. We submitted an affidavit stating that it amounted to ₹32 per person per day in urban areas and ₹28 per person per day in rural areas. These numbers suddenly became controversial with many claiming that the poverty line was too low. Part of the problem was that we had switched to defining the poverty line in terms of expenditure per person per day instead of expenditure per person per month, which was the case earlier. The change was made to conform to international practice. Translated into a budget for a household of five members, the monthly expenditure for a 'poor' household

---

[47]*The Times of India*, 22 March 2012.

was at or below ₹4,824 for urban areas and ₹3,905 for rural areas. This was, of course, very low but it was roughly in line with what a family of five would get if they had one family member fully employed at the minimum wage for unskilled labour.

As explained in the Box, the new Tendulkar poverty line was actually higher than the old Lakdawala poverty line (which had been used uncomplainingly by the previous NDA government) and it actually raised the percentage of the population in poverty in 2004–05 from 27.5 per cent to 37.2 per cent. The new line was roughly equal to the international poverty line of $1.25 per day set by the World Bank and accepted by the UN system (converted into rupees at purchasing power parity exchange rates). We could always raise the line if we wanted, but there was no merit in exaggerating the extent of poverty in India compared to other countries.

I explained our stand on several TV channels. On one such occasion, I discovered that while one half of the screen showed me claiming that poverty had declined, the other half showed visuals of children living in abject poverty in a slum. It was a clever way of suggesting that what I was saying was false. Had the interviewer transparently asked me for my comments on the video, I would have explained that I was not claiming that poverty had disappeared, only that both the percentage of the population below the poverty line and the absolute number of the poor had declined. In fact, I always took care to emphasize that with over 350 million people still below the poverty line in 2009–10, a great deal remained to be done. However, the new line also showed that poverty had declined much faster.

As I battled for acceptance of the poverty numbers, I was aware that we would probably get even better news two years later. This was because 2009 was a drought year, when rural poverty was likely to be higher than normal, and we had therefore requested the NSSO to conduct another consumption survey in 2011–12, a normal year that also happened to be the last year of the Eleventh Plan. The results of the 2011–12 survey became available in the middle of 2013. As I had expected, they presented an even better picture. The percentage of the population in poverty had dropped from 37 per cent in 2004–05 to 22 per cent in 2011–12. This implied a decline of 2.1 percentage points per year in the population below the poverty line, slightly better than our target of reducing poverty by 2 percentage points per year. The absolute number of the poor declined from 407 million in 2004–05 to 269 million in 2011–12.

Pulling 138 million persons above poverty was hailed internationally as a major achievement in inclusiveness. For years, the international development community had lauded the performance of China in poverty reduction. It was heartening that India's performance in this area was also being talked about. At home, however, the opposition remained in attack mode. Senior BJP leader Murli Manohar Joshi was reported in the press to have charged the Government with 'mocking the plight of the poor'. The CPI(M) said the estimates 'made a mockery of life and death struggles'.[48] The UPA allies also distanced themselves and senior NCP leader and Cabinet Minister Praful Patel said the NCP did not agree with the Planning Commission figures.[49]

Loss of entitlements under poverty programmes as a result of going above the poverty line was clearly a source of worry for many people and we addressed this concern by delinking entitlements under the Food Security Act from any linkage to a fixed poverty line. Instead, the entitlements were offered to anyone in the bottom 'x' per cent.[50] With the linkage gone, Minister of State for Planning Rajeev Shukla defended the numbers stoutly in Parliament, stating that the only purpose in estimating the number of people below a fixed poverty line was to judge whether development was benefiting the poor by moving them above the poverty line at a reasonable rate. He argued that the numbers

---

[48]*The Hindu*, 26 July 2013
[49]*Financial Express*, 25 July 2013
[50]The percentage would be determined by the central government and the identification of the individual household would be left to the states.

certainly showed that poverty was falling much faster than in the time of the BJP-led NDA.

Nevertheless, the perception that the new poverty line was too low would not go away and we appointed another High-Level Committee, this time under C. Rangarajan, chairman of the EAC-PM, to take another look. The Rangarajan Committee submitted its report in June 2014 and recommended raising both the rural and urban poverty line above the levels recommended by Tendulkar. This raised the percentage of the population below the poverty line in 2011–12 from 22 per cent based on the Tendulkar poverty line to 29.5 per cent. However, it also showed a decline in the percentage of the population in poverty from 38.2 per cent in 2009–10 to 29.5 per cent, a decline of 8.7 per cent in two years. This vindicated our stand that a higher poverty line would raise the percentage in poverty in both the base year and the most recent year, but it would not alter the phenomenon of an impressive decline over the period.

I remain puzzled why the Congress party was unwilling to claim credit for reducing poverty. Perhaps, they held back because they remembered the India Shining campaign that failed the BJP in 2004. However, that campaign had overtones of overconfidence, seeming to suggest that the country had arrived. That was not the message we were trying to convey. In fact, with 269 million people still below the poverty line in 2011–12, we would have been foolish to claim that all problems had been overcome. But it was important to establish that the UPA strategy was working in a way that earlier strategies had not.

THE QUEST FOR FOOD SECURITY

The Congress manifesto for the 2009 election had promised the enactment of a National Food Security Act, which would give a legal right to every family below the poverty line to receive 25 kg of rice/wheat at highly subsidized prices of ₹3 per kg. This promise was repeated in the President's address to the new

Parliament in 2009, making it an official priority of UPA 2. Food subsidy was part of the pro-poor strategy although it was not a Plan programme.

The proposed Food Security Bill was taken up initially by the National Advisory Council, which had been reconstituted at the start of UPA 2, with Sonia Gandhi as chairperson. Many of its members were deeply interested in food security issues but they wanted the benefit to be made universal and not just limited to those below the poverty line. They believed limiting the benefit to a defined target group ran the risk of excluding deserving poor households.

I was invited to give my views on the scope of a Food Security Act to the National Advisory Council in a meeting chaired by Sonia Gandhi. I expressed reservations on expanding coverage. I said we could easily meet the commitment to provide subsidized food to the poor as then defined, and even extend the benefit to a larger percentage of the population, but I argued strongly against making the coverage universal, or even very large. That would require a much larger amount of foodgrains than the normal domestic procurement, and might require importing 13–14 million tonnes every year. Imports on that scale would raise prices in world markets as well as create demands from our farmers for receiving comparably high prices for domestic procurement. Further, the resulting increase in food subsidy would cut resources available for other UPA priorities such as health, education, irrigation and rural livelihoods.

I also pointed out that the system of physical distribution of foodgrains at very low prices created a huge incentive to divert under-priced foodgrains into the market and pocket the difference between the subsidized price and the market price. Mexico and Brazil had experienced the same problem and had shifted to a system of conditional cash transfers, with very good results. I suggested we should consider something similar.

A pure system of cash transfers would make fair price shops unnecessary. But recognizing that such a drastic change may be unacceptable, I suggested a more limited reform whereby the fair price shops could continue, but would charge a market-related price for foodgrains. The target population (the poorest 'x' percentage) would receive a smart card loaded with a monthly subsidy entitlement. They could use the smart card to transfer the subsidy component to the fair price shop while paying only the subsidized price from their own pockets. I also suggested that the beneficiaries be allowed to use the smart card to purchase not only foodgrains but other items such as edible oils, pulses, wheat flour, eggs and even vegetables, which could be sold by the same shop. This flexibility would allow marginal farmers who produced foodgrains for home consumption on their small holdings to continue to do so and use the food subsidy for other essential food items. In the present system, such marginal farmers could benefit from the food subsidy only by buying subsidized foodgrains from the PDS. This forced them to reduce the production of foodgrains for their own use and grow other crops on their small pieces of land, which was often a more risky proposition.

Sometime in October 2009, Sonia Gandhi forwarded the National Advisory Council proposal on food security to the PM for examination. The proposal did not envisage universal coverage, but proposed to cover 90 per cent of the rural population, of which the bottom 46 per cent was called 'priority category' and would receive 7 kg of rice/wheat per person at ₹3 per kg; the rest would receive 4 kg per person but at a higher, though still concessional, price. For urban areas, the coverage would be limited to the lower 50 per cent, within which the lowest 28 per cent would be designated as priority category and the rest as 'general category'. When the PM asked me for my reactions, I informed him that I had told the National Advisory Council that the coverage proposed was too large. I suggested to the PM that the issues I had raised should be examined in consultation with the concerned ministries, after which he could discuss with Sonia Gandhi how best to go forward.

The PM set up a group under Rangarajan, which included all secretaries from the concerned ministries, to look into the proposal and suggest a course of action. The committee confirmed my informal assessment that the National Advisory Council proposal would require large imports and lead to a large increase in food subsidy.

The proposal went through the usual government processes and the Food Security Act was finally passed in 2013. It differed from the original National Advisory Council proposal in some important respects. The eligible population for rural areas was reduced from 90 per cent to 75 per cent, while the urban eligible population stayed at 50 per cent. The two together covered about two-thirds of the total population. The division of the eligible group into two categories was abandoned and the entitlement per person was set at a uniform 5 kg per person.

I personally thought the number of people proposed to be covered was still too large. The percentage of population below the Tendulkar poverty line was around 20 per cent in 2013. We could have easily expanded the food security provision to cover, say, 40 per cent of the population, but targeting two-thirds of the population was difficult to justify. I also felt we needed to move away from physical distribution to a smart card-based system that could be used to purchase not only foodgrains but other food items and ultimately even a cash transfer. We were able to introduce a provision in the Act that specified that in case physical supplies could not be provided, the Government could use other means to provide an equivalent subsidy. The latter provides a possible opening for shifting to cash transfer. Some pilots have been undertaken to explore this option but no decision has been taken.

The total financial cost of the Food Security Act in 2019–20 was ₹1,84,220 crore or about 1 per cent of GDP, making it the largest programme in the central budget. There is a strong case for subjecting it to critical review to see what improvements are possible while keeping welfare objectives intact.

THE AADHAAR EXPERIMENT

A very important initiative taken by the UPA was the decision to introduce a unique ID with biometric identification. The idea had come from several different sources. Within the Planning Commission, Arvind Virmani, advisor-development policy, had pushed for a more efficient system for distributing welfare benefits based on a smart card with an embedded chip and a unique ID. The single card would eliminate the need for multiple cards for different benefits and the unique ID would avoid the same person claiming benefits under different names. It was also recommended by the Raghuram Rajan Committee on Financial Sector Reforms in 2008 as a way of facilitating financial inclusion. Separately, the MHA had been working on a National Citizens Register, with a national ID card to be issued to all citizens, which was expected to help identifying illegal immigrants.

In January 2009, the Government decided to set up the Unique Identification Authority of India (UIDAI) within the Planning Commission to develop a smart card-based system that could meet both economic and security needs. Shortly after the 2009 election, the PM asked me what I thought of inducting Nandan Nilekani, co-founder of Infosys, into the Planning Commission as a member. I said it was a great idea but I thought he should be brought in as a minister. I learnt that was the original intention but it did not work out, and the Planning Commission was seen as a possible alternative.

I met Nandan and he told me he would be willing to come if he could be given complete charge of the UIDAI project, which he found intellectually challenging. I reported back to the PM recommending Nandan be made chairman of UIDAI and be given cabinet rank as was done for Sam Pitroda. For my part, I said I would ensure that although the UIDAI would be administratively located in the Planning Commission, Nandan would have full operational autonomy.

Nandan quickly put together an impressive team, including some very tech-savvy IAS officers. He also re-conceptualized the project. Instead of the top-down process envisaged earlier, where officials from the Registrar General of the Census office would cover the population going from location to location, Nandan switched to a decentralized approach in which authorized registering agents would be appointed who could be approached by anyone wanting a unique ID number. He reasoned that if the number brought various benefits, people would want to get enrolled. Another important change was to abandon the idea of a smart card with an embedded chip in favour of a system that would only provide a unique ID number (catchily called Aadhaar, meaning 'foundation' in Hindi).

On the first anniversary of UPA 2 in June 2010, the PM announced that the project would provide a platform for direct benefit transfer (DBT) to the poor, and be a means of expanding financial inclusion. The basic idea of DBT was that scholarships, old-age pensions, maternity benefits and even wages under MGNREGA would be transferred directly to bank accounts linked to Aadhaar. The Government also made a commitment that the first Aadhaar numbers would be issued in a few months. As promised, on 29 September, the PM and Sonia Gandhi handed the first Aadhaar numbers to a few people in remote Tembhli village in the Nandurbar district of Maharashtra.

Poor road access to Tembhli meant that the PM and Sonia Gandhi had to make the trip by helicopter and Nandan and I were able to hitch a ride on one of the helicopters accompanying the VVIP flight. The launch went off well. There was a glitch because the effort to demonstrate the process of verifying identity failed as telecom connectivity could not be established. We learnt later that the electronic jammers in the PM's security vehicle prevented telecom signals from getting through! However, this did not spoil the moment. The recipients of the first 10 Aadhaar cards had only a vague idea of the DBT benefits they would get in future but were happy to have an official proof of identity. Everyone in the village turned up to see the helicopters land and take off. I wondered if any of them realized that the digital technology underlying Aadhaar was actually more contemporary than that embodied in the helicopters, and was likely to have much greater impact on their lives.

Any new experiment in government faces resistance from the system and UIDAI was no exception. There was resistance even within the Planning Commission to give UIDAI the autonomy I had promised. I often had to invoke the PM's authority to settle the matter. UIDAI was initially authorized to enrol 100 million people; this was subsequently expanded to 200 million. When we tried to get approval for a further expansion, we ran into resistance from the office of the Registrar General. They took the view that they should have the exclusive responsibility to collect the data, which they would pass on to the UIDAI, which would only generate the unique ID number and maintain the growing database.

Nandan was sure the Registrar General's Office would not be able to expand enrolment fast enough to allow DBT to be introduced within the term of UPA 2. I agreed and we persuaded Home Minister P. Chidambaram to accept a reasonable compromise whereby UIDAI and the Registrar General's Office would split the task of data collection. With this, UIDAI was cleared to enrol about 600 million people, which would suffice to start experimenting with DBT.

Several other steps were needed for DBT to work. A payments bridge had to be set up by the National Payments Corporation, whereby the unique Aadhaar number could be linked to a bank account in any bank. Funds could then be transferred by government agencies to a person via the payments bridge, using only the Aadhaar number. This eliminated the need for distribution of bank checks to beneficiaries, which could become a source for extortion. Another critical step was the RBI's decision to allow banks to accept Aadhaar numbers as fulfilling the Know Your Customer (KYC) requirements for opening 'no frills' bank accounts. This allowed low-income individuals to open accounts easily without having to submit the multiple documents normally needed.

Somewhat to my surprise, NGOs opposed linking welfare benefits to Aadhaar because biometric identification may fail in some cases where physical labour has led to erosion of fingerprints, or where poor mobile connectivity makes operability uncertain. There was also opposition on the grounds that it violated privacy. The Aadhaar database itself did not contain any sensitive information other than name, gender and address, but if Aadhaar was linked to many other databases, it could become a mechanism of surveillance by the state. This would not be a problem if these databases were protected from government scrutiny but any such claim carried little credibility. Privacy concerns were heightened when the Government made Aadhaar mandatory for many other activities, including having a bank account, a credit card or even a telephone. Civil society groups petitioned the Supreme Court that this violated the right to privacy, a fundamental right. The Court has since pronounced that Aadhaar is not unconstitutional as a means of getting welfare benefits, but has struck down sections introducing a statutory basis for compulsorily linking Aadhaar to banking and telephone services.

When a Bill was introduced in 2010 to give UIDAI statutory status, it was strongly opposed by the BJP and this led many people to think that the project would die a natural death after the NDA came to power in 2014. However, Nandan met PM Narendra Modi after the election and explained the many benefits of Aadhaar. The BJP reversed its position and Aadhaar was not only saved but subsequently became a critical element in the NDA's 'JAM' trinity (J for Jan Dhan accounts, A for Aadhaar, and M for mobile). This is another case of a reform conceptualized and implemented by the UPA, which was subsequently taken forward by the BJP and rolled out very effectively.

Another key reform towards financial inclusion was RBI's decision to allow banks to nominate banking correspondents who would be linked to banks by handheld devices. There were only about 32,000 bank branches for about 600,000 villages, making physical access very difficult. Allowing the local village shop or cooperative to act as a banking correspondent meant money could be deposited into one's account by giving it to the banking correspondent, who could move the money from his account to that of the client through a handheld device with mobile connectivity. Cash could be withdrawn from one's account by simply transferring it to the account of the banking correspondent, and taking cash from him.

The telecom revolution that occurred primarily during the tenure of the UPA was obviously critical in facilitating this expansion in financial inclusion. Some decisions became highly controversial later (*see Chapter 17*) but the expansion in connectivity achieved was extraordinary.

16

BUILDING INFRASTRUCTURE THROUGH PPPs

Expanding investment in infrastructure was a critical element in the UPA's strategy for achieving high growth. But the resources available with the Government for infrastructure development were limited because of the competing claims of the social sectors such as health and education, as well as pro-poor programmes. This forced us to follow a strategy that relied upon private investment for infrastructure development. I felt the Planning Commission could play a leading role in this area and decided to set up a new Infrastructure Division in the commission to focus exclusively on PPPs. I persuaded Gajendra Haldea, who had worked with me earlier on PPP projects in the Ministry of Finance, to head the new division.

Investment in infrastructure was opened to the private sector in the 1990s. In some cases, e.g., power generation and civil aviation, sectors earlier closed to the private sector were opened up and new players were allowed to enter and compete on equal terms with other suppliers in the market. There was no role for the Planning Commission in such cases. In other cases, private sector players were invited to bid for a concession to develop a particular road, port or airport under a long-term agreement. In this case, the concessionaire, once chosen, would enjoy limited monopoly as consumers would have no other choice. The private investor was effectively competing 'for the market' but not 'in the market'. Handing over an existing infrastructure facility to a private investor to expand and operate posed many challenges. It became the responsibility of the Government to ensure that the task was entrusted to high-quality players and performed to specified standards, with penalties for non-compliance. It was also very important that user charges were independently fixed to avoid any exploitation of a monopoly or semi-monopoly position. The bid evaluation process had to be transparent to avoid subsequent challenges. We felt the Planning Commission could play an important role in these cases working jointly with the Ministry of Finance, to evolve high-quality bidding documents and procedures that would ensure transparency.

DELHI AND MUMBAI AIRPORTS

My first exposure to PPP as deputy chairman was the modernization of Delhi and Mumbai airports. The previous government had decided that these airports would be expanded and modernized through a build-operate-transfer arrangement on the basis of competitive bidding in which the private partner would get a concession period of 30 years, extendable by another 30 years. Bid evaluations were underway and the UPA sensibly decided to continue with this decision. The process of bid evaluation proved controversial because the criteria specified in the bid documents were vague and open to conflicting interpretations. After much discussion, the contentious questions on how to evaluate competing parties were resolved. The Delhi airport was awarded to GMR partnering with Frankfurt airport while the concession for Mumbai airport was won by the GVK Group, partnering with Johannesburg airport.[51]

Both the Delhi and Mumbai airports came about more or less on time. The timely completion of work on the Delhi airport was particularly welcome as it had to be functional before the Commonwealth Games in October 2010. Stanley Fischer, vice-chairman of the US Federal Reserve, visited Delhi shortly after the new airport opened and sent me an email saying the Government

---

[51]While Hyderabad and Bengaluru airports had been built by the private sector earlier, these were new airports and were not awarded on the basis of competitive bidding.

deserved to be congratulated for having given Delhi an airport that was up to the best international standards. It was a nice compliment from a seasoned international traveller. The airport has received several international awards.

PREPARING IN RIGHT EARNEST

New initiatives in government typically need high-level support and I suggested this was best done by setting up a committee on infrastructure, chaired by the PM, with the finance minister, deputy chairman and other concerned ministers as members. The committee would approve the overall targets for infrastructure development in each sector emerging from the Eleventh Plan and set sub-targets for the PPP component based on the recommendation of the Planning Commission. It would also monitor the performance of the PPP component through quarterly reviews.

The committee was set up in August 2004 and one of its first decisions was to direct the preparation of model bidding documents for use in PPP agreements. The Infrastructure Division prepared a variety of model documents for PPP projects, including the model concession agreements. These were approved by a committee chaired by the secretary of the concerned ministry. The idea of using standardized bidding documents was criticized by some ministries on the grounds that it implied a 'one-size-fits-all' approach. We clarified that any specific part of the standard document could be modified to suit particular project conditions, but it was much easier to handle changes if only some parts of the document were changed. Approving a completely new bid document and concession agreement for each project would be extremely cumbersome as these documents typically run into 250 pages or so, and each sentence would need to be scrutinized carefully to understand its legal implications.

While PPPs in airports and ports could normally generate adequate revenue streams for investors to cover their costs and earn a return, this was not true for all sectors. For example, roads and urban metros generate huge benefits for society at large but as the entire benefit does not accrue to individual users, it cannot be internalized in the user charge. A subsidy is therefore necessary to make the project viable. The most transparent way of determining the subsidy is to invite the concessionaires to bid for the minimum capital subsidy needed and award the concession to the investor seeking the lowest subsidy. We worked with the Ministry of Finance to evolve a system of viability gap funding whereby the maximum subsidy available on a project was capped at 40 per cent of the 'approved capital cost'. The approved capital cost would be specified for each project in the relevant bid document. The first 20 per cent would be met by the central government and the next 20 per cent by the project authority or (in the case of state projects) the state government.

Many PPP projects in roads were approved in the years that followed, not only in the central sector but also in the state sector. This was the period when private investment was booming and credit expansion was strong. I regularly urged CMs during our annual meetings to explore the possibility of PPPs in their states, and several states responded. Madhya Pradesh, in particular, did an excellent job in promoting road development through PPP. On a visit to Indore after I had left the Government, I was struck by the quality of the road we were driving on and happy to learn it had been built through a PPP using the model concession agreement developed by the Planning Commission. The fact that the model concession agreement had been approved by the central government made it easier for the states to adopt it.

Ports were ideally suited for PPPs. There were 13 'major ports' under the control of the central government. All other ports were classified as minor ports and were in the domain of state governments. We had pushed for broader reforms of major ports, including converting the port trusts into corporations to improve the quality of management and speed of decision-making. The Ministry of Shipping was not willing to make such changes. It was only willing to allow private investors to construct new berths in existing major ports on a PPP basis but they failed to meet the modest targets set. As a result, the capacity expansion achieved through this method in the major ports fell considerably short of the targets approved by the Committee on Infrastructure.

State governments acted much more boldly, approving many new ports to be run entirely by the private sector. Gujarat, Maharashtra and Andhra Pradesh showed the way, and Kerala followed. Towards the end of UPA 2, the Kerala government invited Haldea to draft the concession agreement for Vizhinjam port, which had been languishing for over a decade. The project was bid out successfully and is under construction. By the end of my term, some erstwhile minor ports had become larger than some of the major ports. We started calling them 'non-major' ports!

Even as we pushed for PPPs, we also recognized that many projects would continue to be funded by the Government itself. These were typically implemented through what was called the 'item rate system' in which the quantity of each item needed for construction would be estimated and thereafter payment would be made based on measurement of the amount of each item used. The system encouraged long delays, and led to increases in costs and litigation. The system had been given up in most countries in favour of fixed-cost turnkey contracts, but it continued to be used in India. The Planning Commission's infrastructure division developed a model EPC (engineering procurement construction) turnkey contract for construction projects that would ensure both efficiency and economy. There was resistance from departments, possibly under the influence of the contractors who clearly preferred the old system. However, the cabinet approved the new EPC model contract in 2013 and it was adopted for all National Highway projects directly funded by the Government. I thought it was a good example of the commission bringing in system change. Subsequently, the NDA government in 2016 decided that the model would be adopted in all construction projects across all sectors.

RAILWAYS

At a very early stage in UPA 1, in the mid-term appraisal of the Tenth Plan, we had recommended allowing private sector trains to run on the existing rail network in competition with the trains owned and run by Indian Railways. But the Railways were not ready for such radical reform.[52] However, they agreed to allow private sector players to operate container freight trains competing with the Container Corporation of India, a public sector monopoly. The new policy was announced in 2006 and our Infrastructure Division worked closely with the Railways to develop a model concession agreement. Today, there are seven private operators with about 26 per cent share of the market. This remains an area of great potential for further expansion, especially once the dedicated freight corridors finally come on stream.

We got the opportunity to experiment with an entirely new type of PPP when the Railways decided to upgrade their diesel and electric locomotives to heavier haul capacity. The normal practice was for the Railways to produce the locomotives in their own factories under licence from a selected technology provider, with the Railways incurring the capital cost of setting up the facility. Haldea suggested an alternative model in which reputable international locomotive manufacturers could be invited to bid for producing and supplying 1,800 locomotives over a period of about 10 years and maintaining a specified subset of these locomotives for about 15 years. The first few locomotives could be imported but the rest would be produced in India.

The Railways would provide the land for the factory and take a 26 per cent equity stake. They would commit to purchase an agreed number of locomotives over a period of 10 years at a price discovered through competitive bidding and adjusted every year on predetermined parameters. Once the initial purchase was completed, the Railways would be free to switch to any other supplier and the manufacturer would be free to export the product

---

[52]The idea is being considered again and may finally be implemented.

to third-country markets. The arrangement gave the manufacturer a strong incentive to upgrade technology continuously in the interest of obtaining better prices and future orders, and use the Indian production facility to export to third-country markets.

Lalu Prasad Yadav, former CM of Bihar, was railways minister in UPA 1. He approved the PPP proposal with the condition that both factories would be located in Bihar, one at Madhepura (electric locomotives) and the other at Marhowra (diesel locomotives). The CCEA approved the proposal in February 2007 and we started work on the bid documents and concession agreement, but it was a long-drawn process because of frequent changes at the top in the Railways. UPA 2 saw seven railway ministers in five years, along with frequent changes in the chairperson of the Railway Board and the financial commissioner. As a result, the last stage of inviting financial bids and awarding the concession could not be completed during the term of UPA 2.

The successor NDA government sensibly decided to continue with the process and the contracts were finally awarded in 2015. The value of the two contracts was about $8 billion, large by any standards. The contractual framework and bid process attracted no challenge and the first electric locomotive, produced by Alstom, rolled out of the Madhepura factory in April 2018. Similarly, diesel locomotives produced by General Electric were rolled out from Marhowra around the same time.

METROS

Metros had become essential elements of urban infrastructure and most state governments wanted to build metros on the model of the Delhi Metro, which was a 50/50 JV of the Delhi government and the Centre. The central government's involvement was necessary in Delhi, as powers relating to land use were with the Centre, but I did not think a JV with the Centre was the right model for other metros, where the state governments were fully empowered. I was concerned that a 50/50 JV would leave the

Centre vulnerable to meeting half the losses if the metro was not allowed to raise fares over time. I felt we should encourage state governments to explore PPP alternatives using the viability gap funding mechanism, with the Centre offering financial assistance by contributing to a competitively determined capital subsidy.

Andhra Pradesh CM Y.S. Rajasekhara Reddy was the only one who decided to take the PPP route for the Hyderabad Metro. Haldea was invited by the state government to help develop a structure for the proposed PPP. The Hyderabad Metro was initially awarded in 2008 to Maytas Infra, the infrastructure subsidiary of Satyam, but when that company collapsed in January 2009 (*see Chapter 13*), the contract had to be cancelled. Reddy stuck to his decision to implement the project as a PPP and fresh bids were invited. The project was finally awarded to Larsen & Toubro (L&T) in 2010. L&T successfully completed the first line of the metro in October 2017 and it was inaugurated by PM Modi. It is impressive that a project costing about ₹20,000 crore was implemented through a capital subsidy of only ₹1,458 crore, against the maximum possible subsidy of ₹4,853 crore!

FINANCING PPP PROJECTS

A basic problem limiting the pace of implementation of PPPs in infrastructure was the dearth of investors who could bring in a large enough volume of equity. PPP investors in the early stages were typically less-known business groups who could bring in only small levels of equity and hoped to mobilize the rest of the funds needed through debt. This was not easy because lenders needed the reassurance of a sufficient equity buffer to absorb the shock of the revenue stream turning out to be lower than expected. Besides, the corporate bond market in India lacked depth and liquidity because large fiscal deficits flooded the market with government bonds. Insurance and pension funds are the normal sources for infrastructure financing, but prudential regulations forced these funds to invest only in highly rated private paper and the debt issued by infrastructure projects was unlikely to qualify. Many infrastructure projects were therefore financed by shorter maturity borrowing from the banks on the assumption that the loans could be refinanced later with longer tenure debt, once the project moved into the operational stage with a steady revenue stream.

I pushed for setting up a dedicated financing institution for infrastructure to be funded initially by the Government, which could provide long-term debt up to 20 per cent of the project cost. Chidambaram responded positively and the India Infrastructure Finance Company Ltd (IIFCL) was set up in 2006. It played the role once played by the development finance institutions for industrial projects, but only as a supplement to borrowing from other commercial sources, mainly the banks. As originally conceived, it was not expected to undertake a detailed assessment of the viability of the projects as it was ending in partnership with the commercial banks—and it was expected that the banks would do due diligence. In retrospect, I think we should have been more ambitious about the scale of lending by IIFCL and strengthened its project appraisal capability.

The PPP effort did well initially. Total investment in infrastructure at 2006–07 prices increased from about ₹9 lakh crore in the Tenth Five-Year Plan, or 20 per cent of total investment in infrastructure, to about ₹19 lakh crore ($422 billion) in the Eleventh Plan period, or 37 per cent of the total. According to World Bank reports, India was the top recipient of PPP investment during 2008–12. A study assigned by ADB to the Economist Intelligence Unit, London, reported that India was in the same league as Korea and Japan as far as PPP policy and framework were concerned, next only to UK and Australia.

After a good start, several PPP projects in the roads sector started running into problems in UPA 2. Some became unviable because traffic turned out to be lower than expected. Projections were over-exuberant to begin with and actual outcomes were further depressed by the slowdown. In other cases, delays in getting environment and forest clearances or in shifting utilities by state governments led to higher costs. Investors also found it hard to raise finance in the more difficult financial environment that prevailed after the global financial crisis.

As problems mounted, private sector concessionaires began to ask for modifications in the concession agreements to reflect the changed circumstances. However, changing some elements of the agreement in a project that had been awarded on the basis of a competitive bid was not easy and could have attracted legal challenges. The right way to deal with the problem was to make appropriate revisions in the force majeure clause to define a broader set of conditions in which changes could be made. For example, we could have included a provision that if the growth rate of GDP fell short of an agreed benchmark for the first 10 years of operation, the length of the concession period would be extended depending on the extent of the shortfall. However, this could only apply prospectively to new concession agreements. Despite repeated discussions, we never quite got around to finding a solution to everyone's satisfaction for projects currently under implementation.

PPP investors often complained about not getting enough bank credit, but there was also evidence that some investors were getting away with too much credit. Sometime in 2011, Gajendra Haldea brought to my attention that private investors were negotiating large loans from public sector banks by estimating project costs in loan applications much above the approved costs from the project. Approved project costs were relevant only because they limited the extent to which the debt incurred by the project would be reimbursed if the concession was terminated by the Government. The banks were legally free to accept a larger project cost and lend more if, in their judgement, they believed the project could service the debt. However, the extra lending would not be covered by the reimbursement provision and to that extent it represented a greater risk. Unduly high levels of borrowing raised the suspicion that unscrupulous investors may be siphoning off the surplus amounts from the project and then recycling them back as their own equity contribution. I suggested to Haldea that he write up his observations and send the note to the Ministry of Finance and RBI.

Several months later, Haldea received a letter from the RBI governor conveying the comments of the RBI's Research Department. It confirmed that RBI was aware of the danger of 'gold-plating' to increase project costs and they routinely warned banks to be careful about this practice. However, they felt they could not do more until the account actually turned non-performing. The comments also confirmed that the banks had very little experience of project financing. This was understandable at the beginning, but it was odd that they had done nothing to acquire this expertise. This problem was not unique to PPPs; it affected all bank lending to capital-intensive projects and was one of the factors that led to the build-up of NPAs over time.

Sometime in January 2013, I happened to meet Uday Kotak, CEO of Kotak Mahindra Bank, one of our most successful new private sector banks, and we discussed bank lending to infrastructure projects. Uday told me that he was getting worried about the creditworthiness of most infrastructure projects and his bank had started scaling down exposure to these projects. Had the public sector banks been equally vigilant, the NPA problem would not have become so acute.

One complaint of PPP investors, which I felt deserved a positive response, was the absence of an effective dispute resolution mechanism. They complained that disputes, when they arose, were rarely resolved in a spirit of partnership. They felt, the Government treated private investors not as partners but adversaries. The reason was that civil servants found it difficult to depart from a reading of the agreement that was most favourable to the Government for fear of being accused of having caused a loss to the exchequer, which could lead to the charge of corruption. The PM directed us to work on a special arbitration process that could be used for all PPPs. We consulted all ministries and drafted a law for speedy resolution of disputes arising out of government contracts. This work could not be completed during UPA 2 but it needs to be followed up if we want to continue with PPPs.

We also took a note to the Cabinet Committee on Infrastructure, proposing that each ministry with PPP projects should set up a monitoring unit to report on progress and maintenance of service quality of each PPP. A start was made by some ministries but the system had not yet been put in place when the term of UPA 2 ended.

As implementation problems affecting PPPs began to mount, critics began to say that PPP was simply not a viable strategy and we should go back to building infrastructure with public funds. This was not a realistic proposition as the reason for adopting PPPs in the first place was that the public sector did not have the requisite funds. I was convinced that if we wanted an expanded investment programme in infrastructure, we had to find ways to make PPPs for infrastructure work.

One initiative that I thought would help was to bring in a law that would legitimize the resort to PPPs with a clear provision to protect public and consumer interests. This would help bring practices on PPPs in different sectors on common ground and provide a framework to build on the lessons learnt over the past decade. We had hoped to raise the share of private investment in total infrastructure investment to 50 per cent in the Twelfth Plan but the problems that arose with implementing large projects prevented us from achieving this target. However, the case for greater reliance upon PPP remains strong and has continuing relevance for the future. The mechanisms we were exploring to make PPP viable for infrastructure, including a speedy dispute resolution mechanism, need to be pursued further.

17

WINTER OF DISCONTENT:
ALLEGATIONS OF CORRUPTION

The UPA government had barely begun its second term when it was swamped by allegations of scams relating to the Commonwealth Games and 2G licences for mobile telephony. In 2012, there were further allegations about the allocation of coal blocks for captive mining. These allegations were used very effectively by the opposition to tar the Government with charges of corruption, making it a major issue in the 2014 election. It was ironic that this should have happened to a government headed by Dr Singh who was known to be a man of impeccable personal integrity, and about whose family there was never a whiff of suspicion. But it did happen, and it certainly eroded the credibility of the Government in the public mind.

Corruption was obviously not a new phenomenon. It was long known to exist in India, as in most countries, taking various forms from petty bribery all the way to large-scale corruption in government contracts. However, several developments brought the issue more sharply in focus. First, there was a steady increase in the number of legislators with criminal records, especially in state assemblies. There were also regular reports of corruption in states led by different parties; for instance, the Bellary mining scam and land scams in Karnataka under a BJP-ruled government, an iron ore scam in Goa under a Congress government, and the Adarsh housing society scam under a Congress-NCP government in Mumbai, Maharashtra. Further, the introduction of the RTI Act in 2005 and the greater transparency it brought about, combined with a vigilant and free press, made it easier to expose wrongdoing.

There was a perception in some quarters that economic liberalization was adding to corruption. Advocates of reforms had consistently argued that reforms would reduce corruption because industrial and import licencing were major sources of corruption and their abolition would clean up the system in important respects. But the reforms also expanded the role of the private sector in new areas, which provided new opportunities for corruption. In many cases, these were areas where success depended upon access to natural resources such as mineral deposits or spectrum, which were controlled by the Government, or real-estate development, which required numerous government permissions. The system for granting these permissions was not transparent. Companies stood to make large profits if they could manipulate policy to their advantage. Greater transparency and a stronger regulatory framework were needed to deal with this problem.

The public reaction against corruption was intensified by the perception that business was colluding with the political class to get favourable treatment. The publication of the Niira Radia tapes in *Outlook* magazine in November 2010 fed this perception. Radia was a highly successful public relations professional, and her clients included some of the best names in Indian industry. Her telephone had been tapped with legal authorization by the income tax authorities in connection with a tax investigation and transcripts of conversations with prominent businessmen, politicians and media personalities, all pertaining to the year 2009, were leaked. It painted an unsavoury picture of crony capitalism, which greatly raised the level of distrust in the system.

The India Against Corruption (IAC) movement, which emerged in early 2011 in the wake of the Commonwealth Games and 2G controversies, focussed public attention on corruption. The IAC invited veteran social reformer and activist Anna Hazare to be its leader, and this proved very effective in mobilizing urban educated youth and professionals. Projecting itself as a non-political movement, the IAC succeeded in putting the establishment of an independent statutory Lokpal[53] on the national political agenda.

The IAC movement also provided a springboard for its leading activists to join politics later. Arvind Kejriwal founded the AAP and made a successful showing in the 2013 Delhi elections, where he became CM of Delhi in a coalition with the Congress. The AAP once again swept the assembly polls in 2015. By then, Kiran Bedi, another IAC supporter, had joined the BJP and was fielded as the party's chief ministerial candidate in the assembly elections. She lost the election but was accommodated as governor of Puducherry.

SCAM-TAINTED COMMONWEALTH GAMES 2010

The Commonwealth Games was the least complex of the three alleged scams that came to national attention. It related to alleged mismanagement and possible misappropriation of government funds in what was effectively a non-government project, managed by the Organizing Committee (OC) of the Games but funded by the Government. Congress MP and president of the Indian Olympic Association, Suresh Kalmadi was appointed chairman of the committee. Although the OC had almost seven years' advance notice, critical decisions were delayed and projects fell behind schedule, so much so that at one stage the Commonwealth Games Federation in London warned that the Games might have to be postponed.

The central government finally intervened and a team of IAS officers was deputed to set the OC's house in order by taking charge of financial decisions. Games-related infrastructure was completed just in time and the event was successfully staged. My good friend Manohar Singh Gill, who became minister of youth affairs and sports in 2008, put it very pithily: 'As with Punjabi weddings, everything fell in place just in time.' However,

---

[53]An anti-corruption authority empowered to investigate and prosecute government officials and ministers accused of corruption.

government projects, unlike Punjabi weddings, also have to withstand government audits and scrutiny!

The Games were duly audited by the CAG and the report documented numerous instances of mismanagement, including delays in decision-making that led to cost escalation and short-circuiting of bidding procedures, all of which could lead to malfeasance. Complaints were made to the Central Vigilance Commission (CVC) about the handling of particular contracts and these were investigated. While criticizing the delays and cost escalations, the CAG also applauded the end result, saying, 'It is indeed a remarkable commentary on the nation's managerial and sporting capabilities that despite a multitude of adversities leading to the actual conduct of the Games, India emerged successful both as hosts and competitors.'

Isher and I were in the audience in the Jawaharlal Nehru Stadium when Prince Charles, representing Queen Elizabeth II as the head of the Commonwealth, opened the Games. While Prince Charles was roundly applauded and Delhi CM Sheila Dixit also received warm applause, Suresh Kalmadi was loudly booed. In the public eye, the wrongdoings in the run up to the Games were not attributed to the Centre but to Kalmadi. A thorough probe was promised by the PM and it seemed to satisfy the public.

The CAG estimated the total expenditure on the Games, plus associated infrastructure, at ₹13,800 crore and documented that the costs had escalated sharply from initial estimates. Some critics had felt that spending so much money on what they called 'beautifying Delhi' for a few days was wasteful. However, I felt it was not unreasonable for India, as an emerging market country, to invest some money in upgrading infrastructure in the capital to allow the hosting of an international sporting event. The sports infrastructure has made a permanent addition to Delhi's infrastructure and proved to be highly effective in promoting sports activities in the capital. However, those who wanted to feast on large estimates of expenditure found ways of adding on the expenditure on roads, flyovers, the Delhi Metro airport line and several power plants to come up with an estimate of ₹70,000 crore.[54]

In retrospect, Kalmadi should have been subject to much tighter oversight. But, he did not go scot-free. Despite being a member of the ruling party, he was arrested in April 2011 and charged on several counts. He spent several months in jail before getting bail. Astoundingly, his trial has still not been concluded.

THE MOTHER OF ALL SCAMS

The 2G controversy was much more complex because it involved not government expenditure but policy choices regarding the price to be charged for new licences and the allocation of spectrum. These were issues of economic policy on which the final decision had to be evaluated on the basis of whether it advanced the larger objectives of telecom policy.

A. Raja of the DMK, an important coalition partner in the UPA, was the minister of communications and information technology. To expand mobile connectivity at an affordable price, he believed it was necessary to introduce new mobile service providers in each telecom circle to break what he called the 'cartel' of existing service providers. TRAI was asked to advise on whether there should be a limit on the number of licences to be issued in each circle, and how the licence/spectrum should be priced.

TRAI submitted its report in August 2007 and recommended that there was no need to limit the number of service providers in a circle and that whereas all spectrum in future—including the 3G spectrum to be released shortly—should be auctioned, the spectrum available for 2G services should be given to new entrants at the same price discovered by an auction in 2001.[55] The reason for

---

[54]Majumdar, B. & Mehta, N. *Sellotape Legacy: Delhi and the Commonwealth Games*, HarperCollins, 2010.
[55]This was the price discovered by auction in 2001 when the fourth cellular mobile licences were issued. All licences issued since for mobile telephony had been on this price.

retaining the 2001 price was to ensure a level playing field. This was because the established incumbents had not only received 2G spectrum at the low price but had also been given much larger quantities of spectrum and built a substantial client base.

The recommendation to charge the 2001 price was controversial from the beginning, with different stakeholders having different preferences. The Ministry of Finance preferred an auction as the most transparent way of determining the price for a scarce resource; if that was not possible, they wanted a higher price than the 2001 level. Prospective new entrants obviously wanted the low 2001 price. Incumbent service providers fell into two groups. Those operating on GSM technology (that used the 900 and 1800 MHz bands) preferred an auction where they could also bid for additional spectrum to expand their own services. The second group had opted initially for CDMA technology (that used the 800 MHz band) but had subsequently decided to go for a GSM licence as well. As TRAI had recommended that these 'crossover cases' should be charged the same price as new entrants, they had a vested interest in the 2001 price. NGOs generally favoured an auction.

Raja decided to accept TRAI's advice not to auction 2G spectrum and allocate it instead at the old 2001 price. It seems reasonable to conclude — as many did — that an auction would have been the best mechanism to allocate a licence but TRAI's logic could not be dismissed summarily. If the objective is to ensure expansion of connectivity by increasing the number of players, while keeping the price of services low, it could be argued that the new players needed to be supported by charging a low licence fee. The trade-off between the need for revenue and the need to ensure low-cost connectivity is a policy choice and a case could be made for either decision.

Although TRAI had recommended no cap on the number of licences, the fact that the 2G spectrum available for allocation was limited meant only a few new entrants in each circle could receive it.[56] It was therefore necessary to find a transparent and fair method to select from among the applicants for the award of the licence.

Initially, the DoT announced that applications for telecom licences would be accepted up to 1 October 2007. However, as the total number of applications by 1 October had mounted to 575, it was announced on 10 January 2008 that only applications received up to 25 September 2007 would be considered in the first stage. This reduced the number under consideration to about 250. It was also announced that all eligible applicants would get letters of intent (LoIs) on that very day and that these could be converted into licences on payment of the required fee. It was separately announced (an hour later!) that to deposit the fees, a one-hour window would be open that same afternoon from 3.30 p.m. to 4.30 p.m. Those who converted the LoIs to licences first would be given spectrum first. This was a significant departure from the past practice of the first come, first served (FCFS) principle, where licences were processed as they were received and, therefore, those who applied first got the licence and spectrum first.

The end result was that on 10 January 2008, 120 licences were issued for 2G spectrum at the 2001 price to 46 companies to deliver mobile services in 23 circles. Two more licences were issued in July 2008. There were press reports of an unseemly rush to pay the fees and get the licences as well as allegations that some applicants had advance information that enabled them to get bank drafts and other documents ready early. Despite adverse press reports, there was no immediate challenge to DoT's decision. This was a puzzle. If the process was as flawed as it seemed, one would expect those denied licences to challenge the action in the courts.

Towards the end of the year, two companies (Unitech Wireless and Swan Telecom) that were allocated licences and spectrum, issued new equity in the company to foreign investors. The premium at which these shares were issued suggested that the

---

[56]As these were Universal Access Services, licensees could offer landline services if they wanted, but there was no demand for such services.

value of the spectrum (in the assessment of foreign investors) was much higher than what the companies had paid. Controversy began to build up. In May 2009, complaints were made to the CVC about the issue of the licences to some companies and the CBI was asked to investigate. The CAG received letters from the public protesting the DoT decision and in December 2009, it decided to conduct a performance audit.

In September 2010, the Centre for Public Interest Litigation and several others filed a PIL in the Supreme Court seeking a review of the 120 licences. The Supreme Court bench of justices G.S. Singhvi and A.K. Ganguly decided to hear the petition. The court also directed the CBI to pursue the investigation it had been asked to undertake by the CVC, keeping in view the draft report of the CAG that had become available earlier.

The decision of the Supreme Court to take up the petition made the 2G controversy that much more explosive, lending credibility to the charge that something was seriously wrong. With the Supreme Court taking up the legality of the issue of licences and the CBI readying to file a charge-sheet, the DMK leadership was persuaded that it would be best for Minister A. Raja to resign. He did so on 15 November 2010 and was replaced by Kapil Sibal of the Congress.

CAG REPORT ON 2G

The CAG report on 2G was tabled in Parliament on 16 November 2010. It made three important criticisms. Two of these had to do with the manner of processing of applications, which had allowed companies that did not meet the stated requirements to be considered for licences, and the non-transparency in the manner of selection among the multiple applicants. I thought both criticisms had merit. The third criticism was that the low price led to a huge loss of revenue to the exchequer. It is this criticism that caught public attention and contributed to the perception that a major scam had been perpetrated. However, it is here that the CAG was off the mark.

The price to be charged for spectrum is an issue of economic policy and it should be decided on the basis of well-defined principles within the law. The CAG took it as self-evident that the price should have been set at what would have emerged from a 'market-driven process'. This ignored the fact that several policy statements had indicated that spectrum pricing should not be driven by revenue maximization but the larger objective of telecom policy to increase connectivity at an affordable price. The CAG also ignored the specific reason given by TRAI to fix the price at the 2001 level.

Having concluded that the price should reflect what the market would bear, the CAG simply went on to quantify the loss to the exchequer by comparing the revenue *actually* realized with what *could have been* realized based on four hypothetical prices for spectrum. The difference was called 'presumptive loss'. The first three alternative price estimates yielded presumptive losses of ₹57,666 crore, ₹67,364 crore and ₹69,626 crore, respectively[57]. The fourth presumptive loss was based on an equivalent 2G price, calculated from the price for 3G spectrum, when it was auctioned two years later in 2010.

The methodology for deriving a 2G price from the 3G price was highly questionable because 2G and 3G are like apples and oranges. 2G is primarily for voice transmission while 3G is for data (including video). The CAG made some calculations based on a proportional equivalence of 2G to 3G and on this basis arrived at a humungous estimate of presumptive loss of ₹1.76 lakh crore. This became the defining measure of the 2G scam in the public mind. *The New Indian Express* ran a headline with '₹1760000000000' in bold font stretched horizontally across the front page. Not surprisingly,

---

[57]The first of these estimates was based on an unsolicited offer for pan-India spectrum made by S Tel, which did not qualify under the cutoffs announced and in any case withdrew the offer later. The other two were based on pricing the spectrum on the basis of the valuation of new shares sold in Unitech Wireless and Swan Telecom, which got licences and spectrum and raised money to make rollout investments.

the 2G allocation came to be called the mother of all scams.

Coming from an official source, these huge estimates of loss to the exchequer, which implied corresponding huge gains to private parties, stirred up suspicion of massive corruption. The opposition in Parliament demanded the appointment of a JPC. The Government said a JPC was not necessary and that the report should be considered by the Public Accounts Committee (PAC), in the normal process. The opposition reacted by preventing Parliament from functioning for the entire winter session. In the end, the Government conceded the demand for a JPC, if only to ensure that the Budget session to begin in January was not disrupted. A JPC was constituted in April 2011.

As the public debate intensified, the PM stated the position clearly in the Rajya Sabha on 24 February 2011 when he said, 'The basic purpose of the telecom policy is not to maximize revenue [but] to maximize tele-density and [the] public good.' In an interaction with journalists, Kapil Sibal put the revenue loss issue in perspective by referring to the pricing of water. He said the Government could always charge a higher price for drinking water if it wanted, and would gain some revenue, but there are good social reasons why it does not, and no one calls this a presumptive loss. From a public policy perspective, the value of spectrum is not simply realizable revenue: there are spin-off benefits to consumers from a faster expansion of the network that are also relevant. The question to ask was whether fixing the low price of spectrum was in line with telecom policy and whether it had promoted its social objectives.

The CAG held that the decision of the DoT to issue licences despite the objections of the Ministry of Finance was a violation of policy, which required that spectrum pricing be decided jointly by the two ministries. However, this ignored the fact that the final price was not settled when the licences were issued. The terms of the licence allowed the price to be raised subsequently, and the two ministries continued to discuss the pricing issue. The PM clarified the position in the Rajya Sabha when he said that while the Ministry of Finance had favoured an auction initially, the two ministers (Chidambaram and Raja) had finally agreed on a package where the 2G spectrum would be allocated at the 2001 price, while all future spectrum would be auctioned. They reported this agreement to the PM on 4 July 2008 and he accepted it because it fully met the requirements of the cabinet decision of 2003 that spectrum pricing should be decided by the two ministries, and was also in line with the recommendations of TRAI, the technical advisory arm of the Government. He also specifically said that he found the argument of a level playing field for new entrants persuasive.

Did the policy achieve its stated social objectives? The available evidence shows that the outcomes were outstanding with a huge increase in telephone coverage and sharp drop in prices. Telephone density for mobile phones (number of lines per 100 of the population) was only 1.24 in 2003. It increased to 76 by 2012. Average revenue per minute, a measure of the tariff charged to the consumer, declined from ₹2.42 in 2003 to ₹0.29 in 2011. The number of mobile phones increased from around 36 million in 2004 to 919 million by 2012, marking a revolution in expanding telecom connectivity. In fact, as far as the consumer was concerned, the telecom sector outperformed any other infrastructure sector by a large margin. The CAG's 'performance audit' should have brought out these achievements but it only focused on estimates of hypothetical losses to the exchequer.

Vinod Rai was CAG at the time and he has mentioned in his book, Not Just an Accountant,[58] that Murli Manohar Joshi, chairman of the PAC, was questioning officials from different departments on issues related to 2G. Rai was also invited to these meetings. He reported that several MPs expressed concern about the large losses being talked about, based on the sale of equity in Swan Telecom and Unitech Wireless at a premium, and what this implied for the market value of spectrum. He says in his book that if MPs

---

[58]Rai, V. Not Just an Accountant, Rupa, 2014.

were expressing these views, the CAG could not avoid coming out with an estimate. Contrary to the public impression that the CAG 'uncovered' the scam, he only quantified what was already being widely talked about.

It is arguable that instead of succumbing to the pressure to provide an estimate, the CAG should have presented a reasoned assessment of whether the revenue loss issue was relevant given the stated social objectives of the policy. I have no doubt that if the spectrum had been auctioned, it would have realized a higher value, though nowhere close to what the CAG estimated. The question to ask is whether the decision to charge a lower price was justified for achieving the broader objectives of policy. That is what a real performance audit would have done, but the CAG never attempted this.

The CAG recognized that estimating hypothetical revenue losses is inherently difficult and that is why a range of four estimates was offered. However, if the idea was to give a full sense of the alternatives, it is puzzling that the report made no mention of an alternative estimate approved by R.P. Singh, former director-general (audit) in the CAG's department, who supervised the team that prepared the 2G report. Singh testified to the JPC (he had retired by then) that he viewed the ₹1.76 lakh crore estimate of loss as nothing more than a 'mathematical calculation' and had even removed it from an earlier draft, inserting his own estimate of the loss at ₹2,645 crore based on inflation indexing. Singh said he signed the 2G report despite his reservations because he felt he could not question the decision of the headquarters.[59] Adding Singh's estimate to the others would have given a more complete sense of the huge range of variation. Instead, the internal estimate of the team was not even mentioned.

The CAG's approach to calculating revenue loss was also very narrow, focusing only on the initial revenue gain from a higher spectrum price. The logic of the lower price was that it would

---

[59]*Mint*, 11 September 2011.

stimulate a faster growth of telecom, which it clearly did. This would have led to higher revenue from the spectrum charge and other taxes on telecom that would offset the initial loss. In fact, if the faster expansion of telecom also led to a faster growth in GDP, it would generate an additional flow of revenue that needed to be taken into account. These future effects are not easy to quantify, but need to be incorporated for a reasonable estimate of the net impact on revenues. No such effort was made.

In February 2012, the Supreme Court bench of justices Singhvi and Ganguly pronounced that the 2G licences had been given on the basis of a process that was arbitrary and contrary to public interest. All the 122 licences were declared illegal and quashed. The court also categorically stated that auctioning was the best way of allocating scarce resources and TRAI was directed to make fresh recommendations for grant of licences. Subsequently, the Government moved a Presidential Reference before the Supreme Court seeking a clarification on whether auction was the only permissible mode for allocation of natural resources across all sectors.

A five-judge bench, presided over by Chief Justice S.H. Kapadia, pronounced that auctioning was not the only method open to the Government. Justice D.K. Jain authored the leading opinion, and observed that there was no constitutional mandate that any disposal of a natural resource must be guided by revenue maximization and, therefore, be through auction. He observed that such a submission was based neither on law nor on logic. He also noted that alienation of natural resources to the highest bidder may not always subserve the common good, and may in some cases be against the public good. The Supreme Court cited many instances where auctions had been deviated from, and where allocations had been upheld by the courts. It also said that the potential of abuse cannot be the basis for striking down a method of allocation, and this potential existed even in auctions. It took the view that it is for the executive branch to determine how a natural resource is allocated. But the manner of allocation must be transparent and fair and, to that extent, the courts would exercise judicial review.

The Supreme Court's opinion on the Presidential Reference shows a keen understanding of the complexity of economic issues as well as an appreciation of the need for judicial restraint in not overstepping into the realm of the executive. However, it did not affect the decision on 2G allocation because when the Reference was moved, its maintainability was challenged partly on the ground that it was a backdoor means to overcome the 2G judgement. To counter that objection, the Attorney General had categorically stated before the court that the Government was not questioning the correctness of the Court's decision as far as spectrum allocation was concerned. The Supreme Court judgement on the Presidential Reference therefore applied to all natural resources other than spectrum. It also applied to coal, which became controversial later.

The 2G spectrum from the cancelled licences was auctioned as directed by the Supreme Court. I was directly involved as a member of the GoM overseeing the process. We had a false start when the reserve price recommended by TRAI was fixed too high. Rahul Khullar took over as TRAI chairman in May 2012 and recalculated the reserve price on a different basis, significantly lowering it for many circles. The Government realized ₹62,000 crore from the auction. This was seen at the time as a success but it became clear a few years later that the telecom companies had bid over-exuberantly, borrowing heavily to pay for the 2G spectrum and investing in expansion of the network. These loans, mainly from public sector banks, turned into NPAs when the financial performance of the companies did not come up to expectation. In other words, the benefit to the Budget in 2013 from the initial revenues from the auction was at the expense of banking sector losses a few years later, imposing a burden on later Budgets for recapitalizing the banks.

The JPC finally submitted its report in 2013. Signed by the chairman, it categorically rejected the concept of presumptive loss, which was the whole basis of the CAG's argument. However, the value of the report as a parliamentary pronouncement was greatly diminished because it was not a consensus document. MPs representing the Left and the BJP submitted minutes of dissent, which argued that the majority report whitewashed an undisguised scam. The DMK members objected to the criticism. It exemplified that once an issue is politicized and party lines drawn, parliamentary reports cannot rise above the political divide.

Though the Supreme Court judgement cancelled the 2G licences, it explicitly stated that it should have no bearing on the issue of corruption, which was being separately examined in the Trial Court. The trial of Raja and others on criminal charges began in April 2011. The charges included an alleged kickback of about ₹200 crore to a company in Tamil Nadu connected with the DMK. The trial concluded six-and-a-half years after it started; Special Judge O.P. Saini, in a 1,552-page judgement, observed, 'The prosecution has miserably failed to prove its case and all accused are acquitted.' Judge Saini maintained that no credible evidence was presented to prove a charge of conspiring to help any private party. The acquittal by the Trial Court has been appealed by the Government in the High Court.

THE NARRATIVE GOES OUT OF CONTROL

As the 2G controversy built up in the media, I was often asked by friends why the PM did not intervene earlier. I raised the issue with him informally at one stage. The PM said he had already explained his position in the Rajya Sabha. He also pointed out that it would not have been proper for him as PM to start taking punitive action against ministers from a coalition partner merely on the strength of press reports and statements of opposition MPs.

The PM was less constrained when dealing with ministers from his own party. Law Minister Ashwani Kumar had to resign for a purely procedural infringement because he asked to see the CBI affidavit on coal block allocation, whereas the Supreme Court had directed the CBI not to share it with anyone. Railway

Minister Pawan Bansal resigned when there were allegations that his nephew was interfering in Railways recruitment. Minister of Environment and Forests Jayanthi Natarajan was asked to resign when there were rumours of corruption in granting environmental clearances. These were all Congress ministers where the PM and Sonia Gandhi could take the decision, assessing the impact on the image of the party. They could not have acted as unilaterally when dealing with a coalition partner.

The public debate never recognized that the CAG report is not meant to be a final pronouncement even on financial issues. It is only an input into the PAC and it is the PAC's findings that are presented to Parliament. The issues would have been clarified if the matter had been discussed in Parliament but the opposition tactic of blocking Parliament from functioning prevented this. The PM had promised in Parliament: 'The law of the land must punish the wrongdoers.' And the law did get to work. A process of investigation began and a cabinet minister (A. Raja) resigned. However, the process took an inordinately long time. In the meantime, the CAG's apparent endorsement of massive losses made headlines and enabled the opposition to milk the allegations for political gain.

The Government clearly let the narrative get out of control. Manmohan Singh explained his position in Parliament, but statements in Parliament were not enough in a world where negative messages were going viral through digital media. A more proactive communications strategy was needed in a situation where the opposition had effectively prevented the Parliament from functioning and the CAG report was sensationalized.

COAL BLOCK ALLOCATIONS

The controversy on coal block allocations centred on the fact that coal blocks for captive mining were being allocated by an administrative procedure and not through auctions. The policy had been in place since 1993 when it became clear that Coal India, the public sector monopoly supplier, would not be able to meet the ever-increasing demand for coal. Industries using coal were allowed to apply for coal blocks for captive mining and blocks were allotted by a Steering Committee of Secretaries that considered the applications subject to certain guidelines.

The CAG decided to carry out a performance audit of the coal block allocations under the UPA. The PM, in his capacity as coal minister, had approved a proposal in July 2004 to allocate coal blocks by auctions. Its implementation was delayed because the states objected strongly and the Government decided to implement auctions by amending the law, which took time. In the meantime, the Screening Committee continued to allocate coal blocks and the implicit loss of auction revenue became a basis for criticism.

An early draft of the CAG report obtained by *The Times of India* in March 2012 claimed that the allocation of coal blocks had led to unjustified benefits of ₹10.7 lakh crore, of which ₹4.6 lakh crore was attributed to the private sector.[60] The newspaper promptly published the story with a catchy opening line 'The CAG is at it again'. As in the case of 2G, a parallel process of criminal investigation was started in May 2009 by two BJP MPs, Prakash Javadekar and Hansraj Ahir (both later to become ministers in the Narendra Modi government), complaining to the CVC in May 2012 about two specific cases of improper allocations. The CVC directed the CBI to investigate these complaints. Separately, Manohar Lal Sharma and NGO Common Cause filed writ petitions in the Supreme Court seeking cancellation of all coal block allocations made since 1993. A Supreme Court bench consisting of Justices R.M. Lodha and Anil R. Dave took up the petition for consideration.

The final CAG report was released in August 2012, and it reduced its earlier estimate of unjustified benefit by limiting it to coal blocks allocated to the private sector; even for that category, the amount of the benefit was reduced from ₹4.6 lakh crore in the draft to ₹1.86 lakh crore. But this was still a very large amount.

---

[60]*The Times of India*, 23 March 2012.

The Government was faulted on two counts. First, the procedures followed by the Screening Committee for allocation were arbitrary and non-transparent. Responding to this criticism, the ministry appointed an Internal Committee to re-examine past cases of allocations and, on finding some infirmities, recommended the cancellation of 87 allocations.

The second criticism related to the failure to implement auctioning, which the CAG claimed led to huge unjustified benefits. The CAG's conclusion depended critically upon the assumption that auctions could have been introduced by a purely administrative decision and an amendment of the law was not necessary. This view took no account of the strong opposition of the states. Several CMs of coal-bearing states (West Bengal, Chhattisgarh, Jharkhand, Odisha and Rajasthan) had written to the PM opposing auctions. They preferred the existing system in which private sector companies needed recommendations from the CM of the state where the block was located, and claimed they used this power to give preference to applicants who promised to make downstream investments in the state.

The CAG made much of the fact that the Department of Legal Affairs had initially advised that auctions could be introduced administratively. However, the same department changed its advice on learning that state governments were strongly opposed. Parliament was also sensitive to the views of the states. When the Bill for amending the Mines and Minerals (Development and Regulation) [MMDR] Act to allow auctions was referred to the relevant Standing Committee, the committee itself advised the ministry to conduct a second round of discussions with the state governments, further adding to the delay.

Finally, the CAG's estimates of unjustified gains were, in my view, grossly exaggerated because of some basic errors in the assumptions made and the methodology used. First, the price per tonne of coal produced and the cost per tonne were derived from the averages of all mines of Coal India. Former coal secretary Anil Swarup has pointed out that the price of coal from the newly allotted mines should have been much lower because the mines were known to have much poorer quality coal than the average for all mines of Coal India.[61] The cost of extraction should also have been much higher because the new mines were in locations with much poorer infrastructure. Correcting for these factors (i.e. lowering the price and raising the cost per tonne) would have reduced the estimate of benefit per tonne.

Second, the entire difference was called 'unjustified gain' per tonne of coal even though it included what would be called 'the normal profit' on mining. The unjustified benefit could only refer to the excess above normal profit. The CAG provided no indication of what the normal profit should be.

Finally, the total benefit was estimated by multiplying the benefit per tonne (itself exaggerated) with an estimate of the entire recoverable coal reserves. As these benefits would accrue only over three decades or so, depending upon the life of the mine, the CAG should have applied an appropriate discount rate to get a present value. For a professional accounting body to make such elementary mistakes is a puzzle. The use of a discount rate to derive the present value of a stream of benefits spread over time is taught in any basic accounting course. It was something the CAG must surely have known.

The Supreme Court bench gave its judgement in October 2014, a few months after the change of government. The bench pronounced that 214 of the 218 coal blocks allocated under the Screening Committee procedure from 1993 to 2011 were illegal because of arbitrariness in the procedure. The illegality applied equally to mines allocated before the UPA period.

Having declared the licences illegal, the Supreme Court left it to the Government to decide how to proceed. The UPA had already amended the law to facilitate auctions for new allocations. The NDA government informed the Court that it would auction the cancelled blocks. To facilitate this process, the Government

---

[61]Swarup, A. *Not Just a Civil Servant*, Unicorn Books, 2019.

passed a new law in 2015 that provided for prior allottees to be compensated for expenditure incurred in developing the land and mine infrastructure. The law provided that compensation was contingent on successful reallocation of the blocks by auction. The results of the auctions were mixed: the first auction did well, but the second one failed. This demonstrated the uncertainty associated with hypothetical assumptions of loss to the exchequer.

Several problems arose in implementing the process. Where the coal blocks were successfully reallocated, there were disputes on the extent of compensation due and these cases are currently in the courts. Where the coal blocks remain unallocated, no compensation has been paid. This experience illustrates how judicial intervention in an economic process can have unexpected side-effects that need to be considered carefully. The cancellation of an allocation obtained through improper means is one thing and would not affect the investment climate. However, cancellation because the process followed by the Government was judged to be improper, with no demonstrable fault of the investor, is quite another.

The Supreme Court did not directly prescribe what the Government should do to handle this problem. It was left to the Government to adopt a fair procedure but the results suggest that not enough thought was given to how this would be done and the terms on which compensation would be given. The system always resists any demand for compensation, and interprets the law to avoid or minimize compensation. This makes it all the more important that the law and rules be carefully drafted to ensure fairness and enable quick resolution.

The CBI filed a total of 40 cases against officials, industrialists and politicians on grounds of corruption in the allocation of coal blocks. Judgement has been pronounced in two cases: a former CM (Madhu Koda of Jharkhand), a former coal secretary (H.C. Gupta), and some other officials have been found guilty and given prison sentences. The sentences have been appealed.

These convictions created insecurity among civil servants, making them feel vulnerable for actions taken in good faith. The problem arose from the provision of the Prevention of Corruption Act 1988 (section 13.1.d) under which a civil servant could be held guilty of corruption even if he/she had never accepted any bribe or other material advantage, but had 'obtained a valuable thing or monetary reward without public interest for any person'. As any permission given to an individual or company can be said to be a 'valuable thing', the action could be deemed to be corrupt if it is found to be 'without public interest'. As public interest in this context is not well-defined, it increased the feeling of vulnerability among civil servants.

The case of H.C. Gupta exemplifies the problem. He enjoyed a high reputation for personal integrity among his peers, and I know that such reputations are not easily earned. There was no evidence of any bribe or other monetary consideration. He was convicted because he was chairman of the Steering Committee that allocated coal blocks and, in the case in question, the company allotted the block did not meet the eligibility requirements. As chairman of the committee and secretary of the department, he was held personally responsible for this error and convicted for corruption. Many civil servants felt that if they had to operate under these rules, it would force everyone to be exceptionally careful, personally checking everything, leading to delays in decision-making.

The UPA initiated the process of amending the Prevention of Corruption Act and this has since been done. However, the amended Act applies only prospectively. Actions taken earlier will be tried under the old law, which will apply to all the 40-odd cases that have been filed on coal allocation.

TEARING UP THE ORDINANCE

The corruption issue surfaced again in July 2013 when the Supreme Court pronounced judgement on a PIL protesting that legislators convicted of a criminal offence could continue functioning as legislators as long as they had appealed against the conviction and the appeal was pending. A surprisingly large number of legislators had avoided disqualification because the process of appeals took a long time. The Supreme Court put an end to that practice by pronouncing that, henceforth, legislators would be disqualified immediately on conviction, even if the conviction was appealed in a higher court.

The ruling was prospective, but it posed a threat to Lalu Prasad Yadav who had been elected to the Lok Sabha in 2009, and was an important ally and firm political supporter of Sonia Gandhi. He was being tried on various fodder scam cases pertaining to his years as CM of Bihar and the judgement on one of these cases was expected on 30 September. If convicted, he could be disqualified from sitting in Parliament and standing for elections.

The Government responded to the Supreme Court judgement by introducing a Bill to amend the Representation of the People Act 1951 to give convicted legislators the limited privilege of participating in the proceedings of the legislature but without the ability to vote until the appeals process was completed. The Bill was being considered in the Rajya Sabha but in the face of strong opposition, the Government agreed to refer it to the Standing Committee. As it was unlikely to be passed soon, the Government decided to introduce an Ordinance, which would later have to be ratified by Parliament.

The case for the proposed amendment was that politicians were vulnerable to politically motivated charges and the system could be manipulated to secure a conviction at the local level. Justice could only be assured by appealing to a higher level, but the process took so long that disqualification on first conviction was felt to be too strong. That said, resorting to an Ordinance could only be justified by some element of urgency, and the only urgency was the impending judgement in the Lalu's case. The decision to move for an Ordinance was strongly criticized by the opposition even as it was vigorously supported by senior members of the cabinet.

At this stage, Congress Vice President Rahul Gandhi took an unusual step. The party had organized a press briefing on 27 September to explain the rationale for the Ordinance. Rahul made an unscheduled appearance at the briefing and announced that he was personally opposed to the Ordinance. He referred to it as 'a piece of nonsense that should be torn up'. He went on to say it was the sort of compromise with corruption that all parties resorted to, but it was time to stop.

Many young people approved of Rahul's stand. However, leading members of the BJP asserted that the Congress vice president had demeaned the office of the PM, who was on an official visit to the US, and called upon Dr Manmohan Singh to resign. The press had a field day presenting Rahul's action as a direct attack on the authority of the PM. The latter was in New York at the time and issued a characteristically mild statement that the Congress vice president had written to him expressing his views, and the matter would be discussed in the cabinet on his return.

AN IMPORTANT FAULT LINE EXPOSED

I was part of the PM's delegation in New York and my brother Sanjeev, who had retired from the IAS, telephoned to say he had written a piece that was very critical of the PM. He had emailed it to me and said he hoped I didn't find it embarrassing! Sanjeev had been quite unsparing. He said the PM had betrayed himself time and again by turning a blind eye to goings on around him. He also said that when he took up the office, he became 'our' PM and not the Congress party's representative. He went on to say it was not too late to resign: 'Rahul is ripe to take over and we would all welcome his coming out of the shadows.' It was strong, no-holds-barred stuff and, not surprisingly, Sanjeev's article was widely reported in the press with reference to him being my brother.[62]

The first thing I did was to take the text across to the PM's suite because I wanted him to hear about it first from me. He read it in silence and, at first, made no comment. Then, he suddenly

---

[62]*The Times of India*, 26 September 2013.

asked me whether I thought he should resign. I thought about it for a while and said I did not think a resignation on this issue was appropriate. I wondered then whether I was simply saying what I thought he would like to hear but on reflection I am convinced I gave him honest advice.

The incident was still a hot subject of discussion when we returned to New Delhi. Most of my friends agreed with Sanjeev. They felt the PM had for too long accepted the constraints under which he had to operate and this had tarnished his reputation. The rubbishing of the Ordinance was seen as demeaning the office of the PM and justified resigning on principle. I did not agree. Rahul's action was certainly embarrassing and unseemly. He himself admitted this publicly a few days later in Ahmedabad, when he said, 'My mother told me that the words I had used were wrong. In hindsight, maybe the words I used were wrong, but the sentiment was not wrong. I have a right to voice my opinion. A large part of the Congress party wanted it.'[63] The PM also told me that Rahul had called on him personally after he returned from the US to express his regrets and say he meant no disrespect.

I did not think the incident called for a resignation from the PM. Running a coalition government obviously meant making many compromises. In such a situation, it was essential for any holder of political office to resign if political compulsions were pushing them to act differently from what was right. The PM's offer to resign on the issue of the nuclear deal belonged to this category. Resigning because Rahul had rubbished the Ordinance publicly did not. In fact, his opposition to the Ordinance was, if anything, a principled position against tolerating corruption. Resigning on that issue would either look as if the PM was determined to help convicted politicians, even when his party was willing to change course, or be seen as acting out of pique.

In a way, the incident highlighted an important fault line in the UPA. The Congress saw Rahul as the natural leader of the party

---

[63]*The Economic Times*, 3 October 2013

and wanted him to take a larger role. In this situation, as soon as Rahul expressed his opposition to the Ordinance, senior Congress politicians, who had earlier supported the proposed Ordinance in the cabinet and even defended it publicly, promptly changed their position. I had always felt it would have been much better if Rahul had agreed to join the cabinet. The PM had repeatedly asked him to do so but he had preferred to stay out on the grounds that he wanted to strengthen the party. This was an important objective. But given his political position in the party, joining the cabinet would have created a greater sense of political cohesion in that body. Congress cabinet ministers would certainly have looked to him for signals, but the arrangement would have strengthened the cabinet as long as the PM and Rahul were seen to be on the same page.

In January 2014, well before the election notification was issued, Manmohan Singh announced he would not be a candidate for the PM's position after the election, and that Rahul was the best candidate for the job. Manmohan Singh was 81 years old at that time and not in the best of health, so no one was surprised at his decision. It was a dignified way of bowing out after two long innings. There was much speculation on whether Rahul would take over as Congress president before the election. That did not happen and the party went into the election under the leadership of Sonia Gandhi as president, with Rahul campaigning actively as vice president.

DEALING WITH CORRUPTION

Given the extent to which corruption came to dominate the stage in the last three years of UPA 2, it is relevant to ask whether any systemic progress was made in dealing with the problem. I think there was progress on several fronts although the extent was not recognized at the time.

The UPA effectively ensured that all future allocations of natural resources would be done through auctions. In the case of spectrum, it had already been decided, even before the Supreme Court decision, that except for the 2G spectrum, all future spectrums would be allocated by auction. The UPA also amended the MMDR Act in 2010 to provide for coal blocks to be auctioned. Another Bill to make auctions the only way of getting mining rights for minerals other than coal was introduced in 2011 and referred to the Standing Committee. The Supreme Court Judgement on Presidential Reference established that the Government was under no constitutional obligation to adopt auctions for resources other than spectrum. However, it decided to do so because methods other than auctions involve some discretionary decision-making, which is workable only if there is a high level of trust. When there is a significant trust deficit, as seems to be the case in India at present, auctions is clearly the best bet—at least from the point of view of a risk-averse civil servant!

Turning to the broader issue of building institutions that will guard against corruption, the passage of the Lokpal and Lokayuktas Act 2013, along with a parallel Whistle Blowers Protection Act 2014, was an important achievement. It went largely un-applauded because its greatest advocates, the leaders of the erstwhile IAC movement, were unhappy with some aspects of the Bill. Kejriwal even ridiculed the Bill by calling it the 'Jokepal Bill'. The NDA government, which succeeded the UPA, took a long time to appoint a Lokpal, but the appointment was finally made in February 2019.

The Lokpal as an institution is now in place but we have to wait and see how effective it will be in practice. Much will depend upon whether it develops a reputation as an institution immune to political pressure and on the quality of the investigation and prosecution skills it can muster. Equally important is the need to reform the functioning of the judicial system to avoid long delays. These delays cannot be blamed entirely on the judiciary because it does not function in isolation. It is often constrained by the time taken by other institutions. Nevertheless, there is need for deep judicial reform and this has been a missing element in our reform effort thus far.

Several other measures were taken to introduce greater transparency in government which could be expected to reduce corruption. The RTI Act 2005 opened up decision-making in government to external scrutiny and helped ordinary people defend their interests better and instil a greater sense of responsibility in the administration. Several steps were also taken to improve e-Governance for simplifying and reducing documentation. Pilot projects were undertaken to deliver high-volume, citizen-centric e-Governance services in 88 districts across seven states. These initiatives began under the UPA and have been continued and considerably expanded by the NDA.

Reform of election financing is another major area to combat corruption on which little progress has been made. Elections in India have become an expensive business and candidates often spend several times the amount permitted by the Election Commission. This in turn means campaign finance has to depend on unaccounted money. The resulting dependence of politicians on those with unaccounted money is a recipe for cronyism and corruption. The recent initiative of anonymous bonds that can be purchased from the RBI and donated to political parties is questionable because it actually increases non-transparency.

The nexus between money and politics is a matter of grave concern not just because of its implications for corruption, but also because the ability to control politics through money power can delegitimize democratic processes. This issue has been highlighted in recent years in mature democracies such as the US, where extreme inequality in income and wealth is increasingly seen as pushing politics in a particular direction, causing the public to lose faith in democratic processes.

MANMOHAN SINGH AS PM

I could not help being saddened at the way the public mood turned negative towards the end of Manmohan Singh's second term. He had served for 10 years as PM: the longest continuous period anyone had held that position since Jawaharlal Nehru.

The performance of his government in the first seven of its 10 years was outstanding. The economy clocked an average growth of 8.4 per cent in this period, the fastest growth rate ever. It was on his watch as PM that India moved from being a low-income developing country to the lower range of middle-income countries and came to be recognized as one of the fastest-growing emerging market economies in the world. India's private sector came to be perceived as a potentially strong engine of growth capable of developing a global footprint.

It was in his term that the absolute number of the poor in India declined and 138 million people were pulled out of poverty. Primary school enrolment became near universal, though much more needed to be done to improve the quality of education. Life expectancy improved and India was declared polio-free in 2014—in earlier years, the country regularly had about 100,000 polio cases. And he succeeded in bringing an end to the nuclear apartheid that had excluded India from the privileges enjoyed by the other countries in the NSG.

Manmohan Singh never bragged about his achievements. He genuinely believed it was best to let the results speak for themselves. But because neither he, nor his party, projected these achievements, they never formed part of the political discourse. I saw this for myself in 2013, when the Congress seemed unable or unwilling to claim credit for a decline in poverty in India, which was being widely acclaimed as a major achievement in the rest of the world. The elimination of polio, another major achievement that affected the lives of ordinary people, was mentioned in government documents but barely projected by the party.

Dr Singh was not naturally inclined to projecting himself as a leader. His instinct was not to prevail by force of authority but always to appreciate the other person's point of view and look for a consensual way to move forward. In many ways, this made him ideally suited to manage what he called the 'compulsions of coalition politics'. He was experienced and wise, deeply committed to the ideal of a pluralist, secular India and a firm believer that India must be part of a global community. And he had done much to further India's ability to contribute to building such a community.

Public memory is short and it was no surprise that towards the end of UPA 2, the achievements of the first seven years were forgotten and the narrative was dominated by the economic slowdown, a sense of paralysis in decision-making and the continuously repeated charges of corruption. At his last press conference, he was asked what he thought about his tenure. With characteristic modesty, he said he had done the best he could: 'History will judge me more kindly than the press does today.' I have no doubt he will be proved right. However, I reminded him that in saying so, he was quoting Winston Churchill. But Churchill had gone on to explain that history would judge him more kindly because he intended to write it himself! I have often urged Dr Manmohan Singh to write his memoirs but have had no luck so far.

18

THE PLANNING COMMISSION: AN INSIDE VIEW

One of the first things the Narendra Modi government did was to wind up the Planning Commission and replace it with a new institution, the National Institution for Transforming India, or NITI Aayog, which has very different functions. As the Planning Commission is no more, it is worth reflecting on the functions it performed, if only to help think through which of these functions remain important and how they will be performed in the current dispensation.

RETHINKING PLANNING FOR A MARKET-ORIENTED ECONOMY

The need for rethinking the role of the Planning Commission was evident when I joined in 2004. The economy had become much more market-oriented with the private sector expected to drive growth. There were some who believed that there was no role for planning in a market-driven economy: the Government just had to get out of the way and the market would do the rest. I never subscribed to this laissez-faire fantasy, which did not hold even in developed economies. They did not have planning commissions, but they all recognized that the government had an important role to play in achieving national goals.

The UPA had set ambitious targets of faster and more inclusive growth, which called for active involvement of government in multiple areas. This required careful planning but the nature of planning had to be very different from the past. The Government had to provide a policy framework that would enable the private sector to grow rapidly in an environment open to foreign trade and investment. The Government also had to ensure high-quality infrastructure such as seamless transport connectivity, reliable electric power and modern telecommunications. It also had to play a much larger role in the delivery of basic public services such as health, education, clean drinking water and sanitation in rural and urban areas. Rapid growth had also brought new challenges such as a faster pace of urbanization and the need to protect the environment from the pressures of economic growth, both of which required active government intervention.

I saw the Planning Commission as an institution that could help define a development strategy that would deal with these challenges and be acceptable to both the Centre and state governments. Our work revolved around three broad activities: setting national and state targets; helping to finance the development programmes of the Centre and provide assistance to the states for their plans; and helping to shape policies at the central and state levels.

SETTING NATIONAL AND STATE-LEVEL TARGETS

Governments need targets that reflect social aspirations. But they also need to ensure these are realistic and consistent with the levels of domestic savings and investment likely to be available, ensuring an acceptable level of the BOP deficit and reasonable fiscal deficits for both the Centre and the states. The Planning Commission not only set measurable targets for growth of GDP over a five-year period but also tested them for consistency using quantitative economic models. We also set national targets for reducing poverty, generating non-agricultural employment, improvements in education and health, and reduction in child malnutrition, infant mortality, maternal mortality, etc. These were also converted into state-specific targets in consultation with the states and used in monitoring performance.

This endeavour remains relevant even today. The NDA government has done away with Five-Year Plans but it has adopted the target of reaching a GDP of $5 trillion by 2024–25. With India's

GDP in 2018 at $2.7 trillion, the growth rate required in current US $ is required to be about 11 per cent. Allowing for inflation in the US at about 2 per cent, this implies GDP growth of 9 per cent per year in constant US $. If this is indeed the GDP growth the Government aims for, it should be made clear so we can measure performance year on year against this target.

The planning exercise can be seen as deploying a combination of policies and government programmes to achieve these targets. One of the biggest weaknesses in our system was that the Plan had come to be almost completely identified with programmes of public expenditure. The role of policy, which was at least as important, was greatly underplayed. I wanted to bring about a better balance between policies and programmes by using the Planning Commission to push for policy changes both at the central and state levels. We had some success but not as much as I would have liked.

FINANCING THE CENTRAL AND STATE PLANS

Given the importance attached to programmes, a lot of our time in the Planning Commission was spent ensuring that the central Budget provided a sufficient level of gross budgetary support (GBS) to finance the plan programmes of the Centre and provide central assistance to state plans.

We began by reviewing the demands for funds from the central ministries and states over the five-year period of the Plan. These demands would normally add up to a much larger figure than feasible and we would judiciously trim it down to a more reasonable number. We would then try to persuade the Ministry of Finance to commit to what we thought was a feasible level of GBS over the five-year period. The ministry would naturally have its own view given the pressure of the other 'non-plan expenditures' — salaries, defence, subsidies, etc — and the constraint of living within a fiscal deficit target. These discussions would narrow the difference between our assessment and that of the Ministry of Finance; the final number was decided by the PM.

I recall the meeting with Dr Manmohan Singh in 2007 when the GBS for the Eleventh Plan was finally decided. I argued for a GBS that would allow us to fund many programmes the Government had politically committed to, while providing adequately for investments critical for achieving the growth target. Chidambaram argued equally forcefully that we had to learn to live within our means. I was familiar with these arguments as I had made them for years as finance secretary. At one stage, he said, 'Our plan programmes have become a system of very leaky pipes and Montek wants to push more water through the pipes instead of trying to fix the leaks.' He was right that it was a leaky system but fixing the leaks would take time, especially as much of the leakage took place at the state level. If we wanted to increase the flow of benefits in the short run as the Government had promised, we had no choice but to push more water through the pipes while working separately to fix the leaks.

The PM settled the matter by picking a number between the two proposals and we then got down to dividing the GBS pie for the Eleventh Plan between the Centre and the states. The total GBS for the Eleventh Plan was roughly about 4.7 per cent of GDP. Of this, about three-fourths went to the central ministries and the rest was earmarked as central assistance for state plans, supplementing the funds provided by the states in their own budget.

Fixing the GBS entitlement for the ministries and states gave them an idea of the scale of financing to expect over the next five years. The corresponding annual allocations would then be made year by year to ensure the five-year total was achieved. The role of the Planning Commission in this process was to lobby for a suitably large GBS commitment by the Ministry of Finance and ensure that the allocation of this amount across ministries reflected plan priorities. It is not clear how this role will be played in the current dispensation as NITI Aayog is not assigned this function.

While we no longer have Five-Year Plans, we still need a mechanism to determine the total financing envelope over a three-year, five-year or seven-year horizon within which the individual programmes of central ministries are fitted. Otherwise, there is a danger that individual ministries will launch programmes that could become financially unsustainable over time.

The GBS allocated to central ministries was used either for central-sector programmes (national highways, railways, atomic energy, etc.) or to support schemes in sectors that are constitutionally the responsibility of the state governments (primary education, health services, agriculture, rural employment, etc). In the latter case, the individual schemes were called centrally sponsored schemes (CSS). They were implemented by state agencies in the field, following guidelines laid down by the Centre.

As the central government's engagement in education, health and rural development increased, the share of the CSS in the central plan increased steadily and by 2013–14, about 60 per cent of the GBS allocated to central ministries went into CSS.

The states were not happy with the expansion of CSS. They complained that the guidelines specified for CSS were often unsuited to conditions on the ground. The Centre was accused of following a 'one-size-fits-all' approach, very reminiscent of the complaint voiced by developing countries against the World Bank or IMF! As the states also had to bear a share of the cost, they felt they were being forced to divert their own funds to schemes that reflected the Centre's priorities. They wanted the funds from the CSS to be converted into untied central assistance in support of state plans. The central ministries were completely opposed to this suggestion. They saw the CSS as a means of ensuring that central funds went to sectors that the Centre viewed as critical for inclusiveness.

I personally agreed with the states on this issue. They were democratically elected governments and responsible to the electorate. I felt that if we were not able to convert CSS into untied central assistance to the states, we should restructure the CSS to allow maximum flexibility within the schemes, as we had done for the RKVY introduced in 2007. We proposed that in the Twelfth Plan, 10 per cent of funds for each CSS in each state should be unconstrained by central guidelines, provided the funds were used in the sector for which the CSS was designed. I had in mind increasing this to 25 per cent if it worked well.

With the abandonment of Five-Year Plans, central assistance for state plans no longer exists but the CSS continue. The issue of giving the states more flexibility within these schemes remains relevant. A radical alternative would be to consider gathering the funds for all the CSS into a single pool and define an entitlement for each state from this pool on the basis of a transparent formula. The state should then be able to draw upon this entitlement under any of the CSS, abiding by the guidelines of the specific CSS it chooses. This would give the states flexibility to use their total entitlement for central support under any of the CSS, thus introducing competition among the central ministries to devise CSS guidelines that are more acceptable to the states.

EFFECTIVENESS OF PLAN SPENDING

With Plans focusing heavily on public expenditure programmes, it was necessary to ensure the expenditure was productively spent. This was a weak spot in our planning. Priority areas received additional funds, but there was insufficient focus on ensuring that the expenditure led to the outcomes expected. For example, the priority given to primary education led to substantial fund allocations for the Sarva Shiksha Abhiyan, but the funds were used to build new schools and classrooms, hire teachers, and provide mid-day meals. All this helped increase school enrolment but there was little evidence of improved learning levels, which was the desired 'outcome'.

The poor quality of outcomes was evident from the Annual Status of Education Report (ASER) brought out by NGO Pratham; it showed that half the children in Grade V could not even read a text meant for students in Grade II! There was a similar result from the OECD's (Organisation for Economic Co-operation and Development) Programme for International Student Assessment

(PISA), which measures academic achievement in 15-year-olds, in which India participated for the first time in 2009. The Indian contingent was drawn from Tamil Nadu and Himachal Pradesh, widely regarded as two of our best states for school education. The results were a rude shock. Out of 74 participating countries/ provinces both developed and developing, Tamil Nadu ranked 72nd and Himachal Pradesh ranked 73rd, just above Kyrgyztan, which was at the bottom! The Ministry of Human Resource Development simply rejected the results on the grounds that the tests were culturally biased and decided to withdraw from participating. I tried to persuade the ministry to reconsider but failed. I am glad to hear that India will now participate in PISA in 2021.

Ensuring better quality of delivery is especially difficult in the so-called 'soft sectors' of education and health. It is relatively easy to work out what is needed to build a good road or railway line and, once funding is approved, the relevant agencies can do a reasonably good job. It is much more difficult to work out what would make for a good school or health clinic in a rural area.

We invited a team from IIM Ahmedabad to review our system for appraising programmes in the social sectors. The team found that programmes submitted by ministries for approval of funding contained lots of details regarding inputs but hardly any on measurable outcomes, i.e. levels of learning, state of health or burden of disease. It recommended strongly that all programmes clearly indicate quantifiable outcomes expected so that progress could be regularly measured and evaluated in comparison with expectations. Evidence of better performance in some areas would provide pointers for what works well.

Abhijit Banerjee of MIT, who has done extensive work on evaluation of programmes in India and elsewhere and was awarded the 2019 Nobel Prize for Economics, pointed out to me that we were too quick to roll out national programmes in response to political announcements. In his view, we would be much better off launching a number of pilot programmes experimenting with different designs to see what works best in what circumstances.

An obvious implication was that we must provide much greater flexibility to the states to experiment with alternative designs. We followed up on this suggestion by including a provision in the Twelfth Plan that states could experiment with pilot programmes for providing universal healthcare in one or two districts, which the central government could fund. The proposal did not evoke a positive response from the Ministry of Health and we could not take the idea forward.

I came to the conclusion that the best way of improving project design was to subject programmes to high-quality independent evaluation and use the results to modify the programme in future. My brief stint as the director of the IEO of the IMF gave me an exposure to how international financial institutions were benefitting from independent evaluation of their programmes. Such evaluation must be in addition to regular in-house evaluations (also called concurrent evaluations) that the ministries should do in any case. Ministries were generally not happy with independent evaluations, often deeming them unnecessary, but the problem with in-house evaluations is that they tend to be biased in favour of validating existing practices.

We had a Programme Evaluation Division in the Planning Commission and it had done some good work, but I felt it needed to be greatly strengthened by bringing in a professional of the rank of member of the Planning Commission at the helm, with the flexibility to hire specialized consultants if needed, and the provision to publicize their reports, favourable or not. The PM accepted this proposal and I tried to get Abhijit to take up the position. He expressed interest but in the end could not come because he and Esther Duflo, his wife and fellow Nobel Laureate, were expecting their first baby. We recruited Ajay Chibber, who had earlier worked in senior positions in the World Bank and UNDP. He joined in 2013 but his appointment was terminated shortly after the change of government in 2014. I remain convinced that an independent evaluation organization is essential if we want to move towards evidence-based policymaking. In the absence of the Planning Commission, it could be located in the NITI Aayog, the Ministry of Finance or the PMO.

PUSHING FOR POLICY CHANGES AT THE CENTRE

I was convinced that changes in policies were at least as important as public expenditure programmes in achieving plan targets, but it was not easy to persuade ministries to change policies. Our plan documents contained extensive discussions of the policy changes needed in different areas, some in the realm of the states and others in the realm of the Centre. However, these recommendations were not mandatory. When ministers approved the Plan in the cabinet, they knew the financial allocations proposed for their ministries would ultimately determine the funding they would get for their programmes over the next five years. Not surprisingly, they took a great deal of interest in the allocations proposed and would protest if they did not get enough. I don't recall any minister commenting on the policy recommendations made in plan documents for their ministry!

In retrospect, I think the approach of listing a large number of proposed policy changes in the plan document, covering all areas, was not a particularly useful way of getting things done. We would have done better if we had identified the most important and immediate areas for action, picking out critical changes for the next two to three years, fleshing out policy recommendations in some detail, and also indicating the mutually supportive changes needed in other areas. The political feasibility of this package could then have been discussed in the cabinet and approved for implementation within a defined time-frame.

Despite these limitations, I tried to get the Planning Commission to push for policy reforms in a number of areas. Besides the push for PPPs in infrastructure, we focused our effort on three additional areas: energy policy, restructuring of the Railways and water resource management. We had some success in energy policy, very little in the Railways and could only make a start in water.

I also used my interactions with the CMs to push them to act in areas that were constitutionally in the realm of the states.

Energy is critical for rapid growth and we are an energy-deficit country, heavily dependent on imports (mainly of crude oil) to meet our energy demands. We were also beginning to import coal in increasing quantities. We needed to reduce energy imports both for BOP reasons and energy security. This required moderation of the growth of energy demand as well as increased domestic supply. Achieving energy self-sufficiency through our plentiful coal reserves would have harmful effects on the climate. We therefore needed to shift towards renewable energy to make our development more environmentally sustainable. All this called for an integrated approach to energy policy but different sources of energy were under different ministries and policies had evolved in silos with no consistency across sectors. There was no consistent policy on energy pricing or the role of the private sector — domestic or foreign — in the different parts of the energy sector, such as coal, petroleum, electricity and solar energy.

We set up an Expert Committee on Integrated Energy Policy under the chairmanship of Kirit Parikh and its recommendations were reviewed in a meeting chaired by the PM and referred to the individual ministries to consider. One key recommendation was to align the prices of imported fuels with trade parity prices to give domestic producers the right incentives to expand production while encouraging consumers to reduce consumption. It took a long time to get this implemented.

The proposal was approved by the cabinet in December 2008 when oil prices were about $41 per barrel. They began to climb steadily thereafter and with a general election due in May 2009, the necessary price adjustment was postponed. In June 2009, after the elections, by when the price of crude oil had risen to $69 per barrel, the price of both petrol and diesel was raised, but by much less than was necessary to achieve parity with world prices. Crude oil prices continued to rise and the failure to adjust domestic prices put a burden on the oil sector.

What followed was an example of gradualism in which the end objective of aligning domestic prices with world prices was clearly stated, but implemented only gradually over a six-year period. In June 2010, petrol prices were aligned with world prices immediately, but for diesel, the consumption of which was four times that of petrol, the process was much more gradual. In January 2013, the price of diesel for bulk buyers (for power generation in industry) was raised to trade parity, but the price of diesel sold at petrol pumps for trucks, tractors and automobiles, would be raised by 50 paise per litre every month until it reached trade parity. Administering the medicine in small doses made it acceptable but it took six years to get the job done. Oil prices collapsed in October 2014, a few months after the NDA government had taken over, and they were able to decontrol the price of diesel immediately while mopping up some of the bonanza for the exchequer by raising taxes.

The Planning Commission had made several recommendations for reforms in Railways but there was little willingness at the receiving end. The Indian Railways was not very different from Chinese Railways in 1980 but we had fallen steadily behind thereafter. Our Railways officials tended to attribute the superior performance of Chinese Railways to much higher levels of investments. But China had also carried out structural reforms, including the abolition of the Ministry of Railways and spinning off China Rail as the operational entity, while the policymaking role was assigned to the Ministry of Transport. In sharp contrast, Indian Railways continued to be run as a department of the Government, greatly reducing their ability to act commercially.

Passenger fares were kept very low as a political decision and this was compensated by overcharging freight. Underpricing of passenger services led to constant demands from the public to expand train services and successive ministers had approved many more new rail line projects than we could afford. The result was a huge shelf of 'new line' projects for which funds were released at a miniscule pace, which meant projects would remain under construction for a long time. Overcharging freight made the economy uncompetitive and caused freight traffic to switch from rail to roads.

I recall writing to Mamata Banerjee when she was railways minister, recommending the conversion of the Railways into a public sector corporation with a management structure better suited to commercial decision-making, a shift to commercial accounting to accurately assess the cost and profitability of different segments, establishment of a Rail Tariff Regulatory Authority to depoliticize tariff fixation, and reliance on PPP to redevelop railway stations. When Mamata left the ministry to become West Bengal CM in 2011, she recommended to the PM that Dinesh Trivedi, a TMC MP, be made railways minister. Dinesh wanted to make major investments in railway safety, which had been ignored for too long. He asked me if the Planning Commission could allocate more funds. I told him we were already allocating much more to the Railways than envisaged in the Plan, and that the real reason for the financial problems of the Railways was that they had not raised passenger fares for several years while costs were rising. He saw the point and told me that he would convey to the PM that unless he could get extra plan funding from the finance minister or the Planning Commission, he would have no option but to raise passenger fares.

Dinesh was as good as his word and raised passenger fares in the Railway Budget of 2012, defending his action in public. Mamata Banerjee promptly asked him to withdraw the fare increase or face removal from office. When he refused to back down, she wrote to the PM asking him to remove Dinesh and appoint Mukul Roy, another TMC MP, in his place. It was a demonstration of the realities of coalition government, the control exercised by party leaders on their nominees for cabinet positions and, of course, the irresistible pull of populism. The TMC walked out of the UPA in September 2012.

The NDA government took up the issue of reform of the Railways in 2014. A High-Level Committee was appointed under Bibek Debroy, chairman of the EAC-PM. The Debroy Committee submitted a voluminous report that lays out a phased programme for action over a five-year period, but only a very small part of the reform has been implemented thus far. Reform of the Railways remains an urgent priority.

A third area where I felt wide-ranging changes in policy were desperately needed was the management of water resources. With prevailing levels of efficiency in water use in different sectors, available water supply would only meet 50 per cent of the water demand of India by 2030. Unless we reduced the intensity of water use, our growth projections would simply not be realized. Climate change presented an additional threat in terms of greater variation in annual precipitation, with greater frequency of extreme events.

Water is a state subject in the Constitution and policy correctives have to be implemented at the state level, though the Centre could help guide reforms in this area. Our policies towards water management had long focused on building large-scale irrigation projects. However, evidence was accumulating that these large projects were environmentally damaging because they submerged forested areas; socially disruptive as they dislocated large populations that were rarely adequately resettled; had much lower economic return than made out because siltation was much higher than expected, reducing effective storage; and led to highly inequitable distribution of scarce water because farmers at the head of the canal network typically grabbed a disproportionate amount of the water for growing water-intensive crops, leaving little for tail-end farmers. As investment in irrigation projects was mainly by state governments, it was necessary to convince them to shift resources to smaller, more sustainable, water conservation projects, including projects aimed at recharging groundwater.

As more than 80 per cent of total water use was in agriculture, it was clear that water-use efficiency in agriculture had to be increased to make room for other uses. This was technically feasible but if water was not priced to reflect its scarcity, there was no incentive for farmers to adopt economizing techniques. In the absence of rational water pricing, the only way of promoting economic use of water was through water rationing. This is possible, in principle, for water delivered through canal networks by establishing a strong water regulatory authority. However, there is no mechanism for doing so with groundwater as farmers can legally extract as much water as they want from a borewell on their own land. Excess use of groundwater was further encouraged by the fact that electricity for farmers was free in some states and heavily subsidized in others. As groundwater was increasingly the main source of additional irrigation, some resolution of this problem was essential.

Mihir Shah, who had joined the Planning Commission in UPA 2, worked closely with the Ministry of Water Resources to develop the National Water Policy 2012, which called for action on several fronts. An important policy objective was to ensure that water once used is returned to natural water bodies only after being sufficiently treated. This could be legislated, but it could only be enforced by state pollution control bodies who found it difficult to take tough action against polluting industries, especially when many of them were small scale. Only about 30 per cent of the sewage or wastewater generated in the cities was treated before going back to natural water bodies. We tried to incentivize state governments to act in this area by making a sustainable plan for wastewater treatment a condition for accessing funds under the JNNURM.

A second area for urgent action for water was to try to limit the rate of extraction of groundwater in each aquifer to the rate of recharge. We found there was not enough information on the rate of recharge of each aquifer! The Twelfth Plan provided some funds to start the process of measuring this rate in different aquifers across the country. However, this was only a first step. Once we knew the sustainable rate of extraction, we would have to deal with the more difficult job of ensuring that water use within the aquifer for different uses stayed within this limit. This could only be done either by introducing physical rationing to different uses or appropriate water pricing, neither of which would be easy. We were able to do no more than outline the problem and start a programme of work that in due course could put in place policies that would lead to sustainable use of water resources.

The Planning Commission also had an impact on policy through the members being asked by the ministries to chair inter-ministerial committees on policy issues. Many of the members were actively involved in this process, notably B.K. Chaturvedi, Abhijit Sen, K. Kasturirangan, Soumitra Chaudhuri, Kirit Parikh, Syeda Hameed and Anwarul Hoda. This was a good example of 'planning by persuasion'.

INTERACTING WITH THE STATES

Interacting with the states on plan strategies and performance was an enjoyable and educative experience for me. There were meetings of the NDC, usually once a year, to discuss the approach to the plan, the draft plan itself and mid-term appraisals of the Plan. There were also special meetings, such as the one on agriculture in 2007. These were formal occasions where each CM spoke for about 10 to 15 minutes. I had also introduced the practice of discussing the approach to the Plan in more informal meetings hosted by different CMs in their states.

In addition to discussions in the NDC, we had annual meetings in Delhi with each state to discuss and approve the annual plan. These discussions began with a meeting of senior officials from both sides followed by a formal meeting of the CM, deputy chairman, members, and officials from both sides. The meeting lasted two to three hours and usually began with the CM speaking on the state's performance and what they expected from the Centre. Each member of the commission would offer comments on the state's performance in the sector for which they were responsible. There would be responses from the state government, followed by a general discussion.

At the end of the annual plan discussion, the CM and I would meet the press. Most CMs valued the exposure this gave them on national television. Typically, I would make a very short statement on the economic performance of the state and announce that we had approved a plan size of ₹'x' crore with central assistance of ₹'y' crore. The CM would then take over, elaborating the areas where we had complimented them, while ignoring the weaknesses pointed out! They would express happiness that the commission had approved a plan of ₹x crore. Some even phrased this ambiguously, by saying, 'The Planning Commission has given us a plan of ₹x crore.' Perhaps they felt TV viewers in the state would see this as an indication that they had obtained that much money for the state. The reality, of course, was that while we 'approved' the plan, it was funded largely by the states' own resources. What the states actually 'got' from the Planning Commission was only the central assistance for their plan. This was large for the special-category states (over 80 per cent of the Plan on average) but for other states, it averaged only about 8 per cent of the size of the state plan.[64]

Tamil Nadu CM J. Jayalalithaa once commented that she found it odd that she had to come to Delhi to get approval for what Tamil Nadu was doing with its own money! She had a point because the central assistance Tamil Nadu got was only 6 per cent of the plan size. However, as central assistance could only be given for an approved plan, it was technically necessary to 'approve' the plan. The approval was only a formality and no state was ever denied approval. Nevertheless, with more and more states being ruled by opposition parties, the need to get approval began to be resented.

The tendency to equate planning with plan programmes rather than policies was common to both the Centre and the states. CMs would talk with pride of their favourite programmes but almost never about policies they had introduced to help achieve the targets of state plans. The focus on programmes also led to demands

---

[64]There were 11 special-category states, including J&K, Himachal Pradesh, Uttarakhand, Assam and the seven other Northeastern states: Arunachal Pradesh, Sikkim, Tripura, Meghalaya, Manipur, Mizoram and Nagaland.

for additional financial support from the Planning Commission. Over time, successive Finance Commissions had raised the share of central taxes devolved to the states, leaving less available for the Centre. This had led to a progressive reduction in the size of central assistance for the states relative to states' plans, at least for the non-special category states.

The inadequacy of central assistance for the states' plans was frequently mentioned by CMs. I would explain that I had very little flexibility in this matter because the total volume of central assistance was determined at the time the Five-Year Plan was approved, and the distribution of central assistance across states was governed by the Gadgil-Mukherjee formula. This formula allowed only 10 per cent of the total to be distributed at the discretion of the deputy chairman. This was a very small amount and each state had come to expect something. As no state would accept a reduction from the level in the previous year, the discretion I had was effectively limited to giving differential increases to different states on a small portion of the total central assistance.

On one occasion, Punjab CM Parkash Singh Badal made a case for special assistance for Punjab and I painstakingly explained why I could not help. He responded with frankness: 'If that is the case, why should we come to Delhi for these annual plan discussions?' I explained that the purpose of the meetings was not to distribute largesse but to discuss performance, and learn from success stories elsewhere. I could see that he was not convinced.

There were many areas where the state government could improve performance significantly by making policy changes without additional government expenditure. Agriculture, for example, was a sector where states could take several initiatives. They could amend the state APMC Act to allow private markets to emerge to compete with government-run 'mandis'. Corporate buyers could be allowed to pick up the produce directly from the farmers, thus giving farmers better prices, especially for perishable crops. They could liberalize tenancy laws that made leasing illegal in many states. Holders of small parcels of land, which were unviable to cultivate as separate farms, could then lease them out to others. The agricultural extension system could be revived to provide a powerful means of bringing the latest technology to farmers to improve yields and increase farm income.

Electricity distribution was another area that was entirely in the realm of the states and there was enormous scope for policy reform. Privatizing parts of the system would give private operators a chance to prove whether they could be more efficient than state-run distribution companies. Allowing open access in electricity distribution within the state would enable industrial consumers of power to buy power supplies directly from companies generating electricity, while paying the distribution companies a regulated charge to use their wire network. This would introduce competitive pressure on the government-owned power distribution companies. States could also explore the scope for PPP in a wide range of infrastructure projects, including state roads and development of minor ports.

Our efforts did yield some results. A few states began to exempt horticultural produce from coverage under the APMC Acts. Many states took up PPP in road building and port expansion; one state even took up a transmission project. A few small urban projects were also taken up in PPP mode.

Some policies had become too 'baked in' to change. I recall pointing out to CM Badal that Punjab's policy of giving free power for agriculture (which he had introduced many years earlier) was having a very damaging effect, leading to excessive extraction of groundwater. This meant a steady decline in the water table and deterioration in water quality because of chemical and heavy metal content, endangering both soil fertility and human health. He agreed with the logic of my argument but said the policy had persisted for so long that it was now impossible to change! In my concluding remarks to the Punjab delegation, I read out a quote from Machiavelli:

At the beginning, a disease is easy to cure but difficult to diagnose: but as time passes, not having been treated or recognized at the outset, it becomes easy to diagnose but difficult to cure. The same thing occurs in affairs of state. By recognizing from afar the diseases that are spreading in the state (which is a gift given only to a prudent ruler) they can be cured quickly. But when they are not recognized and left to grow to the extent that everyone recognizes them, there is no longer any cure.

The quote was greeted with suppressed laughter from the delegation, but it was no laughing matter. Punjab has not been able to revoke free power to farmers and, indeed, more states have followed Punjab's example. Rajasekhara Reddy, the dynamic CM of Andhra Pradesh, had effectively trounced Chandrababu Naidu in the 2004 election by projecting a strong pro-farmer position, including a promise of free power. He introduced it on his first day in office. When I met him shortly thereafter, I warned him about the experience of Punjab. He said he could not deny free power to farmers as states dependent on canal irrigation provide water almost free, with the state covering the capital and operating costs. Andhra Pradesh did not have a large irrigation system and most farmers had to get water from borewells where the farmers covered the capital cost of the pumping system. Free power was the least the state could do to level the playing field!

The states often used the annual plan discussions to draw attention to central government policies that operated to their disadvantage, and sought our help in getting them modified. We were able to help in some cases. For example, although royalty on minerals accrued entirely to the state government, the rate was set by the Centre and was often fixed as a specific levy, i.e. ₹'x' per tonne. The mineral-producing states wanted ad valorem rates (per cent of the price of the mineral) as this would ensure that the royalty would increase in line with increases in mineral prices. We persuaded the Ministry of Mines to set up a High-Level

Committee under one of our members, Anwarul Hoda, to look into this issue. The committee recommended a shift to ad valorem rates and this was subsequently put in place.

CM Narendra Modi often used the meetings to point out how certain policies of the Centre hurt Gujarat. For example, the state had built a distribution system to take piped gas to urban households but it could not get the allocation of gas needed to feed the system. We could not help because the national policy on natural gas, approved by the cabinet, gave priority to fertilizer production and power generation and there was not enough gas left to allocate for household use. He also complained that power plants in Gujarat were getting coal linkages from distant coal mines owned by central coal fields, while those in Maharashtra were getting linkages from western coal fields, which were nearer and involved lower costs. Here, too, we could not help because coal linkages were determined by the coal companies as a commercial decision. Coal was a nationalized industry and it may have looked like a central government decision but it was not, and there was nothing we could do. He also complained that environmental clearances by the Centre took too much time.

The annual plan discussions for Gujarat in 2013 proved unusually contentious. CM Modi used the opportunity to criticize the Government of India for following policies that hampered states trying to develop. Examples of such policies he highlighted were tolerating a high fiscal deficit at the Centre and rising current account deficit; prolonged delays in clearing important projects, like the Narmada project that had become the target of NGO attention; flip-flops on export policy for cotton; and other cases of what he called 'policy paralysis'. He also said laws such as the RTE imposed burdens on the state without providing adequate support. The CSS were criticized for violating the spirit of federalism. He concluded by saying that in a federal polity, the Planning Commission should exert its influence on the Centre to remove impediments imposed by central government policies. He clearly felt we were not doing enough in this area.

In the interaction with the press after the Plan discussion, I made the point that Gujarat's economic growth performance was very good and had been so for many years. However, I pointed out that its social indicators were behind those of other comparable states such as Maharashtra, and in this respect, the Gujarat model needed to be strengthened.

A few weeks later, the BJP announced that Modi would be the party's prime ministerial candidate in the 2014 elections. I realized then that the audiovisual presentation we had seen in the annual plan discussions was a preview of the issues that would be raised in the hotly contested election campaign.

Bihar CM Nitish Kumar wanted Bihar to be classified as a special-category state because it had the lowest per capita state domestic product (SDP). We were unable to help because the criteria for eligibility had been approved by the NDC and Bihar did not qualify. The fact that Bihar had a low per capita SDP was given weight in the Gadgil-Mukherjee formula for distributing central assistance and in the Finance Commission formula for devolution of sharable taxes. He took up the matter with the PM who asked me what we could do. I suggested it would be best to set up a committee under chief economic advisor Raghuram Rajan to report on which states were really backward. The committee came up with the finding that on a multidimensional comparison, Odisha was actually poorer than Bihar, so any classification of Bihar as a special-category state would elicit the same demand from Odisha. After its bifurcation from Telangana, Andhra Pradesh made the same demand.

The states in the Northeast suffered from poor connectivity with the rest of the country and this was a major drag on their development. This was an area where we could help by urging the central ministries responsible for road, rail and air transport to give full priority to the region. The problem was exemplified by the Bogibeel rail and road bridge across the Brahmaputra. It was the second bridge across the river in Assam and was expected to improve connectivity within Assam across the river as well as access to Arunachal Pradesh. The project had been languishing for many years because the Railways could not spare the funds to complete the bridge on time. The UPA declared it a 'national project' in 2007, which meant 75 per cent of the cost would be provided by the central government outside the Railways budget. Even so, it took 10 years to complete and the bridge was finally inaugurated by PM Modi in 2018.

When B.K. Chaturvedi retired as cabinet secretary in 2007 and was appointed member of the Planning Commission, I asked him to take charge of the Northeast as a regional responsibility. We were able to accelerate action on completing railway lines and building airports in the three states with no air connectivity. Arunachal Pradesh and Meghalaya got connected to the railway network in the UPA period. We also put pressure on the NHAI to give priority to completing the East-West Highway, which gave the Northeast a trunk road connection with the rest of the country.

The four states to the east of Bangladesh—Meghalaya, Mizoram, Nagaland and Tripura—were particularly disadvantaged because they had to follow a circuitous route around Bangladesh to reach the rest of the country through the narrow chicken's nest. Cross-country connectivity through Bangladesh was the obvious solution. A start was made in 2010 when India and Bangladesh agreed to build a rail connection from Agartala in Tripura to Akhaura in Bangladesh, giving Tripura direct access to Chittagong port, a distance of 200 km, in place of a 1,100-km connection going around Bangladesh to Kolkata port.

In February 2014, we organized a two-day conference in Guwahati jointly with CII to showcase infrastructure development in the region and highlight its potential as a link to Southeast Asia. Looking ahead, once the internal connectivity of the rest of the country to the Northeast is completed, the region provides a natural springboard to Southeast Asia through Myanmar. Building transnational transport links should have high priority. Some important initiatives have been taken, such as the Trilateral Highway, which starts in Manipur, traverses Myanmar and ends in Thailand.

I was often asked whether the annual plan discussions were substantively valuable or just a ritual. All top-level meetings have an element of ritual because difficult operational matters are usually sorted out in advance at the official level. However, I felt the meetings served two very useful purposes. First, meeting the CMs personally helped me to get a sense of the big problems worrying them. We would send a note on the outcome of each meeting to the PM, but when something seemed especially important, I would brief the PM personally. Second, the meetings were the only occasion when the CMs were presented with a comprehensive critique of the performance of their state! They were used to dealing with political criticism and a hostile press but facing a professional assessment of strengths and weaknesses of their government's performance was a very different experience. CMs generally took the criticisms in their stride and dealt with them quite effectively.

Interacting with the states also gave me many enjoyable opportunities to travel across the country. In my 10 years as deputy chairman, I managed to visit almost all the states, including visits outside the state capitals. A particularly memorable experience was a visit to West Bengal when Isher and I visited the island of Pakhiralay in the Sundarbans. The West Bengal transportation minister accompanied us. The only means of transportation on the island was cycles. We were supposed to go a little way off the landing point to meet the villagers and the local administration had arranged a 'thela gaadi': a three-wheeled cycle with a flat platform on which goods could be placed for transportation and passengers could also sit. The platform was covered with a nice white sheet, which made it look respectable, if not exactly comfortable. I decided I would do the cycling myself and Isher and the minister could sit on the platform. I was allowed to try my skills but the minister insisted he would walk! *The Telegraph* in Kolkata reported the visit with a nice picture of me riding and Isher sitting at the back with the caption, 'Demonstration of a very different kind of skill'. Isher spoke to the village women in fluent Bengali (having been brought up in Kolkata). The meeting ended with her joining the women in Rabindra Sangeet, with all of them singing 'Ekla cholo re'. Isher's flawless Bengali and singing were a great hit.

DIALOGUES WITH CHINA

Another highlight of my tenure as deputy chairman was a new opportunity to interact with China. Following the visit of Premier Wen Jiabao of China to India in December 2010, the two governments decided to launch a Strategic Economic Dialogue (SED); it was co-chaired by me and Zhang Ping, chairman of the National Development and Reform Commission of China. It was a great opportunity to learn more about the remarkable progress China had made in the past 20 years and draw some lessons for our own planning.

At the first meeting in Beijing in September 2011, we agreed to focus on improving the environment for investment for both sides and find ways of cooperating in specific areas such as energy-efficiency, infrastructure development (especially in Railways), environmental protection including renewable energy, water conservation and clean water technology. Working groups were set up in each area that would meet prior to the next dialogue to outline specific ways of cooperation.

The Chinese government arranged for the entire delegation to call on Premier Jiabao in the Great Hall of the People. Jiabao was a soft-spoken, wise and avuncular sort of person. He had once told PM Manmohan Singh that every time China had closed its borders, it had suffered, and every time it opened them, it had prospered. It was a perspective the two men shared. I conveyed the good wishes of our PM to the premier and gave him a brief account of our discussions. Chinese news agency Xinhua quoted the premier when he said, 'China and India are good neighbours and two of the largest developing countries, and the two countries should enhance communication and coordination at all levels and in all areas, expand cooperation, take each other's concerns into consideration and steadily pursue a means of reciprocity and common development.'[65] Knowing that news reports in China are strictly controlled, we took this as an official signal of the Chinese government's desire to give the SED a high profile.

The subsequent meetings of the SED were held in New Delhi in November 2012, and in Beijing in March 2014. B.K. Chaturvedi was my deputy for the SED. The working groups we had established evolved specific areas of collaboration and study, which we reviewed in our meeting in New Delhi. The Chinese official delegation led by Zhang Ping was accompanied by a large business delegation, which met with their Indian business counterparts. Reporting the event, *The New York Times* quoted me as saying, 'The economic growth of India and China is a critical element of the transformation of the global order that is underway. Our ability to influence global decision-making will be stronger if we work together…India can certainly benefit by studying Chinese experience in the building of infrastructure and handling of urbanization.' The report also emphasized how the large business delegation indicated a parallel pursuit of business possibilities.

We used the SED to raise specific issues where government could help. For example, our major IT companies had set up offices in China but the only business they got was from MNCs operating in China. There was scope for contracts from provincial governments but a positive signal from government was necessary, given China's relatively opaque public procurement policies. I brought up this issue in our meetings. I also raised the issue of allowing easier access for Indian pharma companies to the Chinese market.

The Chinese, too, used the meetings to raise problems they faced in India. When asked whether Chinese investment would be welcome in infrastructure, I explained that investment in certain areas, such as ports, might run into security clearance issues, but they were welcome to invest in many other areas. Chinese

---

[65]*The Economic Times*, 27 September 2011.

construction companies complained about delays in obtaining visas. The problem arose because they preferred to work with Chinese labour, whereas we expected they would use local labour for the most part. I explained that we could only allow a limited number of visas for supervisory personnel depending on the size of the contract, and promised to facilitate the issue of such visas on fast track.

During our meeting in Beijing, I learnt from an academic from Tsinghua University about how the Chinese government was planning to get about 1,000 professors of Chinese origin teaching in US universities to return home to take up academic positions and contribute to the country's economic development. They would first decide on the areas where they wanted to bring in new talent and then reach out to people of distinction. They were flexible about salaries, knowing that academics of Chinese origin in the US (most of whom may have been US citizens) could not be expected to come at Chinese academic salaries. They were also willing to negotiate salaries depending on the individual.

I complimented him on their practical approach and confessed that, in India, we would find it very difficult to negotiate salaries with academics that were much higher than what other professors were drawing. I asked him whether this did not create resentment among the local faculty. He said it did, but added charmingly, 'Mr Ahluwalia, you have to learn to distinguish a dragon from a fish.'

A SYSTEMS REFORMS COMMISSION

At the start of the second term of UPA, the PM had asked us to rethink the role of the Planning Commission in light of changing circumstances. He said that the commission should try to become a 'systems reform commission', by which I understood that we should work to change systems and not just policies. He also clarified that planning in India could not be a 'command control' activity but an 'exercise in persuasion'.

It was a challenging assignment and we had several internal discussions on how to proceed. An earlier attempt at restructuring the commission by an external consultant for the Vajpayee government had found no support and the project was abandoned. Realizing that comprehensive restructuring would require considerable effort to overcome resistance from vested interests, we decided to do things differently within the existing structure and leave formal restructuring to later, based on the experience gained.

Our first conclusion was that the commission should not spread itself too thin trying to cover every aspect of the economy. Instead, we had to choose selected areas and try to become a knowledge hub and change agent in these areas. I felt we needed to focus on policies and programmes to enhance agricultural productivity, infrastructure development, energy policy, water resource management and India's interaction with the rest of the world.

The commission was the only part of government that had in-house capacity to handle quantitative models but it had traditionally dealt with old-fashioned input-output models. There were many new-generation models being developed by research institutions in the country. We had experimented with a 'hub-and-spoke' relationship with these institutions and gained access to a variety of models. I felt this approach needed to be institutionalized and expanded to cover critical sectoral models, especially for agriculture, infrastructure and energy.

We recognized that the function of finalizing the size of the Plan and allocating funds across ministries and states could, in principle, be assigned to other units, notably the Ministry of Finance or the PMO. However, the Planning Commission, under the chairmanship of the PM, could act as an independent lobby for development expenditure within the Government. This was necessary to counter the natural instinct of the Ministry of Finance to limit expenditure. Involvement with financing also gave the commission an organic link with the ministries as well as the states, which could be used to leverage ideas for policy change.

We strongly believed that to perform these new roles, the commission needed to be staffed differently. Rather than relying on generalist officers from the same pool as the ministries, it needed a mix of high-quality civil servants with the right background and experience supplemented by domain experts recruited from outside for fixed-term assignments of three to five years. Getting first-rate civil servants was not easy because the rules required us to choose from a panel prepared by the Department of Personnel and Training, which was bound by its own rules determining eligibility of IAS officers for a central government posting. We had started experimenting with hiring consultants, but the scales of pay allowed were too low to get anyone with real experience. We were able to hire younger people, who made a great contribution, but we also needed senior experts for which much higher salaries would have to be paid.

Looking back, I feel we did not pay enough attention to the need to build institutions that would promote good governance. I was very conscious of the importance of changing policies but even good policies need a supporting institutional framework. A conscious effort was made to reform institutions in the financial sector; but here, too, institutional weaknesses kept surfacing as the financial sector evolved. There were many other areas where institutional reform was equally critical, including strengthening regulatory institutions related to environmental protection and pollution control. Some were entirely in the realm of the states, such as electricity distribution. Improving systems of dispute resolution and contract enforcement were critical for the efficient functioning of a market economy and this called for deep reforms in the functioning of the judicial system.

A week before demitting office, PM Manmohan Singh asked me to prepare a note for him responding to some specific queries. These related to how the commission had changed in particular ways over the 10 years of UPA and my views on changes needed for the future. I gave him a note reflecting much of what is said above. He told me later that he had given the note to his successor.

EPILOGUE

As soon as the election results were declared in May 2014, I went to see PM Manmohan Singh to hand him my letter of resignation. It was an emotional moment for me. He had played a major role in my career: encouraging me to move to India and join the government in 1979, bringing me to the Ministry of Finance at the start of the reforms in 1991, and appointing me deputy chairman of the Planning Commission in 2004. In our long association, I had come to admire his deep knowledge of India, and his patience and perseverance in trying to bring about change.

As I walked out of his office, I could not help reflecting on how things had drifted in the past two years. My mind went back to a late afternoon in the spring of 2012. An array of superstar guests, including cabinet ministers, bankers, industrialists, senior editors, economists, lawyers and civil servants had gathered in a conference room in New Delhi's Vigyan Bhavan. The occasion was the launch of a second edition of a festschrift for Dr Manmohan Singh titled *India's Economic Reforms and Development: Essays for Manmohan Singh*, edited by Isher and Ian Little (his thesis advisor at Oxford).[66] A distinguished panel, consisting of Governor Subbarao of the RBI, T.N. Ninan of *Business Standard* and Raghuram Rajan from the Chicago School of Business, was slated to discuss the challenges of economic reforms in India. PM Manmohan Singh was the chief guest. He had accepted the invitation on the understanding that he would only listen and not speak.

---

[66]The festschrift was first published in 1998 when Manmohan Singh was not in government. It was updated and brought out as a second edition in 2012 by Oxford University Press as an Oxford Perennial on the occasion of their 100th anniversary in India. The royalties from the book have been funding two scholarships at the Delhi School of Economics.

The mood was sombre. Economic growth had slowed down to 5.8 per cent in the last quarter of 2011–12 and inflation was high. Regulatory delays were holding up the implementation of large projects. The government had also been shaken by a flurry of anti-corruption protests in the previous year. The Supreme Court had cancelled the 2G licences barely two months earlier and a draft of the CAG's report on coal block allocation had just leaked to the press. There was also a self-inflicted wound: the retrospective tax amendment to nullify the recent Supreme Court judgement on the Vodafone case (*see Chapter 13*), which weakened an already fragile investment climate.

Isher initiated the discussion by flagging the slowdown and highlighting the need for corrective action. Subbarao made a dignified presentation befitting a serving governor. He said there was no danger of the kind of crisis we had in 1991, but we needed to push ahead with reforms, albeit cautiously. Ninan felt that if the government did more to build a constituency for reform, it should be possible, even within the constraints of a coalition, to make some progress through what he called 'homeopathic doses'.

Raghuram Rajan was the star performer. He began by saying that India's economic reforms had achieved a great deal but things were going wrong. Growth was slowing down but the politicians, instead of responding with more reforms, were trying to buy popularity by increasing subsidies and transfers. He warned against the 'resource raj', which allowed businessmen to use political connections to get access to natural resources. In an indirect reference to the Vodafone decision, he said we should be kinder to foreign investors because we needed their money. He warned that Dr Singh's legacy would be at risk if corrective steps were not taken.

When Isher escorted the PM to his car at the end of the function, she expressed the hope that he would deliver on our message to get reforms going again. He obviously knew a great deal was expected of him, but his response was 'Politics is the art of the possible.'

It says something about Manmohan Singh that despite the very critical stance of Raghuram Rajan's presentation, he was appointed four months later as chief economic advisor in the Ministry of Finance. Isher pointed out to me that by doing so, Dr Singh was living up to the doha (verse) from Sant Kabir which says,

Nindak niyare rakhiye, aangan kuti chawai,
Bin pani, sabun bina, nirmal kare subhai

(Keep your critic close to you; give him shelter in
your courtyard,
Without soap and water, he will cleanse your character)

In the two years that followed, the media turned decisively against the government with headlines declaring that the 'Dream Team' was not delivering.

Walking back from the PMO after handing in my resignation, it was natural to reflect on whether things could have been any different in the last few years. The perceived weakness of the government had encouraged a number of institutions to assert themselves: the press, the courts, the opposition, civil society, and even the CAG. It created an environment in which the public mood turned against the UPA and there was hankering for a strong government that could deliver results. The BJP fashioned its campaign for the 2014 election to respond to this feeling and won a resounding mandate.

Strong, centralized governments have some advantages, but they also have a major disadvantage: the failure to provide room for different views. This reduces the likelihood that policy mistakes will be acknowledged and corrected. Manmohan Singh recognized the importance of encouraging free expression of views and dissent in a liberal democracy. We were now about to go through a different experience with a government enjoying a strong majority and also one which was expected to rely on much greater centralization of power in the PMO.

A PRIVATE CITIZEN ONCE AGAIN

My cabinet colleagues in the outgoing government busied themselves with how they would function in the opposition. I was not a member of any political party. I had neither the desire nor the skills to be a politician. After more than three decades in government, I was at a loose end.

We quickly moved out of the large official bungalow in Lutyens' Delhi to our private home in Greater Kailash in South Delhi. I went through a period of unwinding and relaxing with friends and family, especially our grandchildren. I also played a little more golf. Some friends from Mumbai asked whether I would be interested in serving on corporate boards but I did not want to do that, at least not right then.

I received an invitation from the Stern School of Business of New York University to spend a term as a visiting distinguished professor and give a few lectures on India's economic development. It was a good way of getting away for a few months from the pressure-cooker atmosphere of New Delhi where all economic issues are discussed in an intensely political context. After some reflection, and much encouragement from Isher, I decided to write about my experience in government, pushing economic policies to bring about the change I believed was so necessary.

In the six years I have been out of government, the NDA government under PM Narendra Modi served a full five-year term, and was re-elected in 2019 with an even stronger majority. The next section presents an assessment of the performance and policies of the first six years of the Modi-led NDA. I then present my perspective on future challenges and identify some of the policies and institutional reforms that are crucial if we want to get back to the trajectory of high growth and use the additional revenues generated to support programmes of inclusiveness.

THE NDA YEARS: AN OVERVIEW

The economic performance of the first six years of the NDA government can be described as 'beginning with a bang and ending with a whimper'. The electorate wanted a quick return to high growth, and Finance Minister Arun Jaitley, while presenting the Budget for 2015–16, played to this expectation by declaring 'Aiming for double-digit growth seems feasible very soon.'

The policies that would be adopted to achieve this objective were not specified, but there were some signals. The slogan 'Minimum Government Maximum Governance' suggested continuity in liberalizing the economy. The new government also signalled a commitment to fiscal prudence when Finance Minister Jaitley, presenting his first Budget in July 2014, said he was retaining the fiscal deficit target of 4.1 per cent of GDP set by his predecessor in the interim Budget, and promised to reduce it to 3 per cent by 2016–17. Policy signals on FDI were also broadly positive. PM Modi presented his 'Make in India' initiative as an invitation to foreign investors to set up production facilities. This was a politically important signal because parts of the Sangh Parivar were known to be anti-FDI.

The new government was also careful to avoid seeming 'anti-poor'. Programmes such as MGNREGA, which were earlier criticized as wasteful, were continued and even expanded. Some existing programmes were rebranded and given a higher political profile. For example, the Total Sanitation Programme, which provided toilets to reduce open defecation in rural areas, was rebranded as 'Swachh Bharat' and PM Modi, in his first Independence Day address, announced a target of making India 'open defecation free' by 2 October 2019, the 150th birth anniversary of Mahatma Gandhi. Similarly, the UPA programme of opening 'no-frills bank accounts' for the poor, combined with direct transfer of certain benefits into these accounts, all assisted by the Aadhaar (the Unique Identity Scheme of the UPA) and mobile connectivity, was repackaged and given the catchy title of 'the

JAM trinity'[67]. The National e-Governance Plan was repackaged as 'Digital India'. The Rashtriya Krishi Vikas Yojana was repackaged as 'Paramparagat Krishi Vikas Yojana'.

Economic performance under the NDA improved initially but the improvement was short-lived. A new national accounts series was introduced in 2015. According to this series, growth peaked at 8 per cent in 2015–16, using the GVA measure which corresponds to GDP at factor cost used earlier, and then decelerated steadily, falling to 4.5 per cent in the second quarter of 2019–20. The Advance Estimates, released by the National Statistical Office in January 2020, projected growth for the year as a whole at 4.9 per cent. This implies that the NDA government in its first six years, would have delivered an average growth rate of only 6.9 per cent, compared to an average of 7.8 per cent for the 10 years of the UPA.

Part of the revival of growth in the first three years was simply a continuation of the upturn that had begun in the last year of the UPA, when growth moved up to 6.1 per cent in 2013–14. Performance in the first two years of the NDA was greatly helped by the collapse in world oil prices in October 2014, which created a very favourable external environment compared to the situation facing the UPA when oil prices were very high. However, questions began to be raised about whether the new national accounts series was overestimating growth. Data on sales of trucks, cars, scooters, consumer electronics, etc., as well as the growth of bank credit, suggested that economic growth was much slower than indicated by the new series. Businessmen began to say in private that 'it did not feel like the economy was growing at 7 per cent'.

The issue of whether the new series was overestimating growth was examined by Arvind Subramanian, who was the chief economic advisor in the Ministry of Finance in the first three years of the NDA government, and then moved to Harvard in 2017. He found that the growth rate using the new series for the period

---

[67]All three elements were part of the strategy of inclusiveness of the UPA regime.

from 2011–12 to 2015–16 was much less correlated with growth in many economic variables with which growth in the earlier series was more closely correlated. Probing deeper, he concluded that the new series may be overestimating the annual GDP growth rate over this period by 2.5 percentage points.[68]

Data on employment from the Periodic Labour Force Survey (PLFS) for 2017–18 also cast doubt on the growth narrative. Employment had been a weak spot even in the UPA years, but there was no increase in the rate of unemployment in that period. The problem was that the quality of jobs generated was poor, with new employment being largely of the non-formal type. The PLFS for 2017–18 showed a much worse situation with total employment falling from 474.2 million in 2011–12 to 465.1 million in 2017–18, and the rate of unemployment rising from 2.2 per cent in 2011–12 to 6.1 per cent in 2017–18.[69]

The report on the PLFS was cleared by the National Statistical Commission (NSC) in November 2018 but its release was delayed until after the general election in May 2019. The chairman and one of the members of the NSC resigned over the interference with the release of the report. Government spokesmen dismissed the results of the PLFS, citing other partial data to suggest that employment had increased. However, independent surveys by the Centre for Monitoring Indian Economy (CMIE) confirmed that unemployment rates had increased and continued to do so even after 2017–18. The CMIE estimate for unemployment for the month of October 2019 was 8.5 per cent.

The NSSO household consumption survey for 2017–18 brought further bad news. The *Business Standard*, got hold of the results and reported that per capita consumption in 2017–18 was about

---

[68]Subramanian, Arvind. *India's GDP Mis-estimation: Likelihood, Magnitudes, Mechanisms, and Implications*. Centre for International Development Faculty Working Paper No. 354, Harvard University, June 2019.
[69]The rate of unemployment among youth (15 to 29 years) increased even faster from 6.1 per cent in 2011–12 to 17.8 per cent in 2017–18. For graduates, it has risen from 19.2 per cent to 35.8 per cent.

3.7 per cent lower in real terms than in 2011–12. NSSO surveys had traditionally shown lower consumption than the national accounts, but this was the first time since 1972 that the survey showed per capita consumption to be lower than in the previous survey (2011–12). The government announced that the 2017–18 survey was being junked on the grounds that the results were not 'in line' with other information and a new survey would be carried out in 2021. This decision clearly compromised the independence of the statistical system. Over 200 prominent economists issued a statement on 21 November 2019 protesting the government's decision.

Analysts working on the leaked data have shown that the decline in per capita consumption is primarily a reflection of adverse developments in rural areas. Real consumption has declined in all deciles in rural areas while all deciles in urban areas show an increase.[70] The urban-rural divide has therefore widened. The percentage of the population in poverty has increased from 21.9 per cent in 2011–12 to 22.8 per cent in 2017–18. This increase in total poverty reflects a sharp increase in rural poverty swamping a decline in urban poverty.

The results of the household consumption survey highlight the poor performance in agriculture. The growth rate of agriculture and allied sectors had increased to 4.3 per cent in UPA 2, but it declined to an average of 2.9 per cent in the first five years of the NDA. Rural wages grew at about 6 per cent per year before 2013–14, but stagnated thereafter. Poor agricultural performance has contributed to agricultural distress and lack of demand in rural areas. This is one of the major factors contributing to the deceleration in overall growth in the economy.

Many had hoped that the installation of a government with a strong majority in the Lok Sabha and a declared objective of improving the ease of doing business would reassure investors and revive private investment. This did not happen. Gross fixed capital formation under the UPA had reached a peak of 32.9 per

---

[70]Bhattacharya, Pramit and Devulapalli Sriharsha. "India's Rural Poverty has shot up", *Live Mint, Dec 4, 2019.*

cent of GDP in 2007–08. It declined in 2008–09, the year of the global crisis, but recovered in the later years of UPA 2 to reach 31.3 per cent of GDP in 2013–14. Despite pro-investor statements by the NDA government, the rate of fixed investment declined in the NDA period to reach 28.1 per cent in 2019–20 according to the Advance Estimates.

Investment behaviour is driven by a complex combination of domestic and global factors. There were many domestic factors at work which depressed investment. The failure to meet fiscal targets and the uncertainty that it created about macroeconomic prospects was one factor. The Centre's fiscal deficit for 2016–17 ended up at 3.5 per cent of GDP, half a percentage point higher than the finance minister had promised. More disturbingly, the Comptroller and Auditor General (CAG), in a report on the Centre's fiscal performance for 2016–17, pointed out that the fiscal deficit for that year was understated by as much as 2 percentage points of GDP because of off-budget financing. This infirmity also affects the deficit numbers for subsequent years.

The failure to address the twin balance sheet problem, i.e. corporate balance sheets burdened with too much debt and bank balance sheets burdened with large NPAs, also contributed to the low growth in investment. As corporate managements shifted their attention to mending their balance sheets, they began to focus on reducing outstanding debt rather than investing and expanding capacity. This should have been an opportunity for those with better balance sheets, including mid-size companies, to expand but public sector banks saddled with large NPAs became highly risk averse and bank credit growth slowed down. Reduced growth in bank lending was initially offset by a growth in credit from non-banking financial companies (NBFCs), but these too soon came under stress with ILFS, one of the most prominent NBFCs, collapsing in 2017. The twin balance sheet problem was known in 2015 but was not addressed as quickly as it should have been.

Rahul Bajaj, speaking on the occasion of the 2019 Economic Times Awards function in Mumbai, drew attention to another problem that may have dampened animal spirits and that was the perception that the government was unwilling to hear any criticism. 'During UPA 2,' he said, 'we could abuse anyone… But if we want to openly criticize you, there is no confidence you will appreciate that.' Bajaj was clearly implying that business leaders were hesitant to talk about their problems which also meant that the problems were left unattended. He also talked about an 'atmosphere of fear'. This was probably a reference to the fact that businessmen are highly vulnerable to investigations on tax evasion and alleged violations of the Foreign Exchange Management Act. Once action against an alleged violation is initiated, it triggers a very protracted legal process involving both economic costs and reputation loss.

Some part of the slowdown in the later years of the NDA can also be traced to two major policy mistakes—the demonetization of November 2016 and the manner in which the GST was implemented in 2017.

Demonetization came as a complete surprise when the government on 8 November 2016 announced that all currency notes of denominations ₹1,000 and ₹500, accounting for 86 per cent of the value of currency with the public, were no longer legal tender. Holders of these notes were given up to 31 December to take the notes to banks to convert them into new notes. The decision was originally presented as a decisive attack on black money and corruption, but as that particular justification seemed difficult to sustain, several other justifications were advanced.[71]

---

[71]At first, it was stated that as much as 25 per cent of the currency with the public would not be returned to the banks because the holders would not be able to account for it. When almost all the currency came back to the banks contrary to the initial expectation, a new justification was provided that all those who had deposited substantial sums in their bank accounts when converting old notes would be subjected to investigation by the tax authorities to determine whether this money was acquired lawfully. Other justifications for demonetization were that it would counter the financing of terrorist activity through counterfeit notes and that it would promote digitization of the economy.

Raghuram Rajan, who was then governor of the RBI, was consulted informally about a possible demonetization and he had advised that any long-term benefits would not be worth the short-term costs. In any case, he counselled that if the government was determined to demonetize, there should be careful planning to ensure adequate supply of new notes. In fact, demonetization was hastily announced a couple of months after Raghu's term as governor came to an end.

Raghuram Rajan's fears were amply vindicated. People rushed to banks to exchange their holdings of old notes for new notes, but as there was a shortage of new notes, amounts handed over to banks could only be credited to their bank accounts, from which cash withdrawals were permitted on a restricted basis until the supply of new notes could catch up with demand. The shortage of cash disrupted agricultural markets and operations in the informal sector, both of which are highly cash-dependent.

Eight months later, the economy received a second jolt when the GST was introduced in July 2017. Unlike demonetization, which had very little support from professional economists, the GST was universally regarded as a major reform of the indirect tax system. It was expected to generate larger revenues, and also simplify the system but it failed on both counts because of a flawed design and poor implementation.

An ideal VAT-type tax system normally involves a very wide base, with very few exemptions, and a simple structure of one or perhaps two rates. Instead, the GST in India exempted more than 200 items (accounting for roughly 40 per cent of total personal consumption). There were also far too many rates: 3 per cent for gold and jewellery; and four other rates—5, 12, 18 and 28 per cent. Four important sectors were left out: petroleum products, electricity, alcohol and real-estate development. Frequent changes in the rates added to the confusion, giving the signal that rates could be adjusted through lobbying, which goes completely contrary to the signal of stability that GST should normally convey. There were also a very large number of notifications in the next two months changing one aspect of the procedure or another, suggesting that these issues had not been carefully thought out before introducing the tax.

Large businesses in the formal sector took to the GST fairly well but small businesses found it difficult to comply with the complex procedures. Exporters, in particular, experienced long delays in getting refunds for tax paid on inputs, a particularly unfortunate development at a time when exports were doing badly.

Both demonetization and GST hit the informal sector especially hard. The informal sector accounts for about 25 per cent of non-agricultural GDP but direct information on production in this sector becomes available only every five years from the Enterprise Survey conducted by the NSSO. In the intervening years, the national accounts estimates assumed that production in the informal sector has grown at the same rate as the formal sector for which annual data is available. This assumption clearly exaggerated the official estimates of GDP and therefore growth of GDP for these years.

A negative development on the policy front was the reversal of the policy of gradually reducing import duties to bring them down to the levels prevailing in ASEAN countries. Successive governments, including the Vajpayee NDA, had followed this policy. The Three-Year Action Plan of NITI Aayog, prepared under its first Vice Chairman Arvind Panagariya, had proposed that import duties be brought down to a uniform 7 per cent. However, the NDA government moved in the opposite direction, raising a number of duties. These increases were a response to demands for protection from imports but they also reduced the competitiveness of Indian industry.

The protectionist pressures to raise import duties could have been avoided by relying on better management of the exchange rate to gain competitiveness. This would also have reduced the pressure from some sections of domestic industry that led India not to sign the Regional Comprehensive Economic Partnership (RCEP) agreement. Staying out of a major new trade grouping in Asia will make it difficult for India to link with global value chains. India can still join RCEP and, in my view, we should do so. The time allowed before tariffs have to be reduced for RCEP members can be used to remove domestic impediments to our competitiveness.

As it happened, export performance in the NDA period was disappointing. The average growth of exports of goods and services (in US $) was 24.5 per cent in UPA 1. This declined to 9.8 per cent in UPA 2 in the wake of the global slowdown. It has deteriorated further under the NDA to average only 3.4 per cent. Admittedly, world trade has slowed down in this period, but the Indian export slowdown is much sharper. No country has grown rapidly without also displaying robust export growth. Any plan to get the economy back to faster growth must therefore include a credible plan to improve export performance.

The sharp decline in growth in recent years and the increase in unemployment are serious problems that need corrective action. Unfortunately, the policy response was delayed because the government remained in denial for too long. The extent of denial is reflected in the periodic growth projections made by the RBI in the course of 2019. In the February 2019 meeting of the Monetary Policy Committee (MPC), the RBI projected growth in 2019–20 at 7.4 per cent, implying a significant pickup from the 6.8 per cent growth recorded in 2018–19. This was moderated to 7.2 per cent in the April meeting and further reduced to 7 per cent in June. By the time of the October meeting of the MPC, the national accounts data for the first quarter showed that growth in that quarter was only 5 per cent. Nevertheless, the RBI forecast was lowered only marginally from 7 percent to 6.9 per cent, implying a very sharp pickup in the remaining quarters of 2019–20. It was only by the time of the December meeting, when the national accounts data showed second quarter growth at 4.5 per cent, that the RBI finally lowered its growth projection for 2019–20 to 5 per cent!

The NSO's advance estimates of GDP growth for 2019–20 at 4.9 per cent is actually optimistic since it implies a significant acceleration in the second half of the year which is not yet evident.

However, even if it is realized, it means the NDA in its sixth year would have recorded a growth rate much lower than the low point of 5.4 per cent for UPA 2 in 2012–13 (both growth rates are based on the new series). The wheel has really come full circle!

There is much discussion on whether the slowdown is cyclical or structural. One can readily agree that there is a cyclical component and there will be an upturn if corrective steps are taken. However, this will at best see the economy get back to around 6 per cent growth in another year or so. It would be a struggle to get growth up to 7 per cent, and certainly the double-digit growth that Arun Jaitley spoke of back in 2015 is nowhere in sight. A revival of high growth calls for deeper structural reforms.

There is also an urgent need to create an environment of social harmony. Two recent initiatives of the government, the Citizenship Amendment Act and the proposed creation of a National Register of Citizens, have led to large-scale protests from students and the youth in many parts of the country. These have been met with repressive measures from the State. A protest in Jawaharlal Nehru University saw masked goons attacking protesting students with the police standing by. It is not possible at the time of writing to anticipate how these developments will unfold.[72] The voice of the youth is unlikely to be silenced easily. In any society, students and the youth are the ones most likely to speak truth to power if only because they have the least to lose and the most to gain.

To create an environment conducive to the revival of investment it is necessary for the government to hear these voices and bring a healing touch. The need to create an environment of social harmony and peace is also vital for the survival of the idea of India. Authoritarian systems can afford to suppress dissent with little effect on investment because investors are interested primarily in social stability. In a democratic society, where dissent cannot

---

[72]The repercussions of implementing the Citizenship Amendment Act and creating the National Register of Citizens are beyond the scope of discussion here but the protestors have found the two changes discriminatory to Muslim citizens and against the spirit of the Constitution.

be suppressed, it becomes necessary to listen to voices of protest and try to carry everyone along. India is much admired for its adherence to democratic norms and this reputation needs to be preserved. The 2019 election gave the NDA government a massive mandate and the PM has accumulated enormous political capital. He must use it to tackle the many serious economic challenges that are emerging, and not allow divisive issues to occupy centre-stage.

THE ECONOMIC CHALLENGES AHEAD

With the abolition of planning, we no longer have official targets for the growth of GDP. The target now talked about is making India a $5 trillion economy by 2024–25. This calls for an average growth rate of about 9 per cent in real terms over the six-year period from 2019–20 to 2024–25. With growth below 5 per cent in 2019–20, and only a slow recovery expected next year, achieving an average of 9 per cent for the period as a whole is simply not credible. We will certainly get to $5 trillion, but it will be a few years later!

A more realistic target would be to try to reach a growth rate of around 8 per cent per year as quickly as possible. This is certainly necessary if we want to continue to reduce poverty and generate the employment needed to satisfy our young and aspirational labour force. Is 8 per cent growth feasible? India did achieve GDP growth of 8.5 per cent in the first seven years of the UPA, but a return to that growth rate is easier said than done.[73]

---

[73]The 8.5 per cent average is based on the old national accounts series (base 2004–05). When the new series base 2011–12 was released, no estimates were provided of GDP at 2011–12 base prices for earlier years because some of the data used in the new series was simply not available for earlier years. Subsequently, two alternative 'backcasts' were produced. One was by a committee appointed by the NSC headed by Sudipto Mundle. This committee made some assumptions to fill the data gaps and came up with a backcast that raised the average growth rate in the first seven years of the UPA to close to 9 per cent. This series was rejected by the government and a new committee was appointed that made different assumptions to fill in

We will have to work hard for higher growth and carry out many reforms that have been held up for one reason or the other.

The so-called 'middle-income trap' is relevant in this context. The concept derives from the proposition that in the initial stages of development, growth can be accelerated by carrying out reforms that remove key constraints on productivity. This can take a country out of the low-income category of per capita income below $1,000 to the middle income category from $1,000 to $12,000. However, once the economy gets into the middle-income range and attains a degree of complexity and sophistication, another set of 'second-generation' reforms are needed to ensure that rapid growth is sustained. These reforms include stronger institutions and much greater investment in human resources to help realize the full efficiency gains possible in a market economy.

India graduated out of the low-income category towards the end of UPA 1 and we are currently in the lower end of the middle-income group. In a sense, we are still far from the midpoint of the middle-income group, where the middle-income trap is expected to bite. However, we are a dualistic economy, with a more modern part of the economy consisting of about 300 million people, which is much closer to the middle of the middle-income category. For this part of the economy to grow rapidly and act as an engine of growth for the rest of the economy, it needs deeper reforms.

What follows is not a comprehensive list of the reforms that are needed. There are many important issues that are critical for our long-term survival, such as environmental protection, managing climate change and managing water resources. These larger issues are not discussed below. Instead I focus only on issues of immediate and medium-term importance which are essential to get back to a high-growth trajectory which would also be inclusive. The longer-term challenges also have to be addressed

---

the data gaps, lowering the average growth rate in the first seven years of the UPA to 7.3 per cent. In view of the wide differences between the two estimates, we have used the old series to report growth rates for the earlier years and the new series for the period after 2011–12.

for development to be truly sustainable, but this is beyond the scope of this epilogue.

ISSUES OF IMMEDIATE IMPORTANCE

The most important issues of immediate importance are ensuring macroeconomic stability and fixing the banking system.

Macroeconomic stability and the fiscal challenge

Macroeconomic stability is a precondition for investor confidence in a private sector-led economy. The principal indicator associated with macroeconomic stability is the general government deficit, i.e. the central and state government deficits taken together. The IMF's World Economic Outlook database shows India's general government deficit for 2019 at 7.5 per cent of GDP. This is much higher than the deficit for other comparable countries, such as Indonesia (1.9 per cent), Malaysia (3 per cent), Thailand (0.2 per cent), Bangladesh (4.8 per cent), the Philippines (1.1 per cent) and Sri Lanka (5.7 per cent).

The CAG's observation that the Centre's fiscal deficit may be underestimated adds to the problem because it suggests that the combined deficit, properly measured, may be closer to 9 per cent. As the net financial savings of households—the pool of savings from which the government and the corporate sector can draw—is around 11 per cent of GDP, a combined deficit close to 9 per cent leaves only about 2 per cent of GDP for the private corporate sector.[74]

The crowding out problem may not appear to be relevant at present because private investment is depressed, rural consumption demand has fallen, and there is excess capacity in many sectors. Attention is therefore focused on the need to stimulate aggregate demand, which could involve a temporary increase in the fiscal

---

[74]In 2007–08, the same pool of financial savings offered 7 per cent of GDP to the private sector because the combined deficit had dropped to 4 per cent of GDP. (*See Table 1 of Chapter 13*)

deficit. This may make sense in the short term, although much depends on the nature of the stimulus. A cut in income tax rates will benefit upper-income groups and may have relatively little impact on aggregate demand. Additional expenditures on public programmes that stimulate demand in rural areas will be much more effective, especially if they are linked to productive investments. Whatever the decision on the fiscal deficit in the short run, we must be quite clear that continuing with a high fiscal deficit in the medium term will jeopardize growth because it will crowd out private investment.

As a medium-term objective, we should therefore plan to reduce the combined fiscal deficit by 3 to 4 per cent of GDP over a five-year period. This will be difficult enough, but the scale of the fiscal challenge in the medium term is actually much larger because the government also needs to spend much more in a number of critical sectors such as infrastructure, health, education and defence. An increase in such spending by at least 5 per cent of GDP over a five-year period is necessary.[75] The total fiscal effort needed to reduce the fiscal deficit and increase expenditure in critical areas, therefore, comes to about 8 to 9 per cent of GDP, and this makes no allowance for new basic income schemes that have been much talked about.

Increasing tax revenue will have to be a large part of the solution. India's total tax revenues are about 16 per cent of GDP and have been stagnant at that level. Several studies of taxable capacity have shown that India, with its present level of per-capita GDP, should be able to raise tax revenues by an additional 5 to 6 per cent of GDP. A large part of this has to come from the Centre's taxes.

The first priority for the Centre for raising tax revenues must be to fix the problems with the GST. This will require a complete

---

[75]Increases much discussed are the following: 1.5 per cent of GDP in infrastructure, 1 per cent each on health, education and scientific research (including R&D in agriculture), and, to be realistic, about 0.5 per cent in defence.

redesign, which would mean reducing the large number of exemptions and reducing the number of rates to two—perhaps 10 per cent and 14 per cent—with an additional levy on luxury goods consumed only by the rich. The Ministry of Finance, or perhaps the PM himself, may need to persuade the GST Council that indirect tax rates do not have to be differentiated across commodities to achieve progressivity. It is the direct tax system that should be used to ensure progressivity of the tax system as a whole.

The tax revenue projections in the Medium-Term Fiscal Policy statement accompanying the Budget of 2019–20 reflect no recognition of the need to increase the tax ratio. The tax-to-GDP ratio of 2019–20 is estimated at 11.7 per cent, and is projected to fall to 11.6 per cent in the next two years. The recent reduction in the corporate tax rates after the Budget for 2019–20 will further reduce the tax ratio.

The time is right to start working on a medium-term tax reform plan covering all the major taxes with a clear target for a higher tax ratio to be reached at the end of a five-year period. Such reform cannot be left to the CBDT and CBEC acting in silos, under the direction of generalist IAS officers in the Revenue Department. The government should set up a High-Level Committee, like the Chelliah Committee of 1991, to lay out a complete tax reform programme to be implemented over the next five years, which would achieve a targeted increase in the overall tax ratio. It should consider new issues such as the taxation of e-commerce and digital companies. It should also consider the case for inheritance taxes or wealth taxes which do not exist in India at present, but are being discussed in industrialized countries in the context of rising inequality.

Modernizing tax administration needs to be given top priority. Our tax laws are not clear and leave wide discretion to assessing officers in determining the tax liability. Pushed to meet unrealistic revenue targets, tax assessment officers tend to interpret the opaque laws to raise the highest possible tax demands. Taxpayers see such actions as arbitrary and complain of harassment. It also encourages corruption as assessing officers can use their discretionary powers to threaten large tax demands unless they are paid off.

These concerns are not new. The BJP had blamed the UPA for 'tax terrorism' during the election campaign of 2014 and promised to put a stop to it. However, the problem remains unaddressed and Indian business leaders and foreign investors continue to complain. Rahul Bajaj's comment on an 'atmosphere of fear', which I have referred to earlier, clearly refers to a fear of investigations on tax evasion and money laundering. Tax evasion is a criminal offence everywhere and calls for strong enforcement, but it is possible that our system gives too much discretion to tax authorities to take action on the presumption rather than proof of guilt. A thorough reform of tax administration and procedures to bring them in line with global practices would be a substantive contribution to improving the investment climate.

The scale of the fiscal effort needed is such that higher tax revenues have to be complemented by restructuring to eliminate low-priority expenditure. A large part of the Centre's expenditure is accounted for by interest payments, salaries and pensions, which cannot be reduced. Expenditure restructuring in the Centre therefore has to focus on subsidies, which amount to about 1.6 per cent of GDP, and some development programmes that are not sufficiently productive. There is a case for reducing the fertilizer subsidy and using the resources released to increase investments that will increase farm income (*see Chapter 13*). There is also a strong case for redesigning the food subsidy (*see Chapter 15*). Both require strong political will and effective political marketing to emphasize that the money saved would be channelled back to the same groups in a more productive form.

Similar restructuring of expenditure is needed in most states where budgets are burdened with populist expenditures such as free distribution of cookers, mixers, TVs, lump sum payments for daughters' weddings, waivers of bank loans to farmers, etc., to say nothing of highly distortionary subsidies such as free or near-free electricity to farmers and very low pricing of canal water. This profligacy does not show up in higher fiscal deficits because the states cannot borrow more than the central government allows. It is accommodated by squeezing provision for expenditures in areas such as health and education, and postponing it to future years. State electricity distribution companies are also pushed to run large losses. It is not clear how we can get out of this trap as long as state politicians believe that freebies are the surest way of getting re-elected.

The burden on the budgets of both the Centre and the states for infrastructure development can be reduced by resort to PPPs. We have gained considerable experience in PPPs and the problems that have arisen can be resolved through institutional reform (*see Chapter 16*). However, the recent action of the Andhra Pradesh government cancelling a number of long-term contracts will discourage PPPs in other states.

Fixing the banking system

The banking system is currently under severe stress because of large NPAs in public sector banks arising from loans given during the boom period which have become non-performing. Whatever its origins, the problem must be speedily resolved if growth is to be revived. Banks have to take the haircuts needed and the resulting capital erosion has to be made up by recapitalization, so that public sector banks can expand credit at a pace consistent with resumption of growth.

Until recently, banks did not have reliable ways of getting defaulting borrowers to cooperate. The Insolvency and Bankruptcy Code (IBC) enacted by the NDA in 2016 is a game changer in this respect because it has provided the banks with a credible mechanism to initiate recovery. Predictably, the process was delayed by defaulting borrowers raising various legal issues, but the Supreme Court's decision on Essar Steel, which allows Arcelor Mittal to take over the company, has resolved most of these issues.

The IBC is a major structural reform but it is only a first step. The next step is the recapitalization of public sector banks combined with reforms to prevent the same problems from recurring. The government seems willing to put up capital for recapitalization, but there is no evidence of willingness to give up the government's majority ownership in public sector banks. Internationally, majority government ownership is seen as inconsistent with sound commercial banking, but no part of the political spectrum in India shares this view.

If we have to work within the constraint that the government must retain majority ownership, the only option is to implement the reforms recommended by the P J Nayak Committee in 2014. A key recommendation was that the government should distance itself from the management of public sector banks by creating a holding company and transferring all the government shares of public sector banks to this company. The holding company would appoint reputed professionals to the boards of the banks, and the public sector banks would become board-managed institutions. The top managements would be appointed by the boards, not by the government. The Ministry of Finance would not issue any directions to public sector banks, thus ending the present anomaly where public sector banks are subject to dual regulation by both the RBI and the ministry.

Implementing these recommendations would end much of the interference from the government that prevents public sector bank managements from competing effectively with private sector banks.[76] Not surprisingly, the Ministry of Finance has not been keen to disempower itself. The only step announced thus far is the decision to merge some public sector banks, but merging some unreformed banks to form a larger unreformed bank is no solution. A possible compromise would be to apply the Nayak formula to a selected group of public sector banks, leaving the rest to be managed as they are. This would give us, at the end of 10 years, an objective way of judging whether the involvement

---

[76]It would not, however, end other constraints on the banks, which follow from being more than 50 per cent owned by the government. These include being subject to the CVC and the CBI.

of the finance ministry actually improves performance. It would be an application of experimental economics for which Abhijit Banerjee, Esther Duflo and Michael Kremer were awarded the Nobel Prize in Economics in 2019.

Banking reform should include giving the RBI the same powers over public sector banks as it has over private sector banks, including the decision to approve the proposed appointment of a CEO in advance, based on 'fit and proper grounds', and the power to remove CEOs for non-performance. It is also necessary to implement reform in the RBI to improve its regulatory and supervisory capacity. The need for such improvement is evident from the way NPAs were allowed to build up in the public sector banks until the problem was finally revealed by the asset quality review initiated by Governor Raghuram Rajan in 2015. RBI regulation over the non-bank financial sector also needs to be strengthened as this part of the financial sector has also come under stress.

Those who resist privatization of existing public sector banks must remember that private banks are continuously innovating and inducting new technologies while government-controlled public sector banks have less flexibility and are losing their ability to compete. The result is already evident as the share of public sector banks in total advances fell from 76 per cent in 2014 to 61 per cent in 2019. At this rate, the share of the private sector could increase to over 50 per cent in 10 years. Since, the sector is being effectively privatized in this manner, the option of privatizing some individual public sector banks deserves consideration.

ISSUES FOR THE MEDIUM TERM

I now turn to some issues of importance over the medium term, including accelerating agricultural growth, addressing the employment problem, the approach we should take on trade policy, managing Centre-state relations and implementing institutional reforms.

Accelerating agricultural growth

Accelerating agricultural growth remains critical for inclusiveness and calls for many policy changes by both the Centre and the states (*see Chapter 13*). Some of the reforms needed, for example, in agricultural marketing or legalizing leasing of land, are entirely in the hands of state governments and do not require much funding. However, large public investments are needed in conservation and management of surface water and groundwater, as well as in agricultural R&D to improve land productivity. These issues will gain in importance in the years ahead if we want to adapt to the likely impact of climate change. States are unlikely to be able to make these investments themselves and will turn to the Centre, which is also fiscally constrained.

There is, therefore, an overwhelming case for withdrawing large sums that are currently going into agricultural subsidies and redirecting them to productive investments in agriculture. This also raises the issue of whether the new PM KISAN scheme, announced just before the 2019 elections, is the best use of scarce funds. The Budget provision for this scheme in 2019–20 is ₹75,000 crore, whereas all the other central schemes in agriculture add up to just under ₹40,000 crore.[77]

The states were not consulted when this scheme was announced and it is a moot point whether, if offered a choice, they would have preferred a new centrally sponsored scheme that would make the same funds available to them with greater flexibility to design projects to enhance farm productivity and income. The Centre should explore the possibility of giving states this choice.

Employment generation in a changing world

The PLFS 2017-18 revealed the near-crisis nature of the employment problem. Employment in agriculture actually declined between

---

[77]Green Revolution: ₹12,566 crore; Crop Insurance: ₹14,000 crore; Pradhan Mantri Krishi Sinchayee Yojana (irrigation): ₹9,682 crore; White Revolution (milk): ₹2,240 crore; Blue Revolution (fish): ₹550 crore; and Agri Research: ₹566 crore—totalling ₹40,000 crore

2011–12 and 2017–18. This is actually a desirable outcome because the only way incomes of those in agriculture can catch up with those in non-agriculture is if the population dependent on agriculture declines. But the labour released from agriculture must be absorbed elsewhere—and this has not happened. In East Asia, surplus labour from agriculture was absorbed in manufacturing which expanded rapidly because of an export boom. In our case, PLFS shows that employment in manufacturing has declined. Employment increased in construction and services, but this was not enough to offset the fall in agriculture and manufacturing, so total employment in the economy actually declined.[78] What is worse, the jobs being generated are not regular jobs but low-quality jobs in the informal sector with little job security. This is a recipe for social explosion.

Faster growth will help to produce more jobs. However, we also need to bring about changes in the industrial structure in India, which would help generate more and better-quality employment. We have a very large number of small firms, employing less than 10 people, which account for a large volume of employment but produce a relatively small proportion of output, with very low levels of productivity and wages. At the other end, we have a few large firms that account for a large proportion of output, generating limited but high-quality employment. There is a 'missing middle' of firms, employing between 50 and 500 workers. This is the category with the greatest potential to generate good-quality employment.

Ideally, policy should encourage the more successful small-scale entrepreneurs to graduate quickly from micro to small and then medium size. Employment in the expanding firms will then increase and be of better quality, while employment in the micro sector may contract compared to its present level. This structural change must be accepted as part of the process of formalization,

---

[78]Mehrotra, Santosh, and Jajati K. Parida. *India's Employment Crisis: Rising Education Levels and Falling Non Agricultural Job Growth*, CSE Working Paper, Azim Premji University, 2019

in which lower-quality employment will be replaced by better-quality employment.

Improved infrastructure, especially better quality of power and improved logistics, and an efficient financial system will create an environment in which middle-sized units can become more competitive leading to greater employment-generation. More flexible labour laws are also needed. This has been a contentious issue on which successive governments have made very little progress. PM Manmohan Singh had said at the Economic Times Awards Function in 2006 (*see Chapter 13*) that he was hopeful of getting labour to agree to more flexibility if we could raise the growth rate of GDP to 10 per cent. The growth rate was raised, though not to 10 per cent, but the position of labour leaders across the political spectrum did not change.

The recent initiative of the NDA government allowing workers to be hired on fixed-term contracts is a good development, but it is not enough. We also need to allow greater flexibility in retrenchment and even the closure of units. Technology is changing so rapidly that the economy needs to be nimble in response to such changes, and this requires more flexibility in labour laws.

New technologies such as robotics, the Internet of Things, artificial intelligence and 3D printing will make many existing jobs redundant but they will also create new jobs. We need to ensure that the system is sufficiently flexible to allow full exploitation of these new employment opportunities. Efforts to improve the ease of doing business must be combined with an environment that encourages start-ups and innovation. Foreign investment in these start-ups through venture capital funds and angel investors should be encouraged. The tax treatment of such funds, especially when they come from foreign sources, needs to be streamlined and ambiguities removed.

The Indian educational system has not been very effective in creating the skills needed even for older technologies. It will be a major challenge to redesign the system to meet the demands of rapid changes in technology. This calls for an educational and training system that makes reskilling very easy.

We have to recognize that the solution to India's employment problem will not come from the manufacturing sector alone since it provides only 12 per cent of the total employment. There is a much larger range of employment possibilities in the services sector, including commercial services such as hotels, restaurants, catering, transport, logistics, health services, etc. Some of the growth in these services is a reflection of outsourcing of activities from the manufacturing sector, in which value added is shifted from manufacturing to services.

There is also scope for expanding employment in government jobs for teachers, health workers and even police personnel. However, vacancies for these jobs remain unfilled in state governments because the inadequacy of budget resources discourages the states from recruiting permanent employees. Vacancies in these essential services coexist with overstaffing in lower-level government jobs such as peons and even typists, who will increasingly be phased out as offices become more digital.

A disturbing development in the past few years is the tendency in many states to prescribe local hiring requirements even for the private sector. This happens because the inadequate growth of employment puts CMs under pressure to do something to increase employment opportunities in the state. However, there is an inherent contradiction between taking pride in integrating the national market for goods through a common GST and fragmenting the labour market. States that enforce local reservation provisions strictly will become less attractive to investors and the danger that other states follow suit will increase uncertainty.

Managing Centre-state relations and cooperative federalism

The most important issue in Centre-state relations is the scale and manner of transfer of financial resources from the Centre to the states. With the abolition of planning, one of the old channels of transfer—central assistance to state plans—has ended. There are now only two channels: the Finance Commission transfers that are not tied to any conditions, and transfers through the centrally sponsored schemes that are constrained by the guidelines laid down by the central ministries dealing with these schemes.

The key issue before the Fifteenth Finance Commission (FFC) is whether to increase the share of the states in total central revenues, leaving it to the states to decide how the funds will be spent, or to determine a scale of devolution that leaves a sufficient amount with the central government for the so-called centrally sponsored schemes. The FFC has delivered an interim report for the year 2020–21 and will deliver its full report for the next five years sometime in 2020.

If the commission responds to the demands of the states to increase their share of tax revenues substantially, the Centre will have that much less to provide through centrally sponsored schemes. If the recommended revenue sharing allows a substantial flow of funds through centrally sponsored schemes, the states will want the Centre to give them more flexibility in how to use these funds. I believe there is merit in giving the states more flexibility and I have suggested a way (*see Chapter 18*) of reforming the system to do so. This proposal, as well as others, could be usefully discussed with the states to come to an agreement.

A major gap in the existing system is the inadequacy in the devolution from the states to the third tier, i.e. Panchayati Raj institutions (PRIs) and urban local bodies (ULBs). The states have a constitutional responsibility to ensure such devolution, but this has not been done in most states. The Finance Commission in the past has recommended some grants to be given to the states to pass on to PRIs and ULBs. However, these grants have been very small. A radical approach would be for the FFC to recommend a much more substantial volume of funds to be passed on to the third tier. These transfers would come from the Centre's financial resources, but the FFC could reduce the states' share in the divisible pool of tax revenues correspondingly so that the total devolution to the states, including grants to the PRIs/ULBs, is reasonable.

One consequence of the abolition of Five-Year Plans is that neither the Centre nor the states prepare projections of the expected development expenditure in key areas over the medium term consistent with the total resources likely to be available. For meaningful discussions between the Centre and the states on development issues, it is necessary for the Centre to spell out its medium-term projection of development expenditure in the form of central sector schemes and centrally sponsored schemes, consistent with the total funds available. The states should also prepare medium-term development expenditure budgets on the same basis. It is only by adding up such projections across the Centre and the states that we can get an idea of how much is proposed to be spent by the Centre and the states together on critical sectors such as health, education and infrastructure development, all of which are critical for inclusive growth.

The recent decision of the Andhra Pradesh government to cancel a large number of long-term contracts in the power sector entered into by the previous government poses a new set of problems. While such action can be viewed as the sovereign privilege of any state government, we have to recognize that it has wider consequences. Not only would it affect future investment in the state itself, it also has consequences for the Centre and other states. The Centre is affected because if the cancelled contracts are with investors from countries where we have a bilateral investment treaty, the cancellations could lead to the central government becoming liable. Other states are also affected, as action by one state affects investor assessments of the risks involved in entering into similar agreements with other states.

The issue is particularly important if states want to resort to PPPs to implement infrastructure projects. Perhaps the Centre and the states could evolve a code of conduct that would impose some discipline on states acting unilaterally on these issues. One possibility would be for the Centre to set up an arbitration forum to deal with all state government projects that make provision for such arbitration explicitly in the contract. States that do not wish to include such arbitration in their contracts would be free to do so, but those that accept the arrangement may be viewed by investors as posing lower risk.

Finally, an important subject for discussion in a Centre-state forum is the issue of what should be a maximum size of a state. Uttar Pradesh has a population of 228 million, which is only a little less than that of Indonesia, the fourth most-populated country in the world! In 10 years, this will grow to 260 million. Trifurcation would create three much more manageable states. If there is agreement that any state that exceeds 120 million in population should be considered for bifurcation, both Maharashtra and West Bengal will be candidates in 10 years' time.

The role of institutions

Economic reforms in developing countries have generally focused on reducing government controls and allowing a greater role for the market on the assumption that this would improve efficiency and deliver better economic performance. This assumption was fully justified in the early stages of reforms in India when government intervention was excessive and dysfunctional. But as markets are given freer rein, we also have to consider whether the preconditions have been established for markets to deliver efficient outcomes.

At the most elementary level, effective enforcement of contracts is critical for markets to function efficiently. Within a small community, such as a village, social custom may suffice to ensure delivery of contracts but as transactions occur between people in a much larger community, enforcement of contract depends upon a modern legal system which functions efficiently and without excessive delay. We have a long way to go before we can claim success in this area, with commercial disputes taking an inordinately long time for final resolution.

The institutional support needed for markets to function efficiently becomes more complex as the economy becomes more developed. For example, as more private companies start raising funds from the capital market, it becomes necessary to ensure that the stock markets are not being distorted by inadequate disclosure, insider trading and other forms of manipulation. There is also a role for regulation in goods markets to ensure that large players do not misuse market power. Regulation is also necessary when actions of individuals impose costs on society that are not taken into account in the individual cost-benefit calculation. This is the basic justification for regulation to protect the environment and prevent pollution.

Over the years we have developed a complex web of regulatory institutions but as the global financial crisis showed, regulatory failures occur even in advanced countries. An effective regulatory system is today regarded as essential if capitalism is to be socially acceptable, but creating such a system is not easy. It requires a culture of independence from the government, ability to recruit the human resources needed to staff the new institutions, and also to ensure a high quality of leadership. It also requires watchfulness to prevent 'regulatory capture' by the very entities these institutions are meant to regulate.

Independence from the government is especially difficult to achieve at the state level. This is exemplified by the experience with State Electricity Regulatory Commissions (SERCs). These bodies were established to ensure that the fixation of electricity tariffs would be depoliticized. However, SERCs in most states are staffed by retired civil servants and have gone along with what the state government wants. The result is that the power sector in most states continues to be financially unviable, putting a serious strain on state finances and requiring periodic bailouts from the Centre.

Government itself is an institution that needs to be strengthened. India is a much more complex economy today than when the reforms began in 1991. One of the reasons we were able to break out of the low growth of the '70s was that there was a pool of expertise available to chart a new course, and successive governments—to their credit—utilized it effectively. The increased sophistication of the economy compared with 30 years ago means that the range of expertise needed today is much greater.

Bringing in technical experts on short-term contracts from outside can add great value, but we also need to induct professionals from outside at the middle level and let them grow in the system for longer periods. The technical capacity of the civil service also needs to be upgraded. This can be done by sending promising candidates for advanced training to the top universities, not just in India but also abroad, and following up by posting them in positions that need the expertise they have acquired.

An institutional gap that has been highlighted recently is the need for a strong national statistical system, independent of control by the government. India had a high reputation in this area, but this has been eroded by the controversies about the national accounts data, the delayed release of the employment survey for 2017–18 and the junking of the consumer household survey for 2017–18. If we want the economy to appear attractive to private capital—domestic and foreign—then the Indian statistical system must meet the highest standards observed in emerging market countries. The NSC, which was set up by the UPA government in 2005, must be made the sole supervisory body clearing data from the quality perspective and ensuring its release according to a set timetable. Government should have no role in 'clearing' data for publication.

The observation of the CAG that current government accounting practices lead to understatement of the fiscal deficit also calls for an institutional response. One solution, which was proposed by the Fourteenth Finance Commission and reiterated by the FRBM Review Committee, would be to set up a Fiscal Council suitably staffed with experts that would submit an independent report to Parliament on the fiscal numbers projected in the Budget and their consistency with established accounting norms.

CONCLUDING REFLECTIONS

The slowdown of growth in the past few years, and especially its collapse in 2019–20, has given rise to scepticism about whether we are settling into a 'new normal' very far from the robust growth witnessed earlier. The concern is understandable and hopefully it will lead to serious reflection. I have no doubt we can get back to higher growth, provided we are willing to usher in the next generation of reforms that the economy needs.

It is easy to succumb to pessimism about whether these reforms can be introduced. My mind goes back to 1979, just before we returned to India, when many Indian friends and well-wishers were discouraging me from moving back. They said I would find working in the Government of India very frustrating, that I would be a small cog in a large machine and unable to do much, and that India's economic policies were too set to realistically expect any change. They were wrong. Contrary to everyone's expectations, economic policies in India did change—and so did India's economic performance.

From a purely personal perspective, Isher and I feel fully vindicated in the decision we took in 1979 to return to India. We built a strong family and a wonderful life in Delhi. Both our sons were educated in India and also in universities abroad. Both started their careers in the United States but have chosen to settle in Delhi. Both our daughters-in-law have thriving professional careers in Delhi. As grandparents of five, we feel particularly blessed that both our children and their families are only a 10-minute drive away from us. An important regret is that we have not made substantial progress in protecting the environment and providing clean air for our grandchildren. But awareness has increased greatly and one can hope for more progress on this issue in the future.

India's transition to high growth, which is the story narrated in this book, was not a chance development. It was achieved by deliberate policy steps taken by those who had conviction and belief in the need for change. Changing policies in a country as complex as India has to go much beyond making declarations of intent. It needs an open society where businessmen and other stakeholders are free to criticize the government and draw attention to whatever is not working. It needs a team of technically skilled professionals with the ability to understand economic issues offering honest advice to the political class. It also needs a political class that can combine the unavoidable compulsions of adversarial politics with working towards building consensus on the broad direction of economic policy.

My own experience gives me hope that even though the challenges ahead may look formidable, the system has the capacity to respond. Pressure points are building up that give me confidence that the political system will move in the right direction. An obvious pressure point is that the demand for better economic performance will grow with time. Migration from rural to urban areas is accelerating and the new generation, which is better educated and much more interconnected, will demand more and better jobs, higher incomes and a better quality of living in cities. Appeals to populism and nationalism can distract attention for a while from poor economic performance and we see this in many countries. But poor economic performance will be registered by voters and will generate pressure for better results.

The time has also come for policy changes in the future to be put on a much faster track. Gradualism made sense at the start of the reform process because we were not sure how the economy would respond to economic reforms. We now know that it can respond well. The case for faster change is also reinforced by the fact that growth is bringing about structural change in the economy at an accelerated pace and these changes pose new challenges that must be addressed with urgency. Technology is also changing more rapidly and globalization is accelerating the spread of technological change.

All these factors suggest that we need to make policy changes faster than we have done in the past. This may be easier than we think because the new generation is less wedded to past ideologies. For example, the younger generation is much less opposed to privatization than was the case earlier, provided it is done in a transparent manner.

Good economics may not seem to be good politics in the short run, but wise political leaders will realize that it is almost always the best politics in the long run. How to marry the two is, in some sense, the real test of political leadership. I remain an unrelenting optimist that our political system can resolve this conflict and that the India story of high growth and development will therefore continue. India can and must return to its high growth years—our younger generation deserves nothing less.

ACKNOWLEDGEMENTS

This book is about my journey through policymaking, a journey in which I had many fellow travellers—friends and colleagues— who made it enjoyable and enlightening. Some were on my side on various issues of policy, and others on the opposite side, but both groups helped shape my views and sharpen my instincts, and therefore, deserve my sincere thanks.

This manuscript was shared with only a few, and their comments helped me greatly in preparing a better book. My good friend Sarwar Lateef, whom I have known since our days together in St. Stephen's College, diligently read through the whole manuscript and gave me incisive feedback on each chapter. I found his comments on the importance of good governance and the role of institutions in making reforms work particularly insightful. Anne Krueger, a distinguished trade and development economist who had worked on India's industrial and trade policies in the 1960s, was one of the first to point out the distortionary effects of the policy regime. She filled out my understanding with many micro-level examples of how the system actually worked on the ground in the years before the reforms. I have also benefitted from comments by Andrew Sheng, a distinguished economist from Malaysia; Junaid Ahmad, an international civil servant from Bangladesh and head of the World Bank's India office; and Roberto N. Zagha, a Brazilian economist who had served as head of the World Bank's India office earlier and was secretary of the Growth Commission of which I was a member. All three know India well, and their comments gave me a sense of how the issues discussed in this book may also be of interest to other developing countries spanning East Asia, South Asia and Latin America. Manoj Kumar of Naandi Foundation, a development professional from the NGO world, read the whole manuscript and gave comments from a very different perspective from that of professional economists.

Shankar Acharya, with whom I worked closely in the Ministry of Finance in the 1990s, shared some excellent thoughts, especially on the contentious issue of whether we had overdone the stimulus after the global financial crisis. My view was somewhat different from his, but our discussions helped me to address this issue in a more balanced manner. Josh Felman offered very useful feedback on several chapters. I also benefited greatly from comments by Prof. Vijay Tankha. As an academic from the world of philosophy, he made several suggestions to make the book more accessible for non-economists. My brother Sanjeev, sister-in-law Vidyunmala Singh, and sister Anjali helped to sketch in some family memories. Sanjeev also shared some valuable inputs on the substance of my policy travelogue.

I benefited greatly from a long discussion with Justice Sudershan Mishra, who saw some of the chapters, and gave me his perspective on the interaction between the judiciary and the executive. Shriya Mishra, a young practising lawyer in Delhi, drew my attention to the many circumstances where the courts have pronounced judgements that could easily lead to outcomes that economists would view as suboptimal. I am also grateful to Vikas and Veena Mankar, Tariq Baloch, Satya Poddar, Amarjit Singh Chandhiok, Aman Bahl, Vinay Sitapati, Rahul Khullar, Sindhushree Khullar, Almitra Patel and Richard Danzig for significant comments on a number of different chapters.

As the dedication of this book makes clear, the person to whom I owe the greatest thanks is my wife Isher. In fact, the whole idea that I should write about my journey originated from her. She helped me conceptualize the organization of the book and went through the early drafts of all the chapters, engaging in substantive discussions on my account of particular events. She also constantly reminded me that I was not writing an economics textbook or a government white paper, and that the prose should be smooth and not stilted. Our two sons Pavan and Aman also read the whole draft and gave me the benefit of their views. They were often brutally frank, but they also made many constructive suggestions that helped me improve the quality of my point of view.

My perspectives on India's economic development, which are the basis of much of what I have said in this book, have been shaped by numerous interactions with some very distinguished economists who did not always agree with each other, or with me, but helped me understand the issues better. This group includes Hollis Chenery, Amartya Sen, Jagdish Bhagwati, T.N. Srinivasan, B.S. Minhas, Prabhat Patnaik, Deepak Nayyar, K.N. Raj, Michael Spence, Joseph Stiglitz, Peter Kenen, Ian Little, Max Corden, Edmar Bacha, Roger Noll, Michael Mussa, Lord Meghnad Desai, Stan Fischer, Lawrence Summers, Lord Nicholas Stern, Martin Wolf, Nouriel Roubini, and Ruchir Sharma. They deserve sincere thanks for helping me to understand the complexity of economic policy issues. Many of my colleagues in my early years at the World Bank helped put my perceptions about India in the context of the experience of other developing countries. Thanks are especially due to Stanley Please, Mahbub ul Haq, Ravi Gulhati, Ernest Stern, John H. Duloy, Nanak Kakwani, Clive Bell, Bela Balassa, Marcelo Selowsky and Harinder Kohli. Surjit Bhalla and Suman Bery, who worked in the World Bank in their younger days, also contributed to my understanding of the issues facing the Indian economy.

I learnt a great deal about Indian agriculture from M.S. Swaminathan, Verghese Kurien, Amrita Patel, Ashok Gulati, S.S. Johl, and farmer leader, Sharad Joshi. On public health issues, I benefitted enormously from the insights of Srinath Reddy and Nachiket Mor.

Special thanks are due to the many people with whom I worked in the Government of India in various capacities at different times. Manmohan Singh tops the list, followed by L.K. Jha, P. Chidambaram, Yashwant Sinha, Subramanian Swamy, Y.K. Alagh and Arun Shourie. Others from whom I learnt immensely were Raja Chelliah, Arun Ghosh, Bimal Jalan, C. Rangarajan, Manu Shroff, A. Vaidyanathan, Lavraj Kumar, S. Venkitaramanan, R.N.

Malhotra, P.K. Kaul, B.G. Deshmukh, Vinod Pande, Gopi Arora, Vijay Kelkar, Ronen Sen, N.K. Singh, S.S. Tarapore, Y.K. Alagh, T.N. Seshan, Debu Bandyopadhyay, Nitin Desai, Amaresh Bagchi, N. Ganesan, D.R. Mehta, Rakesh Mohan, Y.V. Reddy, D. Subba Rao, Parthasarathi Shome, Gajendra Haldea, Arvind Virmani, Jayanta Roy, Arbind Modi and K.P. Krishnan.

I owe special thanks to my colleagues, the other members of the Planning Commission in UPA 1 and UPA 2: Kirit Parikh, Abhijit Sen, Anwarul Hoda, B.N. Mungekar, Syeda Hameed, V.L. Chopra, B.N. Yugandhar, B.K. Chaturvedi, K. Kasturirangan, Narendra Jadhav, Saumitra Chaudhuri, Mihir Shah and Arun Maira. We represented a rainbow of opinions and did not always agree with each other, but I always felt that diversity of opinions was important in trying to solve India's complex economic challenges.

Business leaders with whom I interacted over the years and who gave me an insight into the perceptions and priorities of Indian industry include Dhirubhai Ambani, Ratan Tata, Rahul Bajaj, Keshub Mahindra, Mukesh Ambani, Uday Kotak, Kiran Mazumdar Shaw, Jamshyd Godrej, N.R. Narayana Murthy, Nandan Nilekani, Azim Premji, Sunil Mittal, Anand Mahindra, Naushad Forbes, K.P. Singh, Shiv Nadar, Rajendra Pawar, Shobhana Bhartia, Naresh Trehan, Prathap Reddy, Anji Reddy, N. Vaghul, K.V. Kamath, Rajinder Gupta, Victor Menezes, Vikram Pandit, Tarun Das of CII and Amit Mitra from the days when he headed the Federation of Indian Chambers of Commerce and Industry (FICCI).

I have also learnt a great deal from many journalist friends including Swaminathan Aiyar, T.N. Ninan, N. Ram, N. Ravi, Prem Shankar Jha, Prannoy Roy, Shekhar Gupta, Karan Thapar, Anil Padmanabhan, M.K. Venu and A.K. Bhattacharya.

I am grateful to Kapish Mehra, managing director of Rupa Publications, who was one of the first publishers to approach me to write a book about my experiences almost as soon as I stepped out of government. His offer was all the more attractive because he was interested in having the book translated into Hindi and some Indian languages. I am grateful to Yamini Chowdhury for the many structural editorial suggestions and also for the tolerance she showed towards my constant slippages on deadlines. Arati Rajan Menon copyedited the book with great skill. I was particularly impressed by her ability to 'crunch', as she put it, excessively long stretches of prose into a much more compact form. I am also indebted to Janki Shah and Nevin John for very helpful suggestions about cover design.

Utkarsh Patel, Vaibhav Khurana and Ayush Khare provided excellent research assistance at different stages in the preparation of this book. I am grateful to all of them for their efforts in digging out material and checking facts.

In the end, I own sole responsibility for any errors in the book.

INDEX